The Irony of the Ideal
Paradoxes of Russian Literature

Ars Rossica

Series Editor: David Bethea (University of Wisconsin—Madison)

The Irony of the Ideal

Paradoxes of Russian Literature

MIKHAIL EPSTEIN

Translated by **A. S. Brown**

Boston
2018

Library of Congress Cataloging-in-Publication Data

Names: Epstein, Mikhail, author. | Brown, A. S., translator.

Title: The irony of the ideal : paradoxes of Russian literature / Mikhail Epstein; translated by A.S. Brown.

Other titles: Ironiia ideala. English

Description: Boston : Academic Studies Press, 2018. | Series: Ars Rossica | Includes bibliographical references and index.

Identifiers: LCCN 2017012870 (print) | LCCN 2017021255 (ebook) | ISBN 9781618116338 (e-book) | ISBN 9781618116321 (hardcover)

Subjects: LCSH: Russian literature—History and criticism. | Paradox in literature.

Classification: LCC PG2986 (ebook) | LCC PG2986.E7713 2017 (print) | DDC 891.709—dc23

LC record available at https://lccn.loc.gov/2017012870

The publication of this book is supported by the Mikhail Prokhorov Foundation (translation program TRANSCRIPT).

©Academic Studies Press, 2018
ISBN 978-1-61811-982-7
ISBN 978-1-61811-633-8 (electronic)

Book design by Kryon Publishing Services (P) Ltd.
www.kryonpublishing.com

Cover design by Ivan Grave. On the cover: "A Guardian Angel," by Vladimir Lubarov, reproduced by the author's permission.

Published by Academic Studies Press in 2018
28 Montfern Avenue
Brighton, MA 02135, USA
P: (617)782-6290
F: (857)241-3149
press@academicstudiespress.com
www.academicstudiespress.com

Contents

Acknowledgments ix
Translator's Note xi
Introduction xiii

Part I: The Titanic and the Demonic: Faust's Heirs

1. Faust and Peter on the Seashore: From Goethe to Pushkin — 3
   a. Comparativistics and Typology — 3
   b. Toil and the Elements — 4
   c. *The Bronze Horseman* as the Anti-*Faust* — 10
   d. Demonic Irony — 15
   e. Pushkin between Goethe and Mickiewicz — 18
   f. Apocalypse — 22
   g. The Transformation of the Faustian into the Mephistophelian — 25
2. The Bronze Horseman and the Golden Fish: Pushkin's Fairy Tale-Poem — 28
   a. Semantic Convertibility — 28
   b. Textual Parallels — 30
   c. The Subjugation of the Elements, and Their Retribution — 34
   d. Peter and the Old Woman: A Pair of Autocrats — 42
   e. The Fate of the "Little Man" — 44
   f. The Family and the State — 46
   g. The Poem and the Tale as a Single Work — 47
3. The Motherland-Witch: The Irony of Style in Nikolai Gogol — 53
   a. The Irony of Style and the Apotheosis of Russia — 53
   b. An Aesthetic Demonology of Russia — 56
      The Stare or Fixed Gaze — 56
      Rootedness to the Spot — 59
      Light and Chiming — 61

		Ghostly Light	62
		Chiming and Weeping	64
		Dream and Waking	66
		Fast Riding, Flickering	67
	c.	Patriotism and Eroticism	70
	d.	Blok Gives Gogol's Secret Away	74
	e.	Gogol, Betrayed by Words: The Irony of Style	81

Part II: The Great in the Little: Bashmachkin's Offspring

1.	The Saintly Scribe: Akaky Bashmachkin and Prince Myshkin	87
2.	The Figure of Repetition: The Philosopher Nikolai Fedorov and His Literary Prototypes	101
3.	The Little Man in a Case: The Bashmachkin-Belikov Syndrome	113

Part III: The Irony of Harmony

1.	Childhood and the Myth of Harmony		125
2.	The Defamiliarization of Lev Tolstoy		158
	a.	*The Death of Ivan Ilyich*	160
	b.	"Alesha-the-Pot"	167
	c.	Happy and Unhappy Families: *Anna Karenina*	173
3.	Soviet Heroics and the Oedipus Complex		178
	a.	"Big Brother": Between Freud and Orwell	178
	b.	The Mythological Basis of Materialism	179
	c.	Militant Atheism and the Oedipus Complex	181
	d.	The Call of the Underworld: The Erotics of the Worker's Blow	186
	e.	Materialism as Rooted in *Mat*	191
	f.	Mother-Worshippers and Incestors	196

Part IV: Being as Nothingness

1.	A Farewell to Objects, or, the Nabokovian in Nabokov		203
2.	The Secret of Being and Nonbeing in Vladimir Nabokov		215
	a.	The Chain of Negations: Omnipresent "Nonnons"	215

		b.	"A Series of Hinged Lids"	219
		c.	Physical Vacuum and the Buddhist Nirvana	221
		d.	The Secret of the Afterlife	225
	3.	\multicolumn{2}{l}{Andrei Platonov between Nonbeing and Resurrection}	228

	3.	Andrei Platonov between Nonbeing and Resurrection		228
		a.	Russian Literature and German Philosophy	228
		b.	The Nonbeing within Being	231
		c.	Between Martin Heidegger and Nikolai Fedorov	233
		d.	A Strange Language: On the Other Side of Subject and Object	239
		e.	The Boring Void and Deathening	243
		f.	Nabokov and Platonov: A Metaphysical Dispute	246
	4.	Dream and Battle: Oblomov, Korchagin, Kopenkin		251
		a.	Oblomovka and Chevengur	251
		b.	Warrior-Dreamers	256
		c.	Oblomagin: Bipolarity in Russian Culture	261

Part V: The Silence of the Word

	1.	Language and Silence as Forms of Being		271
		a.	Quietude and Silence	271
		b.	The Word as Being	274
		c.	The Beingfulness of the Russian Word	276
	2.	The Ideology and Magic of the Word: Anton Chekhov, Daniil Kharms, and Vladimir Sorokin		280
		a.	The Word-Figment: Daniil Kharms and Anton Chekhov	287
		b.	Three Literary Episodes: The Silence within and around the Word	291
	3.	The Russian Code of Silence: Politics and Mysticism		296
		a.	The Eternal Quiet	296
		b.	Two Silences: Political and Mystical	302
		c.	The Formative, Informative, and Fictive Word: The Self-Devouring of Language	307

Part VI: Madness and Reason

	1.	Methods of Madness and Madness as a Method: Poets and Philosophers	313

		a.	Hölderlin and Batiushkov	314
		b.	Two Half-Witted States: Poetic and Philosophical	322
		c.	Madness as Method	327
		d.	The Self-Critique of Pure Reason	333
	2.		Poetry as Ecstasy and as Interpretation: Boris Pasternak and Osip Mandel'shtam	338
		a.	Alien Language: Poetry and Kabbalah	338
		b.	Pasternak, Hasidism, and the Sparks of the Universe	347
		c.	Mandel'shtam, Talmudism, and the Textbook of Infinity	360
	3.		The Lyric of Idiotic Reason: Folkloric Philosophy in Dmitrii Prigov	375
		a.	Folkloric Philosophism: The Poetics of Platitude	375
		b.	The Stripped Consciousness. A World without a Groove. Allthing and Allbody.	381
		c.	The Banality of Abstraction: The Deeply Thoughtful Unconscious	388

The Cyclical Development of Russian Literature — 391

Conclusion — 403
   a. Literature and Metaphysics — 403
   b. Metanarratives — 407
   c. Metaphysics without a Metanarrative — 410

Works Cited — 416

Index of Subjects — 430

Index of Names — 434

Acknowledgments

This book is the product of many years of research, and I owe my gratitude to many people and organizations.

I am deeply grateful to the Mikhail Prokhorov Foundation for the generous financial support that made the translation and publication of this book possible.

My wife, Marianna Taymanova, read and edited the entire manuscript in both the Russian original and the English translation, and her advice was most valuable and formative in my work.

I am grateful to Irina Prokhorova, director of the Novoe literaturnoe obozrenie Press in Moscow, and to lead editor Evgeny Shklovsky, for publishing the book's original Russian version *Ironiia ideala: Paradoksy russkoi literatury* in 2015.

I owe my sincere thanks to Prof. David Bethea, editor of "Ars Rossica," who kindly invited me to contribute the book to his series; and to the director of Academic Studies Press Dr. Igor Nemirovsky and the editors Faith Wilson Stein and Kira Nemirovsky, who were most careful and patient at all stages of the manuscript's production.

A major role in the production of this book was played by its translator. I am profoundly grateful to A. S. Brown for his most dedicated, responsible, and intellectually generous approach to the process of translation. His devotion to the project was amazing, and he was extremely open and responsive to my opinions. For several months, we exchanged five to eight emails nearly every day, discussing all aspects of the translation, including stylistic subtleties, and there was no issue regarding which Dr. Brown did not offer most thoughtful, illuminating advice. Overall, our correspondence comprises eighteen hundred emails, attesting to the truly dialogic nature of our collaboration. Dr. Brown also substantially edited and practically reworked some chapters that had previously been translated by others and was extraordinary helpful at all stages of work, including the reading of the proofs.

I am sincerely grateful to the artist Vladimir Lubarov for permitting me to use his painting "A Guardian Angel" for the book cover design.

Last but not least, I want to thank my deeply esteemed colleagues and students at Emory University for their intellectual and emotional support of my research. The very opportunity to teach and discuss my ideas in the classroom has had a significant impact on their development.

Translator's Note

This translation was a challenge, both because of the importance of conveying Mikhail Epstein's literary talent and expressiveness and due to the great number and variety of works of Russian literature he cites.

I used existing translations whenever possible (in a very few instances adjusting perhaps a single word; these minor adjustments are always indicated with square brackets).

But even when I did use an existing translation for some text from a given work, it sometimes occurred that another part of that same translation did not suit this book's purpose. (This is not a criticism, of course; so much of translation is a matter of choice, and the original translator had simply made a perfectly warranted choice that does not match the point Prof. Epstein is making, or in some cases the specific word he is emphasizing.) In such instances, I have cited the original Russian text and provided my own translations.

A. S. Brown
Brookline, MA

Introduction

It would be difficult to find a culture more internally self-contradictory, more given to self-negation, than Russian culture. Reflecting its dual, its (conventionally speaking) East/Western identity, this is a culture of paradoxes. On the one hand, it gravitates toward the positive values of the West, toward social and technical progress and all the materially expressed forms of civilization. On the other, even as it adopts these forms, it casts doubt on and at times destroys them, falling into a radical nihilism directed against the values of reason, beauty, freedom, utility, and order. Hence the tendency to erect idols and mercilessly tear them down, "to incinerate everything one has worshipped" and "worship everything one has incinerated."

"Paradox" refers to a situation or statement that, following its own logic, suddenly enters into contradiction with itself, refutes its own premises, lays waste to its own foundations. Aside from this international term, the Russian language also has more colloquial ways to express the lability of existence: the words *vyvert* ("quirk," "eccentricity"), *vykrutasy* ("antics," "twists and turns"), *prevratnost'* (vicissitude), *nadryv* ("rupture," "laceration"), and *nadlom* ("breakdown") … The same situation of unforeseen reversal is expressed in popular idioms: "to keep stepping on the same rake" and to "strive for something only to be flogged by it." This mode of transition from thesis to antithesis through ironic twist is very characteristic of the Russian mentality. This dialectic has little in common with the Hegelian or Marxist variety, wherein thesis and antithesis are sublated in synthesis, and unity emerges from the struggle of opposites. The Russian version is more like an aggravation, an intensification of the thesis, its being taken to excess, when it turns into its own antithesis and begins to negate itself. Such a dialectic may be called ironic, insofar as it returns to its initial thesis, now with a minus sign. As aptly put by Andrei Bely, the triumph of materialism in the USSR resulted in the abolition of matter. In the same way, the affirmation of socialism led to the annihilation of entire classes, the destruction of social, professional, and family ties. Aspirations toward the very highest ideals—freedom, unity, productivity, greatness, reason, harmony—all reveal their dark underside, turning into suffering, poverty, slavery, and the absurd. Russian literature, like Russian history, is full of such unexpected twists, and of the pathos of tragic irony.

The tendency toward paradox is inherent also in the major representatives of Russian culture. When I teach courses in Russian literature and intellectual history at universities in the United States and England, what strikes students most of all are not the particular directions of thought but authors' attitudes toward their own ideas and aspirations. They find it surprising that:

Petr Chaadaev was simultaneously the father of both Westernism and Slavophilism: in his "Apology of a Madman," he inverts the meaning of the first of his *Philosophical Letters*, so that now the insignificance of Russia's past and present is put forth as a pledge to her future greatness;

Nikolai Gogol tries to extirpate his own artistic gift and "blasphemous" laughter, and consigns his own cherished work, the second volume of *Dead Souls* (*Mertvye dushi*), to the flames;

Vissarion Belinsky abjures his Hegelian reconciliation with reality, and is ready, "à la Marat," to exterminate, with fire and sword, one portion of humanity for the sake of the happiness of another;[1]

Fedor Dostoevsky's own ideals are derided, in the most sophisticated manner, by some of his characters, and championed by others, the author oscillating emphatically between voices pro and contra;

Lev Tolstoy renounces his own greatest artistic achievements for the sake of peasantly simplicity and truthfulness;

In Vladimir Solov'ev's "A Brief Tale of the Antichrist" ("Kratkaia povest' ob Antikhriste"), completed not long before his death, the author expounds the cherished ideas to which he had devoted his life of prophetic thought—oneness, universalism, ecumenicism, theocracy, and the

---

1 As Belinsky confesses in a letter (1 March 1841) to V. P. Botkin: "A year ago my thinking was diametrically opposed to what it is now. ... My present self is full of a painful hatred for my past self, and if it were in my power, then woe would be unto those who are now what I was a year ago." http://az.lib.ru/b/belinskij_w_g/text_3900.shtml.

unification of the Roman Catholic and Eastern Orthodox churches—as a worldview inspired by the devil;

Vasilii Rozanov combines in himself Judeophilia and Judeophobia; vigorously advocates both left- and right-wing causes; wages war on Christianity, and dies as a communicant of the Christian sacraments;

Aleksandr Blok, a knight of the Beautiful Lady and the Eternal Feminine, in a carnivalesque move casts this ideal persona as a harlot in *The Fairground Booth* (*Balaganchik*) and *The Stranger* (*Neznakomka*);

Vladimir Maiakovsky, a poet of cosmic tragedy, after the revolution gives himself over to the service of state propaganda, "trampl[ing]," as he put it, "on the very throat of my verse";[2]

Andrei Platonov, a utopian, a communist and technophile, creates the most profound anti-utopia of socialist society as a kingdom of emptiness and death;

Daniil Andreev preaches, as a religious ideal, the universal church-state of the Rose of the World, which paves the way for the Antichrist;[3]

Anna Akhmatova comments on one of Osip Mandel'shtam's works: "The essay is superb in its nobility, but Mandel'shtam revolts first and foremost against himself, against what he has done, and done the most, just as when he revolted against himself by defending the purity of Russian against encroachment by other words, revolted against his own theory, his idea about Italian sounds and words in Russian. ... It would be hard for a biographer to sort this all out without knowing this characteristic of his, this tendency to revolt, with the purest nobility, against what he himself had been doing, or what had been his idea."[4]

Conscious or unconscious irony or even self-derision has been a highly characteristic gesture of Russian writers and thinkers, an irony that overturns that which took decades of concentrated effort to create, a resolute self-negation.

---

2 Cited from Rottenberg, *Vladimir Mayakovsky: Innovator*, 87.
3 I describe the ironic self-refutation of D. Andreev's mystical utopia in detail in my discussion of paradoxes of Russian eschatology in *Religiia posle ateizma: Novye vozmozhnosti teologii* (*Religion after Atheism: New Possibilities for Theology*), 106–58; for a partial translation, see "Daniil Andreev and the Mysticism of Femininity."
4 *Dnevnik Pavla Luknitskogo*, 8 July 1926. http://www.litmir.net/ br/?b=62792&p=89

This book is devoted to the paradoxes of Russian literature, but many of its general conclusions apply to Russian culture as a whole, insofar as in the nineteenth and twentieth centuries it remained for the most part a literary, a verbal one. Russian culture is famously marked by the duality of its values, as has been discussed by early twentieth-century thinkers (N. Berdiaev, D. Merezhkovsky, S. Askol'dov) as well as by cultural scholars in the latter part of the century (Iu. Lotman, B. Uspensky, S. Averintsev). In the well-known formulation of Iurii Lotman and Boris Uspensky, "a specific feature of Russian culture is... its fundamental polarity, expressed in the dual nature of its structure. The primary cultural values (ideological, political, religious) in the system of medieval Russia are arranged in a bipolar field of values separated by a sharp boundary and bereft of any neutral axiological zone."[5] Thus in Orthodox Christianity, the world beyond the grave is divided into heaven and hell, whereas Catholic conceptions include a third space as well—purgatory, to which the souls of the not-entirely-righteous and not-entirely-sinful are consigned, those who have conducted themselves according to ordinary human standards and therefore, once they have undergone a purifying ordeal, may be found worthy of salvation. "In the real life of the medieval West, a broad range of neutral behaviors and neutral social institutions were thus enabled, things that were neither 'holy' nor 'sinful,' neither 'of the state' nor 'anti-state,' neither good nor bad."[6]

If a neutral zone is not fortified in a culture, then it begins to swing from one extreme to the other, from piety to godlessness, from asceticism to debauchery. This duality gives rise to upheaval, to a "rotational" model of development, where opposites rush headlong to change places, and there is no gradual evolution. All extremes are sharpened: God and the devil, saintliness and sin, the spiritual and the corporeal, religion and atheism, Christianity and paganism, the God-Man and the Man-God, state and individual, power and anarchy... Even when Russian culture undertakes to attempt a joining of two poles, it does so not via their evolutionary mediation but rather through their direct coupling, as

---

[5] Lotman and Uspenskii, "Rol' dual'nykh modelei v dinamike russkoi kul'tury (do kontsa XVIII veka)," 220.
[6] Ibid.

in Dostoevsky's characters, who are "too capacious" and simultaneously stare into the abysses above and below, at once encompassing the ideals of the Madonna and of Sodom.

The method Russian culture has developed to work with these opposites consists in "twisting" and "overturning" them: the sublime and majestic is revealed to have demonic features, while the base and minor are suddenly characterized by spiritual depth and devotion. The cultural dynamic is manifest in its hyper-intense paradoxicality. While the greatest of the Russian tsars, Peter I, and Russia herself, manifest demonic traits in the portrayals of Pushkin and Gogol, the littlest of the little men, the literary type of Bashmachkin, evolves into Prince Myshkin, the loftiest of figures in Russian literature.

This model of the ironic "reversal" or "inversion" of opposites affords us insight into the enduring structural features of Russian culture, which are reproduced in its various historical stages: pre-Soviet, Soviet, and post-Soviet.[7]

---

7 See my discussion of these dual and triadic models of Russian culture and the role of mediation between opposites in *Russian Spirituality and the Secularization of Culture*, 31–61 and 121–32.

PART I

The Titanic and the Demonic: Faust's Heirs

1 | Faust and Peter on the Seashore: From Goethe to Pushkin

a. Comparativistics and Typology

From its inception in the mid-nineteenth century, the comparative-historical method was directed against romantic aesthetics, the main purpose of which had been to gain insight into the creative spirit of a work, its singularity and the uniqueness of its author. What made the comparative method novel and valuable was that it discovered a work's dependency upon its literary environment and influences. The artist, till recently thought of as a "free genius," was now viewed as an intermediary in the exchange of plots, images, and ideas shifting from one literature to another.

However, the consistent application of this method, which treated literature not as the fruit of organic creativity but as a medium of cultural exchange, ultimately came to hinder the development of literary scholarship.[1] As Dionýz Ďurišin has justly put it, "From the genetic-contact standpoint, writers of the second rank are often far more illustrative than those of the first, because the continuity of interliterary values in their works is more linear."[2]

In search of a new methodology, one capable of analyzing artistically original phenomena, the field of comparative literature was forced to reject the primacy of "influences and borrowings" and return to examining the creative uniqueness of the works being compared. Thus arose and rapidly spread the field of *typological* research, focused on connections between literary phenomena that result not from direct interaction but in

---

[1] On the crisis in comparativistics and the flaws of this method, see Wellek, *Concepts of Criticism*, 282–95; Zhirmunskii, *Sravnitel'noe literaturovedenie: Vostok i Zapad*, 66–67, 101, 137, 185; and others.
[2] Diurishin, *Teoriia sravnitel'nogo izucheniia literatury*, 212.

4 The Titanic and the Demonic: Faust's Heirs

the course of parallel and independent development. Using the concepts of Leibniz, we may state that from the typological standpoint, artistic worlds are closed monads that do not communicate via doors and windows but rest on a common foundation and correspond to one another through a "preordained harmony."

Thus in the latter half of the twentieth century does the comparative-historical method undergo a comprehensive update. One of the ways in which comparative studies develops is to return to themes previously studied in terms of direct contact, and to broaden these subjects in the light of typological juxtapositions. The greater the artistic phenomenon, moreover, the less subject it is to external influences, and the greater the call, consequently, for a typological approach.

Hence the need to reexamine the theme, already sufficiently studied in terms of literary influence, of "Pushkin and Goethe." V. A. Rozov (*Pushkin and Goethe*), V. Zhirmunsky, D. Blagoi, and other Russian scholars have identified in their studies all the however-many major reminiscences of Goethean imagery and motifs to be found in Pushkin's oeuvre. It is unlikely that new facts in this area remain to be discovered, which renders a typological juxtaposition of the two artistic worlds all the more pressing. It is indicative that not a single comparative study—not even Rozov's book, justly criticized for deriving almost the whole of Pushkin from Goethe—has found room to discuss Pushkin's greatest creation, *The Bronze Horseman* (*Mednyi vsadnik*). And indeed, this long narrative poem does not contain any obvious intertextualities or reminiscences that might enable comparison with any work by Goethe. Nevertheless, a typological analysis allows us to uncover what the direct-contact approach has missed. Between *The Bronze Horseman*, written in 1833, and the second part of *Faust*, completed in 1831 and first published in 1833, there exists, even in the total absence of influence, borrowings, polemics, and the like, a profound correlation, and contrast, in terms of *artistic metaphysics*.

b. Toil and the Elements

After all his tireless seeking, and nearing his life's threshold, Goethe's Faust has resolved to expand coastal lands so as to wrest, step by step, the sea bed from the waves. For Faust, the sea embodies an elementality as mysterious and labile as the air, though amenable to toil and subjugation. Let us recall that at the end of act 3 of *Faust, Part Two*, the hero is borne upward, into the sky, and at the beginning of act 4, he descends from the clouds to a mountain range, from which he surveys the expanse of the sea. The heavens yield to the sea as Faust's dreaming—which had borne him away to distant places and times in search of beauty, and had faded forever upon the disappearance of Helen of Troy—is replaced by the urge to create. But Faust also rejects Mephistopheles's tempting proposals to arrange his life in a palace, to give himself over to enjoyment among "the most delightful women."[3] A "grandiose pleasure-palace" encompassing "straight ... avenues" and "velvet greensward"—all that had enthused him back when he loved Gretchen, this whole clinging and coddling world of nature—now repulses him as a "Babylonian debauch, modern vulgarity" (178). Now he has no use for land amid the land, tranquil and self-sufficient; but neither does he crave the heavens. "Perhaps, since you've learnt to float above the ground, / A mission to the moon is our next task?" asks Mephistopheles, mocking Faust's unwillingness to find earthly peace, to which the latter replies, "Certainly not! This earthly sphere / Is room enough for high deeds; here / I still can achieve wonders. Never / Have I felt such great strength for bold endeavour" (179). But where now is the desired sphere for this endeavor, since Faust can neither adhere to the Earth nor tear himself away from it? Where is this magical element which is on Earth but is not earth; whose elusive iridescence renders it like the heavens, though it is not found there? Faust casts his gaze to the sea. Here and only here can his final life's motto be carried out: "What matters but the deed?" (ibid.). From now on he shall aspire, not to earthly enjoyment, nor airy dreaming, but to work. Water, at once yielding as air and supple as soil, is the element that mediates between the earth and sky. Thus it is on the seashore that Faust's creative will, which aims to cast the heavens down to earth, is destined to be fulfilled.

To work means to impart form to inchoate chaos, and thus is the shore—the boundary between dry land and the waters—a place of intense

---

3 Goethe, *Faust, Part Two*, 178. Further citations in the text are to this translation.

6 The Titanic and the Demonic: Faust's Heirs

toil: here, before the yawning expanse and the waves' elemental onrush, a person is inspired to create:

> At once my plan was made! My soul shall boast
> An exquisite achievement: from our coast
> I'll ban the lordly sea, I'll curb its force,
> I'll set new limits to that watery plain
> And drive it back into itself again. (180)

These lines from Goethe's drama are as familiar to the German reader as the famous lines from Pushkin's epic poem are to the Russian, and likely arouse in both the same proud flush of sovereign ambition to master nature:

> On a shore washed by desolate waves, *he* stood,
> Full of high thoughts, and gazed into the distance.[4]

> На берегу пустынных волн
> Стоял он, дум великих полн,
> И вдаль глядел.[5]

Peter's creative thought is akin to the creative will of Faust; it manifests itself with the firmness of rock (the Greek πέτρος) and the aggressiveness of the fist (the German *Faust*), bestowing a wondrous structure on the senseless seething of the water, and building a dam, an artificial shore, wrested not from dry land by the sea but from the sea by human will.

These two great works thus interpret, in different ways, the same theme: the creation of a firm culture out of elemental instability; the power and labor by which mankind transforms nature. Could not the following words of Mephistopheles apply to Peter as well?

> Why these dark looks, this frowning brow?
> Sublime good fortune greets you now:

---

4 Pushkin, *The Bronze Horseman: Selected Poems of Alexander Pushkin*, 247. Further citations in the text are to this translation.
5 Pushkin, *Mednyi vsadnik*, 285. Further citations in the text are to this edition.

> By your high wisdom, the sea-shore
> And sea are reconciled once more;
> Now from the land in easy motion
> The ships glide swiftly to the ocean;
> And thus, here in this royal place,
> The whole world lies in your embrace! (212)

And could not the following verses of Pushkin sum up the regal project begun by Faust?

> A hundred years have passed, and the young city,
> The grace and wonder of the northern lands,
> Out of the gloom of forests and the mud
> Of marshes splendidly has risen;
> ....
> Now huge harmonious palaces and towers
> Crowd on the bustling banks; ships in their throngs
> Speed from all ends of the earth to the rich quays. (247)

> Прошло сто лет, и юный град,
> Полнощных стран краса и диво,
> Из тьмы лесов, из топи блат
> Вознесся пышно, горделиво;
> ....
> По оживленным берегам
> Громады стройные теснятся
> Дворцов и башен; корабли
> Толпой со всех концов земли
> К богатым пристаням стремятся. (285–86)

Here we might cite the original of the lines of Goethe (quoted above in the translation of David Luke) that most of all echo Pushkin's:

> Vom Ufer nimmt, zu rascher Bahn,
> Das Meer die Schiffe willig an;

8 The Titanic and the Demonic: Faust's Heirs

> So sprich, dass hier, hier vom Palast
> Dein Arm die ganze Welt umfasst.[6]

Most of the words in this excerpt directly correspond to or echo the introduction to *The Bronze Horseman*: "Ufer"—*bereg*, "shore"; "die Schiffe"—*korabli*, "ships"; "Palast"—*dvorets*, "palace"; "die ganze Welt," "the whole world"—*so vsekh kontsov zemli*, "from all ends of the earth"; "willig," "eagerly, ardently"—*stremiatsia*, they "speed"; "rascher," "swift, lively"—*ozhivlennym*, "bustling." Cf. also Goethe's "hier, hier vom," "from here" (212) and Pushkin's *otsel'* (285), "from here" (247); and Goethe's "Dein Arm die ganze Welt umfasst," "The whole world lies in your embrace" (212) and Pushkin's *nogoiu tverdoi stat' pri more* (285), "To stand with a firm foothold on the sea" (247). Also very similar are the syntactic constructions both poets use to contrast the two states of the locale, before and after development: Pushkin has *gde prezhde ... nyne tam* (286), "where once ... now" (247); Goethe has "hier stand ... wo jetzt," "here ... was ... where now" (212). The impression of the two poetic texts' resemblance is heightened by the closeness of their rhythmic structure (iambic tetrameter).

This thematic, in places almost textual coincidence between Goethe's drama (part 2, acts 4 and 5) and Pushkin's poem, which to my knowledge has gone previously unnoticed, is all the more significant in that there is no basis here by which to assign historical priority to either writer. We have no evidence that Pushkin was acquainted with the second part of *Faust*, whose first part so interested him and inspired his writing of *A Scene from Faust* (*Stsena iz Fausta*, 1825). Incidentally, as to the question of who first devised a dramatic situation involving Faust and the sea, that honor belongs to Pushkin: in *A Scene from Faust*, the hero appears on the seashore several years before a similar mise-en-scène was realized in the final acts of Goethe's *Faust, Part Two* (1830–31). The idea that Pushkin wrote *The Bronze Horseman* with Goethe consciously in mind is even more dubious than the reverse notion, that Pushkin's *Scene* spurred Goethe to complete *Faust*.[7] If there was a dispute between the poets, then

---

6   Goethe, *Faust: Der Tragödie erster und zweiter Teil*, 389.
7   This hypothesis, rejected in its time by Sergei Durylin and subsequently revived by the French Slavist André Meynieux, remains essentially as irrefutable as it is unprovable. See Alekseev, "Zametki na poliakh: K 'Stsene iz Fausta' Pushkina."

it existed on a level far deeper than purposeful imitation or polemic: it was a dispute between artistic worldviews, between cultural traditions.

Goethe and Pushkin represent similar stages in the formation of the two literatures—when, out of the chaos of thought and feelings gripping a nation, a harmonious, crystalline form is born, one capable of serving forever as a classical model. The theme of reining in the agitated elements is so important to both poets because they themselves strove for a goal just as exalted: "out of the gloom of forests and the mud of marshes" of an as-yet unconstructed culture, to erect a "young city" (247), to lay the foundation for national consciousness as a model for the architecture of the spirit. Goethe and Pushkin are classical in their outlook in the sense that both in history and poetry alike, they value most of all that moment when chaos ripens into form—a feat performed by objective art. The romantic thrust heavenward, or the realistic or naturalistic clinging to the soil, are equally alien to them. They rejoice in the sea, the most malleable and transparent of plastic materials, in which the sky is reflected, and which the land seeks to master.

The love of Goethe and Pushkin for the sea is a demanding one; at its base, it is the love characteristic of an architect or even an engineer. Creative toil on the shore, the construction of an artificial barrier—this is the quintessential spirit of modernity. Prototypical of Greek classicism, and of Greek technology, was the ship that plied the limpid southern seas. It was by ship that the Achaeans reached Troy, by ship that Odysseus returned to Ithaca. A ship is open to the movement of waves and wind, and is animated by the seas' elements. The earthen rampart or granite bank that curbs these elements is completely different; it does not hurl itself into their embrace but, with their unruliness in view, shackles them. A ship is a particle of terra firma that has been entrusted to the sea; a dam is a mass of terra firma to guard against the water. The Hellene gave himself over to the power of nature; the European began to master it. The Dutch dams, protecting part of the country from the water's onslaught, are among the first and more glaring proofs of humanity's new handling of nature. Whereas during the Renaissance, southern Europe sent ship after ship to unknown lands (Columbus, Vasco da Gama), the north came to maturity with a grim

10   The Titanic and the Demonic: Faust's Heirs

vocation all its own, and began to erect, with the hands of the Dutch, such earthen barriers as would have made no sense to the Greeks: after all, the rocky shores of Hellas afforded reliable protection against the waves' assault.

But when nature provides no rock, when the shores are all marshland and moss, then appears a rock-man, Peter; then is built a rock-city, Petrograd, with a German accent: Petersburg. The Petersburg theme in *The Bronze Horseman* is historically rooted in the same world from which Goethe gleaned the idea of how to conclude his *Faust*. Holland was the first European country to live in defiance of its natural conditions: engineering arose of necessity; because the soil was too low, the whole country (the *Nether*lands, the *low* lands) was literally underwater. The very foundation of living—land itself—had to be constructed artificially. It was to Holland that Peter came to study shipbuilding; and it can hardly be said for sure how much of that training, what portion of the spirit of the Netherlands, was mixed in with Peter's vision of building a city, with the idea of bringing thousands of people to the "mossy, marshy" lowlands (*The Bronze Horseman*, 247) to wrest land from the sea, to build palaces on soil only barely wrung of its moisture. Holland is the common homeland of the Faustian and Petrine ideas: the pathos akin to both, expressed by the mottos: "[May] even the conquered elements ... make / Their peace with you" (*The Bronze Horseman*, 249); "This ... elemental energy.... / This I would fight, and conquer if I can" (*Faust*, 180). What draws Goethe and Pushkin artistically to a harmonious rearrangement of chaos was anticipated by Dutch craftsmen and surveyors' battle with water. Goethe meant to hold up their first modest experiment as an ideal for the edification of the future, while Peter, sung by Pushkin, took it over and carried it out on the grand scale of Russian history.

c. *The Bronze Horseman* as the Anti-Faust

What the two works under discussion have in common allows us to pinpoint their more substantive differences. No less aware than Pushkin of the grave aftermath of the Petersburg flood of 1824, Goethe indeed took a more philosophical and serious attitude toward it than did the young Russian poet, who from his confinement at Mikhailovskoe evinced a lightly mocking tone regarding the disaster befalling the capital from which he'd been banished. There is reason to believe that it was precisely this "great calamity" (to quote Goethe) that gave the German poet the creative impetus to complete *Faust*, specifically, by suggesting the theme of humanity's struggle with the sea. In his remarkable article "Petersburg in Goethe's *Faust* (Toward a Compositional History of *Faust, Part Two*)," B. Geiman goes so far as to say that "had Goethe not been so shaken by the news of the catastrophe in St. Petersburg, the second part of Faust may have remained unwritten."[8] In that case it is all the more striking that in Goethe's consciousness the Petersburg flood should elicit the image of building a city on a seashore. The fact that Goethe in *Faust, Part Two* and Pushkin in *The Bronze Horseman* refer to the same historical phenomenon throws the difference in their artistic conceptions into even sharper relief.

Pushkin's work *begins* where *Faust*, in effect, *concludes*: with the image of a beautiful city having arisen amid swamps thanks to immense labor and innumerable sacrifices. *Faust* presents the conception of the project, the beginning of its execution, the process of toil itself, while *The Bronze Horseman* shows the result. That which *Faust* considers "wisdom's final word" (223)—power over nature, achieved via daily struggle—is, in *The Bronze Horseman*, merely a given, a reality preceding the work's main events. It is as if Pushkin grants, Let's say Faust's labor, however hard and long, has all paid off: where once there were waves, now there are bridges and granite. Now what? Taking history's hint, Pushkin answers: a flood. *Faust* involves the *draining* of swamps; *The Bronze Horseman*, to the contrary—the *swamping* of a city. The elements prove stronger than manmade barriers; they come gushing over granite, they destroy shelter and bring thousands to their doom. Previously it had been easy enough for a Finnish pauper in a humble canoe to avoid the danger of these elements; he had trusted them, not walled himself off from them, and lived in peace

---

8 Geiman, "Peterburg v 'Fauste' Gete (k tvorcheskoi istorii 2-i chasti 'Fausta')," 68.

on the "marshy banks" (247). But now the inhabitants of the majestic capital perish, it having been the city-founder's "fateful will" (256) to set them in opposition to the elements, to order them, in Faustian terms, into "strife" therewith. ("Only that man earns freedom, merits life, / Who must reconquer both in constant daily strife" [*Faust*, 223].)

The sea takes up the challenge: "Siege! Assault! The sly waves" (251) attack. This is what Pushkin emphasizes—the backlash of the elements as they return to the boundaries assigned them by natural law. In Goethe, man's creative will triumphs; in Pushkin, it is put to the most exacting test and found wanting.

Here it is worth recalling that Pushkin's *A Scene from Faust* (1825), which chronologically precedes Goethe's "seashore" scenes, similarly concludes as if clearly rebutting them. The protagonist is a bored Faust, further than ever from fulfilling his wish to stop time. Like Goethe's Faust, he is disappointed, as he nears the end of his life, in the results of all his former questing: for love, glory, and knowledge. But this disillusionment does not induce him to counter all these failed attempts to gain happiness free of charge (i.e., via the "largesse" of Mephistopheles) with daily effort or the habit of work, to look upon time and striving as the only means of achieving eternal bliss. No, for Pushkin's Faust, time and eternity are two very different entities: time is meaningless, since reason judges everything from the standpoint of eternity; but eternity is vacuous, for life proceeds only in the course of time. All that remains is to be bored, to studiously squander one's time, burdened with the bad infinity that lies ahead. (One of Pushkin's Faust-pieces includes the lines "After all, we're not playing for money, / But just to pass the eternity!"[9]) Labor is the acceptance and justification of all that is rational amid the transience of existence, while boredom is the sensation of the senselessness of all that is finite, even as the infinite and eternal are also unattainable. Labor resigns itself to the necessity of time, it understands that effort is gradual, while boredom finds gradualness oppressive, languishing at the thought of it, and takes delight in the destruction of all finite things.

---

9 Pushkin, *Sobranie sochinenii v 10 tomakh*, 2:519.

This is why Faust the worker (Goethe) and Faust the bored (Pushkin) act so differently on the shore: one erects a dam with the help of Mephistopheles, while the other demands that the devil sink a ship. Pushkin's Faust is amused by the sight of a speck of terra firma sinking to the bottom of the ocean of eternity. Goethe's Faust, to the contrary, intends to build an earthen rampart, a structure assembled by humble human effort over the course of time, yet worthy of resisting the eternal ocean. Finally, Pushkin's Peter builds a far stronger rampart, one made of granite—but over it roll the lethal waves.

It should be noted that in both *A Scene from Faust* and *The Bronze Horseman*, Pushkin's theme is not the subjugation but rather the *triumph* of the elements, as summoned by man himself (Faust), or in defiance of his (Peter's) challenge. Waters flood the deck of a ship or a whole city ("plunged to the waist in water" [*The Bronze Horseman*, 251]). Creative toil is fated either never to commence, due to all-destroying boredom, or never to be completed, due to the all-destroying elements. States of being are revealed that render toil impossible, useless. And indeed, in effect, all nineteenth-century Russian literature depicts, following Pushkin, conditions that defy and irrationalize the idea of work. This state of affairs is rooted either in the soul of a person who languishes at the thought of life and does not know what to do with himself,[10] or in the circumstances of historical being, which threatens labor with natural disasters and popular uprisings. When Russian literature depicts a laboring, or at least active, enterprising person—be it Chichikov, Shtol'ts, Nikolai Rostov (in the epilogue of *War and Peace* [*Voina i mir*]), Razumikhin, or Lopakhin—the very activity of these people stands as a sign of their limitedness, of the fact that they are not privy to higher truth. Clearly, a bored Faust and a raging Neva—these Pushkinian antitheses of the German Faust who is intoxicated by the spirit of work—are not incidental to the mindset of Russian literature.

In the interest of avoiding overinterpretation, it should be noted precisely what work means in this case. It is one thing for the business-like Dutch to conduct their land projects; they are forced to deal with the

---

10 The Russian literary type of the "superfluous man" is gendered.

14 The Titanic and the Demonic: Faust's Heirs

unfavorable conditions of their small country and must adapt to nature's caprices in order to survive. An entirely different matter is the transformational activity of Peter, his desire to raise a new capital on a swampy shore, summoning thousands of people from the plains of an enormous country to take up the prideful toil of subjugating the elements.

It would seem that, as Goethe put it, Peter merely wished to "repeat Amsterdam, so dear to his youth, in a metropolis at the mouth of the Neva."[11] But this very secondariness, the "premeditation" of his undertaking, forced him to ignore the natural duty of a builder: that of taking the soil, the foundation, into account. "An old shipmaster" warned Peter that he must build on higher ground, "and prophesied that the people would be drowned every seventy years. There stood also an old tree with various marks from times when the waters had risen to a great height. But all this was in vain; the emperor stood to his whim, and had the tree cut down, that it might not bear witness against him. You will confess that such conduct is very strange in so great a man."[12] There was no pressing need to build a new Amsterdam, nothing of the urgency that led the Dutch to defend their low-lying country.

Hence the mysteriousness Goethe senses in Peter's activity and very character—a quality the poet uses to define the nature of the demonic. To Eckermann's question, "Has not Mephistophiles [sic] ... demonic traits?" Goethe replies, "No ... Mephistophiles is much too negative a being: the Demonic manifests itself in a thoroughly active power."[13] *It is not Mephistopheles, suffused with an appetite for destruction, who is demonic, but rather Faust, who makes plans to create.* Only his "active power" can give impetus to Mephistopheles as a "negative being."

True, Goethe includes an elderly couple whose patriarchal idyll, and very lives, are destroyed by the aggressive progress of Faust's labor, which raises doubt as to the moral value thereof. But here the difference with Pushkin's poem is particularly glaring. Philemon and Baucis have lived a full life; the youthful epoch shunts the old folks aside, and their end is as if predetermined by the natural order of things.

---

11 Eckermann, *Conversations with Goethe*, 408.
12 Ibid., 407.
13 Ibid., 526.

Pushkin's Evgenii and Parasha, by contrast, are young; nature itself has not yet managed to attain its purpose through them—their union is destroyed at the very outset. The blow delivered by the state utopia against the family idyll is here a deeper one, striking its very foundations. The loss is more unnatural, more painful in Pushkin's narrative, and has a different place therein than in Goethe's: not as setting the stage for Faust's final glorious deeds, his grand finale, but as a refutation of what Peter has done, and a challenge to his memory and monument, his own immortalized moment. In both cases—Philemon and Baucis, Evgenii and Parasha—it is precisely marriage that proves incompatible with the builder's singular will as he determines the fate of people. What is ancestral perishes, what is individual is affirmed; the private perishes, while the state is affirmed: the individual heading the state, the individual's state, the power of the ego. But while Pushkin devotes his final word to the deceased Evgenii, Goethe's goes to Faust triumphant. The latter discourse is not a quiet mourning over a poor madman but a loud exulting over a soul that has gained immortality and higher truth. Goethe and Pushkin develop a similar plot in opposite directions: from sacrifice and destruction to the deed's endowment with meaning and justification from above; from a grand organizational achievement to destruction and sacrifice.

d. Demonic Irony

There is another substantive difference we have not yet taken into account: the builders Faust and Mephistopheles are responsible for Philemon and Baucis's perishing, whereas in the case of Parasha and then Evgenii, the guilty party is the raging elements. Peter, it seems, is not responsible for the flood; to the contrary, he had made every effort to fortify the city. But then again, neither does Faust order Philemon and Baucis killed; he merely asks Mephistopheles to negotiate with them, to offer them a relocation on advantageous terms, which results in their house burning down, thus making way for the construction of the future city. At fault, of course, is Mephistopheles, the middleman between Faust and the world, who distorts the kindly initiatives of the hero. But then again, the whole construction of dams, the whole grandiose project of draining the swamps and settling a "free people on free land" (223)—this too is carried out by Mephistopheles, who acts as the over*seer* of these tasks, Faust having gone blind in his old age. The crowds of workers, wielding shovels for days on end, and representing the coming age of laboring humanity, are there only to provide cover, an idyllic gloss for a diabolical design. In reality the night work is carried out by some sort of hellish forces, which light up the darkness, as Baucis remarks: "Slaves toiled vainly: blow by blow, / Pick and shovel made no way. / Then we saw the night-flames glow—And a dam stood there next day" (209).

There is something similarly unnatural, unclean, in the place where Peter has built his city: here too, night and day have got mixed together amid "transparent twilight" and "moonless glitter" (248). In both *Faust* and *The Bronze Horseman*, the violation of the order of things is signified by white nights, by rivers of fire cutting canals through the darkness—a luminescence that has forced its way into the sanctuary of night. The boundary between light and darkness is primordial, established on the first day of creation; which means that forces rebelling against God's world should first of all violate precisely this boundary, an original commandment of the physical order, just as they break the main commandment of the moral order: "thou shalt not kill." Evidently, violating the border between sea and land—a dividing-line established on the third day of creation—must extend to all other boundaries as well: between light and dark, between life and death. All the borders by which the world was originally shaped and harmonized are done away with. This is the true significance of Mephistopheles's work, to which Faust ascribed a higher, beneficent meaning. The essence of it is not to establish a new border (i.e., pushing back the sea) but to destroy the old one and cast the world into chaos. Mephistopheles is busy erecting an artificial shore because he wants to eliminate the natural, original (if "mossy, marshy") one. Thrown off balance, the world will wobble and crash. Forced to retreat from its shores, the sea will never rest; it will make war against the land, and henceforth all borders will be destroyed. This triumph of chaos is in fact Mephistopheles's goal; for him, "[t]he Eternal Void is what

I'd much prefer" (224). Mephistopheles does not conceal his mockery from the reader, saying, out of earshot of the half-deaf Faust:

> And yet it's us you're working for
> With all your foolish dams and dikes;
> Neptune, the water-devil, likes
> To think of the great feast there'll be
> When they collapse. Do what you will, my friend,
> You all are doomed! They are in league with me,
> The elements, and shall destroy you in the end. (222)

Mephistopheles's plan is clear: populate most densely the newly gained land, the shore, so that the elements might ultimately carry off millions of souls. The devil Mephistopheles is not working for humanity's benefactor Faust but for his own brother, the sea-devil Neptune.

Faust the *bored*, the one who makes a gift of a ship to the sea, turns out to be all talk, a piker in comparison to Faust the *worker*, who—with a helping hand from Mephistopheles—is diligently preparing to give a whole country to the sea: not "three hundred scoundrels"[14] (as in Pushkin's *A Scene from Faust*) but the millions of "free people" who have settled near the elements allegedly tamed by Faust's "mastering will" (221). And the first victim after Philemon and Baucis is Faust himself: the clanging of shovels and hoes wherein he fancies hearing the grandiose creative work of the people, in reality means that the lemurs, evil little spirits, are digging his grave. "The clash of spades: how it delights my heart!" (222), exclaims Faust, seeing in his mind's eye the zealous fulfillers of his will but in fact addressing his own gravediggers. This line contains the whole irony of creative titanism, which moves shorelines while preparing the triumph of destructive chaos. "The digging has gone well today; / No ditch or dike, but dust to dust, they say" (223), remarks Mephistopheles under his breath.[15] "Peter's City" (249) becomes just such a sarcophagus for flood victims. Mephistopheles's threat does not come true in the German drama, in which the devil is ultimately disgraced (as angels snatch Faust's soul

---

14 Pushkin, *Sobranie sochinenii v 10 tomakh*, 2:111.
15 "Pun[ning] untranslatably," as Luke notes, "on *Graben* (ditch) and *Grab* (grave)" (282).

from his grasp). But this threat—"The elements ... shall destroy you in the end"—*is* carried out in the Russian poem.

The distinctiveness of Pushkin's Peter lies in the fact that he is not divided into human and diabolic hypostases, as are Faust and Mephistopheles in Goethe's portrayal. Peter is both. When he stands on that "shore washed by desolate waves ... full of high thoughts," when the city he has founded flourishes magnificently on the banks of the Neva, he is Faust, the "wonder-working builder" (*stroitel' chudotvornyi*; *Mednyi vsadnik*, 297). But the miracle that had raised Petersburg has the same troubling, unclean tinge as the night fires' "industry" (212) in *Faust*. The legend that Peter was the Antichrist arose even during his lifetime. It was based not only on his abolition of the patriarchate, and the travesties of religious services he arranged, but also the sacrilege associated with the construction of Petersburg. For instance, construction work on stone churches was halted throughout Russia—all the stone, all the masons, were being forcibly sent to the construction site of the new capital. Thus did Tsar Peter in effect take the famous words addressed in the Scripture to his apostolic namesake—"upon this rock I will build my church"—and turn them inside out; now stone was being confiscated, quite literally, from churches. The very beginning of Pushkin's *History of Peter the First* (*Istoriia Petra I*) includes the remarkable phrase "The people considered Peter to be the Antichrist,"[16] and *The Bronze Horseman* expresses the same apocalyptic view.

e. Pushkin between Goethe and Mickiewicz

This is not a matter only of legend but also of the specific poetic work that served as Pushkin's reference point as he composed *The Bronze Horseman*—namely, the famous "Fragment" from part three of Mickiewicz's *Forefathers' Eve* (*Dziady*, 1832), which is devoted entirely to Russia. Here Peter's city is perceived as a product of the evilest, most satanic forces in history, hence doomed to earn, sooner or later, God's wrath and destruction:

> Rome displays the labors of mankind,
> While lovely Venice was by gods designed;

---

16 Pushkin, *Sobranie sochinenii v 10 tomakh*, 8:12.

> But he who views St. Petersburg will find
> That such a pile demons alone could raise.[17]

For Mickiewicz, Petersburg is a city that has sprouted up from blood, its soil thus incapable of growing anything truly great: "What though a hundred thousand peasants died! / Upon the piles, upon their trampled forms / He built his firm foundation."[18] *The Bronze Horseman* is usually interpreted as Pushkin's polemical response to this Polish rebel's disparaging portrait of the Russian capital.[19] And indeed, Pushkin's introduction is suffused with admiration for the city's *derzhavnost'*, its sovereign and majestic power:

> I love you, Peter's creation, I love your stern
> Harmonious look, the Neva's majestic [*derzhavnoe*] flow,
> Her granite banks, the iron tracery
> Of your railings. (248)

> Люблю тебя, Петра творенье,
> Люблю твой строгий, стройный вид,
> Невы державное теченье,
> Береговой ее гранит,
> Твоих оград узор чугунный. (286)

Pushkin delights in precisely that which Mickiewicz finds repulsive. What seems to the Polish poet an oppressive flatness and straightness ("all as uniform in roofs and walls / As is an army corps, newly equipped"[20]) is for the Russian poet a "stern, harmonious" appearance. To Mickiewicz, the bronze monument to Peter, too, and this whole city-fortress of stone, seem like a frozen waterfall bound to melt under the hot rays of freedom. Pushkin, by contrast, is far from the Polish romantic's aspiration to destroy the citadel, to melt the architectural ice for the sake of some

---

17 Mickiewicz, *Poems by Adam Mickiewicz*, 344.
18 Ibid., 343.
19 See, for instance, Blagoi, "Mitskevich i Pushkin."
20 Mickiewicz, *Poems by Adam Mickiewicz*, 344.

boundless outpouring of the spirit of freedom. For Pushkin, Petersburg is the grand accomplishment of Faust, while for Mickiewicz, it is the fulfillment of Mephistopheles's maleficence.

But in the wake of this odic introduction, in the poem's first part and especially its second, Pushkin not only preserves the "satanic" motif proposed by Mickiewicz, he even develops it, in the image of a statue come to life. Pushkin, of course, does not proclaim Peter the Antichrist, in part due to the restrictions of censorship, and in part because he is largely devoid of the openly rhetorical pathos at times characteristic of Mickiewicz. But the main point is that Peter combines in himself the Faustian and Mephistophelian, and the latter comes through with especial ominousness precisely in the figure of the "wonder-working builder" hymned in the introduction—a bold new Faust.

Peter's satanism is signified first and foremost by the words "prideful *graven image*" (gordelivym *istukanom*, 297) and "*idol* on a bronze steed" (*kumir* na bronzovom kone, 292) (here and below, emphasis mine), which have a biblical subtext: "Ye shall make you no idols nor graven image." As if anticipating the future history of humanity, the book of Revelation lists (9:20) several such "gods," who gradually decrease in material value: "they did not stop worshiping demons, and idols of gold, silver, bronze, stone and wood—idols that cannot see or hear or walk." Significantly, right in the middle of this array we find "bronze." Pushkin's poem furthermore calls Peter "lord of half the world" (256)— that is, the Antichrist is halfway to his goal of world domination. The satanic overtones of the concepts of "idol" and "graven image" were so obvious that the tsar himself, having read the poem with the eye of a censor, crossed these seditious words out, forcing the poet to find the lesser replacements of "giant" (*gigant*) and "cliff" (*skala*). In Roman Jakobson's article "The Statue in Pushkin's Poetic Mythology," the demonic meaning of sculptural imagery (in *The Stone Guest* [*Kamennyi gost'*], *The Bronze Horseman*, and "The Golden Cockerel" ["Zolotoi petushok"]) is explained by way not only of a generally religious but specifically a Russian Orthodox worldview. "Precisely the Orthodox tradition, which severely condemned the art of sculpture, which did not admit it into churches, and which understood it as a pagan or diabolic vice (the two concepts were equivalent for the Church), suggested to Puškin the close association of statues with idolatry, with devilry, with sorcery. ... On Russian soil, sculpture was closely associated with whatever was unchristian, even antichristian, in the spirit of the Petersburg tsardom."[21]

Superimposed upon the biblical motif of idolatry here is a romantic one, that of the inanimate coming to life. Pushkin's Peter is not merely a "graven image" that "cannot see or hear or walk"; this "idol of bronze" hears Evgenii's threat, casts his gaze upon him, and chases him along the "shaking" (257) pavement. The coming to life of a statue, or a mechanism, corpse, doll, or picture, signals the fairly traditional literary motif of the encroachment of demonic forces into the human world. The works of E. T. A. Hoffmann, Edgar Allen Poe, Prosper Mérimée ("La Vénus d'Ille"), and other of Pushkin's contemporaries are full of similarly archetypal images; in Russian literature, these are frequently found in the works of Gogol, in such stories as "May Night, or The Drowned Maiden" ("Maiskaia noch', ili Utoplennitsa"), "Viy," and "The Portrait" ("Portret"). The devil does not have his own creative power, cannot create living tissue—all that godly business of fertilizing and growing is beyond his abilities. His easiest way into this world, which he has condemned and rejected, is from without, through dead matter—the painted surface of a canvas, a statue sculpted in bronze, etc. The mysterious force that suddenly animates these objects betrays its diabolical nature by its hostility to everything living, which it aims to deaden, numb, and carry back with it to hell. A reanimated young witch gets out of her coffin, summoning unclean forces to her aid, and pursues Khoma—and the latter falls dead; a moneylender's portrait comes to life to enslave an artist's soul and lead him to his doom.

And lastly, this infernal motif appears several times in the works of Pushkin himself. In *The Stone Guest*, the commodore's handshake, the squeeze of his right hand of stone, casts Don Juan down to the underworld; the queen of spades (in the eponymous story "Pikovaia dama") winks at Germann from her card, just he is dealt this instead of the ace he needed,

---

21 Jakobson, *Puškin and His Sculptural Myth*, 40.

ruining his life and plunging him into madness. In just the same way, the bronze horseman quits his pedestal and threatens Evgenii with death. There is a direct correlation of this motif in Revelation: "[The Antichrist] had power to give life unto the image of the beast, that the image of the beast should both speak, and cause that as many as would not worship the image of the beast should be killed" (13:15). And of course, the fact that a dead image has been imbued with life does not mean resurrection. The Antichrist is neither himself resurrected, nor does he resurrect the dead; he only ensouls what is dead in order to rob the soul of the living. The graven image has "thought ... on his brow," but as for the human being, his "mind could not endure" (*The Bronze Horseman*, 256, 255).

Significantly, in all these cases of contact with the demonic, the main characters—Evgenii in *The Bronze Horseman*, Germann in "The Queen of Spades," Chartkov in "The Portrait," Nathanael in Hoffmann's "The Sandman"—all first lose their minds, then perish. The destruction of the spirit precedes that of the flesh. The Neva's overflowing its banks, the monument's coming down from its pedestal, and the madness of Evgenii—in all three events, the boundaries of existence are erased, and we sense the primordial "fateful will" of him who shifted the division between the waters and the land, who carried out a literal *upheaval* so that a city might be "founded *under* the sea" (*pod morem gorod osnovalsia*).[22]

Some mysterious commonality seems to exist between the bronze horseman and the raging river, not just in the fact that they both pursue Evgenii and drive him mad, but in their interaction with one another. The enraged river does not touch the horseman, as if pacified in his presence; "over ... the turbulent Neva" stands the horseman himself "with outstretched arm" (252). After all, the Neva's revolt against St. Petersburg is clearly foreordained by Peter's own revolt against nature—and in this sense they are allies.

f. Apocalypse

In *The Bronze Horseman*, Pushkin develops the apocalyptic motifs encountered throughout Mickiewicz's Petersburg cycle. In the poem

---

22 Pushkin, *Mednyi vsadnik*, 297; emphasis mine.

"Oleszkiewicz: The Day before the St. Petersburg Flood of 1824," the following prophesy (here in a literal prose rendering) is placed—on the eve of the flood—in the mouth of a Polish artist living in the Russian capital:

> He who will live to see to-morrow will see great miracles. It will be the second but not the last trial. The Lord will shake the foundations of the Assyrian throne, the Lord will shake the ground of the city of Babylon; Lord, let me pass before the third test comes.[23]

In Mickiewicz, this is foretold. In Pushkin, it is depicted. "The people gaze upon the wrath of God / And await their doom" (251), as if the end-times have come; death itself, escaping its assigned space, has entered the city. "Coffins from the [flooded] / Cemetery ... float along the streets!" (ibid.). Bridges that had formerly hung "poised over [the] waters" now collapse, "swept away by the storm" (248, 251). Like Revelation's "beast of the sea," the Neva "roared ... [and] suddenly / Hurled herself on the city like a beast. / Everything ran before her, everything / Suddenly became deserted" (251).

The picture of this "second trial" unwittingly calls to mind a picture of the "first"; after all, it is precisely the fall of Babylon that is depicted in Revelation:

> Alas, alas, that great city, that was clothed in fine linen, and purple, and scarlet, and decked with gold, and precious stones, and pearls! For in one hour so great riches is come to nought. And every shipmaster, and all the company in ships, and sailors, and as many as trade by sea, stood afar off.... And they cast dust on their heads, and cried, weeping and wailing, saying, Alas, alas, that great city, wherein were made rich all that had ships in the sea by reason of her costliness! for in one hour is she made desolate. (18:16–19)

---

23 Cited from Weintraub, *The Poetry of Adam Mickiewicz*, 181. According to Mickiewicz, Petersburg is fated to suffer the second tribulation, the first being that which befell the capital of the ancient world. The third "trial"—that which the prophet hopes he does not live to see—is the Judgement Day that will end all time.

But it is not just this picture of "wrath" and "doom," but the image of the horseman as well, that ties Pushkin's poem with Revelation: "How terrible / He was in the surrounding murk!" (256). The bronze horseman, at a gallop through the desolate streets of St. Petersburg—is this not one of the four horsemen of the apocalypse, as if transported here straight from the streets of Babylon? "And I looked, and behold a pale horse: and his name that sat on him was Death, and Hell followed with him. And power was given unto them over the fourth part of the earth" (Revelation 6:8). The Petersburg horseman, too, is given great power over the earth—twice as much territory as his Babylonian counterpart[24]: he is, as mentioned above, "lord of half the world" (according to Revelation, on the eve of the third "trial," the last judgement, the Antichrist takes power over the whole world). Pushkin's description even preserves a key characteristic of the apocalyptic horseman—his paleness, the color of death:

> And lit by the *pale* moonlight, stretching out
> His hand aloft, the Bronze Horseman rushes
> After him. . . . (257)

> И, озарен луною бледной,
> Простерши руку в вышине,
> За ним несется Всадник Медный (298)

Thus while the poem's introduction calls the notion of Peter-as-Satan into question, the rest of the work takes up this image and develops it. There is an enormous difference between the two Peters. The individual standing on the shore and gazing into the distance is not even named; there is only the pronoun "he." No specific name has been bestowed on the creator—he encloses the whole world in his thought. His spirit moves over the watery wastes, ready to take up acts of creation ("On a shore washed by *desolate* waves, *he* stood, / *Full* of high thoughts"). But now the void has been filled, the city built, and Peter stands before us, not as creative thought, but as a soulless idol. Hardly accidental, of course, is the horse's deafening clatter

---

24 It should be recalled that by "Babylon," the book of Revelation means Rome.

on the pavement: this is the sound of bronze on stone, solid against solid. The whole horror of Peter's inexorable gait is in this sharp, lapidary sound: "like the rumble of thunder—the heavily resounding gallop" (*kak budto groma grokhotan'e—tiazhelo-zvonkoe skakan'e*, 298), and later, again: "on the resoundingly galloping steed" (*na zvonko-skachushchem kone*, 298).

Only three times in the whole poem does Pushkin call Peter by name, and these are all in the introduction, in the lyric ode to Petersburg: "I love you, Peter's creation"; "Flaunt your beauty, Peter's City, and stand"; "let them not disturb ... Peter's eternal sleep" (248–49). In each of these contexts, Peter's name is inseparable from the name of the city. But further, over the course of the poem's two main parts, Peter's name is not mentioned at all. Here there are only common nouns—"idol," "graven image," and "bronze horseman"—this last epithet, in fulfillment of the whole Petrine theme, rising to the level of a proper name ("the Bronze Horseman rushes / After him"). As a person, Peter is entirely absent from the poem: the beginning features only the super-persona of the creator; the end, the inanimacy of an idol.

The beginning of the poem is the grand thought of Peter; its finale, the madness of Evgenii. Pushkin demonstrates how the Faustian idea, obeying the rigid, alienating force of history, leads to a Mephistophelian outcome.

g. The Transformation of the Faustian into the Mephistophelian

Pushkin's treatment of this theme differs substantially from that of Goethe in that his Faust and Mephistopheles are not separate characters; the same historical figure turns out to be both Faust and Mephistopheles. Goethe divides the two—a fundamentally optimistic move: this way, the devil/destroyer can be disgraced, and the creative genius crowned. But in Peter the two are inextricable. Pushkin loves Peter's creation, and cannot withhold his admiration before its "harmonious" design, but he is also horrified by its destructive outcome. For Goethe, good and evil are separable, as if coexisting in space rather than one turning into the other in time. This is why Faust can be snatched away from Mephistopheles, or rather, his spirit can be, as the angels do in the denouement ("This noble spirit saved alive / Has foiled the Devil's will!" [234]). But what will become of the dam, what will people do on their newly gained land, and how will the sea, which has been forced to retreat, respond?—this is left unsaid. The optimistic appraisal of Faust's labor can be explained by the fact that it has only just begun, and is represented solely in Faust's dazzling visions (or, as Mephistopheles less charitably puts it, the "changeful fantasies" Faust has been "whoring after" [223]). It is only the *anticipation* of that "beautiful moment" (ibid.) when his dream will be fulfilled that enables the "bliss" (ibid.) Faust experiences at death's door. Heavenly salvation is granted him, moreover, only in recognition of his aspirations: he "strive[d] … and live[d] to strive" (234). Faust departs the pages of Goethe's drama the same as Peter appears in Pushkin's poem—full of high thoughts, and gazing into the distance of time.

Mickiewicz, to the contrary, sees Petersburg only as the logical result of tyranny—an agglomeration of stone hostile to people. He senses in it no embodiment of harmony, nor triumph of human thought; and so condemns it entirely, damning it as a creation of Satan. Goethe's optimism and Mickiewicz's pessimism are each in their own way justified.[25]

As for Pushkin, he combines his poem's "Faustian" introduction with a "Mephistophelian" conclusion. Pushkin shares neither the optimism of the German poet nor the Polish one's apocalyptic gloom. In his view, his nation is fated to perform the historical *transformation of the Faustian into the Mephistophelian*; to bring about the triumph of a magnificent state structure, a unifying order of the sort one could take pride in (Mickiewicz was, alas, denied this), *as well as* the destruction of freedom, of the right to a private life, which one cannot help being horrified by (Goethe was fortunately spared this). Faust and Mephistopheles cannot make history alone, only together. Pushkin's poem embodies both the motifs expressed separately by Goethe and Mickiewicz. Here we might recall that the three works were composed almost simultaneously, in 1831, 1832, and 1833, which lends their juxtaposition a particularly concrete historical meaning.

The duality of Pushkin's poem is expressed through the formal strictness of its composition. Two voices are heard in the poem: in the

---

25 Part three of *Forefathers' Eve* was written in 1832 and bears directly upon the defeat of the Polish uprising of 1830.

introduction, the author's ("I love you, Peter's creation"); in the first and especially second part, that of a character (who denounces the "wonder-working builder" with a "just you wait!" [257]). But nowhere is there any dialogic interaction, just as there is no direct confrontation. Neither the author's praise of Peter nor the main character's vituperation of him constitute the whole truth, insofar as the author, being a creator, feels a natural solidarity with the tsar-creator, while it is left to the main character, as a made-up, subordinate figure, to grumble against his lord and creator. It is thus fitting that the voice of Pushkin, maker of the poem, should praise Peter, maker of St. Petersburg, while the voice of Evgenii, a character, a "creature," curses the superhuman might of the "wonder-working builder." The two truths are as divided and conjoined by the poem as the two elements separated by the shoreline, of which both have equal need.

2 | The Bronze Horseman and the Golden Fish: Pushkin's Fairy Tale-Poem

a. Semantic Convertibility

Culture has a feature that may be termed semantic convertibility, or the law of inverse semantic action. This means that every successive work resounds in the works that have preceded it, and changes their meaning.

Thus, as Borges observes, Kafka brings together writers of the past who knew nothing of one another. What, for instance, do the ancient Greek philosopher Zeno, the ninth-century Chinese author Han Yu, the Danish thinker Kierkegaard, and the French prose writer Léon Bloy have in common? They were all Kafkaesque long before Kafka, as seen, for instance, in the ancient Greek parable of how Achilles never catches up with the tortoise; or the ancient Chinese one about how encountering a unicorn is a good omen, except that this animal is impossible to identify. Even if these authors do not resemble one another, "[i]n each ... we find Kafka's idiosyncrasy to a greater or lesser degree, but if Kafka had never written a line, we would not perceive this quality; in other words, it would not exist. ... The fact is that every writer *creates* his own precursors."[1] If not for Kafka, all these authors and works would stand apart; now they become links in a single tradition.

Paradoxical as it may seem, different works by one author may also evince a deep resemblance thanks to the texts of another, produced later. One would think that every line of Pushkin, indeed every draft of a line, has been investigated as to all possible strands of influence and borrowing—especially such classic works as *The Bronze Horseman* and

---

1 Borges, *Labyrinths*, 201.

The Tale of the Fisherman and the Fish (*Skazka o rybake i rybke*), which were written at the same time, during the "Boldino autumn" of 1833. But, as far as I know, these works have never been juxtaposed in terms of concept, composition, and imagery. And indeed, what does a moralizing fairy tale for the edification of children have in common with a masterpiece of historiosophic poetic thought?

My unexpected middleman in juxtaposing these two works by Pushkin turns out to be Dostoevsky. At least three times—in "A Faint Heart" ("Slaboe serdtse"), "Petersburg Visions in Verse and Prose" ("Peterburgskie snovideniia v stikhakh i proze"), and *The Adolescent* (*Podrostok*)—the same fantastic scene is repeated:

> A hundred times, in the midst of this fog, a strange but importunate reverie has come to me: 'And if this fog breaks up and lifts, won't this whole foul, slimy city go with it, rise up with the fog and vanish like smoke, and leave only the former Finnish swamp, and in the middle perhaps, for the beauty of it, a bronze horseman on a hot-breathed, overridden steed?[2]

Of course, this phantasmagoria on the theme of Petersburg echoes Pushkin's *The Bronze Horseman*, the prototype of the whole Petersburg theme in Russian literature. It is as if the city disappears for a time, sinking underwater… But in the narrative poem something is missing, some final stroke to make the city disappear entirely, and restore the desolation and wildness that preceded it; to lay bare its illusoriness, the "intentionality" of everything between its appearance and vanishing. Meanwhile, Dostoevsky's motif of the city disappearing like a reverie and phantom also alludes to something in Pushkin…

And then I recalled *The Tale of the Fisherman and the Fish*. Where there had once been a ramshackle hut of mud, a high tower arises, then a royal palace, until finally it all disappears, and the old woman is back at square one, on the threshold of that same hut, with her broken washtub.[3]

---

2 Dostoevsky, *The Adolescent*, 135. See also in drafts of *A Writer's Diary* (*Dnevnik pisatelia*) in Dostoevskii, *Polnoe sobranie sochinenii v 30-i tomakh*, 17:372, note.

3 Because of Pushkin's tale, to be "left with a broken washtub" (*ostat'sia u razbitogo koryta*) has become the Russian equivalent of what in English is "back at square one"—trans.

Furthermore, one motif after another, a deep interconnection is revealed between the long narrative poem and the fairy tale, as if they were two variants of the same plot.

b. Textual Parallels

Both in the poem and the tale, the action unfolds on the seashore, which poses a similar arrangement of countervailing forces: the powerful human will and the elemental freedom of nature. Both works begin by depicting the poverty and miserable everyday existence about to be encroached upon by the characters' grand aspirations:

The Tale of the Fisherman and the Fish (hereafter, *TF*)

>They had lived in a ramshackle mud-hut
>Exactly three and thirty years.
>The old man caught fish with his fishing net,
>The old woman spun her yarn.

>Они жили в ветхой землянке
>Ровно тридцать лет и три года.
>Старик ловил неводом рыбу,
>Старуха пряла свою пряжу.[4]

The Bronze Horseman (hereafter, *BH*)

>... where once
>The Finnish fisherman, the sad stepson
>Of nature, standing alone on the low banks,
>Cast into unknown waters his worn net (247)

>Где прежде финский рыболов,
>Печальный пасынок природы,
>Один у низких берегов

---

4   Pushkin, *Skazka o rybake i rybke*, 338. Further citations in the text are to this edition.

Бросал в неведомые воды
Свой ветхий невод. (286)

Of course, the poem's imagery is much richer than that of the tale, but key motifs coincide in these initial situations, and are indicated by rare, hence stylistically marked, words: *vetkhii* ("ramshackle," "worn"); and the archaic *nevod* (a trammel or seine-net). Such is the natural milieu of godforsaken primeval existence in both works' exposition.

The opposite pole, in the poem's imagery: "[T]he young city, / The grace and wonder of the northern lands, / Out of the gloom of forests and the mud / Of marshes splendidly has risen." Similarly, in the tale, the run-down hut on the shore is succeeded by dwellings of increasing grandeur: first a "hut with an attic" (*izba so svetelkoi*), then a "high tower," and finally a "royal palace" (*tsarskie palaty*) (340, 341, 342).

The optical background changes entirely: "On the crown of her head was a brocade *kichka* / ... / There were gold rings on her hands, / There were red boots on her feet" (*TF*, 341). Similarly, the desolate locale, once drab with huts, now acquires color and brightness: "dark-green gardens," "girls' faces brighter than roses" (*BH*, 248). The poem and tale also keep to a definite order in their conception of the "royal" life that plays out on their once-dead shores:

First comes opulent architecture:

TF:
And what does he see? A high tower.
Что ж он видит? Высокий терем. (341)

And what do you know?—before him stands a royal palace.
Что ж? пред ним царские палаты. (342)

BH:
Now huge harmonious palaces and towers
Crowd on the bustling banks.

Громады стройные теснятся
Дворцов и башен.

32   The Titanic and the Demonic: Faust's Heirs

Then luxurious feasting:

TF:
They pour her wines from overseas;
Her dessert is gingerbread with high-relief designs.

Наливают ей заморские вины;
Заедает она пряником печатным. (342)

BH:
[T]he hiss of foaming goblets
And the pale-blue flame of punch. (248)

Шипенье пенистых бокалов
И пунша пламень голубой. (287)

And lastly, a military retinue:

TF:
Around her stand fierce sentinels
Holding hatchets on their shoulders.

Вкруг ее стоит грозная стража,
На плечах топорики держат. (342)

BH:
[T]he uniform beauty of the troops
Of infantry and of the horses... (248)

Пехотных ратей и коней
Однообразную красивость, (287)

The poem's "martial capital" (248) and the tale's "royal palace" are both defended the same way, by force of arms, with a "fierce" retinue. Also mentioned are members of the service class guarding the throne: "boyars and noblemen" (*TF*, 342), "generals" and "government officials" (*BH*, 252, 254)—all the signs of entrenched power ascending to hegemony over the world.

A variant of the tale that did not make it to the final text has the old woman, having been enthroned as tsarina, ascend even higher—to the Tower of Babel:

> Before him stands the Tower of Babel,
> At its very tippy-top
> Sits his old woman ...

> Перед ним вавилонская башня,
> На самой на верхней на макушке
> Сидит его старая старуха ...[5]

Whence this Tower of Babel motif in the tale's draft? As is well known, *The Bronze Horseman*, which Pushkin was working on at the same time (October 1833), was the poet's polemical response to part three of Mickiewicz's *Forefathers' Eve* (1832), published not long before, in a fragment of which—titled "Oleszkiewicz: The Day before the St. Petersburg Flood of 1824"—Petersburg is compared to Babylon. Did the Babylonian motif find its way into the fairy tale from here as well? The fact that the draft mentions Babylon reinforces the tale's parallel with *The Bronze Horseman*.

> He who will live to see to-morrow will see great miracles.
> It will be the second but not the last trial.
> The Lord will shake the foundations of the Assyrian throne,
> The Lord will shake the ground of the city of Babylon;
> Lord, let me pass before the third test comes.[6]

The Polish artist Oleszkiewicz, who lives in St. Petersburg and studies the Bible and Kabbalah, predicts that, like the capitals of the ancient world, Petersburg will be destroyed, after which shall follow the "third" tribulation—the end

---

5 Pushkin, *Sobranie sochinenii v 10 tomakh*, 3:478.
6 Cited from Weintraub, *The Poetry of Adam Mickiewicz*, 181.

of the world and Judgement Day. In Mickiewicz's fragment, Petersburg is referred to allegorically as "Babylon" much as the book of Revelation uses "Babylon" to refer to Rome, at the time the capital of the pagan world.[7]

What is essential here is not Pushkin's particular dispute or concurrence with Mickiewicz[8] but the motif itself of steadily growing power and the raising of a Tower of Babel where once was only "gloom" and "marshes" (*BH*), a "ramshackle mud-hut" (*TF*) and "the shelter of the hapless Finn" (*BH*, 247).

c. The Subjugation of the Elements, and Their Retribution

In both works, the most significant moment of the same "power" plots is when the natural elements are subjugated. Both Peter in the poem and the old woman in the tale reach the height of *earthly* power, as symbolized by the new capital and the "royal palace" respectively. But they both yearn to master another element as well—that of the *sea*. An earthly throne is not enough for the old woman, and her whole triumphal elevation by the golden fish's will culminates in her most cherished desire: "I don't want to be [just] an unconstrained tsarina [*vol'noiu tsaritsei*], / I want to be mistress of the sea, / I want to live in the Ocean-Sea / I want the golden fish to serve me / To be at my beck and call" (342). This is the audacity that causes the cup of patience of the sea's *true* ruler to finally spill over.

Here we might note that in "The Fisherman and His Wife," the tale of the brothers Grimm from which, as is well known, Pushkin borrowed his plot, the wife's wish-crescendo culminates in her desire to command the sun and moon, to become queen of the universe.[9] In Pushkin's treatment,

---

7 The history of Pushkin's acquaintance with part three of *Forefathers' Eve*, which in particular includes the poems "The Monument to Peter the Great" and "Oleszkiewicz: The Day before the St. Petersburg Flood of 1824," is given in A. S. Pushkin, *Mednyi vsadnik*, ed. N. V. Izmailov (Leningrad: Nauka, Leningr. otd-nie, 1978), 137–39.

8 For more detail on the two poets' dispute/concurrence regarding Petersburg, see the chapter "Faust and Peter on the Seashore: From Goethe to Pushkin."

9 That this Pomeranian tale from the Grimms' collection served as Pushkin's source was first proposed by V. V. Sipovskii (in *Pushkin i ego sovremenniki*, vyp. 4, 80–81) and subsequently corroborated by S. M. Bondi, who published a draft of Pushkin's tale that features, in particular, the transformation of the old woman into the Pope of Rome— an episode lacking in all other folkloric variants of the plot but found in the Grimms' version (Bondi, *Chernoviki Pushkina*, 50, 52). M. K. Azadovskii concludes (*Literatura i fol'klor*, 74) that the congruence of a number of details enables us to "establish that Pushkin's tale relies directly upon the Grimms' text." However, the Grimms' tale, while referring to the Pope, does not mention the Tower of Babel — a clear indication of

by contrast, the plot unfolds not in a straight line but a closed circle: having received power from the mistress of the sea, the old woman now wants to rule the sea herself. This motif is absent in the brothers Grimm and, while distancing *The Tale of the Fisherman and the Fish* from its German source, it does directly associate Pushkin's tale with his *Bronze Horseman*. After all, as depicted in the poem, Peter's main activity is the subjugation not of earthly kingdoms but of the element, alien to mankind, of water. And the author, summing up Peter's deeds at the end of the introduction, proclaims: Let "even the conquered elements ... make / Their peace with you; let the Finnish waves / Forget their enmity and ancient bondage, / And let them not disturb with empty spite / Peter's eternal sleep!" (249). The feast that Peter holds in store for all peoples on "waves unknown to them" (247)—this is, in effect, a festival of the victory over the sea.

Thus does the "ascending" line culminate in both works: the aspiration "to stand with a firm foothold on the sea" (*BH*)—"to be mistress of the sea" (*TF*). The subjugated elements must recognize human dominion: let "the conquered elements ... make / Their peace with you" (*BH*)— "I want the golden fish to serve me" (*TF*).

But at the same time, a "descending" line runs through both works: the rising lust for power is met by a corresponding movement of these selfsame "conquered" elements, increasingly angered by human audacity; elements whose seething, whose fierce retribution are conveyed gradually via a steady intensification—in the tale, however, with sharper, more staccato strokes than in the poem.

TF:
The sea was choppy.
... море слегка разыгралось. (339)

The blue sea was troubled.
Помутилося синее море. (340)

---

another source, Mickiewicz's "Oleszkiewicz," which Pushkin read at this very time in the course of his work on *The Bronze Horseman*. This double intertextual reference, to the Grimms and Mickiewicz, explains the strange intermingling of the two images in the same episode in the draft of Pushkin's tale: "Before him stands a Latin monastery... Before him stands the Tower of Babel" (*Pered nim monastyr' latynskii... Pered nim vavilonskaia bashnia*; Bondi, *Chernoviki Pushkina*, 50).

The blue sea was not calm.
Не спокойно синее море. (ibid.)

The blue sea went black.
Почернело синее море. (341)

On the sea, a black storm:
So swollen were the angry waves,
So astir, howling their howl.

… на море черная буря:
Так и вздулись сердитые волны,
Так и ходят, так воем и воют. (343)

BH:
[T]he Neva tossed
Like a sick man in his restless bed. (249)

Нева металась, как больной,
В своей постеле беспокойной. (288)

[The] Neva swelled up and roared,
Bubbling like a cauldron; (251)

Нева вздувалась и ревела,
Котлом клокоча и клубясь, (290)

There the waves rose up … [a]nd raged,
There the storm howled, there wreckage
Rushed to and fro. (252)

Вставали волны там и злились,
Там буря выла, там носились
Обломки… (292)

There is a congruence here, and not only in the overall picture of enraged waters rising balefully against human coastal settlement; also coinciding are the particular, most characteristic details of this picture, the verbs and epithets conveying sound and color. To cite parallels between poem and tale:

The movement of the waves:

BH:
[The] Neva *swelled up*
Нева вздувалась

TF:
the angry waves *swelled*
вздулись сердитые волны (343)

Sound:

BH:
there the storm *howled*
там буря выла

And the wind blew, *howling* sadly. (249)
И ветер дул, печально воя. (288)

TF:
howling their *howl*
так воем и воют

Color:

BH:
over *darkened* Petrograd (249)
над омраченным Петроградом (288)

the *sullen* [or "dark," "gloomy"] wave (255)
мрачный вал (296)

TF:
The blue sea *went black*.
Почернело синее море.

on the sea, a *black* storm
на море черная буря

Emotional state:

BH:
in his *restless* bed
в своей постеле беспокойной

angrily the rain was beating ... against the window (249)
сердито бился дождь в окно (288)

TF:
The blue sea was *not calm*.
Не спокойно синее море.

So swollen were the *angry* waves
Так и вздулись сердитые волны

Upon comparison, the extent to which the tale and poem share imagery becomes clear. The tale stands as a sort of transposition of the poem's deep historiosophic design into simple folkloric language.

Let us compare the works' finales. The tale ends quite laconically, constituting a simple return to the beginning: "And lo: before him once more stands the hut of mud. / On the threshold sits the old woman, / And in front of her, the broken washtub" (343). The golden fish, sovereign of the sea, has taken back everything it had given the self-styled earthly "tsarina."

The Bronze Horseman has, for all intents and purposes, a circular composition as well, closing upon its own beginning. The action shifts to the most flood-stricken part of the city, thereby returning to the previous life on the "mossy, marshy banks" (247).

> [S]o close to the waves, almost by the gulf
> Itself, is an unpainted fence and a willow
> And a small ramshackle house.... (252)

> Близехонько к волнам,
> Почти у самого залива—
> Забор некрашеный, да ива
> И ветхий домик... (292)

Now primordial, meager reality becomes visible through the veneer of this capital of half the world, as if all this architecture, the palaces' splendid décor, were made a phantasm, wiped away by the enraged Neva. The flood has laid bare the city's metaphysical spectrality; we see the same desolate shoreline landscape as in the beginning, as if there had never been any Petersburg, as if it had been just a dream of the madman Evgenii, or remained a "high thought" of Peter himself.

> A small island can be seen off-shore. Sometimes
> A fisherman out late will moor there with
> His net [*s nevodom*] and cook his meagre supper ...
> ....
> [On] the barren island.
> No grass grows, not a blade. The flood, in sport,
> Had driven a ramshackle little house there.
> Above the water it had taken root
> Like a black bush. Last spring a wooden barge
> Carried [it] away. It was empty
> And completely destroyed.[10] By the threshold

---

10 I have added this sentence to make the translation more literal—trans.

> They found my madman, and on that very spot
> For the love of God they buried his cold corpse. (257)

> Остров малый
> На взморье виден. Иногда
> Причалит с неводом туда
> Рыбак на ловле запоздалый
> И бедный ужин свой варит. . . .
>
> ....
>
> . . .Пустынный остров. Не взросло
> Там ни былинки. Наводненье
> Туда, играя, занесло
> Домишко ветхий. Над водою
> Остался он, как черный куст.
> Его прошедшею весною
> Свезли на барке. Был он пуст
> И весь разрушен. У порога
> Нашли безумца моего
> И тут же хладный труп его
> Похоронили ради Бога. (298–99)

The echo of the poem's finale with its beginning is not as obvious as in the fairy tale, but it is all the more significant for that. In the introduction, Peter stands "on a shore washed by desolate [*pustynnykh*] waves," in the conclusion Evgenii meets his end on a "barren [*pustynnom*] island" where "no grass grows, not a blade." In the olden days, a fisherman used to throw his run-down trammel net (*nevod*) into the uncharted waters here—and in the poem's finale, a fisherman docks here with his net, signified by that same archaic word *nevod*. In the beginning of the poem, "here and there, / Like black specks ... / Were huts" (247), and in the finale, "a ramshackle little house ... / Like a black bush." Where are the grand marinas, the lively shores crowded with ships from every corner of the earth? A word crucial to the beginning and end of both works is *vetkhii* ("ramshackle," "dilapidated"): in the tale, the old folks are left to dwell in that same "ramshackle [*vetkhii*] mud-hut" from the opening; in the poem, prologue and epilogue are connected via "a worn [*vetkhii*] net"; "a small ramshackle [*vetkhii*] house"; "a ramshackle [*vetkhii*] little house."

And to sum it all up, a "broken washtub," which corresponds metaphorically to the little house that "was empty and completely destroyed." The image of the broken washtub, which is lacking in the Grimm version, is hardly accidental; it is with this image that Pushkin's tale both opens and concludes. The broken washtub is a corollary of the sea's elementality, and is analogous to a sinking ship; in fact, in Russian, an unseaworthy boat can be referred to as a "washtub" (*koryto*). It is a fairytale analogue, moreover, for the whole city as it appears in the poem: split to its foundations. There is an original, irreparable defect, a "leak" in the very concept of building civilization on these swampy shores.

Significantly, in both works the action concludes on thresholds. "By the threshold [*u poroga*] / They found my madman" (*BH*); "On the threshold [*na poroge*] sits the old woman" (*TF*). The threshold symbolizes the same boundary as does the shore (the threshold of water and land). In both works, threshold and shore alike signify human defenselessness before the surrounding element of water. The threshold is where we find, in the end, those catastrophe victims from whom the sea has taken back all that had been raised upon its shore.

In reworking a Grimm tale, Pushkin thus aligns it with the plot of his poem, strengthens its connection with the sea, with life on the shore, thereby underscoring both works' shared leitmotif.

BH:
Or is all this a dream? Is all our life
Nothing but an empty dream, heaven's jest [upon the earth]? (252)

Или во сне
Он это видит? иль вся наша
И жизнь ничто, как сон пустой,
Насмешка неба над землей? (292)

In tale and poem alike, a whole succession of ambitious endeavors, from a "new washtub" to "royal palaces," passes by in such an "empty dream": the glittering world disappears like a mirage.[11]

d. Peter and the Old Woman: A Pair of Autocrats

The two works are not only close in their image system, they were also written at the same time, or more precisely, one after the other, during the Boldino autumn of 1833. The draft of *The Bronze Horseman* was begun on 6 October, and the fair copy was completed on 31 October.[12] The tale is dated 14 October, written, that is, between the two stages of work on the poem. It is as if, while producing a rough draft of the poem, Pushkin created still another version of it, a conventional fairy tale, before getting down to finishing the fair copy.

The two works echo one another also in their title images, the names of metals: the "bronze horseman" is the embodiment of power; the "golden fish," that of wealth. In Pushkin's symbolic system, metal is contrasted with water, which represents mankind's attempt to subjugate "the free elements" to its will. Power and wealth, bronze and gold captivate and charm both the "wonder-working builder" and the old woman who has "gone madly capricious" (*vzdurilas'*, 340, 341, 342).

But there is a fundamental difference between the poem and tale in their plot construction and genre parameters. In the poem, the tsar's power over the sea has already been realized as a matter of exposition, in the introduction, and serves as a point of departure for the plot. In the tale, the old woman/tsarina's power over the sea is her final, unrealized wish, and sets the stage for the finale. This is not simply a compositional distinction. Because Peter's creative action is completed at the outset, the driving force of the plot becomes the action of the elements themselves. This is characteristic of tragedy: retribution

---

11 Both these Pushkinian motifs, the "empty *dream*" and "*heaven's* jest," are combinedly replicated by Dostoevsky both in "A Faint Heart" and "Petersburg Visions in Verse and Prose": the city on the Neva "resembles a fantastic, magical reverie, a dream that suddenly vanishes in turn, evaporating in the dark-blue sky" (*Polnoe sobranie sochinenii v 30-i tomakh*, 2:48, 19:69).
12 Abramovich, *Pushkin v 1833 g. Khronika*, 418, 426, 456–60.

from above is visited upon the city. "Tsars cannot master / The divine elements" (251). By contrast, the theme of competing with the elements is treated comically in the tale, insofar as the challenge is thrown down by a capricious old woman. In tragedy, a person's fate is meted out by destiny, but in comedy an individual lays claim to the role of master of fate, and such outlandish pretensions cast him or her in a ridiculous light.

As a tragic hero, Peter is grand and fierce, for he, "by whose fateful will the city had / Been founded under the sea,"[13] has, even without realizing it, summoned the destructive force of destiny's retaliatory will against his own creation. Insofar as in the introduction, Petersburg is already presented as a start-point, an undeniable given, the subject matter of the poem's two subsequent parts becomes the merciless revenge of fate. In the fairy tale, by contrast, the whole plot is constructed on the play of the subjective in its incongruence with the objective. The woman's behavior defies common sense and the warning signs of the elements. "The old woman became even more outrageously capricious [*vzdurilas'*] than before" (340). This "cantankerous" (*svarlivaia*, ibid.), "accursed" (*prokliatoiu*, 343) woman, who is constantly "scolding" (*branitsia*, 339, 340) and "cussing out her husband like there's no tomorrow" (*na chem svet stoit muzha rugaet*, 340)—departs from her assigned role, that of human and womanly meekness, for which she gets her comeuppance. In the poem, the sea-born retribution itself is developed into a whole plot, whereas the tale compresses it into the finale: in a moment, destiny overturns the multitiered constructs of the human will.

In other words, in the poem, the action of the subject (the tsar) constitutes a brief prologue to the poem's two parts, which depict the action of fate (the sea's elements). In the tale, it is the other way around: the action of fate (these same elements) make up the brief epilogue of a work that depicts the action of a subject (an old woman attempting to ascend to her kingdom). This is the difference between the tragic and the comic: while the former unfurls the inevitability of the objective, the latter emphasizes the futility of the subjective.

---

13 Pushkin, *Mednyi vsadnik*, 297.

e. The Fate of the "Little Man"

If the old woman is a cut-rate, ridiculous version of an autocrat, then the old man is a cut-rate version of the "little man" (*malen'kii chelovek*) whose tragic fate is revealed in Evgenii. Both of the latter are humble, gentle, unassuming; their desires go no further than a "ramshackle mud-hut" (*TF*), a "humble, simple shelter" (*BH*, 250). For them, what is alluring is "coziness"—the family idyll, the prose and simplicity of everyday life; pretensions to power and "glory" strike them as nonsensical. In fact, Evgenii dreams of the humble lot in life that the old man has already achieved.

> *TF*:
> They had lived in a ramshackle mud-hut
> Exactly three and thirty years.
> The old man caught fish with his fishing net,
> The old woman spun her yarn.

> Они жили в ветхой землянке
> Ровно тридцать лет и три года
> Старик ловил неводом рыбу
> Старуха пряла свою пряжу.

> *BH*:
> [S]omehow or other
> I'll fix myself a humble, simple shelter
> Where Parasha and I can live in quiet.
> ....
> We shall begin to live, and thus we'll go
> Hand in hand to the grave. . . . (250)

> Уж кое-как себе устрою
> Приют смиренный и простой
> И в нем Парашу успокою.
> ....

И станем жить, и так до гроба
Рука с рукой дойдем мы оба... (289)

But there is a substantive difference between these two "little men." Evgenii dares threaten the autocrat: "Just you wait!"—while the old man is afraid to contradict his own wife ("The old man did not dare talk back, / Dared not say a contrary word," 343). For a moment, there awakens in Evgenii a greatness that makes him tantamount to the elements all around that ragingly resist the autocrat's will. "*Flames* ran through [Evgenii's] heart, his blood *boiled* [*vskipela*]" (256)—this repeats, almost word for word, the picture of the rampaging Neva: "the waves / Still *seethed* [*kipeli*] angrily, as though beneath them / *Fires* were smouldering" (253).

In general, a number of epithets are applied to Evgenii that were previously used to characterize the elements crashing down upon the city:

"his eyes were sealed by mist" (256); "somberly [*mrachen*] he stood" (256)—"the mist of the foul night"; "darkened [*omrachennym*] Petrograd" (249)

"possessed [*obuiannyi*] by a dark power" (256)—"wearied / By her insolent violence [*buistvom*]" (253)

"he whispered ... trembling / With wrath [*zlobno*]" (256)—"the waves / Still seethed angrily [*zlobno*]"

It is as if the storminess of the landscape is bursting into the portrait frame: the Neva's revolt is transmitted to Evgenii, and makes him rebellious. And even the hero's madness is a form of the elements' "impetuous folly" (*buinaia dur'*, 290) having taken hold of him. "The rebellious noise / Of the Neva and winds rang / In his ears" (*Miatezhnyi shum / Nevy i vetrov razdavalsia / V ego ushakh*, 295)—he was "deafened by / An inner turmoil" (255).

Evgenii's madness, and his challenge to the statue, which then comes down from its stone pedestal, signals a tragic break in the order of things. In terms of his plight, Evgenii is one of the "little men," but he overcomes this lot via his own internal refusal: he chooses madness. It is precisely because the autocrat is a tragic figure in the poem that the "little man" rising up against him is tragic as well. Just as the fate of Petersburg is beyond Peter's control, and historical reality is beyond the control of reasons of state ("high thoughts")—so too, to the contrary, is the mind of the "little man" Evgenii beyond the control of reality. This rupture is indicated in two ways, each equally tragic: in the elementality of the flood, reality proves to be beyond the control of Peter's reason; in Evgenii's madness, reason gets out of reality's control and does not survive its collision with it.

A different law is in effect in the fairy tale: not that of rupture but repetition. The old man's submissiveness as he keeps humbly conveying his wife's commands to the fish is a comic element, based on the mechanism of pure repetition.[14] The old woman, and then the old man, summon the fish again and again. This multiplication of desires and requests without any qualitative shift is characteristic of the comic. If the old woman and her petty tyranny constitute a parody of the tragic autocrat, then the old man and his passivity are a comic version of the helpless victim.

f. The Family and the State

Also comical in the tale is that it brings matters of state into the realm of family life, where they appear in devalued form and upside down. This is why the tale's resemblance to the poem is at first hard to notice: the comic alternative to the tragic plot is brought off radically, that is, via the transposition of this plot into a different generic and thematic scheme.

The Bronze Horseman presents an opposition between the family and the state, with the former sacrificed to the latter. Here we might recall that in Goethe's *Faust*, the patriarchal couple Philemon and Baucis perish at the behest of the "wonder-working builders" who construct, at the behest in turn of Faust and Mephistopheles, a dam to claim land from the sea. In just the same way, for Peter's design to be carried out, the logic of things requires the destruction of another couple—Evgenii and Parasha.

---

14 According to Henri Bergson, mechanical repetition is the essence of the comic, precisely because it is the opposite of life.

In the tale, the state is not opposed to the family but rather identified with it, with husband-wife relations whose traditional polarity is, moreover, inverted. At the outset of Pushkin's tale, the old man and woman are an idyllic couple, a sort of Philemon and Baucis, who have lived a long life together in a ramshackle mud-hut. But soon the situation flips, to comic effect. The "head" of the family, the husband, becomes a subject of the empress who is his own wife, and who treats him like dirt, gives him the bum's rush, and makes him a laughingstock ("And the people laughed at him: 'Serves you right, you old ignoramus!'" [342]).

We have already noted the circular structure of the plot of both *The Bronze Horseman* and *The Tale of the Fisherman and the Fish*. But in the former work, in its progress from beginning to end, a young couple perishes; while in the latter, it is as if nothing has happened—the old couple winds up in exactly the same situation as at the outset. "And lo: before him once more stands the hut of mud." This is, again, a manifestation of pure repetition. There turns out to be an internal kinship between the idyll and the comedy, although the former is hardly reducible to the latter. Whereas an idyllic world is static in its perfection and self-containment, in comedy, scenes of tempestuous change lay bare the whole internal stillness of a situation, its self-repetition. While the family idyll is destroyed in the poem, in the tale, the calm of the old couple's existence is violated and restored, like an act of addition and subtraction amounting to zero.

g. The Poem and the Tale as a Single Work

The same plot plays out in poem and tale in tragic and comic versions. Let us recall that in ancient Greece, stage performances of tragedy were immediately followed by satirical drama to form a single cycle; the point was to produce catharsis and show the flip side of existence, where the fierce will of fate exists side by side with the vain pursuits of human beings.[15] Horror and laughter complement one another in a holistic aesthetic experience. Thus does Pushkin, too, turn to the comic amid work

---

15 "The grave impression made by the serious action of tragedies was alleviated by the lighthearted farce of satirical drama, with facetious conversations, songs, and humorous dances" (Radtsig, *Istoriia drevnegrecheskoi literatury*, 191). Characteristically, in

on his tragic poem, as if following the ancient law of all-encompassing artistic vision. *The Bronze Horseman* and *The Tale of the Fisherman and the Fish* are not only joined by the date of their composition but in fact form a singular *action* or *rite* (*deistvo*) in the ancient sense. The poem and tale are in effect a single work, not just written "consecutively" but comprising a whole. They should be interpreted as two versions of the same aesthetic event.

It is possible that working on the draft of *The Bronze Horseman* clarified for Pushkin a certain plot pattern, one he undertook to play out in a comic register, so that its tragic incarnation might then be raised to new heights. In Shakespeare, we might recall, high tragedy includes crude street humor and parody. Pushkin, whose dream was precisely a Shakespeareanly holistic art, consciously or otherwise created something similar in his Boldino autumn of 1833.[16]

From these two works it is clear what general themes were uppermost in the poet's consciousness at the time—themes he found in the experience of his country's history and in a folkloric fairytale plot. Power and the elements. A royal palace and a desolate shore. What is the peculiarity and the mystery of Russian history, in which the "intentional," the "planned" element has subjugated what is given by nature?—and how does nature respond to this attempt to command her?

Dostoevsky follows through on the artistic intent of both these works of Pushkin, which like two parallels eventually meet in the complex, curved space of Russian literature. That which in Pushkin is divided into separate plot variants, tragic and comic, in Dostoevsky becomes, in a highly compressed, single-sentence formula, a fantastic image combining

---

the case of Aeschylus for instance, satirical drama formed a single plot cycle with the tragedies preceding it, and included the same characters.

16 This new, "integrated" quality of Pushkin's mature art, in which outwardly standalone works unite across genre barriers, was intuitively sensed already by Pushkin's first biographer P. V. Annenkov, who remarked on the Boldino autumn of 1833, precisely in connection with *The Bronze Horseman* and *The Tale of the Fisherman and the Fish*: "He wrote several works in this interval in the remote seclusion of Boldino that in their character make up a new kind of art, the art he was practicing when he met his end" (*Materialy dlia biografii Pushkina*, 373). Annenkov does not clarify what this "new kind of art" consists of.

the tragedy of a vanished city and the absurdity of its founder's statue being mired in a swamp (the founder, that is, of something that never managed to acquire a firm foundation). Thus, combining the tragic and the comic gives rise to the *grotesque*—a new sort of imagery not found in Pushkin. Dostoevsky especially underscores its artistic peculiarity with his half-mocking, half-hysterical insertion of "perhaps, for the beauty of it" ("only the former Finnish swamp, and in the middle perhaps, for the beauty of it, a bronze horseman on a hot-breathed, overridden steed"). This is an image constructed on incongruity—the aesthetics of the tragicomic absurd.

If Dostoevsky's image provides a key to two works by Pushkin, the same law of semantic convertibility is in effect even further back, applying also to Pushkin's sources, which, thanks to Pushkin himself, echo forward in their turn. Art is metaphorical in nature, and this applies not just to particular words or images but to whole works as well. Why in October 1833 did Pushkin creatively respond precisely to two works as different as Mickiewicz's poetic drama *Forefathers' Eve* (part three), with its denunciation of autocratic Petersburg, and a fairy tale from the collection of the brothers Grimm meant to expose female pickiness and petty tyranny? Pushkin apparently found the German tale and the Polish verse to both metaphorize the same design, to allegorize the same meaning he embodied "fairy tale-wise" and "long poem-wise," respectively.

Thanks to Pushkin's mediation, we can find wording in "The Fisherman and His Wife" that seems to allegorically convey the clash, in part three of *Forefathers' Eve*, between the will of the individual and the state's alienating power as embodied in the autocratic stronghold of the northern capital. When the Grimms' fisherman returns to find his wife reigning over all Christendom as pope, he humbly expresses the hope that this is her final aspiration. "But she sat stiff as a board and neither stirred nor moved."[17] This inflexibility, likened to a tree in the original ("styf as en Boom"[18]), is rendered by the Russian translator (the writer

---

17 Grimm and Grimm, *The Complete Fairy Tales of the Brothers Grimm*, 72.
18 http://gutenberg.spiegel.de/buch/die-schonsten-kinder-und-hausmarchen-6248/48

and poet Grigorii Petnikov) as *sidit ona pered nim istukanom*[19]—metaphorically sitting "stock still," but literally as that same "graven image" (*istukan*), as if the power-hungry wife in the Grimm tale anticipates the "prideful graven image" (*gordelivym istukanom*) of *The Bronze Horseman*. Precisely this "algorithm" enables the content of Pushkin's tale to be transferred to his poem, and allows us to understand why two so dissimilar and different-genred source works should have crossed paths in the poet's consciousness. After all, Mickiewicz too depicts a royal graven image—the monument to Peter that crowns the whole architecture of great-power hegemony that is so odious to the Polish rebel. "So this gigantic image of the tsar / Bestrides the bronze back of a mettled steed."[20] This means that this remote imagistic echo already exists in the brothers Grimm and Mickiewicz, a potential that is realized by the creative will of Pushkin, like a magnet pulling in specks of a single design from far-flung literary sources.[21]

Thus are the Polish poet's work and the German folklorists' tale connected, indirectly, through Pushkin, becoming metaphors for a single generalizing plot. A super-meaning emerges from both sources, bringing into direct contact two truths, those of the individual and history, the *chelo* ("brow") and *vek* ("century") that together form *chelovek* ("human being"). The human will, hastening and foreordaining the course of events, sets itself in opposition to existence itself, and is ultimately left with nothing, cast back down to its start-point.

The Petersburg myth, which has taken root in Russian literature thanks to Pushkin, evinces at its very origin a connection with the cosmic myth of the creation of the world, of drawing boundaries

---

19 Brat'ia Grimm, *Skazki*, 49.
20 Mickiewicz, *Poems by Adam Mickiewicz*, 349. The associations with the golden calf of Exodus 32 are more pronounced in the original: "Już car *odlany* w kształcie wielkoluda / Siadł na brązowym grzbiecie bucefała"; the tsar is "poured" or "cast" (*Utwory dramatyczne*, 275).
21 Here we might apply Roman Jakobson's apt comment on the sculptural imagery Pushkin borrowed from various sources (Irving, Moliere, etc.): "He selects from these foreign prototypes only such elements as conform to his own conception; and whatever contradicts this, he reshapes in his own way" (*Raboty po poetike*, 151).

between the elements (let us recall the biblical days of creation). The division of dry land from water that takes place on the second day of creation is necessary for cosmic balance; the attempt to circumvent this balance, to create a city on, or rather *under*, the water and subject the sea to human will, is answered by the elements' hostility. This cosmic retribution, "heaven's jest upon the earth," is at the heart of the irony of history. Claude Levi-Strauss famously posits myth as a logical tool for solving fundamental oppositions via a progressive mediation. Juxtaposing *The Bronze Horseman* with *The Tale of the Fisherman and the Fish* on the one hand, and on the other with part two of Goethe's *Faust*, allows us to view the Petersburg myth as an attempt to mediate between the creative and the destructive in human power over the elements, and in the concept of power generally. Pushkin is trying to solve the contradiction between a monument and a phantom, between the greatness and the spectrality of a civilization erected upon shores "washed by desolate waves."

Obviously, Pushkin's simultaneous reference to a Mickiewicz poem and a tale of the brothers Grimm is connected with the very nature of the "coastal city" plot, with the intersection therein of historical and cosmic motifs. These two different-tongued sources have come together in Pushkin's creative consciousness as a double signification of the October (1833) plot in his thinking. History would subsequently unfurl this plot to its October (1917) finale, when Russian history's whole Petrine epoch would, in Dostoevsky's words, "evaporate in the dark-blue sky" and "vanish like smoke," leaving ruined palaces in its wake, and black peasant huts on a once-again desolate shore. History reverses course, so that again and again it might flow through its own beginning, obeying the law of the "broken washtub," the inexorable return to "square one."

This intertextual composition, created by several great authors echoing one another, culminates in words the philosopher Vasilii Rozanov wrote in 1917: "God, Russia is empty. ... Dreaming of the 'golden fish' of

52   The Titanic and the Demonic: Faust's Heirs

futurity and historical grandeur."[22] Here are summed up, briefly as possible, all the motifs of Pushkin and Dostoevsky that, in this first year of the new, revolutionary epoch, come to a close in the plot of Russian history itself.

---

[22] From the piece "Scattered Chichikovs ("Rassypavshiesia Chichikovy"); Rozanov, *Religiia. Filosofiia. Kul'tura*, 367.

3 | The Motherland-Witch: The Irony of Style in Nikolai Gogol[1]

a. The Irony of Style and the Apotheosis of Russia

As is well known, irony is a stylistic device that plays on the incongruence between the obvious and implicit meaning of an utterance. For example, praise might conceal mockery or contempt, while self-deprecation, pride. Irony permeates Gogol's entire artistic worldview: from brief lines ("the lady agreeable in all respects"[2]) to the construction of whole collective images, such as Petersburg in "Nevsky Prospect" ("Nevskii Prospekt") or the county seat in *The Inspector-General* (*Revizor*).

Irony is typically understood as a means for an author to express his particular attitude toward the world, toward characters and situations. But aside from authorial irony, there is also the irony of style, which can turn against the author's own aesthetic goals. This is a far rarer, underinvestigated type of irony, one that arises contrary to the author's intention and endows their statements with some other or outright opposite meaning. The author means one thing but expresses something entirely different. In this case it is not a conscious artistic device but the "unauthorized" irony of art itself; it gets out of the author's control, imposing its own will.

It is just such a case—when it is not the author who plays with a certain style but the other way around, when a style plays with the author and foils his intention—that is examined in this chapter. *The irony of style* is a crucial category if we are to understand Gogol, insofar as this irony holds sway over the "constructive," mythopoetic consciousness of Gogol himself as a patriot, humanist, and preacher.

---

1 Some wording in this chapter draws on the translation of a previous version of this piece by Jonathan Z. Ludwig and Sven Spieker.
2 Gogol, *Dead Souls*, 207. Further citations in the text are to this translation.

Gogol's works have been studied in terms of negative aesthetics, which foregrounds "the laughter visible to the world and the tears invisible and unknown to it" (*Dead Souls*, 152), that is, the aesthetics of ridicule and lamentation. This aesthetics was presumed to have a positive pole as well, a realm of the ideal, thematized as humanism (especially in "The Overcoat" ["Shinel'"]) and patriotism (especially in *Dead Souls*). But in "How Gogol's 'Overcoat' Is Made," Boris Eikhenbaum demonstrated the purely ludic, almost parodic nature of its "humane passage,"[3] and since then the positive pole of Gogol's oeuvre has narrowed in scholarly perception to focus on the patriotic digressions in the "epic poem" *Dead Souls*.

The lyrical apotheosis of Russia in this work's volume 1 (chapter 11) seems genuine. Gogol's own statements demonstrate that for him, the famous "patriotic passage" was no mere game or device. Thus, in the second of his "Four Letters to Different Persons Regarding *Dead Souls*," Gogol defends the sincerity of his "lyrical appeal" to Russia and repeats, now on his own behalf, the same pathos-filled assertions that are woven into *Dead Souls*' imagery.[4] Upon first reading these lyrical digressions, Belinsky experienced a "sacred trembling," an ecstasy before "this lofty lyrical pathos, these thunderous, melodious dithyrambs of a national self-consciousness luxuriating in itself [*blazhenstvuiushego v sebe*], dithyrambs so worthy of a great Russian poet."[5]

The tradition of taking Gogol's hymning of Russia "literally" continued into the twentieth century. This was not simply a matter of paying

---

3 This refers to the episode when Akaky Akakievich is being ridiculed by his officemates. "'Let me be. Why do you offend me?'—And in those penetrating words rang other words: 'I am your brother'" (Gogol, *The Collected Tales*, 386; further citations in the text to this translation of "The Overcoat" and other stories are indicated by *CT*). According to Eikhenbaum, this "humane" moment constitutes "an introduction of the declamatory style into the system of comic *skaz*." Eikhenbaum, "How Gogol's 'Overcoat' Is Made," 36.
4 "[T]he lyric digressions, which the journalists have attacked [most of all]. ... I mean that passage in the last chapter where ... the writer ... in a lyrical appeal addresses himself to Russia herself, asking her for an explanation of this incomprehensible feeling with which he is filled. ... These words were taken for a pride and boasting unheard of till now, while they are neither the one nor the other. They are simply an awkward expression of a real feeling. It seems the same to me now." Gogol, *Selected Passages from Correspondence with Friends*, 99.
5 Belinskii, *Polnoe sobranie sochinenii v 13 t.*, 6:222.

homage to state-sponsored patriotism, whether Russian or Soviet, as witness the substantive works of contemporary Western scholars. In an article on Gogol's negative aesthetics, Robert Maguire emphasizes that the writer's "apophatic statements" serve the positive goal of the sacred transformation of the world—and as the main example of Gogol's "language of affirmation," he cites the lyrical appeal to Russia: "But what is the incomprehensible, mysterious force that draws me to you?"[6]

Mikhail Weiskopf draws a parallel between Gogol's "bird troika" and Plato's "chariot of the soul," elevating the image of Russia in *Dead Souls* far higher than the usual patriotic pedestal, up to where Russia now abides alongside the Lord himself as his Eternal Companion, the Wisdom of God. "Rising up together with Russia into metaphysical spaces, the narrator communes with lofty Wisdom; Rus itself becomes Sophia, providing him with prophetic knowledge."[7]

Gogolian patriotism as expressed in *Dead Souls* is perhaps the only thing that still seems undeniable amid the ambiguity surrounding this writer: a realist and fantasist, humorist and hypochondriac, teacher of life and necrophile. It is widely held that if in his capacity as artist, Gogol directly proclaims his ideal anywhere, then it must be in the lyrical digressions of *Dead Souls*. From an early age, the Russian reader keeps Gogol's poignant-sweet image of Russia impressed upon their soul—Russia as a wonderland, shining with some unearthly light, through which mighty steeds careen, exulting and disappearing in the magical distance. What sort of Russia would we have in our imagination if not for these luminous hues of Gogol, these swirling lines, these rolling peals, which inspiredly convey the rapture of a wide-open expanse and a boundless future? "And menacingly the mighty vastness envelops me, reflected with *terrible* force in my depths; my eyes are lit up by an unnatural power: ohh! what a *shining*, wondrous yonder, unknown to the world! Rus!" (253–54; here and in subsequent quotes, emphasis is mine).

---

6 Maguire, "Gogol and the Legacy of Pseudo-Dionysius," 49. This was the first work to coherently unfold the apophatic side of Gogol's aesthetics, namely, the negation of the aesthetic itself, overcoming the word itself as a means of religious ascension, which is akin to the devices of the negative theology of Pseudo-Dionysius (the Areopagite).
7 Weiskopf, "The Bird Troika and the Chariot of the Soul: Plato and Gogol," 139.

But something in Gogol's wording causes the reader to prick up their ears—ears trained by Gogol himself. Some sort of echoes of a completely different Gogol work are heard in this hymn. We have already seen the shining of this wondrous, enchanted beauty somewhere before. "Such *terrible, dazzling* beauty. ... Indeed, the deceased girl's ... beauty seemed *frightful*" (*CT*, 177). In the quotes just cited, the first from *Dead Souls*, the second from "Viy," "terrible" and "frightening" render the same word (*strashnoiu, strashnaia*); as do "shining" and "dazzling" (*sverkaiushchaia*). The reader might feel the urge to suddenly exclaim, like Khoma Brut: "'The witch!' he cried out in a voice not his own, looked away, turned pale, and began reading his prayers" (*CT*, 171).

Let us attempt to get a good look at the outlines of this "wondrous yonder," listen closely to its sobbing roulades—through the prism and echo of Gogol's prose itself. What exactly is Gogol describing under the name of "Russia"? Using Gogol's own earlier works as a commentary on *Dead Souls*, I will show that the lyrical digressions concluding volume 1 of *Dead Souls*, where the Gogolian voice reaches its supreme, prophetic, "Platonic" note, actually incorporate demonic motifs from the writer's previous works, which have emanated from his soul seemingly unbeknownst to him. What is perceived as the positive pole of Gogol's oeuvre, countering his aesthetic of negation, in fact represents a different stratum—the deepest one—of that same aesthetic.

b. An Aesthetic Demonology of Russia

The Stare or Fixed Gaze

The writer's gaze is fixed on Russia's "shining, wondrous yonder," and the latter in turn seems to look back at him. "Why do you gaze so, and why is everything in you turned towards me with eyes full of expectation?" (*Dead Souls*, 253) Encounters of Gogol's characters with evil spirits typically involve precisely such a steady, bewitching gaze. This motif may be found in "A Terrible Vengeance" ("Strashnaia mest'"), "Viy," and "The Portrait," that is, in all three of Gogol's books that preceded *Dead Souls* (*Evenings on a Farm near Dikan'ka* [*Vechera na khutore bliz Dikan'ki*], *Mirgorod*, and *Arabesques* [*Arabeski*]).

The image of a sorcerer's open eyes comes up in "A Terrible Vengeance": "Instantly the sorcerer died and *opened his eyes* after death. ... Neither the living nor the resurrected have such a *terrible gaze*" (*CT*, 99). This motif continues in "Viy": while Khoma stands in the church by the young witch's coffin, "it seemed to the philosopher that she was looking at him through closed eyes" (*CT*, 178); "The corpse was already standing before him, right on the line, fixing her dead green eyes on him" (*CT*, 181); "through the web of hair *two eyes stared horribly*. ... They all *looked at him*, searching" (*CT*, 187). In general, the motif of the piercing gaze—"Lift my eyelids" (*CT*, 187)—is central to "Viy."

Finally, it is the gaze seemingly bursting from the canvas that betrays the demonic nature of the portrait purchased by the artist Chartkov. "He went up to the portrait again, so as to study those *wondrous eyes*, and noticed with horror that they were indeed *staring* at him" (*CT*, 339). "Two *terrible* eyes were *fixed* directly on him, as if preparing to devour him" (*CT*, 338). "The eyes were *fixed* still more *terribly*, still more meaningly, on him, and seemed *not to want to look at anything but him*" (*CT*, 340).

Quite often encountered in this context is the expressive Russian verb *vperit'*, which means to gaze intently, point-blank, as if piercing with a look and pausing fixedly on an object. The same verb is used in the second draft Gogol made of *Dead Souls*: "[W]hy do you *look me right in the eye*, why have you *fixed* [*vperilo*] your *eyes* upon me with everything that is in you?"[8] Gogol also uses the verb *vperit'* when paraphrasing *Dead Souls* to defend the sincerity and genuineness of his patriotic sentiment. "The writer," he remarks in the third person, "in a lyrical appeal addresses himself to Russia herself, asking her ... wherefore and why does it seem to him as though everything in her, from inanimate things to animate, *fixes its eyes on him* and expects something from him?"[9]

The concentration and fixedness of the gaze indicated by the verb *vperit'* associates the Russia of the lyrical digression with the demonic imagery of the early Gogol. As far as I know, the first to point this out was Ivan Ermakov, an undeservedly forgotten researcher who focused on

---

8 Gogol', *Polnoe sobranie sochinenii v 14 tomakh*, 6:885.
9 Gogol, *Selected Passages from Correspondence with Friends*, 99.

psychoanalytic aspects of classic Russian literature. "In Gogol, everything connected with the eyes (which are the windows of the soul, but the souls are dead) is characterized by horror and terror.... The ancient corpse who has grown into the earth and rocks it to its foundations will find another incarnation in 'Viy,' and still another in the Rus (Viy is the earth, the land) who looks at Gogol himself in a lyrical digression in *Dead Souls*."[10]

It should be noted in particular that the fixed or staring eyes of Gogol's demonic characters frequently give off a mysterious radiance—they "shine" and "sparkle" (*sverkaiut, svetiatsia*). Thus in "A Terrible Vengeance," the sorcerer, Katerina's father, kisses her "with a *strange glint* in his eyes. Katerina gave a slight start: the kiss seemed odd to her, as did the strange glint in his eyes" (*CT*, 72). In "Viy," the "old woman stood in the doorway, fixing her flashing eyes on him, and again began to come toward him" (*CT*, 159). In "The Portrait," the "old man's fixed stare was unbearable: his eyes absolutely *sparkled* [*svetilis'*], absorbing the moonlight."[11] And even when the portrait is covered with a bedsheet, "the old man's gaze *shone* [*sverkal*] through the cloth.... The old man's eyes *glowed* dully and *transfixed* him [*vperilis' v nego*] with all their magnetic power."[12]

Is this not the source of the light dazzling the writer's eyes ("my eyes are lit up by an unnatural power")—the eyes staring back at him? Russia looks upon Gogol with the same sparkling or resplendent gaze that Gogol's sorcerers and witches cast upon their victims. The epithet "unnatural" renders these eyes' light an otherworldly one. In a draft of *Arabesques*, the similar epithet "supernatural" is applied to the light emanating from the eyes of the old man in the portrait.[13]

This is why the image of Russia wittingly or unwittingly takes its place in the same associative array alongside the sorcerer from "A Terrible

---

10 Ermakov, *Ocherki po analizu tvorchesta N. V. Gogolia*, 49, 95.
11 Gogol', *Sobranie sochinenii v 7 t.*, 3:217.
12 Ibid., 218.
13 Ibid., 217.

Vengeance," the young witch from "Viy," and the moneylender from "The Portrait."[14]

In general, the motif of wide-open eyes has a primordial connection with the experience of sin, with demonic temptation. After Adam and Eve have succumbed to the temptation of the serpent, "the eyes of them both were opened, and they knew that they were naked" (Genesis 3:7). At first glance, this seems contradictory: Adam and Eve had always had the power of sight, but it is only after the Fall that their eyes are opened. Open eyes are a sign of satanic pride, the wish to lift the veil on a mystery known only to God.

Rootedness to the Spot

Not only does the wide-open gaze itself contain an element of fixedness, but this fixedness is transferred to the object upon which the gaze is directed. In Gogol, to bewitch means to immobilize, to root one's victim to the spot.

A sorcerer is obsessed with the "godless design" (*CT*, 90) of seducing the soul of his own sleeping daughter—but he himself is bewitched by the still more terrible power of the gaze of an avenging knight: "A white cloud came to hover in the middle of the room, and something resembling joy *flashed* in his face. But why did he suddenly stand motionless, mouth gaping, not daring to stir. ...? In the cloud before him, some strange face shone. ... [I]t grew more distinct and *fixed its gaze on him*. ... An invincible horror came over him. And the strange, unfamiliar head kept looking at him *fixedly* through the cloud. ... *the keen eyes would not tear themselves away* from him" (*CT*, 90). In this scene of magic, two motifs are intertwined: eyes that are gleaming (*sverkaiushchie*) and fixed (*nepodvizhnye*); and a head enshadowed by cloud, which likely sheds light also on the magical significance of the "cloud" in the lyrical digression on

---

14 For a profound commentary on the demonic nature of vision in Gogol, see Annenskii, "Portret." The exclusive role in Gogol's works played by vision-related imagery was subsequently elucidated by Andrei Siniavsky in his book *In Gogol's Shadow*: "'Lift my eyelids' and 'don't look!'—it is between these extreme poles that Gogol's narrative is torn, abounding as it does with visual lusts that seem to constitute an enormous sea of meaning, happiness, and sin." Terts, *Sobranie sochinenii v 2 t.*, 2:304.

Russia. The resonance between the two works is nearly word-for-word: "eyes ... turned towards me ... my head ... overshadowed by a menacing cloud" (*Dead Souls*, 253); the "head kept looking at him fixedly through the cloud" ("A Terrible Vengeance").

Here are a few more episodes of magic in which sparkling eyes are connected with the motif of stillness and being rooted to the spot. In "Viy": the "old woman stood in the doorway, fixing her *flashing eyes* on him, and again began to come toward him. The philosopher wanted to push her away with his hands, but noticed to his astonishment that *his arms would not rise, nor would his legs move*; with horror he discovered that *the sound of his voice would not even come from his mouth*: the words stirred soundlessly on his lips" (*CT*, 159). In "The Portrait": "[T]he old man ... did look behind the screen, with the same bronze face, *moving his big eyes*. Chartkov tried to cry out and found that *he had no voice*, tried to stir, to make some movement, but *his limbs would not move*" (*CT*, 340). "In *motionless* fear he ... saw living, human *eyes peer straight into him*. ... He wanted to back away, but felt as if *his feet were rooted to the ground*" (*CT*, 341).

Faced with a witch or sorcerer, a person cannot move from the spot, cannot utter a word. And both these details are repeated in the author's stance of awe under the eyes of Russia:

> Rus! [...] Why do you gaze so, and why is everything in you turned towards me with eyes full of expectation?... And still, all in perplexity, I stand *motionless*, but my head is already overshadowed by a menacing cloud, heavy with coming rains, and thought *stands numb* before your vastness. (*Dead Souls*, 253)

Iurii Mann has devoted a special analysis to the Gogolian image of petrification, noting in particular that it occurs under the impression of "divine" or "perfect" beauty.[15] Typically, however, this beauty is seen rather than seeing. In both examples cited by Mann—in "The Portrait," when Chartkov freezes in front of a painting by a Russian artist who has

---

15 Mann, *Poetika Gogolia*, 371.

arrived from Italy, and in "Rome," when passers-by "stop as if transfixed" before Annunziata's beauty—the petrification is caused by the beauty of the object, not by the gaze of another. By contrast, the author's standing "motionless" before the eyes of Russia, eyes trained upon him and full of expectation, should be seen in the context not of admiration before divine beauty but rather the power of the sorcering gaze. In Gogol, divine beauty allows itself to be contemplated, while demonic beauty itself stares at you, immobilizing you and striking you dumb.

Light and Chiming

Magical space has an intense coloration and acoustics; in particular, it features radiance and ringing. If we imagine Gogolian Rus from a distance, then we are struck first and foremost by its sparkling and chiming, as in these examples from *Dead Souls*: "[M]y eyes are *lit up* by an unnatural power: ohh! what a *shining, wondrous* yonder, unknown to the world! Rus!.. (254); "was it a bolt of lightning thrown down from heaven?... *Wondrously the harness bell dissolves in ringing*" (284).

And once again, this wondrous ringing has already been heard in the early Gogol, and already associated with wondrous radiance. "With a soft *chiming*, the *wondrous light* seemed to spread throughout. ... And again *with a wondrous chiming the whole light-chamber [svetlitsa] lit up* with a rosy *light*, and again the sorcerer stood *motionless* in his *wondrous* turban. The sounds grew stronger and deeper, the thin rosy *light* grew *brighter*, and something *white*, like a *cloud*, fluttered in the middle of the hut."[16] This is the sorcerer in "A Terrible Vengeance" casting his spells, summoning the soul of his daughter Katerina in order to entice her into a "godless" connection.

And here is another magic-user, from "The Portrait": "The moonlight intensified the *whiteness* of the sheet. ... [T]he old man began to unwrap the packets. *Gold gleamed*. ... [Chartkov] gazed at the gold, *staring fixedly* as it was unwrapped by the bony hands, *gleaming, clinking* thinly and dully" (*CT*, 340–41). Here we have the same combination: the fixed

---

16 Gogol', *Sobranie sochinenii v 7 t.*, 1:148.

gaze, radiance ("gleaming"), and a ringing or tinkling sound.[17] It is as if the circumstance of sorcering passes from work to work, taking on different details but preserving the requisite connection of visual and acoustic imagery. Does this not explain, incidentally, Gogol's strange expression in the description of the wonder-steeds of the troika that is Russia: "Is a keen ear burning in your every nerve?" (*Dead Souls*, 284). The "ear" "burns." In "A Terrible Vengeance," light itself chimes, in "The Portrait," moonlit gold jingles, and in *Dead Souls*, a little "harness bell" rings.

In "Viy" we find a direct connection between the chime of a bell and the charms of light: "He saw some *sun shining* there instead of the moon; he heard *bluebells tinkle*, bending their heads" (*CT*, 159).[18] And further, when Khoma manages to saddle the witch who has been riding him, and rides her in turn, her screams eventually turn "soft, barely *ringing*, like fine *silver bells*, penetrating his soul" (*CT*, 160). And right away, as if by magic, two other elements of the same Gogolian archetype appear: eyes and radiance. "He got to his feet and *looked into her eyes*: dawn was breaking and the *golden* domes of the Kievan churches *shone* in the distance" (*CT*, 161).

The particular semantics may change: we may be dealing with bluebells, the flower; actual silver bells; or gold coins—but the archetype itself of radiance and chiming remains, spreading throughout the resplendent expanse. This is the seductive sound-and-light show that goes from Gogol's demonic scenes to his lyrical apotheosis of Russia.

Ghostly Light

Magic light emanates not from the sun but from the kingdom of darkness. There is something ghostly and shimmering about it: perhaps the moon is practicing its witchery; perhaps, as in the example from "Viy" quoted above, it is the shining of some sort of mysterious nighttime sun. In "The Night before Christmas" ("Noch' pered Rozhdestvom"), a devil carries Vakula through the skies at night: "Everything was *bright aloft*. The air

---

17 It should be emphasized that the ringing or chiming of a bell and the clinking of coins are in Russian effectively the same: *zvon, zvenet'*—trans.
18 The connection of imagery is more stark in the original: the harness bell in *Dead Souls* is literally just a "little bell," and bluebells are literally "little blue bells"; and the ringing, chiming, or clinking of either is that same verb *zvenet'*—trans.

was *transparent*, all in a light silvery mist. *Everything was visible*, and he could even observe how a sorcerer, sitting in a pot, raced past them like the wind, ... how a whole swarm of phantoms billowed in a cloud off to one side" (*CT*, 50–51). Here we have not a bright daytime and dark night, as in the natural order of things, but a transparent night, illuminated from within.

In "Viy": "The timid *midnight radiance* lay lightly as a *transparent* blanket and steamed over the earth. Forests, meadows, sky, valleys—all seemed to be *sleeping with open eyes*" (*CT*, 159). In "The Portrait": "The *radiance of the moon* intensified the *whiteness* of the sheet.... The *moon's radiance* still lay upon the rooftops and *white walls* of houses."[19]

We find this same chronotope of a magic night illuminated or even blanched from within in one of the lyrical digressions in *Dead Souls*: "The ... *moon shines* there and there, as if *white linen kerchiefs* were hung on the walls, the pavement, the streets ... the slantly *lit* ... roofs gleam like *shining* metal.... But the night! heavenly powers! what a night is transpiring in the heights!" (254). The verbal parallelism in "The Portrait" and *Dead Souls* is particularly striking, as the moon's witchery is augmented by the whiteness of a sheet/kerchiefs and walls/rooftops. Such is the light of that enchanted land over which Vakula rides a devil, Khoma a witch, and Chichikov his troika. At night nature surrenders to sleep—only the forces of the underworld are wakeful: this is why everything in the demonic episodes is illuminated from within, everything sleeps with its eyes open, obeying the "supernatural influence of the moon, whose miraculous light harbors the mysterious attribute of conferring on objects some portion of the sounds and hues of another world" (first draft of "The Portrait"[20]).

Such magically luminous nights in Gogol recall the episode in which, "lit by the pale moonlight," the proud idol—the graven image of him who has displaced the sea—gallops after Evgenii in *The Bronze Horseman* (257). Here the white night, too, serves to signify the unnatural violation of the boundaries set by nature. These boundaries—between day and night, land

---

19 Gogol', *Sobranie sochinenii v 7 t.*, 3:70, 71.
20 Ibid., 3:217.

and water—were established at the very outset of creation, and displacing them acquires a demonic meaning in Pushkin and Gogol alike.[21]

Chiming and Weeping

In the bewitched world, sounds, like light, arise as if from nowhere; borne about by the expanse itself, they stick in the soul by some inexplicable charm in which happiness and melancholy are merged. Compare the following passage from "Viy," as Khoma rides the witch—"But *what* now? Wind or music: ringing, ringing, and *whirling*, and *approaching*, and *piercing the soul* with some unbearable trill" (*CT*, 160)—with one of the lyrical digressions in *Dead Souls* marked by the same interrogative intonation: "*What* is in it, in this song? What calls, and weeps, and *grips the heart*? What sounds so *painfully* caress and *stream into the soul*, and *twine* about my heart?" (*Dead Souls*, 253). The same words, their same melodic combination: *v'etsia* ("whirls") and *vonzaetsia v dushu* ("pierces the soul"); *stremiatsia v dushu* ("stream into the soul") and *v'iutsia* ("twine" or "whirl").

This is a sonorous song, but even so, it has something of the painful and piteous in it, a certain weeping. From this sound-image, we understand: the feeling with which Russia reverberates in the author's heart is the same as that with which the young witch's "dazzling" beauty reverberates in the heart of Khoma: "She lay as if alive.... Yet in... these same features, he saw something *terribly piercing*. He felt his soul begin *to ache somehow painfully*, as if in the whirl of merriment and giddiness of a crowd, someone suddenly struck up a *song about oppressed people*" (*CT*, 171).

In *Dead Souls*, this same mournful song seizes the heart of the author himself as he looks into the eyes, trained upon him, of the glittering Russian expanse. "But what *inconceivable, mysterious force draws one to you*? Why do the ears hear and ring unceasingly with your *melancholy song*, coursing through the whole length and breadth of you from sea to sea?... What calls, and *weeps*, and grips the heart?" (*Dead Souls*, 253).

---

21 For more on the "Mephistophelian" meaning of the violation of these borders, see the chapter "Faust and Peter on the Seashore: From Goethe to Pushkin."

The melancholy song, from which one's "soul aches *painfully*" and which "*painfully* caresses the soul," is transferred from "Viy" to *Dead Souls*. And while in the former, it conveys "something terribly piercing" in the features of a dead witch, in the latter it expresses the "inconceivable, mysterious force" that constitutes Russia's allure.

This lyric-demonic passage, which is spread throughout Gogol's "magic" works and ultimately merges with his image of Russia, may be found in embryo in Pushkin's "The Devils" ("Besy," 1830). Here the lyric persona has, like Gogol's, got himself lost in a "vastness" (*Dead Souls*, 253), one similarly filled with the sounds of a "plaintive" song:

> How many there are! Where are they being driven?
> Why do they *sing so plaintively*?
> Are they burying a house-spirit [*domovoi*]?
> Are they marrying off a witch?[22]
> ....
> Swarm by swarm, the devils rush,
> In the boundless heights,
> With *plaintive squeals* and howls
> *Rending my heart*...[23]

> Сколько их! куда их гонят?
> Что так жалобно поют?
> Домового ли хоронят,
> Ведьму ль замуж выдают?
> ....
> Мчатся бесы рой за роем
> В беспредельной вышине,
> Визгом жалобным и воем
> Надрывая сердце мне...[24]

---

22 Trans. of first stanza cited from Aizlewood, "'Besy,' Disorientation, and the Person," 304.
23 Trans. of second stanza cited from Weiner, *By Authors Possessed: The Demonic Novel in Russia*, 131.
24 Pushkin, *Sobranie sochinenii v 10 tomakh*, 2:298.

"Rending my heart"—"weeps, and grips the heart." Also matching is the illumination of this chronotope: in Pushkin and Gogol, the melancholy song is accompanied by a ghostly nighttime landscape under the "murky play of the moon."[25] Insofar as the moon is "invisible," it seems as if light is being emitted by the darkness itself. This devilish landscape occurs to both writers simultaneously: "The Devils," like "The Night before Christmas," was written in 1831, and they feature an almost word-for-word coincidence: "Swarm by swarm, the devils rush, / In the boundless heights [*vyshine*]"; "Everything was bright aloft [or "in the heights," *v vyshine*] ... a sorcerer ... raced past them like the wind, ... a whole swarm of phantoms billowed in a cloud off to one side." But what in Pushkin has the whiff of horror is for Gogol still steeped in folkloric merriment; it is only later that this radiant midnight landscape will be tinged with a "demonically sweet feeling" ("Viy"; *CT*, 160).

The play of the moon, a weeping song, a swarm of rushing phantoms—such is the Gogolian chronotope of the "bewitched place"—"a devilish place, a Satanic apparition,"[26] to borrow the wording from the story "A Bewitched Place" ("Zakoldovannoe mesto")—which is what, in a lyrical digression in *Dead Souls*, the whole of Russia becomes.

Dream and Waking

Hence the constant transition, in Gogol's scenes of magic, from dream to waking, and the erasure of the boundary between the two: now this country exists, now it only seems to. In it the features of reality are washed out; this is some sort of "ecstatically wondrous" (*Dead Souls*, 283) reverie, invoked by person unknown. "Is he seeing it, or is he not? Is he awake or asleep?" ("Viy"; *CT*, 160).

"[D]rowsiness steals up so temptingly, and your eyes are closing. ... You wake up again— there are fields and steppes before you, nothing anywhere. ... [W]hat wonderful sleep enveloping you again!" (*Dead Souls*, 255). What in "Viy" is posed as a question—"Is he awake or asleep?"—in *Dead Souls* becomes a principle for depicting the

---

25 Trans. of Pushkin cited from Aizlewood, "'Besy,' Disorientation, and the Person," 304.
26 Gogol', *Sobranie sochinenii v 7 t.*, 1:197.

road itself: dream alternates with waking reality, one blurring into the other. A single page devoted to a description of the road includes three instances of falling asleep and three of waking up: "[N]ow through sleep you hear. ... You wake up: five stations have raced by. ... [The night air] lulls you, and now you are dozing, and sinking into oblivion. ... You wake up again—there are fields and steppes before you. ... [W]hat wonderful sleep enveloping you again! A jolt—and again you wake up" (255). Such is the flickering of all creation, as one is caught up in the whirlwind of dreams and awakenings. The psychology of the demonic chronotope, its mirage-like nature, is marked by this perceptual fuzziness.

Fast Riding, Flickering

A key motif in Gogol's lyrical digression is speed, the swift, headlong movement of the Russian troika, which seems at once to gallop along the ground and fly above the earth:

> And what Russian does not love fast driving? How could his soul, which yearns to get into a whirl, to carouse, to say sometimes: "Devil take it all!"—how can his soul not love it? Not love it when something ecstatically wondrous is felt in it? It seems an unknown force has taken you on its wing. ... Ah, troika! bird troika, who invented you?" (*Dead Souls*, 283–84)

This is the first instance of the devil being directly mentioned in the epic's "patriotic passage." Gogol hides this long-cherished character under the guise of a worn-out phrase ("Devil take it all!"), but the context itself, mentioning as it does "an unknown force," emphasizes this personage's direct, demonic meaning. Other of Gogol's works suggest that the force invariably laying hold of his characters and taking them up "on its wing," as the bird troika does here with Chichikov, is quite "known"—it is an unholy force. In "The Night before Christmas," a devil carries Vakula through the air, while in "Viy" a young witch whisks Khoma off on a flight through the night. The bird-troika that seizes Chichikov in *Dead Souls* and takes him for a whirl has the same significance.

Notably, the comparison of the troika with a bird in *Dead Souls* is preceded, in Gogol's earlier writings, by a comparison of devil and bird. The blacksmith Vakula orders the devil: "Carry me like a bird!" The devil duly lifts Vakula aloft, up "to such a height that he could see nothing below" (*CT*, 44, 50). Thus the descending image of "devil" and ascending image of "bird" are already merged in an early Gogol tale. A stable figurative triangle ("troika-bird-devil") is constructed around the motif of "fast riding."

Vakula's flight aboard a devil and Chichikov's aboard a troika are described similarly. Significantly, upon landing with Vakula, the devil "turned into a horse," as the blacksmith finds himself riding a "swift racer" (*CT*, 51). The whirling movement of this devil-racer, moreover, coincides with that of the steeds who in the "patriotic passage" embody Rus. "My God! the clatter, the thunder, the glitter ... the clatter of horses' hooves and the rumble of wheels sounded like thunder and echoed on four sides ... bridges trembled; carriages flew by ... huge shadows flitted over the walls" (*CT*, 51). Compare to the troika's racing in *Dead Souls*: "[Y]ou are flying, and everything is flying; milestones go flying by ... the whole road is flying off no one knows where into the vanishing distance. ... [B]ridges rumble, everything falls back and is left behind. ... [W]hat unknown force is hidden in these steeds unknown to the world?... [T]he air rumbles, shatters to pieces, and turns to wind; everything on earth flies by" (283–84). Riding the devil and riding this troika involve the same "horrific movement" (*Dead Souls*, 284): "bridges trembled," "bridges rumble"; "carriages flew by," "the whole road is flying off"; the "wheels sounded like thunder," "the air rumbles." To avoid the speeding devil-horse, "passers-by pressed against and huddled under houses" (*CT*, 51); "looking askance, other nations and states step aside to make way" for the troika that is Rus (*Dead Souls*, 284).

Gogol's glorification of the Rus-troika reaches a mystical apotheosis as we are told that "all inspired by God it rushes on!" (284). This expression, however, is not without a certain ambiguity. In "The Night before Christmas," an image of ostensibly similar pathos is given a humorous ring. Vakula, having been transported to St. Petersburg by a devil, tucks the latter into his pocket before meeting with certain Zaporozhian Cossacks, who hail him thus: "Greetings, countryman! why has God brought you here?"[27] The devil is thus "accidentally" referred to as God. The same sort of dizzying transformation occurs, seemingly unnoticed by the author himself, in the lyrical digression in *Dead Souls*: the fast rider's "soul ... yearns to get into a whirl, to carouse, to say sometimes: 'Devil take it all!'"—but "all inspired by God it rushes on!" Now the troika is spun along by the devil, now impelled by God; in this imagery system, antonyms become synonyms.

Still more striking is the resonance between the "fast riding" imagery of *Dead Souls* and the passage in "Viy" in which Khoma rides the witch. The fairytale elements of "The Night before Christmas" are still present in the latter, but rather than featuring the folkloric humor of that earlier work, the poetics is far closer to the exalted lyricism and pathos-filled sweetness of *Dead Souls*. The intonation of "Viy" easily switches to the intonation of the lyrical digressions. In the following citations it is difficult to tell the two works apart, so smoothly do they flow into one another, thus demonstrating the stylistic unity of Gogol's "demonic chronotope":

"But the night! heavenly powers! what a night is transpiring in the heights! And the air, and the sky, far off, far up, spreading so boundlessly, resoundingly, and brightly, there, in its inaccessible depths!" (*Dead Souls*, 254). "Such was the night when the philosopher Khoma Brut galloped with an incomprehensible rider on his back. He felt some languid, unpleasant, and at the same time sweet feeling coming into his heart. ... The earth just flashed beneath him. Everything was clear in the moonlight, though the moon was not full. The valleys were smooth, but owing to the speed everything flashed vaguely and confusedly in his eyes" (*CT*, 159–60). "There is something terrible in this quick flashing, in which the vanishing object has no time to fix itself" (*Dead Souls*, 283–84).

In episodes of magic, this fleetingness corresponds to shimmering moonlight or the modulating chime of bells; in everything one senses a shakiness and wavering. Objects scarcely manage to appear before one's eyes before vanishing; a whirlwind whisks them off to some unknown faraway or abyss. The fabric of reality itself wears thin, allowing illusoriness and nonbeing to pass through this headlong galloping. And time

---

27 Ibid., 1:233.

and again the troika crumbles to ashes and dust and is borne away to nowhere: "And like a phantom, the troika disappeared in thunder and dust" (*Dead Souls*, 254).

c. Patriotism and Eroticism

A comparison with Gogol's earlier works may also help clarify the mystical-erotic subtext of the "fast riding" Gogol sees as so characteristic of the Russian. After all, Khoma's gallop with the young witch is permeated with an extreme erotic tension, albeit supplanted by fear in the consciousness of Khoma himself. This is the fear of being lost in a huge, immense expanse—a feeling accompanied by the simultaneous and intense desire to penetrate that expanse, to fill it with oneself.

In his remarkable book *The Sexual Labyrinth of Nikolai Gogol*, Simon Karlinsky convincingly traces many of Gogol's artistic peculiarities to his latent homosexuality. In Gogol, the feminine is often presented as negative, cast in such types as the threatening temptress (the young witch; the stranger in "Nevsky Prospect"); the woman who is parodically belittled (Agaf'ia Tikhonovna; the governor's wife and daughter in *Dead Souls*); or who is idyllically sexless (Shponka's auntie; Pul'kheriia Ivanovna). But Gogol's treatment of the feminine is hardly limited to such unflattering portrayals. Eroticism, in particular, has an ambiguous tendency in his work. On the one hand, it places masculine friendship higher than woman's love; but on the other, it deifies the feminine, transferring its erotics from the level of the individual to that of the landscape and the cosmic. This may explain something unmentioned in Karlinsky's book: the erotic subtext of Gogol's patriotism. Karlinsky begins his study with the early piece "1834," in which Gogol invokes not the Muse (as was traditionally done in Russian poetry) but Genius, a masculine representation of inspiration, whom he calls "my beautiful brother."[28] This, according to Karlinsky, is the symbolic start-point of Gogol's artistic thematizing of homosexuality.

But Gogol has a still earlier piece titled "Woman" ("Zhenshchina," 1831)—the first work he ever published under his own name. This is a

---

28 Ibid., 6:17.

mystic hymn to the "female land," to the motherland. Telecles, a young disciple of Plato, complains to his teacher that his beloved has cheated on him, and curses the devious nature of woman; Plato's answer to this constitutes the whole of Gogol's piece. A woman might prove unfaithful, he says, but she stands above blame or disillusionment, because she reveals in herself the absolute, all-encompassing feeling of motherland. If the young man can come to know woman as "an artist's idea—limitless, infinite, incorporeal," then "from within himself, as if in response to the call of the motherland, shall echo both that which is dashing away forever and that which is irresistibly imminent." Further: "What is love?—The fatherland of the soul ... the indelible trace of innocent infancy, where everything is one's motherland."[29]

From Gogol's first signed piece to the lyrical conclusion of his final completed work, volume one of *Dead Souls*, the eternal feminine stands as an erotics of patriotic feeling, an equals sign between woman and nature. In *Dead Souls*, alongside the satirical representation of women and marriage (Korobochka, the Manilovs, the "agreeable" society ladies), we find in this final chapter an erotic representation of space as an open womb (*lono*) into which Chichikov's britzka rushes.

Before this, the sharpest rendition of such imagery in Gogol had come in "Viy." In Karlinsky's reading,[30] Khoma's night gallop with the young witch includes a metaphorical description of an orgasm: "But what now? Wind or music: ringing, ringing, and whirling, and approaching, and piercing the soul with some unbearable trill. ... He felt a demonically sweet feeling, he felt some piercing, some languidly terrible pleasure" (*CT*, 160). But if this is a description of an orgasm, then it is one that transitions here from the bodily dimension to the cosmic. The lust provoked by riding the witch is transferred to a tempting mermaid Khoma sees flitting through the water below him; this desire then evanesces in the surrounding space, in the whirlwind of flight, in the music of the wind. The next stage of this erotic transference comes in the utterly uncorporeal "orgasm" of *Dead Souls*—a purely "landscape"

---

29 Ibid., 9.
30 Karlinsky, *The Sexual Labyrinth of Nikolai Gogol*, 90–91.

orgasm. Significantly, "Viy," which was begun in 1833, was substantially revised in 1841, that is, just when volume one of *Dead Souls* was completed. Khoma rides a witch, Chichikov a troika—images that seem to express the same lyrical impulse. This erotic-demonic obsession also dictated to Gogol the famous "patriotic passage," whose chronotope might be termed that of the "coital landscape."

We can distinguish four basic elements of this chronotope. The first is strictly spatial: the "womb of the landscape." Here Russia is described as a wide-open expanse ready to be conquered: "In you all is openly deserted and level"; "What prophecy is in this uncompassable expanse?"; "sweep[ing] smoothly and evenly over half the world"; "you yourself are without end" (253, 284).

The second element is the presence of a conquering masculine force, one that is contained by this expanse and seeks free passage from it: "Is it not here that the mighty man is to be, where there is room for him to show himself and walk about? And menacingly the mighty vastness envelops me" (253). The sequence of these two sentences effectively equates the "mighty man," the epic hero (*bogatyr'*) amid this powerful expanse, with the lyric persona himself.

The chronotope's third element is strictly temporal. It is the feeling of an impending languor, one that must be vented into something or otherwise resolved. "Rus! what is it that you want of me? what inconceivable bond lies hidden between us? Why do you gaze so, and why is everything in you turned towards me with eyes full of expectation?. ... [M]y eyes are lit up by an unnatural power: ohh! what a shining, wondrous yonder, unknown to the world! Rus!" (254) What is referred to here is a persistent expectation, upon whose elapse there must come a discharge of accumulated and lustful force into the open womb. The drawled interjection of "ohh!" especially conveys the lyric persona's swooniness before the "wondrous yonder," before the inevitability of what must come to pass.

The fourth and final element is spatiotemporal: the rapid penetration into this space ("fast riding"). Space and time are unified by speed; the immensity of space seems to multiply by the compression of time. The result is the headlong rush, a whirlwind of movement. "It seems an unknown force has taken you on its wing ... [T]he steeds go like

The Motherland-Witch 73

[a whirlwind] ... the road simply shudders ... there she [the troika] goes racing, racing, racing!... And already far in the distance you see something raising dust and drilling the air" (284).

The first three elements of this coital chronotope are prepared early in chapter eleven of *Dead Souls*, in the digression on the Russian expanse; the last element appears at the end of the same chapter, in the image of Chichikov's troika. It is in the interval between the first and second lyrical digressions that Chichikov's story unfolds, that of his bachelorhood and renunciation of family bliss, which is to be compositionally crowned with a mystical coitus—not with a woman, that is, but with Russia herself. Hence the instantaneous shift from the biographical to the geographical, to Chichikov's headlong movement deep into the Russian expanse, as described by such wording as "soaring," "moving like the wind," "leaping," "flying up," "racing."

The gap between these two lyrical digressions on Russia merits particular attention. The landscape-chronotope of coitus, at first vividly presented as openness and expectation, is suddenly cut off by the appearance of a courier galloping from out of that "wondrous yonder," which forces Chichikov to "hold up" his driving in the face of a blatantly homoerotic substitution: the courier has a "yard-long" moustache.

> What a shining, wondrous yonder, unknown to the world! Rus!
> "Hold up, hold up, you fool!" Chichikov shouted to Selifan.
> "You'll get a taste of my saber!" shouted a courier with yard-long moustaches, galloping in the opposite direction. "The hairy devil take your soul: don't you see it's a government carriage?" (254)

A symbolic interpretation of this scene suggests itself: instead of Russia's feminine expanse spreading invitingly before him, Chichikov suddenly finds himself confronted by a masculine representative of the government with a protruding mustache. It is as if the state has encroached upon the relations between the lyric persona and Russia, hindering the consummation of their desires (and befitting Chichikov's always uneasy relations with the law and state). Appearing just as Chichikov is most obsessed with Russia, the courier is like the phantom of another, same-sex love, one threatening to lash out with its "sabre." But this does not happen; the two carriages simply pass each other by. Russia, it turns out, has no rival, neither male nor female. The hero thus proves his mystical right to complete this coitus; now nothing stands in his way, and he can drive as fast as he wants. The troika hurtles like a whirlwind "no one knows where into the vanishing distance," "drilling the air."

The erotic subtext of the love of "fast riding" is clear: this is what the young Gogol in "Woman" had described in mystical terms: "the soul drowns in the ethereal womb of the woman's soul."[31] But the mature Gogol partly covers up this motif: the troika that "drills" Russia is, itself, Russia. The erotics of the cosmic landscape in these two lyrical digressions embraces autoeroticism—rendering all the more fitting Belinsky's formulation regarding Gogol's "thunderous, melodious dithyrambs of a national self-consciousness *luxuriating in itself*."

d. Blok Gives Gogol's Secret Away

The demonic-erotic subtext of Gogol's image of Russia is clear not only in his own early work but in the subsequent movement of Russian literature, first and foremost in the poetry of Aleksandr Blok, where these two motifs, the "demonic feminine" and "inspired patriotism," are firmly linked. Blok's lyric poetry, especially in the period of "The Snow Mask" ("Snezhnaia maska"), is entirely permeated with the image of the sorceresses, the "stranger" or "unknown woman" (*neznakomka*), the "snow maiden," etc., all working their spells, their witchery and magicks—and this imagery naturally transitions into Blok's patriotic verse, which glorifies the magical racing of the troika and the brigandish beauty of Russia, enthralled to a conjurer (the poem "Russia"). We recognize the mystic sensuality of "Viy" in such verses, where Blok's lyric persona, bewitched by "the eyes of a spell-weaving maiden,"[32] is borne up into the heights, cast into an abyss, evanesces in a blizzard, and again and again experiences the paroxysm of "fast riding" in the embrace of a witch he calls "Russia." This is a tempting, baleful beauty that will carry you off, gasping, to

---

31 Gogol', *Sobranie sochinenii v 7 t.*, 6:9.
32 Blok, *Sobranie sochinenii v 6 t.*, 2:14. Further citations in the text are to this edition.

infinity, only to vanish and leave you there. Let us recall the huntsman Mikita in "Viy," an earlier victim, prior to the philosopher Khoma, of the young witch's allure. "Either he was really smitten, or she'd put a spell on him. ... He bent his back, the tomfool, grabbed her bare legs with both hands, and went galloping like a horse all over the fields. And he couldn't tell anything about where they rode, only he came back barely alive, and after that he got all wasted, like a chip of wood. ... he burned up, burned up of his own self" (*CT*, 174–75). Such are the escapades of a witch seen from the side; but here is how her charm is perceived by the spellbound himself:

> And, subject to the earthly world,
> Amongst all—you alone do not know
> To what fervor you are privy,
> In what faith you have been baptized.
> ....
> Creep into my room, creeping serpent,
> Deafen me in the voiceless midnight,
> Torment me with your languid lips,
> Strangle me with your black braid.

> И, миру дольнему подвластна,
> Меж всех—не знаешь ты одна,
> Каким раденьям ты причастна,
> Какою верой крещена.
> ....
> Вползи ко мне змеей ползучей,
> В глухую полночь оглуши,
> Устами томными замучай,
> Косою черной задуши. (2:35)

> And to the sultry moan of snow
> Your features blossomed.
> Only a troika races along, jingling,
> In snow-white oblivion.
> You shook the sleigh-bells,

Lured me off into the fields...
You strangle me with your black silks,
You flung wide your sable-furs.

И под знойным снежным стоном
Расцвели черты твои.
Только тройка мчит со звоном
В снежно-белом забытьи.
Ты взмахнула бубенцами,
Увлекла меня в поля...
Душишь черными шелками,
Распахнула соболя... (1:423)

What light is it
By which you tease and lure me?
When will you weary
Of this whirling?
Whose songs? And sounds?
What am I afraid of?
Plaintive sounds
And a free Rus?

....
You race along! You race along!
You've thrown your arms
Ahead...
And a song is heard...
And your features glow with a strange glow.

Каким это светом
Ты дразнишь и манишь?
В кружении этом
Когда ты устанешь?
Чьи песни? И звуки?
Чего я боюсь?
Щемящие звуки
И—вольная Русь?..

....
Ты мчишься! Ты мчишься!
Ты бросила руки
Вперед...
И песня встает...
И странным сияньем сияют черты... (2:68–69)

The upshot of this poetic love affair with a sorceress called "free Rus" comes as the latter answers the man under her spell:

I was faithful for three nights,
I coiled and called,
I let you look me in the eye,
I gave you light wings...

So, burn, o bright and ardent one,
As for me—with a light hand
I'll scatter your light ashes
Across the snowy plain.

Я была верна три ночи,
Завивалась и звала,
Я дала глядеть мне в очи,
Крылья легкие дала...

Так гори, и яр и светел,
Я же—легкою рукой
Размету твой легкий пепел
По равнине снеговой. (2:32)

Blok states outright what classic authors of the nineteenth century left unsaid—something they hardly suspected, something they feared and dared not admit even to themselves. Blok restores the "devilish" landscape of snowstorms and blizzards to its Pushkinian prototype from "The Devils," but where Pushkin features only the fear and despair of a lost wayfarer, Blok experiences the "demonically sweet feeling" of flying with abandon after some unknowable force that calls out to him in the name of the motherland. "What calls, and weeps, and grips the heart?" asks Gogol. "What sings to me? What chime do I hear? That of another life? Deaf death?"—echoes Blok (2:38), and gives his answer.

What in Gogol is revealed unwittingly, through the irony of style, in Blok becomes a conscious pathos. Gogol would probably have been horrified to recognize the demonic imagery of "Viy" or "A Terrible Vengeance" in his lyrical apotheosis of Russia; but for Blok, this "alluring beauty" who leads angels to their downfall, laughs at faith, and tramples the most sacred shrines, is revealed and hymned as his own muse ("To the Muse" ["K Muze"]). "Whosoever has looked into the desired gaze knows who she is," says Blok (2:37) of his "unknown woman" (*neznakomka*). Indeed, Russia-the-witch, with her terrible, resplendent beauty, becomes Blok's muse; his poetry comes from "Viy" no less than, say, Dostoevsky's prose comes from "The Overcoat."

Reading Blok in a Gogolian light allows us to understand, in particular, how and why in "The New America" ("Novaia Amerika"), Russia turns from an old woman into a young beauty: after all, this transformation has already taken place in "Viy," where the demonic flight begun by an old woman is completed by a wondrous beauty. This literary motif may be termed that of the "rejuvenated witch."

> First you pretend to be devout,
> Then you pretend to be a little old lady,
> ....
> No, [it's not] an elderly countenance, and not one of lenten leanness
> Under a colored Muscovite kerchief!
> ....
> The whispering, quiet talk,
> Your cheeks aflush...
>
>
> Там прикинешься ты богомольной,
> Там старушкой прикинешься ты,
> ....

> Нет, не старческий лик и не постный
> Под московским платочком цветным!
> ....
> Шопотливые, тихие речи,
> Запылавшие щеки твои...

Here we sense a variation on a Gogolian theme: "Is this really an old woman?... He got to his feet and looked into her eyes. ... Before him lay a beauty with a disheveled, luxurious braid and long, pointy eyelashes" (*CT*, 160–61). And one has the urge to repeat Khoma's immortal cry: "The witch!" Incidentally, the "cheeks aflush" here also constitute a reminiscence from Gogol—recall in "A Terrible Vengeance" the maiden who, having committed suicide ("destroyed her soul"), now tempts one as a *rusalka*: "her cheeks flush, her eyes lure one's soul out. ... Flee, Christian man!" (*CT*, 95).

> In the bleak, in the wild expanse
> You're just as you were before, and yet not,
> You turn your new countenance unto me,
> And another dream stirs me...
>
> На пустынном просторе, на диком
> Ты все та, что была, и не та,
> Новым ты обернулась мне ликом,
> И другая волнует мечта... (2:200)

Khoma, too, had earlier dreamt only of being rid of the accursed old woman, and found himself stirred by a different dream: "[S]ome strange excitement and timidity, incomprehensible to himself, came over him. ... [H]e was quite unable to explain to himself this strange new feeling that had come over him" (*CT*, 161). This sweet torment has seized him at the sight of a rejuvenated witch.

> But I do not fear, o bride, Russia,
> The voice of your stone songs!

> Но не страшен, невеста, Россия,
> Голос каменных песен твоих!

In Blok, the fear that had gripped Gogol's character is gone. All that remains is longing—the young witch is to become the lyric persona's bride. Now, when "languidly terrible" songs are chanted, when the "horns of onrushing night peal" in the fields (Blok 2:13), this is what they are chanting and pealing about. Pushkin's wayfarer had asked in horror: "Are they marrying off a witch?" Blok's errant hero understands that he himself is the bridegroom—and he races toward that clarion like a lover tired of waiting for his betrothed.

Blok thus seems to give away the secret of Gogol's Russia—one that had been hidden from its creator himself. In his 1909 article "Gogol's Child," Blok espouses his own faith in and fascination with Russia as hymned in the lyrical digressions, claiming that Gogol carried Russia under his heart the way a pregnant woman carries her fetus—and then comes a stunning comparison: "Gogol trembled before the inevitability of childbirth, before the appearance of a new being: as in the case of a *rusalka*, a 'black spot' showed black in his soul" (4:131). It can hardly have escaped Blok what Gogolian image this comparison refers to. In "May Night, or The Drowned Maiden," the titular maiden asks Levko to figure out which of the girlfriends that make up her mermaid roundelay is her disguised wicked stepmother—the "frightful witch" who had led her to suicide. Levko notices that one of the young women seems to take inordinate pleasure in playing the part of a predatory raven, and that "her body did not shine like those of the others: something black could be seen inside her.... 'The witch!' he said, suddenly pointing at her."[33] So it is this mermaid-witch, or rather, the blackness inside her, to which Blok compares the "new motherland" that Gogol carried under his heart.[34]

---

33 Gogol', *Sobranie sochinenii v 7 t.*, 1:77.
34 It may be that the title line of Blok's "demonic" love-poem "A black raven in the snowy twilight" ("Chernyi voron v sumrake snezhnom")—which was written in February 1910, soon after Blok had been rereading Gogol in connection with the centennial jubilee and his work on the article "Gogol's Child"—also contains a reminiscence from "May Night," i.e., the image of a sorceress playing at being a raven amid a roundelay of snow-white girls.

e. Gogol, Betrayed by Words: The Irony of Style

"The word must be treated honestly," says Gogol;[35] but a word may in fact betray a writer, honestly attesting to what he had been trying to hide from himself. That "demonically sweet" bewitchment that Gogol depicts in "The Night Before Christmas," "A Terrible Vengeance," "Viy," and "The Portrait," goes on to be called, in *Dead Souls*, by the name of Russia.

This demonic obsession of Gogol can be interpreted in different ways. One could take the psychoanalytic route and detect in Gogol a peculiar "patriotic libido," one that eroticizes its object to the extent it perverts, defiles, or demonizes it; thus an unconscious debasement of Russia runs parallel to her conscious exaltation. One could apply the Bakhtinian concept of ambivalence: tying Gogolian imagery to the carnival tradition, we could speak of the simultaneous crowning and uncrowning of Russia. One could apply the concept of deconstruction, uncovering implications in the lyrical digressions that are diametrically opposed to the author's stated meaning—further evidence of the sheer semantic ambiguity of any text.

Amid these interpretations, which are all clearly warranted, it is worth highlighting something Gogol himself might have proposed—something we might most simply designate by a phrase applied in "The Portrait" to the artist who produced the painting of the mysterious old man. "Well, brother, you cooked up quite a devil!" (*CT*, 379). The artist has recorded a devil-moneylender on canvas and unwittingly set this frightful portrait loose upon the world, himself becoming its first victim. In his early works, Gogol handles the demonic with a light touch, merrily playing with it; he calls the devil by name. But the author undergoes the same metamorphosis as does his character the artist: he wants to be cleansed of this obsession with the devil, and instead draw sacred figures: not the moneylender of "The Portrait," nor the sorcerer of "A Terrible Vengeance," nor the young witch of "Viy," but Russia, "all inspired by God."

What becomes of this is shown and in part predicted by Gogol himself in "The Portrait." The artist produces a new work, a religious

---

35 Gogol, *Selected Passages from Correspondence with Friends*, 23.

painting—one of his best creations ever—and enters it in a competition to decorate a church. The painting is admired by all, but one of the judges, a clergyman, remarks: "There is, indeed, much talent in the artist's picture. ... but there is no holiness in the faces; there is, on the contrary, something demonic in the eyes, as if the painter's hand was guided by an unclean feeling" (*CT*, 377). Couldn't this be said as well of the lyrical digression Gogol conceived as a verbal icon of Russia: "there is something demonic in the eyes"? The same thing the young witch and the moneylender have in their eyes, and what Gogol wants to be rid of but cannot, for it guides his hand, this "terrible force"; his "eyes are lit up by an unnatural power."

Let us recall that the final version of "The Portrait" was written in late 1841 and early 1842, immediately after volume one of *Dead Souls* was completed. It may be that "The Portrait," the fate of this artist, already expresses Gogol's inkling that he has committed an artistic mistake, has falsely adopted a mystical tone—a sense that would grow to torment him as he worked on the second, "ideal" volume of *Dead Souls*. It is as if Gogol himself, having undertaken to paint a picture of Russia and the incalculable richness of her soul—with a "man endowed with divine virtues" here, a "wondrous Russian maiden" there[36]—"saw with horror that he had given almost all the figures the moneylender's eyes. Their gaze was so demonically destructive that he involuntarily shuddered" (*CT*, 377).

Anticipating our primary conclusion, Innokentii Annensky remarks that "the longer Gogol spent working on his portrait of Russia, putting endless finishing touches on its bottomless, immeasurably populated eyes, the more grievous and dreary his own existence must have seemed to him. Gogol was not only frightened by the profound meaning of the [negative—M.E.] types he had revealed, but most importantly, he felt that there was no getting away from them."[37] And Gogol's subsequent path—his renunciation of his art, his hermitism, his ascetic mortification of the flesh and incessant praying—bears a remarkable resemblance to the fate

---

36 Gogol', *Sobranie sochinenii v 7 t.*, 5:209.
37 Annenskii, "Portret," 18.

of his own character, an artist who despite all his pious intentions cannot help giving everything he draws a demonic expression.[38]

Gogol's negative aesthetics may be analyzed according to the following key aspects:

1) a description of the negative elements of being, artistic satire (emptiness, nonentity, illusoriness, deadness, the "banality of a banal person," etc.);
2) a renunciation of description itself, artistic apophaticism: the object is described via the negation of its characteristics, e.g., Chichikov is neither old nor young, neither good- nor bad-looking—a "person without qualities"; in this category we would put the progressive silence of the artist Gogol himself; and
3) an artistic style that itself negates the author's intentions, lending them an opposite meaning.

The image of Russia in *Dead Souls* indeed becomes, in Gogol's fate, the very "portrait" that reveals the full meaning of negative aesthetics in his art: the power of this aesthetics turns out to extend further than the intentions of the author himself. This is not simply an aesthetics of negation (satire), or a negation of aesthetics (apophaticism), but the negativity of aesthetics itself, negation via aesthetics. The demonic nature of this or that Gogolian image is not the point here, but rather the demonism of the very style that plays fatal tricks on its author.

Significantly, Gogol would not only incarnate this aesthetic "twist" in his work (becoming, that is, its victim) but also may have been the first in Russian literature to sense it as a danger lurking on the writerly path. As he puts it in the section of *Selected Passages from Correspondence with*

---

[38] According to Annensky, "The Portrait" had a particular meaning in Gogol's fate. This is a "wondrous tale, one that Gogol wrote twice, and put more of himself into than any other of his works.... The tale's secret meaning becomes clear to us only in the light of Gogol's subsequent life, and clear to the poet himself, perhaps, only upon his own death.... Gogol flees, too, and also into asceticism, and also from an unfinished portrait.... Gogol dies, overcome by the despair of an artist who has lost track of a portrait he has not finished, but which has become hateful to him—a portrait he considers sinful." Ibid., 14, 16.

Friends titled "On What the Word Is": "It is a terrible thing when rotten words start to be heard regarding subjects sacred and sublime; let rotten words rather be heard regarding rotten subjects."[39] The tragedy of Gogol as writer began not when he "shamed the shameful," but when, at the end of volume one of *Dead Souls* and in its second volume, he began to glorify "the sacred"—and sensed the "rottenness" at the very "roots" of his words. What befell Gogol through no will of his own was precisely what he most feared, what he even warned contemporaries about, convinced by his own artistic torment that—as he admonishes in the same passage just quoted—"you can wind up smearing that which you seek to exalt; at every step, our language betrays us."[40]

It would be hard to find a more exact definition of this "traitorous" type of aesthetics than that given by Gogol himself. It is precisely language that betrays Gogol when he begins to speak of the sacred and exalted. It is Gogol's aesthetics that negates what he himself seeks to affirm as a moralist and patriot, negates the very basis of his prophetic mission.

---

39 Gogol', *Sobranie sochinenii v 7 t.*, 6:186.
40 Ibid., 189.

PART II

The Great in the Little: Bashmachkin's Offspring

1 | The Saintly Scribe: Akaky Bashmachkin and Prince Myshkin

There are characters who are representative not just of a particular author or epoch but of literature in general—symptom-characters or tendency-characters. This category would undoubtedly include Gogol's Akaky Bashmachkin and Dostoevsky's Prince Myshkin. These two are quite disparate in our consciousness, and for that matter in the actual scope of Russian literature; they are diametric opposites, standing at the extremes of what might be considered human greatness and human smallness.

Akaky Akakievich is a "little man," perhaps the littlest in all Russian literature; a littler one could hardly be imagined. Next to him, even those usually put in this category—Pushkin's Samson Vyrin, say, who has a wife and daughter, or Dostoevsky's Makar Devushkin, who carries on a correspondence with his beloved Varen'ka—are persons of a greater caliber, who have managed to engage someone's affection, to fence off for themselves some share of life-space in which even they mean something. Akaky Akakievich does not mean anything to anyone; the only "pleasant life's companion" to have "agreed to walk down the path of life with him ... was none other than that same overcoat" (*CT*, 396).

Prince Myshkin, on the other hand, may very well be first among Russian literature's "positively beautiful" heroes. No other creation of Dostoevsky can match the loftiness of the ideal this character embodies, commensurate as it is, for Dostoevsky, with the figure of Christ (Myshkin is called "Prince Christ" in drafts of the novel); just as there are few writers who could match the pathos of Dostoevsky's aspiring to this absolute, this unreachable ideal. One could arrange every character in Russian literature between Myshkin and Bashmachkin as personifications of the two poles of spiritual loftiness and abjection, of internal freedom and dependency.

The more significant a character's place in literature, the more important every detail in their image becomes. For all their dissimilarity and even oppositeness, Myshkin and Bashmachkin do share one feature in common—their passion for scribal copying. This is quite prominent in the figure of Akaky Akakievich, immediately seizing the reader's attention. "Outside this copying nothing seemed to exist for him. ... There, in that copying, he saw some varied and pleasant world of his own" (*CT*, 397). In the more complex figure of Myshkin, this feature is less obvious, but it is in effect the only thing linking Myshkin to the real world—the realm of occupations, professions, ways of obtaining means for subsistence. Scarcely has he come to St. Petersburg and shown up at his distant relation General Epanchin's residence when Myshkin demonstrates, at the general's request, his scribely gift—the only hope for his future financial security.

> "I don't think I have any talents or special abilities; even the contrary, because I'm a sick man and have had no regular education. ... [But] my handwriting is excellent. That's perhaps where my talent lies; I'm a real calligrapher. Let me write something for you now as a sample," the prince said warmly.[1]

Like Akaky Akakievich, Prince Myshkin is not just a good calligrapher but a passionate one, for whom letters are in and of themselves—aside from the meaning they express—a source of powerful emotion. Let us recall that for Akaky Akakievich, "certain letters were his favorites, and when he came to one of them, he was beside himself: he chuckled and winked and helped out with his lips, so that it seemed one could read on his face every letter his pen traced" (*CT*, 387). Just so does the prince speak, "with great pleasure and animation," of the various handwriting styles, of flourishes and hitches, of English and French fonts. His ecstasy and personal preoccupation is not conveyed as

---

1 Dostoevsky, *The Idiot*, 28–29. Further citations in the text are to this translation.

physiologically as in the case of Akaky Akakievich, with his face and lips, but with no less emotional force.

> They had superb signatures. ... sometimes so tasteful, so careful!... Look at these round *d*'s and *a*'s. I've transposed the French characters into Russian letters, which is very difficult, but it came out well. Here's another beautiful and original script. ... The writing is black, but remarkably tasteful. ... Discipline shows in the writing, lovely!... Elegance can go no further, everything here is lovely, a [bead], a pearl. ... A flourish is a most dangerous thing!... A script like this is incomparable, you can even fall in love with it. (34)

At this moment there is something peeking through Prince Myshkin that smacks distinctly of Akaky Akakievich. He will subsequently have occasion to experience no little amount of romantic agitation, but for now he is capable of falling in love only with letters and fonts, like Akaky Akakievich, who "served with love" and "would go to bed, smiling beforehand at the thought of the next day: What would God send him to copy tomorrow?" (*CT*, 387, 389)

The resemblance is completed via the matching of one further detail: for his copying, Akaky Akakievich receives "four hundred roubles or thereabouts" (*CT*, 389); and General Epanchin, ecstatic at Myshkin's calligraphy, promises him "thirty-five rubles a month ... from the first step," that is, roughly the same four hundred rubles a year. It seems as if Myshkin might become a colleague of Bashmachkin's, sitting with him in the same office, perhaps at the next desk over, and the two could have heartfelt discussions about their favorite letters...

The image of Myshkin as a copyist, outlined in chapter three of the first part of *The Idiot*, is developed no further in the plot, and is somewhat lost from the reader's attention. Such a detail, moreover, does not match the overall conception of Myshkin as a pure concentration of spirit, an existentially refined personality hardly akin to any sort of office paperwork. How could Titular Councilor Bashmachkin sit side by side with Prince Myshkin, or rather, within him? Does this unexpected resemblance not ruin the integrity of Myshkin's image—or is it somehow part of Dostoevsky's design, the intent of an author for whom Gogol's "The Overcoat" was always a reference point in Russian literature (even if we do not ascribe to Dostoevsky the comment, of controversial attribution, that "we all come from Gogol's 'Overcoat'")?

2.

First let us note that Dostoevsky himself, being an individual of a "Myshkinian" cast (the writer endowed his character with both his own illness and his own epiphanies), evinced an extreme carefulness when it came to his own handwriting. It is as if this self-control at the level of outer manifestation was to compensate for the ecstatic unrestraint of his bursts of pathos and imagination. Among nineteenth-century Russian writers, his is perhaps the clearest, the most rounded, the most precise handwriting—the letters are threaded like beads. According to Anna Grigor'evna Dostoevskaia, "Fedor Mikhailovich loved good writing instruments and always wrote his works on finely ruled vellum. He demanded of me, too, that I copy what he dictated only on vellum of a particular format. He loved a sharp, hard pen. He hardly ever used pencils."[2] It is possible that even as a young man studying draftsmanship at the Military Engineering Academy, Dostoevsky acquired the habit and tendency to convey meaning on paper in a graphically strict and professionally responsible manner. Nor should it be forgotten generally that, at least until the coming of the typewriter age, a writer was at the same time a scribe, a painstaking copyist of his own compositions, and so the tendency to psychologically inhabit the world of letters would not be something professionally unfamiliar.

But in this case, the main thing is not the subjective experience of a writer but rather the objective meaning of the profession of copyist itself, its cultural semantics, which have deep historical roots. In the ancient civilizations of the Near East (Egypt, Babylon, etc.), as well as in medieval Byzantium and Western Europe, the activity of the scribe and copyist was surrounded by respect and reverence, insofar as the meaning being imprinted was worthy of commemoration.

---

2 Dostoevskii, *Polnoe sobranie sochinenii v 30-i tomakh*, 9:43.

"Oh that my words were now written! oh that they were printed in a book! That they were graven with an iron pen and lead in the rock for ever!" Thus does the great martyr Job (19:23–24) lament not merely the disease of his fleeting flesh but also the fleetingness of his word, which is worthy, in his opinion, of being heard by God and humanity. The profession of scribe is central to the cult and culture of particular epochs and peoples because the eternal descends and reveals itself in time through the written word (the tablet and the Holy Scripture as cult objects), while the temporal elevates itself thereby and enters into communion with eternity (texts as works of culture). "The Middle Ages," notes S. Averintsev, "were indeed ... the 'Ink' Ages. This was the era of the 'scribes' as guardians of culture, and of 'Scripture' as life's landmark; the time of reverent worship at the shrine of parchment and letters."[3] The greatest minds, the major figures of the Church—Thomas à Kempis, Sergius of Radonezh—had no qualms about taking up the labor of copying; for them, this was hardly something "mechanistic" or "soulless," but rather a path to humility and piety.[4]

With the invention of print, the copyist's labor began to be perceived as mechanistic, hence something to be disdained. It was as if a dual transposition took place: when the copyist was replaced by the printing press, the copyist himself began to be seen as a substitute for same—an inferior substitute at that, fit only for low-quality texts of strictly temporary, narrowly departmental interest. The first books to be reproduced in print were religious ones, then those of artistic and scientific content; and the profession of copyist, relegated to the very periphery of culture, gradually became tantamount to the truly "mechanistic" reproduction (*after* machines, merely replacing them) of the lowliest verbal strata: office documents destined, at best, for an archive, but never for a library.

The social role and image of the copyist was correspondingly reduced to the lowly, pathetic state we encounter in Gogol's figure of Akaky Akakievich. But this social relegation of the copyist not only does not contradict the age-old moral and existential meaning of this profession but in fact reveals it in its proper light. A copyist, after all, is truly a novitiate

---

3 Averintsev, *Poetika rannevizantiiskoi literatury*, 208.
4 Ibid., 205.

of the text being copied; meekness is the technical foundation itself of a profession whose mastery requires total self-renunciation, a humble adherence to the characteristics of an original. To cite a medieval admonition to scribes made by Alcuin of York:

> Let them guard against the great impertinence of inserting additions,
> Let the hand not commit the sin of impertinent carelessness.[5]

Akaky Akakievich piously keeps this commandment and is organically incapable of emending anything in a text he is presented with. On one occasion he is assigned, as a form of encouragement, to change certain verbs from the first to third person, but here "he got all in a sweat, rubbed his forehead, and finally said, 'No, better let me copy something'" (*CT*, 387). Originality becomes a privilege, to one's credit, only in the consciousness of modernity. Akaky Akakievich is a copyist to the marrow of his bones, to the very depth of his character, and the shape of his existence is defined by the stooped posture of the scribe. If in the Middle Ages such a pose was perceived as consecrated from above, in modernity it is associated with an unnatural abjection, the loss of dignity. Championing the rectification (both literal and figurative) of the human being, modernity sees the figure of the copyist as a concentrated expression of moral and social degradation such as gives rise to humanistic protest. This is what has made the figure of Akaky Akakievich central to Russian literature, a focal point of its critical and denunciatory motifs: this is a character, after all, whose day-to-day existence consists in bowing his head, keeping his back hunched, and renouncing his own self. The motif of the repression of human dignity finds here a most explicit and visible incarnation.

But to analyze the cultural semantics of the copyist's profession, it is important to consider, aside from his hunched posture, just what he is hunched over, what elicits his insatiable interest and all-consuming love: the phenomenon of the letter—the letter, moreover, taken as a thing, as some sort of material occurrence, insofar as it is precisely this aspect of

---

5 Cited from Grabar'-Passek and Gasparov, *Pamiatniki srednevekovoi latinskoi literatury IV–IX vekov*, 261.

it that the copyist has anything to do with. Even as, in the material world proper, the letter might occupy the lowest rung in a hierarchy of objects: its flesh is of the very least substantiality. The letter is a sign, one even more conventional and less self-sufficient in its physicality than most other sign-types (pictorial, iconic, figurative). The copyist, then, deals with *matter*—but as it were, on the verge of its rupture; he deals with materiality reduced to a minimum, through which a maximum of meaning is to emerge. To fall in love with letters, to give oneself wholly to their perfect patterning, to have preferences among them—does this not mean to love "the least of these," that is, to keep a commandment central to the medieval worldview, that of condescending (in the positive sense), merciful love? To love not meaning, however important and edifying that may be, but the letter itself, as the least, the weakest of things.

If, moreover, for the copyist of sacred books, love of letters stemmed from love of meaning, the copyist of office documents like Akaky Akakievich has nothing, no grand meaning, to support his feeling. The tragic collision between such a love for letters and the insignificance of their content does not abase the love or insult it but, to the contrary, lends it a meek, almost heroic perseverance. They, these copyists of the age of print, are no longer votaries nor clergymen but lowly clerks; the spirit of obedience, even novitiatehood, has not been extinguished in them but has assumed a more abject, a more disdained—hence purer, closer to its original—form. The "sanctity of letters" even grows in its touching and somewhat absurd (like faith itself) grandeur if it requires no content to support it, no "logical" explanation.

Myshkin and Akaky Akakievich are akin in that their love of copying expresses meekness, which harks back, conventionally speaking, to a scribal archetype deeply rooted in world culture. But it should be noted that within the artistic systems of Gogol and Dostoevsky, this archetype takes on different meanings. The meekness of Akaky Akakievich is first and foremost read as abjection and limitation; Myshkin's, as wisdom and insight. Gogol plays on the alogism of Akaky Akakievich's calligraphic preferences as if to demonstrate the emasculation of the original meaning. Dostoevsky, to the contrary, uses the image of Myshkin to restore this meaning, to induce the reader to comprehend it. The first sample of the prince's talented handwriting, executed in medieval script, is the phrase: "The humble hegumen Pafnuty here sets his hand to it," which he follows with some unambiguous commentary: "They had superb signatures, all those old Russian hegumens and metropolitans, and sometimes so tasteful, so careful!" (33). The prince's art may find practical application only in an office setting, but it is unveiled here amid its immediate ties to the medieval worldview. In the figure of Akaky Akakievich, these ties have been severed (or at least are left unmentioned), whereas in the figure of Myshkin they are revived, imbuing him with a moral force and spiritual rootedness that is present only vestigially in the character of Gogol's "absurd" scribe.

But Myshkin's calligraphy does not merely bring back its former meaning, it also takes on a new one, a "psychological" meaning not found in ancient and medieval civilizations, and immanent specifically in the culture of modernity. For the prince, reproducing the handwriting of another grants insight into the spirit of the person whose hand inscribed the original.

"[Y]ou see, it adds up to character, and, really, the whole military scrivener's soul is peeking out of it: he'd like to break loose, his talent yearns for it, but his military collar is tightly hooked, and discipline shows in the writing, lovely!" (34) Akaky Akakievich would hardly be capable of making such a character sketch; for him, the beauty of letters is absolute, sufficing unto itself. But what Myshkin values and finds significant is not so much the letter itself as whosoever has, tracing it out, left personal traces in it. It is no accident that in this very same chapter of the novel, immediately after his calligraphic exercises, the prince first encounters the photographic portrait of Nastasia Filipovna in Epanchin's study, and gives a profound interpretation of her character based on her appearance. And in chapter five, the prince applies this perceptiveness, this ability to read faces, to the whole Epanchin family. Thus Myshkin's "only" talent, having first manifested itself in calligraphy, gradually penetrates deeper and deeper into the very essence of events, revealing itself as the seed begetting the whole conception of the novel and of its main character.

Myshkin and Bashmachkin share a passion for copying; but from this point of contact, the two characters veer in opposite directions. Bashmachkin betrays his calling, his allegiance, as soon as the minimal material of letters to which he'd been faithful is replaced by a fleshly, physically weighty and self-sufficient material—an overcoat, in which the hero wants to vest himself in order, so to speak, to gain a foothold in the substantiality of the world. So steeped is he in thoughts of the overcoat that "[o]nce, as he was copying a paper, he even nearly made a mistake, so that he cried 'Oh!' almost aloud and crossed himself" (396). Akaky Akakievich's service to letters, or rather his ministration thereto, is holy, while his reverie of the overcoat is like a temptation of the devil.

In this connection we might cite an interesting study in which E. A. Surkov demonstrates that Gogol's frame of reference in the "The Overcoat" is the genre of hagiography (a juxtaposition is made in particular with the "Life of Theodosius of the Caves").[6] The hagiographic hero disdains the rewards of this world and prefers to be vested in poor, tattered clothing. Such is Akaky Akakievich's decrepit overcoat, through which the bitter cold blasts him "especially in the back and shoulder" (CT, 389). We should note that at the very outset of Dostoevsky's novel, Myshkin appears in similarly unsuitable garb; the prince has been "forced to bear on his chilled back all the sweetness of a damp Russian November night, for which he was obviously not prepared" (5–6). Meager clothing, alongside a zeal for copying, rounds out the hagiographic countenance of both characters. And indeed, loving the exceedingly spectral and ephemeral material that is letters goes naturally hand in hand with a disregard for the more needful sort of material in which a person vests his flesh.

Characteristics of the saint's life in the narrative of Akaky Akakievich include his pious mother and godmother, "a woman of rare virtue" (385), the painstaking selection of his name from the Church calendar, and the compositional sequence characteristic of a hagiography. But in the image of Bashmachkin this canon is violated and overturned, first because he turns away from the contemplation of eternal letters (a kind of Platonic ideal) in favor of the fleetingness of the earthly shell, of worldly rewards, which as punishment, and as if to corroborate this fleetingness, are taken away from him; and secondly because Akaky Akakievich becomes an avenger, responding to

---

6 Surkov, "Tip geroia i zhanrovoe svoeobrazie povesti N. V. Gogolia 'Shinel'."

fate's chastisement with punitive measures of his own (in the form of a ghost), which suggests the sale of his soul to the devil. As mentioned in Part 1, ch. 1 (e), the reanimation of a corpse is a fairly traditional motif, appearing frequently in Gogol himself, for instance, in "May Night, or the Drowned Maiden," "Viy," and "The Portrait," and typically involves some deal-making with unholy forces. "The clerk's face was pale as snow and looked exactly like a dead man's," from his mouth comes "the horrible breath of the tomb" (412), and the ghost points menacingly and shakes his fist. All these eerie details in the epilogue of "The Overcoat" signify that the tale, begun in the spirit of hagiography, has gradually turned into the opposite, an anti-hagiography, the story of a moral and mystical downfall. Endowed with the features of a saintly ascetic, the main character becomes a taker of vengeance. It is not only the human that is suppressed and deformed in Akaky Akakievich, transitioning into the inhuman, but, in accordance with his potential and his possibilities, the sacred, too, is deformed, giving way to the satanic.

As for Myshkin, he has the same potential, the same makings of a "little man"—worn-out clothing and a love of copying—but in his case, these develop in an ideal, "ascetic-heroic" direction. If we consider "The Overcoat" an inverted hagiography, then with the character of Myshkin Dostoevsky has revived the medieval canon of saintliness, albeit, of course, enriched with psychological insight and the aesthetics of "realism in a higher sense." *The Idiot* is a nineteenth-century hagiography, an indicator of this genre's potential amid the same bourgeois bureaucracy wherein Gogol demonstrates hagiography's bereftness of meaning. From the "little man," the ascetic hero rendered banal, Dostoevsky moves to the height of the "positively beautiful" hero. In the process, one can sense Bashmachkin as Myshkin's point of departure.

3.

Dostoevsky was "sick" with Gogol his whole life, and never did manage to get over this "illness." The correlation of the images of Myshkin and Bashmachkin may be clarified with reference to Iurii Tynianov's study *Dostoevsky and Gogol: Toward a Theory of Parody* (1921). Here Tynianov famously establishes that Dostoevsky, striving to free himself from Gogol, transposed certain of that author's themes and images into his own works, but with an opposite sign, in the spirit of parodic twist. Being a "dialectical play of devices," parody does not necessarily produce any comic effect at all—that would be only one instance of it. "If a parody of a tragedy is a comedy, a parody of a comedy may be a tragedy."[7]

Tynianov himself only developed the proof for one part of his argument, showing how the exalted, pathos-suffused image of the author—Gogol himself in *Selected Passages from Correspondence with Friends*—is deflated, even directly caricatured by Dostoevsky in the figure of Foma Opiskin in *The Village of Stepanchikovo and Its Inhabitants* (*Selo Stepanchikovo i ego obitateli*). But it follows from Tynianov's theory that Dostoevsky's poetics harbors the reverse possibility: the transference of the "lowly" Gogolian hero to an elevated register, from the comic to the tragic-mysterial. This has apparently occurred with Bashmahckin, who via several successive transformations pervasive in Dostoevsky's entire oeuvre has been turned into a mysterial and antipodal double of himself—Prince Myshkin.

The first such transformation—the figure of Makar Devushkin in *Poor People* (*Bednye liudi*)—is particularly remarkable in that the relationship to his Gogolian prototype is stated outright. The episode in which the main character of *Poor People* reads "The Overcoat" is well known; here we might just recall Devushkin's main grievance with the figure of Bashmachkin: it's too much, he feels, of a view from the outside, showing an everyday penury, but without insight into the meager life's spirit, the positive values that are of primary importance for the "poor person." Devushkin is displeased with Gogol for abasing his character too low; he would like to see him elevated a bit. It would have been more conscientious had the author added that "for all his faults [Bashmachkin] was a decent, virtuous citizen ... [who] wished no one any harm [and] believed in God."[8] Dostoevsky, of course, is snickering at his character's inclination to lecture a great writer on how to write—but at the same time he is showing what sets this "little man" apart

---

7 Tynianov, *Poetika. Istoriia Literatury. Kino*, 226.
8 Dostoevsky, *Poor Folk and Other Stories*, p. 68.

from his predecessor: an active moral self-awareness and personal identity, albeit of limited intellectual scope.[9]

The next transformation of this character on the path from Bashmachkin to Myshkin comes in the figure of the copyist Vasia Shumkov in Dostoevsky's tale "A Faint Heart" ("Slaboe serdtse," 1848). Let us note, incidentally, the typological resemblance of all these surnames, which contain the diminutive *k*-suffix; whereas in neoclassical works, a surname directly "spoke" via its lexical meaning, in Gogol and Dostoevsky its morphology (and often even its phonetic structure) becomes more significant. *K* indicates the characters' diminished position in the world, which elicits, from some, condescension or disdain; but from sensitive souls, compassion.

Vasia's handwriting is remarkable—"in all Petersburg you won't find a handwriting like" it.[10] But what is essential here is not the materiality of the letters itself but the ideal element in the human heart, whose ardency is such that it seems to burn this matter up. In the tale's central episode, Vasia Shumkov is running out of time to finish copying papers for his beloved supervisor and benefactor, and hastens his quill so much that he begins to write dry, without ink. "He went on writing. All at once Arkady noticed with horror that Vasya was moving a dry pen over the paper, was turning over perfectly blank pages, and hurrying, hurrying to fill up the paper as though he were doing his work in a most thorough and efficient way!... 'At last I have made the pen go faster,' he said."[11] Now it is not a simple obedience to what is written that guides Vasia's hand but obedience to the call of his own heart, which has gotten far ahead of the slow flowing of letters. Here it is as if humility is duplicated in the demands it makes of itself: not only does it accept the world as it is, it also makes the leap into a nonexistent world created by its own need for sacrifice and devotion. This perfectionism is still so unripe and hurried that it causes a breakdown into madness.

Vasia Shumkov differs sharply from previous "little men" in a certain sense: he is young, which lends his "littleness" a fundamentally new meaning,

---

9 This same tendency to elevate or "romanticize" the "little man" may be seen in such other writers of the 1840s as A. Maikov and Ia. Butkov; see Iu. Mann's informative article "Put' k otkrytiiu kharaktera."
10 Dostoevsky, *White Nights and Other Stories*, 161.
11 Ibid., 192.

related not so much to this figure's fate as his character, which has a tendency toward self-diminishment. Being older, Samson Vyrin, Akaky Bashmachkin, and Makar Devushkin are in a sense "completed": their humility has been molded by fate. Transitioning from the "little man" to the "positively beautiful" allows humility to be laid bare as goodwill, as the hero's approach to life, and not a consequence of his "brokenness." Unlike in the case of other "little men," everything in Shumkov's life works out well— incredibly well, too well. Vyrin, Bashmachkin, and Devushkin suffer the slings and arrows of fate. Vasia Shumkov, by contrast, inhabits an utter idyll: he is beloved by everyone—his fiancé Liza, his friend Arkady, and his supervisor Iulian Mastakovich. The only thing tormenting Vasia and driving him out of his mind is the feeling of his own unworthiness. "'My heart is so full, so full! Arkasha, I am not worthy of such happiness!... Why has it come to me,' he said, his voice full of stifled sobs. 'What have I done to deserve it? Tell me.'"[12]

Akaky Akakievich's heart does not withstand the dressing-down he receives from the "very important personage." Vasia Shumkov's heart does not withstand the gratitude he feels toward another important personage, his benefactor. The faintness of this heart is revealed not by the eruption of someone else's wrath but under the pressure of its own love. No one humiliates him; he himself feels unworthy, small, unable to perform the moral demands he makes of himself: "Vasya felt guilty in his own eyes"[13]—thus does Arkady explain his friend's madness. Vasia is still a "little man," but in a different sense than Akaky Akakievich: he is small not so much in comparison to the force of circumstances but in the face of eternity—the eternal love that unites people. One more step—let the mind grow to match the size of the heart, the spirit that of the soul—and a "positively beautiful" image shall arise... But not even Myshkin is able to withstand his ascetic vocation to the end; he too loses his mind. This littleness of all that is human in the face of higher, superhuman demands harbors the new and final meaning of that "littleness" whose fate is shared by all the characters mentioned.

Even Akaky Akakievich harbors the eminence of predestination... Even Prince Myshkin harbors an accomplishment unfulfilled...

---

12 Ibid., 168.
13 Ibid., 188.

This marks a limitation: a man can neither sink lower than his own greatness nor rise higher than his own littleness.

This measure of the human, apparently, defines the relationship of the two "parodies" (in Tynianov's sense) by which Dostoevsky responds to Gogol's writings. When Gogol wants to rise above the human measure, making himself out to be a prophet and teacher of humanity—Dostoevsky plays this overblown pathos for comic effect, deflating it in the figure of Foma Opiskin. When Gogol abases a character below the human measure, presenting his life as senseless and pointless—here Dostoevsky sets the imbalance aright in the ascending figures of Devushkin, Shumkov, and finally Myshkin. Dostoevsky held "The Overcoat" in reverence, and with irrevocable antipathy referred to *Selected Passages from Correspondence with Friends* as a book whose author was "lying and playing the fool."[14] The most exalted and positive figure in the mature Gogol's oeuvre, that of the author himself in his selected correspondence, is grotesquified in the figure of Opiskin. And for precisely the same reason, Akaky Akakievich, the leastest nonentity among Gogol's characters, passing through several stages of literary development, is turned (in the spirit of Tynianov's "parodic twist") into the tragically elevated figure of Prince Myshkin.

It is fair to assume that we are dealing with something more than just the drama of the creative relationship between two authors. When it comes to writers like Gogol and Dostoevsky, and to such figures as Bashmachkin and Myshkin, one cannot help taking the whole of Russian literature into one's sights. In what other literature would the distance between its poles be so short, between its least significant and most magnificent heroes, who stand here as variations on the same type? It is as if we have before us, not a whole literature, but a single work, rich in design and modulation, in the genre of tragic parody: the "poor in spirit" is reincarnated as "Prince Christ."

---

14 Dostoevskii, *Polnoe sobranie sochinenii v 30-i tomakh*, 3:503.

2 | The Figure of Repetition: The Philosopher Nikolai Fedorov and His Literary Prototypes

The previous chapter showed how Gogol's parody of the medieval scribe is in turn "parodically" flipped by Dostoevsky, such that it ascends from Bashmachkin to Myshkin, Russian literature's most "ideal" character. We shall further examine the metamorphosis of this "miserable holy man" type, so important for Russian culture, as he outgrows his strictly literary framework and takes on the contours of a historical individual. Usually when we speak of the real-life analogues of this or that literary character, we have in mind the prototypes thereof. But it is sometimes the other way around: the literary image seems to precede its real-life incarnation. Before taking on a life of his own, the real individual is refracted through the "crystal" of the literary imagination—and only then does he separate from his artistic prototype and enter into history. Typically, the literary basis of such historical individuals is easily discerned: they become myth even before managing to die—which is akin to becoming a character without managing to actually be born.

There would seem to be little in common between Nikolai Fedorovich Fedorov (1829–1903), the great thinker and father of Russian cosmism, and Akaky Akakievich Bashmachkin (1790s?–1830s?), the littlest of Russian literature's "little men." Fedorov set the scale of the cosmic daring and theurgic experimentation of the twentieth century, and perhaps even of the third millennium. Conquering death, resurrecting "the ashes of the fathers," taking control of the forces of nature, settling humanity throughout the whole universe... Bashmachkin, meanwhile, can hardly see beyond his own letters, and rarely says anything intelligible—an insignificant clerk, a copier of other people's papers, "a being dear to no one, interesting to no one" (*CT*, 409)... On the one hand, the all-encompassing *Philosophy of the Common Cause* (*Filosofiia obshchego dela*), on the other: "So it's that, that's what it is" (*CT*, 394) (one of Akaky Akakievich's favorite phrases).

Even so, there are numerous features, seemingly minor and random, that symbolically connect this giant and this Lilliputian, and perhaps also stand as the historical succession of a single type, which we might tentatively call the "copyist" who in his ascension becomes a "resurrector." What the two have in common is the *figure of repetition*, so significant for Russian culture, which in the nineteenth century retains features of the medieval "aesthetics of identity" (to use Lotman's term[1]). To resurrect means to copy "in the flesh," to reproduce not symbolic tracings of thought but the bodily existence of people. We will examine the "repetitions" surrounding Nikolai Fedorov on several levels: his name, and the attitude toward his ancestors inscribed therein; the thinker's cultural and everyday etiquette vis-à-vis his literary prototypes; the "common cause" of resurrection as congruent with the occupations of copying and librarianship; reanimating the dead in Fedorov and Gogol, and its demonic subtext...

I would like to emphasize that examining a historical individual alongside fictional characters in no way belittles the former; this is, rather, an attempt to find the common denominator of "reality" and "literature." In this sense, taking a literary-critical approach to historical figures is no less (and no more) ethically justified than turning them into characters in a work of literature.

1.

One is struck with a sort of doubling in the very name Nikolai *Fedorovich Fedorov*. No suitable name was found in the Church calendar for Akaky Akakievich—he had to be given his father's name. No surname could be found for Nikolai Fedorovich, nor even a patronymic, as he was an illegitimate son of Prince Pavel Ivanovich Gagarin. It is not even certain which Fedor or Fedorov had his name repeated in the future philosopher's

---

1 Lotman, *Struktura khudozhestvennogo teksta*, 350–51.

The Figure of Repetition 103

patronymic and surname: the priest Nikolai Fedorov who christened him, or his godfather Fedor Karlovich Beliavsky.[2] In any case, the void of his own paternal name and surname was filled by a mechanistic repetition.

This repetition is inscribed not only in the names but in the professions and worldviews of Bashmachkin and Fedorov alike. Bashmachkin is a copyist; he reproduces word for word the papers put on his desk. Fedorov is a preacher who has dedicated himself to resurrecting ancestors in the very same flesh they were born and died in. But in his secular profession too, as librarian of the Rumiantsev Museum's reading room, Fedorov stood for the preservation and gathering of every letter ever traced by human hand, and ascribed special significance to bibliographic summary-cards. "Given the foreseen destruction, the annihilation, the perishing of books, cards cannot be a means to save them from such perishing, but they are more likely than books to survive a catastrophic epoch; should books perish, the cards will remain, and will allow us to bring their corresponding compositions back from oblivion, to return them to life" ("What Is the Meaning of the Card Attached to a Book?"[3]). In Fedorov's interpretation, then, this highly specialized bibliographic question is internally connected with the idea of universal resurrection: the card is the kernel or trace of a book, by which it can be restored.[4]

Bashmachkin and Fedorov did not merely serve in the presence of letters; they threw themselves body and soul into the ideal-fantastic world thereof, devoting themselves to the written word both out of duty and out

---

2 Semenova, *Nikolai Fedorov: Tvorchestvo zhizni*, 10–11.
3 Fedorov, *Sobranie sochinenii v 4 t.*, 3:228.
4 The library card-catalogue, the technique of repetition, copying and resurrection, projects of universal archiving and museumification, the figure of Bashmachkin, and the ideas of Fedorov are all connected with modern conceptualism, as may be seen in the work of Il'ia Kabakov and Lev Rubinshtein. Thus, Kabakov's meta-installation *The Palace of Projects* (London, 1998; New York, 2000) not only includes a section devoted to Fedorov's "Resurrection of All the Dead," but uses the same concept as a template for sixty-four more "world-saving," grotesquely messianic projects in other sections of the exposition, including: "The Idea Generator," "The Universal Motion Machine," "The Optimal Prison Layout," "Paradise Just Below the Ceiling," "A Universal System for Depicting Everything," "Memory Therapy," "A Common Language with Trees, Rocks, and Animals," "Administering the External World," etc. Rubinshtein's manner of writing his texts on library catalogue cards also pertains to the Fedorovian idea of a universal repository, a museum of words and voices.

of love. Even at his leisure, Akaky Akakievich can find no better pastime than to copy documents, and the shapes of his dear letters shine before his imagination as if imprinting themselves on his very face. Nikolai Fedorovich viewed the written word as the basis of civilization and was sharply critical of shorthand, stenography, and all the "wanton" forms characteristic of writing in the hurried century of progress (the nineteenth). In love with the beauty of letters regardless of their meaning, he defended the intrinsic worth of slow writing as akin to a sacrament:

> Dealing as it does with the shapes of letters, literally with letter-eating,[5] this science [paleography] is held in great contempt by some lovers of progress, even as the shapes of letters say far more than do words, and are more sincere than they; the shapes of letters are less corruptible than words. ... It is precisely letter-eating that enables paleography to define the character of epochs. ... Gothic and uncial letters, traced *with deep reverence, with love, with pleasure even, performed like artistic work, like a prayer.* ... These people, the copyists, who lived in expectation of future blessedness, already anticipated it in the present, finding pleasure in the labor itself.[6] (Emphasis mine)

Not just the idea, but the very intonation of this passage harks back to Gogol, representing a profound and learned elaboration on the Bashmachkin theme:

> It is not enough to say *he served zealously*—no, *he served with love.* ... *Delight showed in his face*; certain letters were his favorites. ... Outside this copying, nothing seemed to exist for him. (*CT*, 386–87)

And of course, the copyist would certainly have agreed with the thinker's statement that "the shapes of letters say far more than do words, and are more sincere than they": Gogol's character finds it unbearable to change verbs from the first person to the third because he is used to

---

5 *Bukvoedstvo*; metaphorically, "pedantry"—trans.
6 Fedorov, *Sochineniia*, 82.

dealing with letters and not words—with the beauty of pure forms, not the conventionality and dissimulation of meanings.

Bashmachkin the copyist and Fedorov the librarian have the same salary—400 rubles a year.[7] They could have been office mates, peers who got together in the evenings to drink tea at a fellow clerk's apartment. But if we look further at this imagined "workplace" of Russian letters, we might notice, at a neighboring desk, another unexpected figure—this literature's loftiest, most "positively beautiful" character: Prince Lev Myshkin. Let us recall that for his elegant handwriting, General Epanchin hires Myshkin at nearly the same salary as that of Bashmachkin and Fedorov. All three share a feature in common: the visionary holy man Myshkin is as passionate a lover of letters as the little man Bashmachkin and the great thinker Fedorov. With "great pleasure and animation" does Myshkin speak of the various handwriting styles, flourishes, and fonts. "Elegance can go no further, everything here is lovely, a bead, a pearl. ... *[A] script like this is incomparable, you can even fall in love with it.*"

As a "saint of the office," an "archivist-resurrector," a "librarian-messiah," Fedorov is of course consecrated and prepared for by Dostoevsky, and is possible only after Prince Myshkin, heir to the medieval scribes and old Russian sanctity. But Fedorov also has a direct kinship with Bashmachkin, the prototype of all meek Russian letter-eating holy men. Both took a solitary route, never acquiring a life's companion or leaving any progeny, keeping to their austere endeavor in their circle of colleagues or followers. Both were extremely unassuming—eating, dressing, and sleeping God knows how, unmindful of the hardships of their everyday lives. To cite further parallels from their hagiographic descriptions:

> [Akaky Akakievich] gave no thought to his clothes at all. ... The broadcloth was so worn out that it was threadbare, and the lining had fallen to pieces. (*CT*, 389)

---

7 "Receiving a minuscule salary (less than 400 rubles a year), he refused any raise" (Losskii, *Istoriia russkoi filosofii*, 104); "There exists in Petersburg a powerful enemy of all who earn a salary of four hundred roubles or thereabouts. This enemy is none other than our northern frost" (*CT*, 389).

> Fedorov never wore a fur coat.[8]

> [Fedorov] went around in winter and summer in the same old overcoat.... The impression of his considerable years was intensified by his very old and worn-out clothing.[9]

> Coming home, [Akaky Akakievich] would sit down straight away at the table, hastily slurp up his cabbage soup ... without ever noticing [its] taste, and he would eat it all with flies and whatever else God sent him at the time. (*CT*, 388)

> He occupied a tiny room... His food consisted of tea and stale rolls or salted fish. Fedorov would often go months on end without a hot meal.[10]

And in both the literary and biographical plot, life comes to an end in nearly the same manner—a winter-related illness caused by a change, unaccustomed for such ascetics, in clothing. For Bashmachkin, so used to his decrepit overcoat, buying a new one proves fatal. And for Fedorov, who was in the habit of going without a fur coat even in winter, the fateful day came when, amid freezing temperatures in December 1903, friends convinced him to wear a fur coat. Fedorov apparently overheated, catching pneumonia and dying, just as Bashmahkin dies of "a quinsy" (*CT*, 408) precipitated by the bitter cold of St. Petersburg.

2.

The hagiographic image of Nikolai Fedorov imprinted in the consciousness of his contemporaries is the highest evolution of a type originally outlined by Gogol in "The Overcoat." This is a Bashmachkin who has graduated the higher school of the moral and religious self-consciousness of the characters of Dostoevsky. The link connecting Bashmachkin and Fedorov is Prince Myshkin, in whom the image of the copyist is elevated

---

8 Losskii, *Istoriia russkoi filosofii*, 104.
9 Semenova, "N. F. Fedorov i ego filosofskoe nasledie: predislovie," 11, 12.
10 Losskii, *Istoriia russkoi filosofii*, 104.

from office drudge to "Prince Christ." If Bashmachkin is a sentimental and humorous parody of the medieval scribe, of the godly novitiate, then Myshkin stands as the restoration of the prototype: a parodic flip occurs once more, and out of a little man, a meek copyist, there again arises a saint.

Now, after Dostoevsky's uplifting literary transformation, it only remains for the type of the little man/savior to step from the page and take on a life of his own; but not, however, without first entering, as befits a "character," into correspondence with the author himself. As is well known, Nikolai Fedorov first began putting forth his ideas on universal resurrection, which he had been incubating in silence over the course of many years, in a letter to Dostoevsky. Begun in 1878, it continued to be written even after the death of its addressee (1881), eventually growing to 400 pages and becoming the principal composition with which Fedorov would enter the history of philosophical thought and sanctity: "The question of brotherhood, or kinship; of the reasons for the unbrotherly, unkindred, that is, unpeaceful state of the world, and of the means to restore kinship. A memorandum from the unlearned to the learned, to the religious and secular, to believers and unbelievers."

Turning from lifestyle to manner of thinking, we encounter once more a striking resemblance: Fedorov's "question of brotherhood," too, has been prompted by the question beating in Akaky Akakievich's breast, which he asks of all those who are stronger, happier, more learned, and richer than he:

> "Let me be, why do you offend me?"—and in these penetrating words rang other words: "I am your brother." And the poor young man [a coworker of Akaky Akakievich who witnessed this scene—M.E.] would bury his face in his hands [upon recalling it], and many a time in his life he shuddered to see how much inhumanity there is in man. (*CT*, 386).

These words of Akaky Akakievich continue to reverberate in the writings of Fedorov, culminating in the proclamation of the COMMON CAUSE:

"This is the question of what must be done so as to escape the unbrotherly condition. And as such, this question is obligatory for all the sons of men, and especially for those baptized in the name of the God of all the fathers."[11]

It turns out that nineteenth-century Russian literature is not the only thing that, as Dostoevsky famously put it, came from Gogol's "Overcoat"; to some extent Russian philosophy, too, with its visions of universal brotherhood and fatherhood, continues to voice the grievance and complaint of Akaky Akakievich.

Neither of our heroes knew their fathers. As a young child Fedorov was taken from his father, never again to encounter him. Bashmachkin was born after the death of his father—apparently, in part, miraculously, because at the time of his birth, his mother, notes Gogol, was already an old woman (like the biblical Sarah). But unlike Fedorov, Bashmachkin is his father's legitimate son, not only bearing his surname and patronymic, but even repeating his first name. "'Well, I see now,' the old woman said, 'it's evidently his fate. If so, better let him be named after his father. His father was Akaky, so let the son also be Akaky'" (*CT*, 385). Duplicating a name symbolizes that children continue the lives of their parents—and are thus not so concerned by their posthumous existence, as in the case of Fedorov, who bore someone else's patronymic and was denied the name of his own father, from whom he was early separated. The resurrection of one's ancestors, which for Nikolai Fedorovich became the highest and universal task, for Akaky Akakievich is already a given, because he is himself, as is said in the Bible, the "fruit after his kind" (Genesis 1:11). He is himself Akaky and himself Bashmachkin, that is, he bears the same surname as "his father, his grandfather ... and absolutely all the Bashmachkins" (*CT*, 384). Thus the question raised by Akaky Akakievich of a lost brotherhood becomes, for Nikolai Fedorovich, the question of a salvific fatherhood.

Both our heroes are perceived, to use the words of N. Lossky, as "holy men, uncanonized saints,"[12] and their lives fit easily into the genre

---

11 Fedorov, *Sochineniia*, 62.
12 Losskii, *Istoriia russkoi filosofii*, 103. Cf. Lev Tolstoy's son Il'ia L'vovich Tolstoy's impression of Fedorov: "If there are saints, they must be just like that" (*Moi vospominaniia*, 190).

of hagiography. Gogol's tale is indeed a stylized hagiography, its ironic revamping, while literature on Fedorov aligns directly with the hagiographic canon. But as it turns out in the epilogue, these saints vengefully shake their fists at humanity, literally and figuratively stripping the rich and highborn of their overcoats and furs—Bashmachkin in his posthumous existence as a ghost, and Fedorov in his posthumously published writings, in which the prophet of universal resurrection denounces the learned and the rich, as well as progress, serving, as it allegedly does, only abstract knowledge, pointless luxury, and sensual comfort. Just as Bashmachkin gets back at the rich and powerful of this world for their selfishness, so does Fedorov condemn "idleness as the mother of vice, and solipsism (or egoism) as the father of crime"—the whole "learned estate ... as the spawn of idleness ... and individualism."[13]

3.

A central motif of both Gogol's tale and the philosophical system of Nikolai Fedorov is that of death and its overcoming. In both cases, a posthumous existence, the "repetition of the unrepeatable," is motivated ethically, necessitated by justice and retribution. In the case of Bashmachkin, the law of vengeance from beyond the grave is in effect: a clerk deprived of his overcoat posthumously takes overcoats from his tormentors. A symmetry is also in effect in Fedorov: dead fathers, who had given life to their sons, must now receive it from those same sons' hands. A mirror-like symmetry may be seen, moreover, between the dénouement of a little man's life according to Gogol and the dénouement of world history according to Fedorov: the dead undress the living—the living dress the dead in flesh. This from-beyond-the-grave triumph of the "ethics of identity" (to rephrase Lotman's "aesthetics of identity"), the transference of repetition from this life to the next as a sign of supreme truth and justice—this lends a new dimension to the image of these holy men, as if they have acquired demonic doubles.

"[The important person] saw the dead man's mouth twist and, with the horrible breath of the tomb, utter the following words: 'Ah!

---

13   Fedorov, *Sochineniia*, 69.

Here you are at last! At last I've sort of got you by the collar!'" (*CT*, 412) The vengeful and denunciatory pathos of the phantom is remarkably eerie, given the righteous meekness of its former life, a most quiet one, full of labor and hardship, of calligraphic raptures and dreams of brotherhood. The animation of a lifeless body—be it a sculpture, corpse, doll, mechanism, or picture—is a traditional demonic motif in literature, one found frequently in Gogol, and typically involving the deceased having made a deal with evil spirits. Poor Akaky Akakievich, too, takes his place in these infernal ranks; his devil-tempter is the tailor Petrovich (that "one-eyed devil"), after meeting whom Akaky Akakievich, "instead of going home ... went in the entirely opposite direction, without suspecting it himself. On the way, a chimney sweep brushed against him with his whole dirty[14] flank, blackening his whole shoulder" (*CT*, 394).[15] Akaky Akakievich's hagiography, which begins with scenes of the main character's pious baptism and humble devotion, in the epilogue turns into an anti-hagiography, a Gothic travesty about a terrifying ghost with an enormous fist and crooked mouth.

The spiritually discerning reader also gets a strange, ambivalent impression from the doctrine of Nikolai Fedorov, who aspires to raise

---

14 Or "unclean" (*nechistyi*), the same word used to describe evil spirits—trans.

15 Among the infernal hints surrounding the figure of the tailor in "The Overcoat" we might highlight the following: Petrovich's kitchen, to which Akaky Akakievich ascends along a blackened staircase "anointed with swill" (*Sobranie sochinenii v 7 t.*, 3:120), is filled with "so much smoke that even the cockroaches themselves could no longer be seen" (*CT*, 390)—an image of ritual impurity; Petrovich's blasphemous habit of "drinking rather heavily on feast days"—"wherever a little cross appeared on the calendar" (*CT*, 390); his "crooked eye and the pockmarks all over his face" (*Sobranie sochinenii v 7 t.*, 3:119); the "disfigured nail" on his big toe, "thick and strong as tortoise shell" (*CT*, 391), as if a vestige of a devil's hoof; the way Petrovich goes "along each seam" of the newly sewn overcoat "with his teeth, imprinting it with various designs" (*CT*, 397), as if leaving his stamp; the manner in which he presents the new item to Akaky Akakievich, taking "the overcoat out of the handkerchief in which he had brought it" (*CT*, 397) as if performing a concluding trick; and the way the tailor, having seen Akaky Akakievich out, himself runs outside, taking a "detour down a crooked lane" (*CT*, 398) to admire his handiwork one last time; and finally, the threefold mention of the devil in the description of Petrovich: he "got himself tight on rotgut, the one-eyed devil"; he is "liable to demand devil knows what price"; "as if the devil gave him a nudge" (*CT*, 391, 394).

the dead from their graves by the power of science, by assembling the remains of the fathers scattered throughout the universe. "Solov'ev had reason to wonder, wouldn't this be *'animating corpses'*? There is a definite tinge of some sort of necromancy in Fedorov," remarks Father Georgii Florovsky, underscoring Fedorov's peculiar veneration of the dead, his fascination with death. "It remains unclear: *who* is dying, and *what* is being resurrected—the body or the person?. . . Fedorov hardly mentions the afterlife of the deceased. He speaks more of their graves, of their sepulchral remains."[16] Berdiaev expresses a similar concern that a blasphemous substitution has been made: "Fedorov's project requires that the life of humanity be concentrated in cemeteries, near the ashes of the fathers. . . . It is hard to say whether Fedorov believed in the immortality of the soul. When he speaks of death and resurrection, he always means the body, bodily death and resurrection in the body. The question of the fate of the soul or spirit is not even raised."[17]

In their respective "epilogues," both the little man rising up to take vengeance on a very important personage and the great thinker rising up to do battle with the forces of nature have about them the whiff of, not reconciliation, not the eternal life of the soul, but the phantom and the grave, the magic of reanimating corpses. The figure of repetition becomes the figure of sinister substitution. It is precisely the ultimate victory of "repetition," its final chord struck from beyond the grave, that interrupts the little man's ascension to sainthood. In the figure of Myshkin, the meekness of the little man attains the fullness of a spiritual ideal, but in the doctrine of Fedorov, it goes even further: beyond literature, into reality; beyond life, into the afterlife. But when a person takes on the business of God, there is no safeguard against forgery. Perhaps there is a Nikolai Fedorovich hiding in every Akaky Akakievich, just waiting for the right moment to show absolutely everyone the shining path to the tombs and stars?

---

16 Florovskii, *Puti russkogo bogosloviia*, 324, 326.
17 Berdiaev, "Religiia voskresheniia," 294, 296.

The Great in the Little: Bashmachkin's Offspring

The Fedorovian project of universal resurrection has been seen by some thinkers as truly world-saving: "Since Christianity first appeared, your 'project' is the human spirit's first movement forward on Christ's path" (Vladimir Solov'ev[18]). By others, as the subtlest of temptations of the sort the devil subjects Christ to in the wilderness: "This strange religio-technical project combines industry, engineering, magic, eroticism, and art in some sort of enchanting and eerie synthesis" (G. Florovsky[19]).

But whatever one thinks of Fedorov's "common cause," there is no doubt that the utterly little cause of Akaky Akakievich lies at the base of it. A threadbare overcoat. The bitter cold of Petersburg. And a question about brotherhood.

---

18 Letter to N. Fedorov, 12 January 1882. Fedorov, *Sobranie sochinenii v 4 t.*, 4:629.
19 Florovskii, *Puti russkogo bogosloviia*, 326.

3 | The Little Man in a Case: The Bashmachkin-Belikov Syndrome

Various lines of literary succession flow from Gogol's Bashmachkin. One path is that of the moral-religious ascent from little man to Prince Myshkin. Another is that of the humble copyist to Chekhov's "man in a case."

If the grand age of Russian realism opens with Nikolai Gogol's tale "The Overcoat" (1842), then Anton Chekhov's "The Man in a Case" ("Chelovek v futliare," 1898) is to some extent a summing-up of this age. One is struck by the similarity of the two main characters, though it would seem they should have nothing in common. Akaky Akakievich is disparaged and insulted by all, while to the contrary, the whole of local society trembles before Chekhov's Belikov. But at the base of each type lies a certain "littleness," expressed both physically and in the diminutive suffix of their surnames. Bashmachkin is "short, somewhat pockmarked, somewhat red-haired, even with a somewhat nearsighted look" (*CT*, 384). Belikov, "small" and "hunched up,"[1] wears dark glasses and constantly hides his face behind his upturned collar. Their appearance and their lifestyles are grayness itself—effacement, colorlessness, timidity, and alienation from the reality around them. Both seek to hide in another world, a sterile and abstract one, like a case, shielding themselves from modernity. It is as if they have not yet been born into the world, have not entered into real and adult life, and so the primary concern and theme of their existence is a secondary maternal womb—an overcoat or case that might protect them from the vagaries, climatic and otherwise, of the external world.

Both lead an abstemious, almost monastic way of life, shutting themselves away, as if in a cloister, in an ideal world of essences, eternal and pure as Platonic ideas. For Akaky Akakievich, this means letters, to which

---

1 Chekhov, *Selected Stories*, 303. Further citations in the text are to this translation.

he ministers in his capacity as copyist-scribe. "Outside this copying nothing seemed to exist for him. ... Not once in his life did he ever pay attention to what was going on or happening every day in the street" (*CT*, 387). Belikov, for his part, takes refuge in the ancient Greek language. "Reality irritated him, frightened him, kept him in constant anxiety, and, maybe in order to justify his timidity, his aversion to the present, he always praised the past and what had never been; the ancient languages he taught were for him essentially the same galoshes and umbrella, in which he hid from real life" (300). Detached from all everyday life, each character exchanges the world of people for a world of signs, taking an almost sensual delight in it. There are moments of almost word-for-word correspondence between the descriptions of Belikov and Bashmachkin, as if Chekhov were occasionally glancing at Gogol's text. "'Oh, how sonorous, how beautiful the Greek language is!' [Belikov] used to say, with a sweet expression; and, as if to prove his words, he would narrow his eyes and, raising a forefinger, pronounce: 'Anthropos!'" (300). This is a variation on a theme from "The Overcoat": "There, in that copying, he saw some varied and pleasant world of his own. Delight showed in his face; certain letters were his favorites, and when he came to one of them, he was beside himself: he chuckled and winked and helped out with his lips" (387). "Delight showed" on Bashmachkin's face, while Belikov speaks with a "sweet expression," the descriptions mirroring one another in the original (*naslazhdenie vyrazhalos'; so sladkim vyrazheniem*). Both are at a loss for words, conveying their delight in gestures: Bashmachkin "winked and helped out with his lips"; Belikov "would narrow his eyes and [raise] a forefinger."

Both works moreover feature, at their base, a similar motif, expressed in the very titles "The Overcoat" and "The Man in a Case." A case in the form of Bashmachkin's overcoat or Belikov's warm quilted coat both physically and symbolically shields these characters from the world they find so frightening. Both of them are extremely unsociable, even asocial, beings. Hence Bashmachkin's silence and tongue-tiedness, his tendency to utter "not one word of response" to the taunts of those around him and, when he absolutely must express himself, to use "such particles as have decidedly no meaning" (*CT*, 386, 391). Belikov, as befits a gymnasium teacher, speaks smoothly but prefers to be silent, which has an oppressive effect on those around him. Dropping in on his fellow teachers in their homes, "he would sit down, and say nothing. ... He would sit like that, silently, for an hour or two, and then leave. ... It was obviously painful for him to come to us and sit" (301).

For both Bashmachkin and Belikov, the hardest thing of all is to interact with other people. "No one could say [Bashmachkin] had ever been seen at any party" (*CT*, 389); "you could see that the crowded school [Belikov] was going to was frightening, contrary to his whole being, and that for him, a naturally solitary man, walking beside me was very painful" (302). In both cases this is a matter of severe *social phobia*—a dread of interaction, of engaging in relations of friendship, romance, family, or what have you. A great number of "little" people the world over suffer from this infirmity, their main wish being to seclude themselves in their case. (For instance, thirteen percent of the population of the United States belongs to this category.) This complex used to be called "misanthropy," which is why *anthropos*, so delightedly pronounced by the misanthrope Belikov, sounds, in his mouth, like Chekhovian sarcasm.

Social phobia includes a number of additional phobias: *enochlophobia*, the fear of crowds; *agoraphobia*, the fear of open or crowded spaces; *heterophobia*, the fear of persons of the opposite sex. It is "impossible even to imagine [Belikov] married" (303). So sexless and unsociable is his whole being that those who know him cannot even fathom "[w]hat generally was his attitude towards women, and how did he resolve this essential question for himself?" (303). Still less can be said of Bashmachkin: the only girlfriend amenable to accompanying him on his life's journey is that same overcoat. It is only in his advanced years (he is already past fifty) that Bashmachkin first sees—and this, only in a picture—a bare female leg, chuckling thereupon as if "he had encountered something totally unfamiliar, of which everyone nevertheless still preserves some sort of intuition" (*CT*, 400). His coworkers make fun of Bashmachkin, asking when to expect the wedding with his seventy-year-old landlady (*CT*, 386). Belikov, for his part, "didn't keep a serving woman for fear people might think ill of him" (302). Thus both characters may be safely diagnosed as "social phobics" and "heterophobes."

Significantly, Chekhov's tale opens with a story about the village elder's wife Mavra, said to have been hiding behind her stove for years, only going outside at night. The narrator Burkin explains this people-phobia as a psychological holdover, an atavism. "There are not a few naturally solitary people in this world, who try to hide in their shells like hermit crabs or snails. Maybe what we have here is the phenomenon of atavism, a return to the time when man's ancestors were not yet social animals and lived solitarily in their dens" (299).[2]

One would think those such as Mavra, so utterly fearful, and cowering in their corners, are only to be pitied. Even Belikov himself elicits sympathy: "'What bad, wicked people there are,' [said Belikov], and his lips trembled. I even felt sorry for him" (306). This "quiet complaint" of Belikov echoes the famous "humane" moment in "The Overcoat," when Bashmachkin exclaims: "'Let me be. Why do you offend me?'. . . . Something sounded in his voice . . . conducive to pity" (*CT*, 386). This something "piteous" is the Bashmachkinian element in Belikov: they find it difficult to get on in this world, and even when they manage to inspire fear themselves, they don't stop being afraid.

But the point is that this "atavism" has the tendency to be reborn not just as a pathological personality trait but as the sociopathy of a whole group, community, or society at large, which is suddenly seized by a fear of "the other," or even of each other. Here a distinction should be drawn between the two types of social phobia: the purely passive, and the active, even aggressive kind. The paradox is that social phobics, despite doing their best to avoid interacting with people, may nevertheless be quite socially active. They impart their fear of society to society itself, corroding it from within, inciting people to fear one another. The little, meek, piteous Belikov, who is constantly afraid that "something may come of it" (301; his famous exclamation *kak by chego ne vyshlo*), acquires a magical power over the city: "[T]his little man, who always went about in galoshes and with an umbrella, held the whole school in his hands for as long as fifteen years! School, nothing! The whole town!

---

[2] The modern science of human ethology does not consider social phobia an atavism but rather a pathology (psychopathy and sociopathy). From an evolutionary standpoint, people descend from humanoid simians, who themselves already had a fairly complex social organization involving numerous ties of kinship and friendship. Thus, evolutionary psychology does not consider social phobia to be a recurrence of some presocial way of life of primordial humanity or its ancestors.

... During the last ten or fifteen years, under the influence of people like Belikov, our town developed a fear of everything. A fear of talking loudly, of sending letters, of making acquaintances, reading books, helping the poor, teaching reading and writing" (301). Unlike Mavra, who hides from people behind her stove, Belikov not only cowers in his case, he drives others into it as well.

The stories of these two overcoated or encased men unfold in parallel. Both remain long faithful to their ascetic and "minimalist" lifestyle—Bashmachkin is past fifty, and Belikov is well over forty, but both are still immersed in their paper-and-ink protocols or ancient Greek. And it is only when each decides to acquire a "female life partner," one in the form of that very overcoat, the other in the person of Varen'ka, a giggly young woman who loves to sing, that they experience a sudden and precipitous cataclysm. Stepping out into social life, going to a party or the theater, throws these men off balance and brings them into contact with forces unknown to them. The scene in which Belikov, so close to the sweet bonds of matrimony, is chased from his fiancée's house in a fiasco that puts "an end to everything: both the engagement and the earthly existence of Belikov" (308) harkens back to Akaky Akakievich's nighttime robbery, which suddenly deprives him of his new bride, his overcoat.

We might note that those who come between these little men and the objects of their desire are characters of a larger physical scale, incarnations of a strong masculinity. "'Hey, that's my overcoat!' said one of [the robbers] in a thunderous voice, grabbing him by the collar. Akaky Akakievich was about to yell 'Help!' when another man put a fist the size of a clerk's head up this mouth" (*CT*, 402). Kovalenko, who takes his sister away from Belikov, bears an outward resemblance to the robbers who take the overcoat from Bashmachkin: he has "enormous hands, and by the looks of him you could see he had a bass voice, and indeed he boomed like a barrel: boo boo boo" (302). Again, the key details coincide: "thunderous voice," a "bass voice ... boomed like a barrel"; "a fist the size of a ... head," "enormous hands."

Another character in "The Overcoat" belongs to this same superior category—the "very important personage." The general stamps his foot and raises his voice at Bashmachkin to such a degree that the latter trembles, "quite unable to stand," and would have fallen "if the caretakers had not come running ... to support him. ... How he went down the stairs, how he got outside, nothing of that could Akaky Akakievich remember. He could not feel his legs or arms. ... [H]e reached home ... all swollen and took to his bed" (*CT*, 408). Belikov, for his part, does not even descend the stairs himself but is thrown down them by the enraged Kovalenko, all his glasses and galoshes rattling along the way. "He did not hear what Varenka said, nor did he see anything. Returning home, he first of all removed [her] portrait from the desk, and then he lay down and never got up again" (308).

The nearly identical ending of both stories and life-paths of their main characters—going down a staircase, coming home, getting into bed never to arise again—underscores once more the resemblance of the two plots:

— The empty, uneventful life of a little man, adorned by a single, "emblematic" infatuation "not of this world";
— The attempt to get on in life and be "like everyone else";
— As if in retribution for this betrayal of one's vocation, a sudden upheaval and death caused by "strong," "big" people.

Of course, it should be kept in mind that in the epilogue of "The Overcoat," another restless fate awaits Bashmachkin beyond the grave, that of a ghost on the hunt for other people's overcoats who terrorizes the city. Gogol already fancied something demonic in the figure of the most humble Bashmachkin, and the theme of diabolical temptation, personified in the "one-eyed devil" Petrovich the tailor, runs through the whole tale, which is topped off with an epilogue in which the whole "hagiography of a little man" is turned upside-down to show its infernal underside, to become an anti-hagiography. But what in Gogol's treatment is a phantasmagoric parable about a poor office clerk who unbeknownst to himself (and in part, to the reader as well) has entered into romantic relations with the devil, for Chekhov becomes the content of realist, almost newspaperish or feuilletonistic prose. Belikov does not rip the overcoats off of townspeople; to the contrary, he tries to pack them all up in a coffin-like case of his own making. Such is Chekhov's artistic discovery: it is customary to behave in a Christian way toward the little man, pitying him; or to treat him humanely, defending him from social oppression and inequality—but Chekhov has revealed this type to be socially dangerous: the little man seeks to level everyone according to his own littleness, which he turns into a sign of civic loyalty.

This type reaches its apogee in the following century, in postrevolutionary society. Andrei Platonov presents a vivid variation on the Bashmachkin-Belikov theme in the figure of Simon Serbinov in the novel *Chevengur* (1929). Serbinov is a "little man in a case" of the early Soviet period. Like Bashmachkin, he is a desk-man, his primary work tool being a fountain-pen. As the real fighter Kopenkin defines him: "You're a clerk, not a party member."[3] And like Belikov, Serbinov finds it very important to have a case, a shell to hide from life in; he is an unripe newborn, not fully gestated. Indeed, his mother has continued to be just such a protecting womb for him. He "was alive because his mother had at one time long enclosed him in her need for him, protecting him from other people who had no need whatsoever for Simon. ... His mother had served as Simon's defense, as a blind against all strangers. ... Now this hedge had fallen. ... his mother had disappeared, and without her, everything was exposed" (276). Serbinov is wracked by loneliness, replete with the "sadness of the boring person in the world"—"an unhappy man, at a standstill amid life" (270, 272).

Even so, he travels around the country rearranging the life of the masses, "so as to obtain for the party the exact truth from the toiling life" (265). "Like some weary revolutionaries, Serbinov did not love the worker or the villager—he preferred to have them en masse, not individually" (265). Here we can clearly hear the motif of Belikov's 'Anthropos!'—an admiration for mankind in general along with a fearful and suspicious attitude toward the living beings surrounding one. Serbinov is closer to letters than to people: he keeps a ledger of human credits and debits, entering therein the names of even random acquaintances, everyone he has happened to meet and part with. And lo and behold, toward the end of his life, he "could not write anything in his ledger; he only read it and saw how his entire past had been for a loss: not a single person had stayed

---

[3] Platonov, *Sobranie sochinenii v 5-i tomakh*, 2:282. Further citations in this section are to this edition.

with him his whole life, no one's friendship had become an affinity he could count on" (283). Without himself knowing how to be happy, he is authorized by the party to build "happiness for all," even as he cannot stand happy people. "The happy were alien to him; he did not like them and was afraid of them" (266).

At the same time, Serbinov has a "vampiric" attraction to the full-blooded and the rosy-cheeked. Chekhov's Belikov suddenly falls in love with his complete opposite, Varen'ka, who is possessed of an excess of happiness: "a new Aphrodite," she "laughs, sings, dances" (303). Just so is Serbinov drawn to Sof'ia, a "happy woman endowed with some sort of refreshing life": he is stirred by her "surplus endowment with life" (265, 271). Varen'ka is "saucy and loud" (302), just as Sof'ia's "life resounds all around like noise" (271). And finally, for both these case-dwelling wallflowers, meeting a "noisy" woman serves as the prologue for their destruction, as if any deep contact with an excess of life destroys their self-preservation mechanism.

It is surprising how persistent this archetype is from Gogol through Chekhov to Platonov, across the intervals of completely different epochs, ascending from an office copyist through the teacher of a dead language to a revolutionary clerk.

Significantly, one of the first to note the resemblance of Bashmachkin and Belikov was Vladimir Lenin, who juxtaposes them in a 1901 article in his characteristic denunciatory manner: "Our reactionaries—including, of course, all the top bureaucracy—show good political instincts. ... They are suspicious of anyone who does not resemble Gogol's Akaky Akakievich, or, to use a more recent comparison, a man in a case."[4] The first communist leader's surprising literary insight regarding the type of the "man in a case" seems all the less coincidental upon the triumph of that same "case" mentality in the activity of Lenin's own successor, the builder of socialism in one country.

A little man, Stalin, towers over the twentieth century, tailored as if to Akaky Akakievich's measure: "short, somewhat pockmarked ... with a complexion that is known as hemorrhoidal" (CT, 384), a "shorty" 155 centimeters in height, with a sallow, pitted face. Immured in his

---

4 Cited from Chekhov, *Polnoe sobranie sochinenii i pisem v 30-i tomakh*, 18:377–78.

permanent Overcoat. And with the infantile nickname Soso,[5] as if in imitation of a childish lip-smacking and the repetition of the "indecent" syllable in Akaky's name.[6] The people-fearing leader of a leader-loving people. Like the shivering copyist of the previous century, from a young age "he accustomed himself to going entirely without food in the evenings; but instead he was nourished spiritually, bearing in his thoughts the eternal idea of the future overcoat" (*CT*, 396)—and while he was at it, the eternal idea of future ranks and barracks.

This little man forged of steel bears a remote resemblance to Serbinov, whose surname has the clang of steel (*serp*, a "sickle"). The rare (in Russian) name "Simon" takes its place alongside another biblical name, "Joseph." Strange as it may seem, "Simon Serbinov" can be interpreted, in the context of this epoch fixated on a single man, as a muffled, distorted, most likely unconscious echo of the thunderous name "Joseph Stalin." This is a little Stalin, a lonely and encased one, shrunken back to the size of a Bashmachkin/Belikov. (Albeit also endowed with reflectivity, an ennui of the soul, and other characteristics of the "superfluous man.") Stalin was a social phobic of world-historic proportions; it is well known that he was maniacally suspicious, mistrustful, and organically incapable of friendly, intimate, or personal relations with other people. The analogue of Belikov's "case" is the Kremlin office and the Kremlin dacha, traveling between which occupied the whole governmental life of "the mountain-man of the Kremlin" (to use Mandel'shtam's jibe[7]). Only rarely and reluctantly did he stray from his beloved route, which, given all the advances in modern transportation, was not much longer than Bashmachkin and Belikov's commutes to their office and high school—paths from which they too did their best never to deviate. The social phobia of this super-Belikov, however, did not keep him from becoming head of the most socialist state in the world, at the base of which lay a "negative cohesion"—everyone's fear of everyone.

Significantly, Stalin liked to use "the man in a case" as a bogeyman, directing it against his political opponents. "The former leaders of the

---

5 Derived from Stalin's name Iosif, the diminutive "Soso" echoes the Russian *sosat'*, "to suck."
6 The Russian *kakat'* means "to poop, make caca."
7 Mandel'shtam, *The Moscow Notebooks*, 74.

right opposition ... have the same illness as Chekhov's famous character Belikov, the Greek teacher, the man in a case. Do you remember Chekhov's story 'The Man in a Case?'"[8] And Stalin goes on to devote a whole page of his speech at a party congress to retelling Chekhov's story and denouncing the right opposition's encasedness, predictably eliciting "general laughter and applause" from those in attendance.

If we ponder the meaning of the most radical versions of communism and take a good look at the character of its leaders, including its founding father Karl Marx himself, we are struck by features of a most active social phobia:

— a pronounced misanthropy, hostility toward existing society and bickering with all one's contemporaries, including even "comrades" and fellow-fighters, who at the drop of a hat are accused of every sin of deviationism, revisionism, and opportunism;
— suspiciousness toward anyone of a different lifestyle or way of thinking; a fear of being, of its immediacy, spontaneity, unpredictability, and disorderliness (the fear that "something may come of it");
— closed-mindedness, rigidity, monomania, concentration on "The Letter," "The Idea," "The Uniform," "The Overcoat," "The Case," or other idée fixe.
— The encasedness these communist leaders denounce in little men, in "philistines," "bumpkins," "bureaucrats," "clerks," and "petty bourgeoisie," grows, in the denouncers themselves, to Napoleonic proportions, turning into a siege mentality.

Such are the super-serious jokes thrown our way by the history of Russian literature and the freakish fantasy of history. The joke would not be understood in all its depth if the littlest man of the nineteenth century and the most exalted Superman of the twentieth were not mediated by a character "encapsulated" by Chekhov—the little man in a case.

---

8 Stalin, *Voprosy leninizma*, 575–76.

PART III

The Irony of Harmony

1 | Childhood and the Myth of Harmony

1.

As some thinker has put it, humanity gets younger as it matures. And it will reach its spiritual height when it attains childhood's happy lightness, its freedom from everyday needs, its trustfulness and openness to the world. But if so, childhood must be seen not as a preliminary stage of development but as an ever-appealing exemplar, a source of renewal.

In his autobiography *Poetry and Truth*, Goethe recalls that in his childhood (he was born in 1749) there were no books specifically written about children or for children—whereas, by the time of this autobiography's writing (1811–33), numerous such books had appeared. Why did children's literature arise in precisely this historical interval (the latter half of the eighteenth to the early nineteenth centuries), and what caused it to break away from "normal," adult literature?

Goethe himself provides an answer: "No libraries for children had at the time been established. The old had themselves still childish notions, and found it convenient to impart their own education to their successors."[1] In order to contemplate childhood, one must feel the burden of a different age. Classicism is still infinitely alien to the poetry of childhood—it is interested in the universal, the exemplary in people, while childhood stands as an age-specific deviation from the norm (im-maturity), just as madness is a psychic digression from the norm (un-reason). Eighteenth-century enlighteners began to show an interest in childhood, but with pedagogy rather than poetry in view: in their democratic aspirations, they undertook not only to write for the third estate, taking literature beyond the circle of an aristocratic elect, but also for children (the lowest in the hierarchy of age), seeing them as fertile ground for the

---

1 Goethe, *Poetry and Truth: From My Own Life*, 1:22.

cultivation of the worthy fruits of reasonableness and morality. It was precisely enlighteners who first began to publish literature for children (in Russia, N. I. Novikov), in which utterly "grownup" scholarly and moral content was presented in an accessibly didactic and illustrative format.

The very concept of childhood as a stage of spiritual development having its own intrinsic value could only arise amid sentimental-romantic contemplation. Having rapidly matured from the turn of the eighteenth century to the nineteenth, experiencing the French Revolution and German romanticism, humanity lost the naiveté of complacent reason and became attuned to the poetry of the irretrievable childhood. There arose a nostalgic, elegiac distance vis-à-vis the happy childhood of all humanity, of every nation and every individual. Only romanticism perceived childhood not as an ancillary, preparatory phase in a lifespan but as a precious world unto itself. All relations between ages are as if turned upside-down in the romantic outlook: if formerly, childhood was perceived as an insufficient degree of development, now, to the contrary, adulthood is a period of decline, bereft of immediacy and purity. The romantics effected a similar overthrow in the field of history, setting great store by folklore—the prattle of the infancy of peoples, something to which none before them had ever lent a serious ear. So it was that the first works to be well-loved by children and free of Enlightenment-style didacticism were collections of fairy tales (of Arnim and Brentano, the brothers Grimm, Hauff, Andersen, and others), in their plots and style harking back to folk art. The childhood of humanity and the childhood of the individual received their citizenship in literature at the same time.

The fundamental upheaval effected by the romantics not only defined new literary forms for children, it also introduced the theme of childhood into literature for adults.

In Russia, the image of childhood is endowed with the deepest significance in the works of that most romanticist of writers, Lermontov. For Pushkin, due to his classical worldview, childhood, like old age, is just a moment in the cycle of time: the shift from one to the next is sad but at the same time comforting. "Should I happen to caress a sweet infant, / I already think: fare thee well! / I yield my place to you: / It's time for me to molder,

Childhood and the Myth of Harmony 127

for you to blossom."[2] For Lermontov, this even-minded acceptance of the future and past, this kindly hailing of the young sprouting up through the decomposing remains of the fathers, is impossible. Lermontovian time is not cyclical but unswervingly linear, eliciting a pining for that which is irredeemably lost. The motif of the soul's early aging and withering is linked to the elegiac recollection of childhood, which is conceived as a shakily flourishing "little island" amid the wastes of life's sea.

> And if I ever should manage for a moment
> To forget myself,—In my memory, to a time not so long past
> Do I fly, a free, free bird;
> And I see myself as a child; and around me
> All my native places: the high manor-house
> And the orchard with the dilapidated greenhouse.
> ("How often, amidst a motley crowd…")

> И если как-нибудь на миг удастся мне
> Забыться, — памятью к недавней старине
> Лечу я вольной, вольной птицей;
> И вижу я себя ребенком; и кругом
> Родные все места: высокий барский дом
> И сад с разрушенной теплицей.
> ("Как часто, пестрою толпою окружен…"[3])

For Pushkin, the mental disposition of every age matches its physical state. "Blessed is he who was young in his youth, / Blessed is he who matured on time"[4]—for all the author's ironic attitude toward this order of things, it does remain an order.[5] In Lermontov, the soul grows old ahead of one's physical age: "Rich we are, virtually from the cradle, in the mistakes of our fathers and their late-come intelligence" ("Thought" ["Duma"], 1838)—and this

---

2 Pushkin, *Sobranie sochinenii v 10 tomakh*, 2:264.
3 Lermontov, *Stikhotvoreniia*, 393.
4 Pushkin, *Sobranie sochinenii v 10 tomakh*, 4:159.
5 For a more detailed interpretation of this line of Pushkin's, see the chapter "The Defamiliarization of Lev Tolstoy" of part 3.

tragic mismatch demands an equally sharp impulse backward, into the lost harmony of childhood. In Lermontov's oeuvre, a person matures suddenly, extraordinarily, a process so acutely experienceable only in one's youth—in England, by Byron; in Italy, by Leopardi. Such poets' lyric personae evince a sort of split personality: the moment they feel themselves to be older, they want to be younger—the aging of the soul has determined their craving for infancy. This is characteristic of reflection generally: the further it estranges its object, the more impetuously and futilely does it strive for it.

The theme of childhood entered Russian literature as a sign of the intense self-consciousness of an individual and a nation far removed from their elemental, unconscious origins—and turning back thereto. It may not be accidental that the Russian writers most clearly expressing an interest in childhood are those most committed to the idea of olden times, the soil, the patriarchal way of life: Aksakov, Dostoevsky, Tolstoy, Bunin… The poetry of the past has an invaluable meaning for the development of the individual and nation, by no means less than fantasies of the future. A love for the past confers self-containment, self-worth upon a life lived, which thus stands not as an avenue of approach to the present, but as a goal in itself; guarding the past, the personality thereby protects the continuity of its own development, the wholeness of its spiritual existence.

A new theme does not enter literature accidentally or in isolation—it alters the whole organic fabric thereof, requiring generic and stylistic restructurings. To a certain extent childhood, being the furthest reaches of the individual past, constitutes the zone of epic consciousness in literature that has largely been diluted by the encroachment of the novel, with its active orientation on the new, the present. The individual, having attained the highest acuity of self-consciousness, searches in their past for something to counter the lonely, tattered present. Childhood thus becomes the theme of a new "individual epic" (to use an oxymoron) about the being of a personality in harmony with itself and the world.

2.

It has long been recognized that Lev Tolstoy's first novella *Childhood* (*Detstvo*) already features many of the artistic breakthroughs that would subsequently bring him fame as a great epicist and psychologist. But to what extent were these breakthroughs foreordained by the very content of the tale—the worldview of a child? Is this not the famous "dialectics of the soul" revealed by Tolstoy in his characters, that primal, shakiest and most fluid layer of inner existence most transparently expressed in children? Writers prior to Tolstoy—Gogol, Turgenev, Goncharov—generally focused on adulthood, with its fully formed, consistent individuality. Tolstoy was the first in Russian literature to break down these rigid contours of "character" and discover, behind them, the flowing, unfixed matter of the soul—laying bare the eternally childlike, the immature element retained by everyone in their depths. Here is the first chapter of *Childhood*: the tutor Karl Ivanych swats a fly right over the head of little Nikolen'ka, who, offended by this disregard for himself, thinks how nasty Karl Ivanych is: "And his dressing gown and cap and tassel—they're all nasty!"[6] But within a minute, so much kindness and concern is heard in the tutor's voice, that "now, on the contrary, [these things] all seemed extraordinarily nice to me and even the tassel seemed clear proof of his kindness" (4). The inner fluidity of feeling, easily transitioning from negation to affirmation, from the whole to the particular, is a most typical feature of childhood. And when subsequently, Natasha Rostova will define Pierre as "blue" and "rectangular," and Anna Karenina will begin to feel revulsion toward her husband, suddenly noticing his protruding ears, then, shining through these highly "Tolstoyan" details will be that oneness, that "adhesiveness" of worldview ("synesthesia," "associativity") that is originally and naturally characteristic of a child. Tolstoy's favorite characters, those closest to his heart, invariably have something childlike about them; his least favorite are those that have lost their liveliness and sensitivity, have hardened in their stereotypically adult thinking (Berg, Drubetskoi, et al.).

---

6 Tolstoy, *Childhood, Boyhood, and Youth*, 4. Further citations in the text are to this translation.

The epicness of Tolstoy's oeuvre is also largely owed to its penetration into the depths of children's consciousness, wherein everything is permeated with everything. *Childhood* has no definitive plot, no line of "personal" fate. Childhood is not subject to a "line," it lives multidirectionally, multidimensionally, eagerly coming into contact with everything around it. After the nursery presided over by Karl Ivanych, we find ourselves, following Nikolen'ka, in the parlor with *maman*, then father's study, then in classes, engaged in hunting, games, dances, etc. Here the teleological sequence of actions characteristic of a novel is lacking—the action is, rather, broadly scattered, radiating out from the center occupied by the all-inquisitive Nikolen'ka; the result is the same sort of epic picture as in *War and Peace*, only on an incomparably smaller scale. Childhood by its nature is centrifugal, diffuse, all-responsive—as is the epic, which looks at the world through the eyes of peoples who are children, peoples in their infancy.

It is no accident that Tolstoy was the first in Russian literature to express the specific psychological features of a child and, at the same time, of a people as a whole. Tolstoy overcomes the stereotype of the "adult individual" by proceeding in two directions at once: from the adult to the childlike, and from the individual to the all-national. Tolstoy insistently returns his characters to the elemental, natural basis of their existence, which is why for him, the child and the people (each constituting the very beginning of things) prove to be the authentic and primary realities upon which the myths of adult consciousness are layered: the myth of reason, on whose laws reality is supposedly based; and the myth of the individual whose will supposedly governs history. The whole pathos of Tolstoy's oeuvre, his aspiration to unmask and purify, is directed precisely against the lie of isolated existence, of abiding in prestige and eliteness. In general, in his critique of rational self-interest from the standpoint of the childlike and ingenuous, Tolstoy has inherited a Rousseau-tinged romanticism (hence the technique of "defamiliarization" or "making it strange," *ostranenie*—the introduction of a layperson who perceives everything the way a child does). But in the dialectics of the conscious and the unconscious, the adult and the childlike in the human soul, Tolstoy surpasses the romantics, and takes a supreme step toward a new art, an art of the twentieth century.

Tolstoyan traditions are quite palpable in modern world literature that depicts infantile consciousness, for instance, Proust and Faulkner, although in those authors, the moment of the unconscious stands in all its purity, often bereft of critical reference to the world of the prosaic and conscious. Proust is constantly superimposing images of childhood and dreams, such that the world seems doubly blurred, submerged in a vacillating tissue of metaphorical associations and things that are half memory, half reverie—a consciousness not yet fully born, "hesitating at the threshold of times and shapes."[7] A profound kinship exists between the soul-state of the sleeping and the child: one's self is not separated from the world. Fittingly, an infant spends most of its time asleep, which is why remembering one's earliest years and recalling a dream after waking are equally difficult. In Tolstoy, the unconscious constitutes the latent but most sensitive tissue of mental life; in Proust, it is pulled from its latency and unfurled over the course of a huge narrative as the sole authentic reality. Objects are presented in a fuzzy state, like ephemeral "exhalations" of the soul. This is a crucial step in the artistic evolution of the twentieth century. To continue and develop Lermontov's metaphor, whereby childhood is a blissful island amid the oceanic wastes: for Tolstoy, childhood is rather the ocean itself, from which particular little islands of adult consciousness crop up; while for Proust, hardly any little islands remain—they are gone, swallowed up in the abyss.

3.

In the twentieth century, childhood transitions more and more from a particular literary theme to a method of perceiving the world. The romantics sought refuge in the remoteness, the "not-here-ness" of childhood; a century later, writers begin to treat childhood as the most immediate and natural inspiration for their art. A total infantilization of poetic language takes place. Thus does Iurii Tynianov say of Pasternak in his article

---

7 Proust, *In Search of Lost Time*. Vol. 1: *Swann's Way*, 5.

"The Interval": "The peculiarity of Pasternak's language is that his difficult language is more precise than precise—it is an intimate conversation, a conversation in a nursery. (Pasternak needs the nursery in poetry for the same reason that Lev Tolstoy needed it in prose.)"[8] In their writings, Andrei Bely, Velimir Khlebnikov, Boris Pasternak, Andrei Platonov, Iurii Olesha, and others carry on the revolution, launched in Russian literature by Lev Tolstoy, of depicting the world through the eyes of a child.

This is indeed a phenomenon not just of literature but of art in general. All twentieth-century painting—Picasso, Chagall, Kandinsky, Matisse, Modigliani—owes much to the "naiveté" of childhood, its particular "turn of vision" (to use Tynianov's term). Gone is the direct perspective that had presupposed some delimited, sharply individualized (adult) point of perception; now comes the reign of a mixture of various planes and projections of existence, a medley characteristic of children's drawings. In them you can instantly see what happened yesterday and what will happen tomorrow. From a crevice in a house crawls a mouse bigger than the house itself. We see the like in Picasso—a runner's legs hover in the air off to the side; and in Chagall—a small country lane lies behind the muzzle of a sad horse. If a swing is reflected in a pier-glass, then that means that "the pier-glass runs to meet the swing" (Pasternak): a child inherently perceives things with the referential relativity of Einsteinian physics.

In Pasternak's *Liuvers's Childhood* (*Detstvo Liuvers*), things appear on some sort of trembling, blurry bezel of their own, lacking even the clarity of Proust's associative bonds—here it is not a matter of something being connected to something else but of everything being connected to everything, without limit, "the more random, the truer." Childhood's blurriness is intensified here by that of illness, just as in the case of Proust it is by that of dreaming. Liuvers is ill, lamps swell and burst over her head, space is engauzed by the ceiling. Illness has a particular relationship to childhood—in it Pasternak discovers a new symptom of that openness, fluidity, and elementality that Tolstoy sought in the folk soul, and Proust in the soul of a person dreaming. Illness breaks down

---

8 Tynianov, *Poetika. Istoriia literatury. Kino*, 184.

the existing shape of body and soul, loosens it, restores its incompleteness; it allows one to plunge into the embryonic essence of life—and like many children, Liuvers does not resist but rather surrenders to illness, experiencing the sweetness of stressless existence in total oneness with the world and exposure to it (which in fact, in the language of adults, is called illness). A child is constantly being pushed toward something: schooling, attention, obedience, patience; but illness restores all his rights as a child, the warm care and nearness of parents, and helps shed the bonds of enforced adulthood—allows a child, that is, to be himself. Romanticism ennobled such deviations from the "classical" norm as infancy and dreams, a category also including the poetry of illness.

The infantilization of all existence takes an even more extreme form, reaching its outer limit, in Faulkner, in the part of *The Sound and the Fury* told from the viewpoint of Benjy, a thirty-three-year-old man with the cognitive ability of a three-year-old child. Benjy is so tightly enclosed in the depths of his own being that he has no real engagement with people. This image ironically demonstrates the romanticist ideal in action: there it is—the ancient exhortation to "become as little children." An unmatured childhood, or more precisely, a childhood that has outgrown itself, is just as flawed as an adulthood that has lost its childhood, this latter condition being incarnate in the figure of Benjy's older brother Jason, a person of narrow-minded "good" sense. The whole tragic tension of the novel lies in the disconnect between poles that ought to merge in a living soul: the poles of childlike immediacy and adult reflectivity. In Faulkner's image of childhood degraded in madness, the romantic tradition is taken to its logical extreme, and negates itself.

4.

The romantic conception of childhood begins to be reconsidered already in the nineteenth century, most profoundly by Dostoevsky. One would think Dostoevsky takes the romantic image of innocent, sinless childhood to the extreme of its pathos when he has Ivan Karamazov renounce "all higher harmony"[9] if it is purchased at the cost of a single little tear

---

9 Dostoevsky, *The Brothers Karamazov*, 245. Further citations in the text are to this translation.

of a child. At the time, the theme of children's suffering was not new in literature: Hugo in *Les Miserables*, Dickens in *Oliver Twist*, and James Greenwood in *The Little Ragamuffin* depicted the culmination of iniquity social and otherwise precisely in the misfortunes of an innocent child. The image of the "little man," whose undeserved suffering elicits a warm feeling of protest—an image highly popular in the literature of critical realism—acquired a particular cogency when the person in question was literally little, a child.

But in Dostoevsky, children are not just mistreated by fate, not merely victims of universal injustice—they are victims of the inventive, sensual cruelty that childhood in particular attracts: "[T]his peculiar quality," asserts Ivan Karamazov, "exists in much of mankind—this love of torturing children, but only children. ... It is precisely the defenselessness of these creatures that tempts the torturers, the angelic trustfulness of the child, who has nowhere to turn and no one to turn to—that is what enflames the vile blood of the torturer" (238, 241). In Dostoevsky, childhood has an aura not of tenderness but of lustful passions: parents torment their five-year-old daughter and lock her in the outhouse all night; a general sics his hunting dogs on a serf boy; Svidrigailov and Stavrogin seduce underage girls...

But the main thing is that the child does not remain a holy martyr; rather, his own inexorable tendency toward evil awakens. Let us recall Svidrigailov's final dream, in which a small girl having run away from her neglectful mother appears before him, and in reply to his fatherly solicitousness toward her, attempts to seduce him. There is something oppressively horrifying in the way the figure of the tiny girl exudes a ruinous, ingrained perversion. Things undergo a radical rebirth, all relations are overturned: the evil that Svidrigailov had sown in children's souls is now hard on his own heels, and it is after this same dream that Svidrigailov kills himself. Or, to take a non-dream example, consider the embittered boy Iliusha Snegirev, who throws rocks at Alesha Karamazov, though the latter has never wronged him. Again, everything is flipped: this is not a case of an adult tormenting an innocent child but of a boy, enraged by Alesha's humbleness, hitting him in the back with a rock, then in the face, and finally going "wild, like a little beast" (179), sinking his teeth into his finger. This is a specifically childlike cruelty, desperate and senseless. Liza Khokhlakova, herself practically still a child, describes for Alesha an imagined scene in which she takes pleasure in cutting off a little boy's fingers and crucifying him, then drinking compote as she watches him die. This is a bivalent image: here the child is hypostasized as both martyr and torturer, as crucified and crucifier.

Charles de Coster's *Legend of Thyl Ulenspiegel and Lamme Goedzak* includes a narrative of the childhood of Philip II, the inquisitor-king—from an early age, he loved to torture animals. But his nature does not change with age, it just manifests itself more broadly, with the cruelty toward insects subsequently extended to people. In Dostoevsky, children are pure with some sort of particular, matchless purity, but also cruel in their unreasoning cruelty: "separately they're God's angels, but together, especially in school, they're quite often merciless" (205), says Captain Snegirev of the schoolboys bullying his son. For Dostoevsky, the child is both the traditional Christian symbol of saintliness, and a demonic being, ready to trample any Christian sanctuary; the poles of human morality—the divine and the satanic—are expressed more absolutely in the child than in the adult.

Dostoevsky's supreme ideal is the adult who has preserved childlike innocence and immediacy but combines these with the experience of moral consciousness. It is only the kindly authority and seniority of Alesha that regenerate Iliusha and the other boys, turning them from desperate, destructive hostility to mutual tenderness, fraternity, and the feeling of a common fate. In just the same way, in *The Idiot*, the mean-spirited children who had been teasing Marie make peace and become her best friends on the sincere initiative of Prince Myshkin, who is himself "a perfect child" (52), but with an adult's ability to distinguish good and evil.

A child is pre-moral; as Dostoevsky puts it, he has not yet eaten of the apple. Unable to tell good from evil, he is therefore absolutely good and absolutely evil at the same time—is amoral. In the twentieth century, some Western writers sharpened this interpretation to foreground childhood as immoral, or anti-moral: bivalency gives way to unambiguity once more, but now of the opposite kind.

William Golding shows in *Lord of the Flies* how easy it is for a child to lose the moral rules inculcated in him and turn into an unbridled, savage being who worships a pig's head, and in the image thereof, Beelzebub himself, the "lord of the flies." Notably, the children's Crusoe-esque sojourn turns out just the opposite of Crusoe's own desert-isle adventure. Finding himself outside society, Defoe's character reconstructs the practical and moral precepts thereof on his own, creating a fully mature human civilization, into which he initiates the local "savage" Friday. In Golding, by contrast, children degrade to savagery. Childhood is the state closest to nature, and returning it to nature turns out to be an experiment in the destruction of all that is human.

5.

Quite popular in twentieth-century Western art is the motif of childhood's dehumanization. Here it transpires that the child is not, as the romantics thought, a full, primordial, higher sort of person but rather a nonperson, alien and even inimical to humanity, like some hostile extraterrestrial civilization. Symptomatic in this regard are Ray Bradbury's stories "The Veldt" and "Zero Hour" (manuscript title: "The Children's Hour"), in which children kill their parents with systematic cruelty. Interest in children nicely matches the aesthetics of suspense and horror. With a particular poignancy did the twentieth century grasp the lonely existence of a human being in outer space, among forms of matter alien and inscrutable. Lem gave us Solaris, a thinking ocean whose intentions toward humanity are obscure and frightening. In *The Birds*, Hitchcock shows, with a methodical, frightening consistency, people assailed by birds possessed of their own reasoning, contrary to that of humanity.

Among these countless alterior life-forms, these beings from an alien space and time, children are perhaps the scariest of all, for they are begotten of us, seemingly entirely dependent on us, but in their interiority are completely inscrutable to us. What children think about, we will never really know, because they do not express themselves in our language; they are aliens from an unknown world. In Bradbury's "Zero Hour," children play a strange game called "invasion," barring any above nine years of age from joining in—the older adolescents are committing the treason of "growing up"; they have already taken on the *human* way of thinking. The parents do not understand what the children are so engrossed in, but gradually their preparations become truly terrifying. Kierkegaard says that innocence is always bound up with dread. Here it is the adults who prove innocent before children, while the latter are in possession of some sort of knowledge and are plotting something wicked. As a result, the alien civilization invades the life of humanity and takes power through the children, through their imagination. "[The aliens] couldn't figure out a way to surprise Earth or get help.... Until one day ... they thought of children!... Grown-ups are so busy they never look under rose bushes or on lawns!"[10] The alien civilization serves Bradbury as something like a metaphor for childhood, which is just as cunning and merciless, its motives just as mysterious and unpredictable.

Widely popular in the 1970s was a series of works (mainly films, but books as well) about the devil taking up residence in the body and soul of a child or in the womb of a pregnant woman. Roman Polanski's *Rosemary's Baby* and William Peter Blatty's novel *The Exorcist*, which was made into a blockbuster, inaugurated a whole slew of movies that developed the theme of childhood satanism. If the romantics' hearts melted at the thought of the childhood years of Christ, and always recalled his eternal "become as little children," then a century and a half later, childhood is more and more often connected with the myth of the coming of the Antichrist (as in Richard Donner's film *The Omen*). Judging by certain trends in Western culture, the theme of childhood seems to have completed at least one cycle of its evolution, from romanticist tenderness and exaltation to mystical fear and trembling, from consecration to damnation, from the idyll to the horror movie.

6.

The figures created by Tolstoy and Dostoevsky trace the main contours by which the theme of childhood emerges in world literature. But Russian literature, like any other, developed its own nationally tinged image of

---

10 Ray Bradbury, "Zero Hour," https://archive.org/stream/Planet_Stories_v03n08_1947-Fall/Planet_Stories_v03n08_1947-Fall_djvu.txt

childhood; what is specific to it may be considered its profound interest in the world of nature and things as it is gradually inhabited by the soul of an infant. Initiating this tradition was Sergei Aksakov, and it was continued by Bunin, Aleksei Tolstoy, Prishvin, Kataev, Paustovsky, etc.

Just comparing the chapter headings in Lev Tolstoy's *Childhood* with those of Aksakov's *The Childhood Years of Bagrov the Grandson* (*Detskie gody Bagrova-vnuka*) is enough to get a sense of the difference between a socio-psychological image of childhood and, provisionally speaking, a natural-coloristic one. The former abounds with portraits, the latter with landscapes. Tolstoy has "Karl Ivanych, the Tutor," "*Maman*," "Papa," "The Hunt," "Playing," "Something Like First Love," "Parting," "The Ivins," and "Sorrow." Aksakov has "The Road to Parashino," "Parashino," "The Winter Road to Bagrovo," "Bagrovo in Wintertime," "First Spring in the Country," and "A Summer Trip to Churasovo." Tolstoy's Nikolen'ka is primarily interested in people and relations between them. For Aksakov's Serezha, by contrast, first and foremost is nature: the seasons and one's places of residence are, for him, the most essential aspects of life. Toponyms are as characteristic for Aksakov's tale as names and surnames are for Tolstoy's; in the former, chapter breaks are determined by the main character's relocation to a new place, in the latter, by his meeting a new person. For Nikolen'ka, what is most relevant is the process of socialization, while Serezha's world seems uninhabited, as if we are traveling somewhere in the backwoods, where a person is one-on-one with nature (one's parents being a part thereof).

Significantly, Tolstoy makes the main character of *Childhood* a ten-year-old boy, whereas Aksakov narrates his life of Bagrov the grandson to age nine—any further, according to him, would be the beginning of adolescence. This is not just a matter of differing terminology but of differences in the whole artistic conception of childhood. So clear and transparent is the internal life of Serezha Bagrov, so unburdened by any consciousness of his own singularity or significance, that in it one can clearly and easily make out the contours of the external world, of things as they are. A child represents prelapsarian humanity, the sort of person who gives names to everything, all the animals that come up to him—and the charm of Aksakov's narrative lies precisely in the fact that it presents the world of things and nature in such a purity as only infant vision can allow.

Prior to Aksakov, it was perhaps only Gogol who was so attentive to things. But in Gogol, things become grandiose, swelling to the point of enslaving people, and attesting to how like things people are, the deadness their souls. In Aksakov, by contrast, things have human proportion and are as if animated, warmed by human presence. Gogol has "dead souls," Aksakov has living things; and this difference is due largely to the fact that in the former, thingness is marked by the congealed, calcified world of adults, while in the latter, by a child's sympathy and engagement with everything around him. The joy of making a bonfire; pity for a tiny blind pup; the delight of gathering multicolored pebbles on the shore—here every object elicits a corresponding animation. Being interested primarily in things rather than people is usually considered morally objectionable; there is only one period in which privileging things thus is justified—infancy, which establishes not a utilitarian but rather a magical contact with objects. In infancy, things are particularly kind and docile souls, well-disposed to us, and free of human impatience and insincerity—and Aksakov is perhaps the first in Russian literature to reveal the warmth and kinship of person/thing relations. Serezha is as sensitive to subtle nuances in the appearance of objects unknown to him as Nikolen'ka is to those in people he does not know. Here is how the burning of a pine-torch is described:

> The burnt and charred stump sometimes bent out to the side, sometimes fell with a crackling noise and broke; sometimes the torch suddenly began to hiss and send out a puff of grey smoke, like a jet of water from a fountain, to the right or left. ... I was much taken up by all this, and was vexed when a candle was brought in from the carriage and the torch put out.[11]

To perceive the world so comprehensively and with an eye toward its inherent value, without drawing any ethical or psychological conclusions

---

11 Aksakov, *Years of Childhood*, 28–29. Further citations in the text are to this translation.

but rather with insight into the pure poetic form of things—only a child is capable of this, or an artist. Bunin once said that he would like to describe the moist cord joining a samovar and its lid—not the samovar itself, and not the person serving the tea, but only the moist cord. This steadfastly "narrow" gaze is natural to a child, who perceives the world in small parts, which, however, he endows with the grandeur, the worthiness and intrinsic value of the whole. Strange as it may seem, aestheticism, the admiration of a thing in and of itself, often seen as characteristic of a highly refined or even decadent consciousness, is hardly alien to infancy, which values not the hidden cause or purpose of a thing but its givenness—its appearance, shape, and color. It is only later that adult experience teaches a child that the functional yield of an object, its "use," is significant, that appearances may deceive, and that one must dig into the depths and roots of phenomena—initially, he trusts the visible and loves it, as if following Oscar Wilde's paradoxical dictum that deep judgments about a thing must be made according to its surface: "The true mystery of the world is the visible, not the invisible."[12] Couldn't the growth of aestheticism in some currents of twentieth-century art be due to a return to an infant (that is, non-ethical, non-utilitarian) vision of the world? The experience of major Russian writers—Bunin, Nabokov, to some extent Olesha and Kataev—is strongly persuasive in this regard. The freshness and radiance of the material world's appearance in their works is largely connected with their profound interest in children's perception.

Works on childhood that follow in the Aksakov tradition share another common characteristic, which may be defined as a feeling of homeland. With Aksakov, this feeling is cheerful and tender, with Bunin (in *The Life of Arsen'ev* [*Zhizn' Arsen'eva*]) it is tragic, bound up with losing one's homeland forever; but either way this blood tie with the land, with nature and one's ancestors, is far more essential to both than is the connection with one's contemporaries. Horizontal connections (with one's environment, with the times) are weaker in infancy than vertical connections (with one's patrimony, with the soil), which is why the primordial feeling of homeland is usually accompanied by a sweet but sad

---

12 Wilde, *The Picture of Dorian Gray*, 26.

sense of solitude. There are no people around—just that endless "depth of the ... sky" and "vista of the fields." Bunin writes of childhood: "Still, there were people, there was some life. ... So why has my memory retained only moments of utter solitude?"[13] It is precisely in these moments that the hidden essence of childhood is expressed, that which may be defined by Bunin's words: "What a blessed desolateness!"[14] You feel all alone in the whole world—and how else are you to feel, having emerged on your own from the unknown darkness and narrowness into an empty, wide-open earthly expanse? But it is precisely thanks to solitude that you are forever joined in particularly firm kinship with your scant, unique surroundings: this steppe, this hillside, this line of the horizon, the like of which you will never meet again.

7.

What is specifically Russian about this literary image of childhood? This is clearly a manorial village childhood, recreated with the subtlety characteristic of a nineteenth-century outlook—conditions rarely repeated in other European countries; after all, nineteenth-century Europe foregrounded the city and the bourgeois way of life, while the preceding "aristocratic" era had no interest in childhood whatsoever. This is why the genre of the "Aksakovian childhood tale" is so characteristic specifically of Russian literature—this sensation of kinship with the things inhabited by one's ancestors, with the land that is one's destiny forever. All of this is utterly absent in the image of "bourgeois" or "urban" childhood modeled by Dickens in *Oliver Twist*: a little person pushed around by adults at every turn, all black and blue from physical and moral injuries. And even when this latter childhood is relatively free of hardship, as in the case of David Copperfield, it is nevertheless marked by a terrible ponderousness and monotony from which the only release is to grow up and gain the right to be one's own master. A forbidding state-run school where the pupils are drilled in conformity to a set standard; a bleak house wherein a son's good conduct is cruelly seen to, so that he might behave like a respectable

---

13 Bunin, *The Life of Arseniev*, 19.
14 Bunin, *Zhizn' Arsen'eva*, 21.

gentleman bereft of emotion—under such conditions, childhood is not just some modified adulthood, it is something far more harmful than actual adulthood, which at least consciously follows those same hobby-horsical dogmas that are forcibly drummed into a child.

Dostoevsky's *Diary of a Writer* includes an essay titled "The Land and Children" about the ghastliness and monstrosity of a childhood deprived of one's own land to grow on. "Millions of paupers have no land, particularly in France, where there is little enough land to begin with; and so they have no place where they can give birth to children and are compelled to give birth in some cellar, and not children but Gavroches, half of whom cannot name their own fathers, and the other half, perhaps, their own mothers. ... Children ought to be born on the land and not on the street. ... One may live on the street later, but a nation—in its vast majority—should be born and *arise* on the land, on the native soil in which its grain and its trees grow."[15] This thought is inscribed in nearly every Russian book about childhood, whether the gentry variety (Aksakov, Bunin) or the peasant (Nekrasov, I. S. Nikitin). Childhood is the beginning of life, but as such, everything in and around it must begin from the beginning, that is, from the earth, its smells and colors. Dostoevsky sees Russia as uniquely fortunate in that here there is enough land for every child, which guarantees that all future humanity shall be spiritually provided for with a supply of primary, organic, vivifying impressions. Nothing could be more akin to a child's perception than phenomena childlike in their very basis: not specially made toys, but the rise and setting of the sun, the flight of a beetle, the silence of the fields—everything that lies in the abyss of his unconscious memory.

Toys have an insignificant part in the childhood recollections of Aksakov, Tolstoy, Leskov, and Bunin. Toys are a fake; they conceal a technical rationality straining to replace nature. It is as if the adult world is using toys as a Trojan horse to sneak into childhood's abode and subjugate it. Toys are invented for children, but they are invented by adults; all these balls, trains, cars, shovels, and guns are merely simplified simulacra of industrial civilization. In the regularity of their geometry, in the

---

15 Dostoevsky, *A Writer's Diary*, 204–6.

given functionality of their forms, toys envelop a child in the system of utilitarian and technical ideas: a ball is to roll, a shovel is to dig with, a gun is to shoot. ...

But what is to be done with a beetle or a lake—that, no one can say; this is a spontaneous encounter of beings equal in their uniqueness. "Everything is silent; only at times, a little russet corn-beetle, entangled in the stubble, starts humming, starts a gloomy buzz. I disentangle it and examine it eagerly, with surprise: what is it, who is it, this russet beetle? Where does it live? Whither and for what purpose was it flying? What does it think and feel?"[16] A tiny, minute-long episode, but how much feeling and knowledge it contains, thanks to the fact that here the living has come in contact with the living. Give Oliver Twist but one such minute with a beetle, and he would truly partake of childhood. But beetles do not even occur to Oliver (they are primordial, are nature—already beyond his spiritual reach). Even toys are for him just a dream; in earliest childhood he was placed in a workhouse, where mechanical equipment is all too real, not the toy but rather the factory variety.

8.

Oliver Twist is not the only version of childhood to take place "on the street." Consider what would seem to be an opposite example: little Jean-Paul, raised under the roof of a well-off family home—the autobiographical main character of Jean-Paul Sartre's book *Words*. Of course, the presence or absence of a roof over one's head is an important question, one that separates poverty from wealth. But no less important is the issue of whether there is living soil beneath one's feet—this is what separates the healthy childhood from the diseased, the natural childhood from the mere construct. Jean-Paul lives in total bourgeois abundance. Oliver Twist is destitute, like a member of the Lumpenproletariat. But Jean-Paul, too, may be numbered among the children who, as Dostoevsky puts it, have grown up on the street. Only it is not a cobblestone street, nor paved with asphalt, but with the powerful blocks of intellectual concepts. "In Platonic fashion, I went from knowledge to its subject. I found more reality in the

---

16 Bunin, *The Life of Arseniev*, 19.

idea than in the thing because it was given to me first and because it was given as a thing. It was in books that I encountered the universe: assimilated, classified, labeled, pondered. ... From that came the idealism which it took me thirty years to shake off."[17] For Sartre, his own childhood, which he calls typically bourgeois, is full of a terrible unnaturalness: its essence is words (hence the title of the book), which are used in two functions: reading and writing (the headings of the book's two sections). The child lacks his own foothold in the real world—everything is done for him by others, he is artificially fenced off from reality and submerged in a world of pure figments. Such is Sartre's conception of childhood as fueling the bourgeois "idealistic" worldview, which one must long struggle to overcome if one is finally, in maturity, to attain a courageous engagement with reality.

But Sartre is constantly falling into a self-contradiction: in his struggle against idealism, he also denies that which might serve as its fundamental refutation—the materially given and ethically anchored necessity connecting a son with his father. This is the feeling of the hereditary full-bloodedness of existence brilliantly expressed by Bunin: "Is it not a joy to feel that connection, that communion with 'our fathers and brethren, friends and kinsmen'?" (17)—this feeling of natural and ancestral roots affords a person the opportunity to immerse themselves in the flesh of the world and thus not get carried away by the phantoms of idealizing consciousness. But such a feeling is utterly abhorrent to Sartre: he considers the early death of his father to be one of the most liberating facts of his own biography.

> There is no good father, that's the rule. Don't lay the blame on men but on the bond of paternity, which is rotten. To beget children, nothing better; to *have* them, what iniquity. Had my father lived, he would have lain on me at full length and would have crushed me. As luck had it, he died young. Amidst Aeneas and his fellows who carry their Anchises on their backs, I move from shore to shore, alone and hating those begetters who bestraddle their sons all their life long.[18]

---

17 Sartre, *Words*, 51.
18 Ibid., 19.

Was it worth it to spend thirty years of one's life struggling against child-like idealism so as finally to joyously cut the very umbilical cord that makes childhood something more than reading and writing, something that cannot be reduced to "books"—being in the bowels of being, a reality higher than "words"? When Sartre was already thirty, that is, when the struggle with idealism had been successfully concluded, his "friends were surprised. 'One would think you didn't have parents. Or a childhood.' And I ... [felt] flattered."[19] What a strange "non-idealism"—feeling oneself unrooted to anything, having come from nowhere! The main character of Sartre's autobiography, like its author, is a child of the *intellectual* street. Half these poor Gavroches don't know their own fathers, wrote Dostoevsky of the children of the French proletariat. Jean-Paul Sartre has no interest in knowing his—and well he might say of himself that he was not thrown out on the street but himself chose to be there.

9.

American fatherlessness differs markedly from the European version. Mark Twain's famous Huckleberry Finn is just as much of a homeless castoff from an unfortunate family as Oliver Twist. But here is the difference: having had his share of woe, Oliver accepts the comforts of home and parental custody offered him by Mr. Brownlow with tenderness and gratitude; whereas Huck does whatever he can to escape the solicitousness of the Widow Douglas and Aunt Sally, who by turns attempt to adopt and raise him. "It was rough living in the house all the time, considering how dismal decent and regular the widow was in all her ways; and so when I couldn't stand it no longer I lit out. I got into my old rags ... and was free and satisfied."[20] Both the Englishman Dickens and the American Twain poeticize: the former, the family idyll of childhood; the latter, the romance of wanderings and adventures, the joy of homelessness. For Dickensian characters, a "bleak house" is unbearable because it is bleak, bereft of the warmth of kinship, constructed on a foundation of businesslike practicality; for Twain's characters, the ancestral home is a closed space, not big

---

19 Ibid., 239.
20 Twain, *The Adventures of Huckleberry Finn*, 4.

enough to contain their bold enterprising spirit. And while Oliver cannot recall his deceased mother without tears of affection and pity, Huck hates his living father with a passion and hopes for his demise. Where for Oliver there is a loss of the soil and the horror of homelessness, for Huck is the joy of being a wanderer, the lure of a vast country's expanse. The childhoods of Tom Sawyer and Huckleberry Finn are in their way no less happy than those of Nikolen'ka Irten'ev and Serezha Bagrov, but they are built on an opposite basis: for the Russian children, a deep sense of the land, lineage, and home; for the Americans, total freedom of action and fancy.

This difference is easily seen with regard to things: for Bagrov, things are interesting in and of themselves—in their form, characteristics, manifestations; for Tom Sawyer, on the other hand, things are important mainly because of their application and exchange value. A blue ticket and a bull's bladder may be exchanged for a dead cat; a glass stopper from a decanter for the right to paint a fence; etc. What is key here is how a thing may be quantified and applied toward a goal, not its physical arrangement or "nature." A thing is deprived of its substantive givenness, its fixedness, the presence that gives it sensory significance—and turns into merchandise, something freely tradable. This is a matter not of calm contemplation but of purposeful action.

The same difference is seen in the characters' first experiences with love: Nikolen'ka trembles, feels faint, becomes fearful of his own self, and jealous of everyone around and of who knows who; whereas Tom, having fallen in love with Becky, immediately in the middle of a school lesson scrawls "I love you" on his slate, and during recess seals the "engagement" with a quick kiss. The actions of Twain's characters almost seem unmediated by internal emotion, while in Tolstoy, a character's emotions frequently burn out inside them, without ever making it to the point of external expression—an action. Tolstoy's main character is possessed of a greater mental fluidity than any adult; his connection with the unconscious, the sea of secret, ineffable sensations, has not yet been severed. Twain's main character has a greater behavioral fluidity than any adult; he is unimpeded by law or decorum, a born nonconformist. The "paradoxes of behavior" in Twain's boys are no less glaring than the "dialectics of the soul" in the central figure of Tolstoy's *Childhood*: both cases involve going beyond "adult individuality," albeit in different directions. Nikolen'ka and Serezha are more sensitive, and Tom and Huck more active, than one's typical adult, and both these qualities, equally fascinating, are manifestations of a child's organicity, their living nature.

Similarly, and perhaps particularly glaringly in this time of life, national-psychological types begin to differentiate in childhood. In this, the Russian and American versions each differ from the European one. In the latter, the feeling of the soil is largely lost, but the feeling of the road has not been found; the rupture in kinship, the loss of one's home are sickly rather than joyous; fantasy runs uninhibited and bold but remains confined to the narrows of the mind, never breaking through into reality (as with Sartre's Jean-Paul or Thomas Mann's Tonio Kröger). In general, all the bonds of soil, kinship, and home, so captivating and defining for a Russian childhood, are tragically shattered and disintegrated in the European world; whereas for an American teenager, inspired by their country's novelty, its sense of being unburdened by history, the disintegration itself of these bonds is full of allure and, cutting off the past, sweeps one away into an unknown future. Following Mark Twain, other American writers, too—Hemingway (in his Nick Adams stories), Faulkner, Thomas Wolfe (*Look Homeward, Angel*), and Salinger (*The Catcher in the Rye*)—underscore the power of naturalness in childhood, its active rather than contemplative intolerance for falsehood, its rejection of conformism.

10.

In Soviet literature the theme of childhood has been imbued with particular significance. With humanity divided according to social class and ideology, it was only the child, or at least the infant, who was allowed to remain a human being in general, the incarnation of pure, non-classed humanness. Significant in this regard is the ending of Mikhail Sholokhov's *Quiet Flows the Don* (*Tikhii Don*): Grigorii Melekhov, devastated by civil war, which has seen him take self-inimical positions, returns to his native farmstead—and the son who scarcely recognizes him or responds to his caresses is the most painful of all reminders of the brokenness and doom of a life in which a peasant is not fated to be reunited with the land, nor a father with his son.

The image of orphanhood, which appears frequently in Sholokhov (in *Tales from the Don* [*Donskie rasskazy*], as well as "A Man's Fate" ["Sud'ba cheloveka"]), symbolizes clashes in the fates of a whole country tearing itself away from its ancestral past. History encroaches on the life of people, alienating them from the soil in which they'd been rooted for centuries—from the land, from the family. Such is the role played by war in the fates of Mishatka, Vaniushka, and other children in Sholokhov: they grow up outside that wholeness in which a child usually feels tightly enclosed—outside domestic tradition, outside a steady way of life, outside the all-around security of the family. In "A Man's Fate," a miracle of restored ancestral connection occurs when two lonely people, an adult and a child, find one another; for them, orphanhood has become a tragic step on the path to a new, created sonship and fatherhood.

Anton Makarenko approaches this theme from a different standpoint. His homeless children of revolution and war have been thrown from their family nests onto the pavement. The peculiarity of Makarenko's approach to children, both in his pedagogical practice and in literature, lies in the attempt to replace the severed ties that formerly bound a person to their past with ties binding them to the collective of their peers. This is another way to replace sonship and fatherhood—not through adoption, but via the fraternity of the fatherless. Soviet literature in the 1920s-30s investigates the possibilities of replacing the family with society: how a child might develop into a full-fledged person without feeling dependent on something singular, absolute, preexisting. With the power of the past having been overthrown, the present becomes the whole determinative factor, even as the essence of morality consists in adhering to something absolute and abiding—just as a lineage always abides in its offspring. Makarenko's *Pedagogical Poem* (*Pedagogicheskaia poema*) shows what great difficulties are involved in "a familyless upbringing," which casts the child into a world of fluid social relations before he has had time to take shape as a patrimonial being. On the other hand, a child raised by a collective does not subsequently experience any significant friction with it. Nineteenth-century Russia featured a sharp gap between the life of a child in a gentry family—a freewheeling, gentle, trusting childhood—and the life of an adult in society, where one comes across callousness, formalism, and bureaucratism. In his autobiographical trilogy, Tolstoy shows Nikolen'ka gradually proceed from the serene world of childhood to the adult world, where he will have occasion to feel alien and unneeded, to be ashamed of himself. In large part it can be said of literature that in it, the child lives an idyll, the adult a tragedy.

With Makarenko, it is the other way around. What is tragic is a childhood bereft of solid, sheltering pillars of its own, a childhood spent among strangers, however benevolent, who can never love you for being of one kin with them, yet singular. But in time, upon internalizing the norms of collective life, such children grow to be "healthy" members of society, with a feeling of belonging to it and sharing its ideas and aims. In Makarenko, a person goes from a tragic childhood to a painless, "conflictless," socially useful maturity via a path diametrically opposite to that taken by Nikolen'ka Irten'ev. The particularity of homeless children in Makarenko (unlike, for instance, in Dickens) is that their state of being cut off from ancestral foundations is not an exclusive phenomenon, something in contradiction with society's moral norms, but a mass phenomenon, expressing the spirit of a whole postrevolutionary society that has broken with its past.

The attenuation of ancestral ways influenced another aspect of children's subject matter in literature as well—that of adventure. Nineteenth-century Russian literature had nothing like Mark Twain's tales of Tom Sawyer and Huckleberry Finn: these are figures born of specifically American soil, amid a spirit of vagabondism and free enterprise to which the Old World is unaccustomed. In Russian literature, a youthful vagabond, for example an autobiographical character of Gorky's, is not having a happy childhood but rather fleeing a disadvantaged and downtrodden one, forced to "make his way in the world."[21] Well-situated children enjoy love and affection, and only rarely scheme to make some romantic escape to America so as to encounter the life of freedom of Twain's mischievous youths (as in Chekhov's "The Boys" ["Mal'chiki"]).

---

21 The second book in Gorky's autobiographical trilogy is *Out in the World* (*V liudiakh*)—trans.

Soviet literature of the 1920s-30s is ever more occupied with Twainian tales of rascally boys, irrepressibly entrepreneurial, daring, freewheeling, and intrepid. Aksakov's main character openly admits to his childlike cowardice—such a boy would be out of place on the pages of a Gaidar work, unless as a negative character. What is primary and morally defining for Serezha Bagrov are kindness, mildness, sensitivity, and love of one's parents. For Gaidar's Timur or Kataev's Gavrik, all of that is minor, and at times even scornworthy, as it is also for Huckleberry Finn. The main thing is bravery, a hankering for the unknown, disdain for danger, and being up for any challenge. It is enough to compare the two main child-characters of Kataev's novella *A Solitary White Sail* (*Beleet parus odinokii*) to note the difference between Petia Bachei, a boy of intelligentsia origins, raised in strict and kindly traditions, and Gavrik, the bold, boisterous offspring of the Odessa streets. All the charisma and moral authority is on the side of Gavrik, whom Petia tries to imitate, albeit not succeeding particularly well: he is hindered by his family prejudices, his fear for his parents' wellbeing.

Twain's boys "said they would rather be outlaws a year in Sherwood Forest than President of the United States forever."[22] The difference between the Soviet adventure tale and the American lies in the fact that Timur, Gavrik, the characters of A. Fadeev, V. Kaverin, etc., do not dream of being outlaws or freebooters; they are not opposed to adults as a class, and do not take issue with every commonsensical law. The charisma and preeminence these boys enjoy among their peers lies precisely in their early maturity, consciousness, and clear-thinking. If nineteenth-century writers like Lev Tolstoy and Dostoevsky make their best adult characters (Natasha Rostova, Alesha Karamazov, Prince Myshkin) childlike, the most positive children-characters of the 1920s-30s are striking in their adultness. But while Soviet and Western literature of the 1920s-30s alike reject the romantic ideal of the "innocent and carefree childhood," they do so from opposite directions. From the Freudian standpoint, a child is hardly innocent, manifesting sexuality, elements of sadism, the Oedipus complex, the "family complex"—jealousy and envy of younger brothers

---

22   Twain, *The Adventures of Tom Sawyer*, 57.

and sisters, etc. Overturning the romantics' inventions concerning the angelicness of the child, Freud laid the basis for a new myth, that of the child's demonicism. In contrast to Freud, Lev Vygotsky, the most prominent Soviet psychologist of the 1920s-30s, considered children to be profoundly social beings whose every psychic movement has an analogue in social communication with a partner, representing a sort of "interiorized" speech. In effect, Vygotsky's psychological conception is the theoretical foundation and scientific parallel of those images of mature, conscious, and socially engaged childhood that became popular in the first decades of Soviet literature, in the works of Makarenko, Gaidar, Kataev, and others.

11.

However, already in the 1940s-50s, in the works of M. Prishvin and K. Paustovsky, there arises a different image of childhood, one that is sentimental rather than heroic. Here the child is surrounded by the reality of nature and the atmosphere of a fairy tale, and now what is lovingly described in him, even sanctified, is naiveté, great simplicity, and childlikeness as such. Beginning with Prishvin, nature plays an ever more active role in narratives about children, whom Soviet literature had previously depicted almost exclusively within the framework of society, the collective. It should be noted that in American literature, too—in Hemingway, Faulkner, and Wolfe—the image of childhood becomes inseparably fused with the image of nature; this may be seen as a sort of "return-to-the-soil" reaction against the general urbanization of literature that had taken place in the first decades of the twentieth century. But it is characteristic that in Faulkner, as to some extent in Hemingway, the adolescent is involved in the experience of nature mainly through hunting or fishing. In Prishvin, and in the Russian tradition generally, nature stands before the child in a different form: not animal, but rather mineral and vegetable. We might recall *Shiptimber Grove*[23] ("Korabel'naia chashcha") and *The Ruler's Road* (*Osudareva doroga*): nature here is kindly and open-armed, and a child feels herself happily dissolving in it, wholeheartedly accepted, whereas in the American tradition, nature is more like an arena for a contest of

---

23 As translated by David Fry (London: Lawrence and Wishart, 1957).

wills or a test of vitality. Compare Melville's *Moby Dick* or Jack London's "Love of Life," in which a person comes up against the predatory will of an animal, to Turgenev's *Notes of a Hunter* (*Zapiski okhotnika*), wherein no trace whatsoever remains of hunting itself, that is, of any struggle to the death—the hunting motif evaporates in a landscape-laden, absent-minded, starry-eyed contemplation of nature. Such hunting is more like perambulating, the pleasure of which consists in merging with nature, not conquering it.

Characteristic of Soviet literature of the 1950s-70s was the image of the child within the framework of a family portrait. Possibly the first to conduct such an experiment, as early as the mid-1950s, was Vera Panova in her novella *Serezha*, at the time received with an enthusiasm that is now surprising. Serezha performs no heroic feats, does not aid adults in their labor or battles, and is of no social use—he plays in the courtyard, collects stamps, and tattoos himself ridiculously. All these concerns and events of a child's life touch upon a very close family circle and mean nothing outside it. But the closeness itself of these relations, the fact that for Serezha his mom is simply a mom, a warm-heartedly close and empathetic being—this was all new in the mid-1950s, and would prove important for the decades that followed.

Of course, this is not simply a rebirth of the type of childhood that had charmed us in the narratives of Aksakov and Bunin. Aksakov's Serezha lives on his family's ancestral manor, and through everything around him, he breathes in the spirit of olden times—his parents are only the near foreground of a heredity receding into the impenetrable depths. Everything Panova's Serezha has, meanwhile, is new, factory-made, just as is the case with all his peers; the building he lives in is new as well, and it is highly unlikely he knows anything about his ancestors, about their fate in Russia—he only has a mom and a stepfather. And this closed nature of family relations, their limitedness to the persons nearest you, explains a great deal about late-Soviet childhood and its literary incarnations.

By the late 1960s and early 1970s, the issue of parent-children relationships was deeply rooted in literature, having in a sense become its moral center. This was due in part to the fact that the writers of the middle generation, those creatively most productive, had by now completely outgrown their status as Aksenovian "star boys" and become parents themselves; they had acquired new life experience that demanded artistic incarnation. But the main thing is that society, which in the late 1950s had still felt very young, still bound hell-for-leather for the communist future, had itself matured. In the late 1960s and 1970s, the romance of vagabondism—of wandering and unsettledness, Grin's "scarlet sails" and Hemingway's "men without women"—gradually disappears from literature, replaced by the poetry of hearth and home. Illustrative in this regard is the evolution of Iurii Kazakov: in his collected stories, only two are dated in the 1970s, and both are about childhood, about the home. In the 1950s-60s, Kazakov loved to write about vagabonds blown God knows where by the winds of wandering, about the charm and perils of the nomadic life. "Riding a train at night is good!... The wheels clang, and you're headed for the new and unknown," he writes in the story "The Easy Life" ("Legkaia zhizn'").[24]

But in the story "The Little Candle" ("Svechechka," 1973), Kazakov proclaims, with the same upbeat intonation: "You know, kiddo, it's good when you have a home you grew up in."[25] So great is the pull of the settled way of life, of rootedness, that Kazakov's lyric persona, who has his own home, misses that of his father and grandfather—misses, that is, a lineage going back generations. It is precisely his son who wakens in him a craving to know his ancestors: after all, he now takes his place among their ranks, having given life to Alesha. The feeling of lineage appears afresh in fatherhood: once wounded, nearly cast off by revolution, it is now restored but has become very personalized and forward rather than backward oriented—toward one's children rather than ancestors. The child becomes the moral center of the family; he represents the hope that one might commune with the truth, at its very source, that used to be gleaned in the covenants of old. And this is why the father now has the same relationship of spiritual dependency and piety toward his child that the child used to have toward the father. Kazakov's character never had in his own childhood any spiritual or physical refuge—he was raised not by

---

24 Kazakov, *Vo sne ty gor'ko plakal: Rasskazy*, 276.
25 Ibid., 422.

a family but by war; hence his avid attention toward his own child, toward the experience of lineage, which is already impossible to make out in the past, through the mists of unpeaceful times. The fullness and holiness of the ancestral life is palpable not in the forefathers taken away by the catastrophes of bygone decades but rather in children.

Reading Kazakov's final stories "The Little Candle" and "You Wept Bitterly in Your Sleep" ("Vo sne ty gor'ko plakal"), you experience at times a joyful recognition: is this not the return, after almost two centuries, and so many negations and transformations, of that same primal romanticist intuition of childhood that introduced this theme into literature? In Kazakov, in Chingiz Aitmatov's *The White Steamship* (*Belyi parokhod*), childhood is once again restored to its position of primacy over adulthood; once again its edifying holiness and purity is revealed. Kazakov is himself aware what a great and ancient tradition he is partaking of, and does not shy from writing about it as he addresses his little son thus: "And again I had the wistful thought that you are wiser than me, that you know something of the sort I once knew but have now forgotten, forgotten… That everything on earth was created just so that it could be seen with the eyes of a child! That yours is the kingdom of God! These words are not said nowadays, but doesn't this mean that thousands of years ago, people felt the mysterious superiority of children? What was it that exalted them over us? Innocence, or some higher knowledge that disappears with age?"[26] Kazakov seems to reproduce the entire complex of romantic motifs: the innocence of the infant, its superiority over adults, the impossibly of regaining its gaze upon the world, and even the idea that when an infant smiles sweetly while sleeping, it means that "angels are making him laugh."[27]

But there is something here that is absent in romanticism, something we might define as a troubled and torturing fatherly feeling: this is not just a tender adoration of childhood but also sensitivity to its pains, the inexplicable and unwarranted insults it suffers. For Kazakov, a child is an innocent and pure being but at the same time a profoundly suffering one,

---

26 Kazakov, *Izbrannoe*, 334.
27 Ibid., 329.

bitterly weeping in his sleep; this is something unknown to the romantic stereotype, which admires childhood from a remove as something inapproachable and serene.

In Kazakov's remarkable story "You Wept Bitterly in Your Sleep," the two "afflictions of being"—that of childhood, and that of adulthood—are directly connected. The narrator's friend, the talented, hard-working, successful writer Dmitrii Golubkov, inexplicably to everyone who knows him, commits suicide. Little Alesha, the narrator's son, is unaccountably crying in his sleep after a happily spent day.

> Your tears flowed so copiously that the pillow quickly got wet. You sobbed bitterly, with a desperate hopelessness. This wasn't at all how you cried when you hurt yourself or were being cranky. Those times, you would just bawl. But now, it was like you were lamenting something gone forever... What have you had time to discover in the world, besides the quiet happiness of life, to make you cry so bitterly in your sleep?[28]

Upon waking from this inexplicable weeping, Alesha is strangely transformed, as if he is transitioning to a different age—but he is only a year and a half old.

> I suddenly realized that something had happened to you: you didn't tap your little foot on the table, didn't laugh, didn't say "hurry!"—you looked at me seriously, staring and silent! I felt that you were withdrawing from me; your soul, till now merged with mine, was now far away, and with every passing year it would be more and more remote; I felt that you were already not me, not a continuation of me, and that my soul would never catch up to you, that you'd go away forever. In your profound, unchildlike gaze, I saw your soul leaving me behind; it gave me a compassionate look, and bade me farewell forever![29]

---

28   Ibid., 334.
29   Ibid., 335.

An unseen bitterness and anxiety make a small boy cry in his sleep as he experiences the spiritual ripping-away of his ego from its primordial oneness with being. And this same disease of being pushes an adult, a strong and seemingly happy person, to his unaccountable suicide.

12.

Whence, then, this notion of childhood as the brightest, most dazzling of times? Lev Tolstoy and Sergei Aksakov, Ivan Bunin and Vladimir Nabokov... The happy feelings, the self-abandon, the enormity and immediacy of impressions that predominate in their reminiscences—are these not the very essence of childhood? But perhaps their writerly gaze is directed *at* childhood, not *from* it? It is one thing to look into the light, another to peer from within it; in the latter case, everything seems darker. For adults, childhood means a self-abandon lost; for children, a self-consciousness gained. And when Bunin tries to look not *at* but *from*, through the eyes of a child, he lets loose a mournful cry:

> Every childhood is sad; barren is that quiet world in which a timid and tender soul not yet quite awakened to life is dreaming its dream of life, still alien to everybody and everything. Golden childhood, a happy time!... No, it is an unhappy, morbidly sensitive, miserable time. (*The Life of Arseniev*, 18)

Of course, when adults consider childhood, what they see is mainly that which they themselves have outgrown: a touching naiveté, innocence and integrity. But children themselves constantly experience a feeling of loss, a splintering of their wholeness, the separation and hostility of a space that had previously enveloped them lovingly. A child is constantly abandoning a world he has hitherto inhabited and being resettled in another, broader and more menacing space. The former unconscious connection with all creation weakens; the new, conscious connection is shaky, and does not instill confidence or comfort. Childhood is a wilderness, a desolation, a headlong plunge into the void, thousands of external irritants one does not know how to respond to, and thousands of internal impulses one does not know how to satisfy. This is a time of utmost bewilderment and loneliness, of gigantic alienation unlike anything that comes after.

An adult may feel alienated from one thing or another—from certain customs or people, from nature; and should *everything* feel alien, then this is a condition that leads to suicide. But a child *begins* life in the same condition, traversing, in their first years, a fearsome zone of alienation sufficient to break a seasoned adult. Maturing, a child reaches a new shore and landing—consciousness, which has now firmly closed ranks with reality. For an adult, these are united anew—in conscious action, in the ability to adapt the self to circumstances, and to adapt them to oneself. But childhood has been wrenched from a sleep and dream without yet attaining waking reality, suspended like a wobbly footbridge between two infinities—how could it be happy? If adults pine for childhood and its wholeness, how childhood itself must pine: it is losing this same quality so precipitously, not year by year, but day by day, hour by hour!

The ability to immerse oneself in *deepest* childhood, the attempt to chase it down and draw nearer to it even as it is moving away—this constitutes the spiritual truth of a literature that stands higher than both an alienated admiration for childhood and an alienated horror before it.

2 | The Defamiliarization of Lev Tolstoy

As is well known, defamiliarization is an artistic device whose essence is to take something seemingly habitual and obvious in everyday life and present it as strange and unusual. Defamiliarization renders our perception of the world more difficult and fresher, inducing us to see things anew, as if for the first time. Explaining the principle of defamiliarization in his 1919 article "Art as Technique," which became a manifesto for the formalist school in literary scholarship, Viktor Shklovksy illustrates it mainly using the works of Lev Tolstoy, counting hundreds of instances in which the device is used. And indeed, Tolstoy is the great defamiliarizer: it is enough to recall the famous episode of the opera as conveyed by the naïve perception of Natasha Rostova...

But defamiliarization may be used as a device not only of literature but also of *literary analysis*. Much as a writer defamiliarizes the lives of characters, so too may the critic defamiliarize the writer and the writer's own works, such that the reader might cast fresh eyes on what has become overly familiar, on literary canon. One example of this critical defamiliarization would be Lev Tolstoy's own essay "On Shakespeare and Drama," in which, for instance, the plot of *King Lear* is presented so as to heighten the impression that this play is strange and incongruous. "Absurd as it may appear in this rendering (which I have tried to make as impartial as possible), I can confidently say that it is yet more absurd in the original."[1] D. Pisarev's study "Pushkin and Belinsky," Kornei Chukovsky's articles on contemporary writers (Merezhkovsky, Andreev, Sologub), and A. Siniavsky (A. Terts)'s book *Strolls with Pushkin* may similarly be seen as examples of critical defamiliarization, meant to expose what is absurd in works usually perceived as "encyclopedias of Russian life," models of

---

1 Tolstoy, *Last Steps: The Late Writings of Leo Tolstoy*, 230.

artistic logic or profound tragedy, etc. In this the defamiliarization itself has a dual effect: on the one hand, it strips a given work of its classic glamor, bringing it into an unceremonious and at times humorous contact with critical thought; on the other, it sharpens features that contradict the author's design, enabling a fresh reading, de-automatizing reception. So, even Shakespeare, given a mocking reading by Tolstoy, or Pushkin by Pisarev, has something to gain from the multivalence involved in so irreverent a treatment.

Insofar as the great master of defamiliarization was Lev Tolstoy, it is natural that we should apply this favorite device of his to him, also examining how and toward what end he uses it—that we should, that is, perform a sort of defamiliarization of defamiliarization.

***

Lev Tolstoy has two mutually resonant narratives on human life in all its extent—and on how its meaning may be squandered or, to the contrary, increased. They conclude with almost identical wording:

> He drew in air, stopped at mid-breath, stretched out, and died.[2] (*The Death of Ivan Ilyich* [*Smert' Ivana Ilicha*])

> Only asked to drink and kept being surprised at something. He got surprised at something, stretched out, and died.[3] ("Alesha-the-Pot" ["Alesha Gorshok"])

At the moment of death, the main characters reach for something, and their lives appear, due to this death, as a single whole. Infants stretch. A person stretches upon waking. "To stretch" signifies making a transition into a different state of being. In this case, it is life's final gesture, the sign of an awakening or new birth of which we are vouchsafed no knowledge.

---

2   Tolstoy, *The Death of Ivan Ilyich and Other Stories*, 91. Further citations in the text are to this translation.
3   Ibid., 373. Further citations in the text are to this translation.

However, the commonality of these endings only underscores how profoundly the two compositions differ. While *The Death of Ivan Ilyich* (1882–86) is one of the first works of fiction written by Tolstoy after his spiritual upheaval, "Alesha-the-Pot" (1905) is one of the last. And if in the former, Tolstoy mercilessly exposes social mores, the latter is conceived as an edifying incarnation of a moral ideal. The main characters of these narratives stand at opposite ends of the Tolstoyan "megatext" (the totality of everything written by him). *The Death of Ivan Ilyich* is the story of an empty, "lifeless" human life, one externally full of weighty governmental meaning, and congruent with the generally accepted system of values and customs. The novella's only positive character is the servant Gerasim, who, motivated not by reasoning but humility and conscience, takes care of Ivan Ilyich and carries out his deathbed wishes. This figure is developed in the short story "Alesha-the-Pot," where the life of a servant stands as an exemplar of the same Christian humility and unreasoning virtue.

In my view, these narratives not only do not fulfill the goal set by their author, they actually refute the very ideas Tolstoy sought to incarnate in them, those he was expressing in parallel in his religious and publicistic writings. To put it crudely, Tolstoy the artist *defamiliarizes* Tolstoy the preacher, exposes the conventionality and artificiality of his outlook—which "inversely" corroborates how true-to-life these works are, containing as they do a sort of self-refutation code.

a. *The Death of Ivan Ilyich*

This work constitutes a most bitter and sober insight into human life, which is revealed in its horrifying, glaring emptiness. Nothing in it is real except childhood, all the rest is lies and dissimulation. The novella begins from the end, the epilogue, where friends and colleagues of Ivan Ilyich learn of his death in the newspaper, and the first thought that occurs to them is what sort of career moves might come of it. Instead of experiencing grief or thoughts of their own end, they are simply glad it didn't happen to them. People flit about the coffin, engrossed in their ambitions and thoughts of petty pleasures, and among them it is Ivan Ilyich in his repose who alone produces the dignified impression of an *accomplished individual*: "[A]s with all dead people, his face was more handsome, and above all more significant, than it had been in the living man. There was on his face the expression that what needed to be done had been done, and done rightly" (42).

But already in the second chapter it becomes clear that Ivan Ilyich's own life had also conformed to those same rules of substitution, and he had been exactly the same sort of mannequin as the friends outliving him. The title *The Death of Ivan Ilyich* itself begins to change its meaning, referring not to the death that awaits him in the end but to the entire course of his life. "And this deadly service, and these worries about money, and that for a year, and two, and ten, and twenty—and all of it, the same. And the further, the deadlier.... In public opinion I was going uphill, and exactly to that extent life was slipping away from under me... And now that's it, so die!" (84–85).

From here on we might abbreviate Ivan Ilyich as I. I., which in Russian is equivalent to "and-and," to underscore the mechanicism and repetition of Ivan Ilyich's life as portrayed by Tolstoy, consisting as it all does of "and ... and ... and": "that for a year, and two, and ten, and twenty—and all of it, the same." As if I. I. is not himself living this life, but rather this life is slowly outliving him, or rather, not him, but the man who bears his name, someone *comme il faut* who has faithfully played the part befitting persons of his background and status. And it is only in the end, when death is coming for him, that I. I., as if rousing himself, begins to see his whole previous life as death—that is, begins to internally revive and awaken. "The Death of I. I." overturns the meanings of life and death; that which is considered life is presented as death, and vice versa.

But what exactly leads Tolstoy to present the life of I. I. and his whole circle as a kingdom of death? Behind nearly every Tolstoyan condemnation, we sense a turn of events and living movements of the soul that the author does his best to deaden, to demonstrate the manufactured, inauthentic nature of. The struggle of the living and the dead takes place constantly in every person and, strange as it may seem, Tolstoy is far more attuned to the dead, readily, we might even say malevolently, depicting its triumph, the rigor mortis and vacuity of his characters. Some characters in *War and Peace* and *Anna Karenina* are internally necrotic, incapable of movement or development; but there are living characters as well, full of the energy of thought and feeling. *The Death of Ivan Ilyich* leaves room for none but the dead. They don't live but perform the conventional ritual of life that someone has thought up, one whose meaning they do not understand but from which they do their best not to deviate, so as not to be cast out of their circle.

But then what is that real life that, by contrast, makes the life of I. I. and those around him mere carrion? Tolstoy does not tell us. I. I. had been in love with his future wife Praskov'ia Fedorovna, but we never find out what this love consisted in, what poetic feelings it inspired. I. I. has a pair of children, and likely has experienced a fatherly tenderness toward them, but we learn nothing of this either. Giving a general description of I. I., Tolstoy notes that this was an "intelligent, lively, pleasant, and decent man" (47), but it remains unclear what his mental and emotional life has comprised, what he has contemplated, what he read, what ideas he found attractive or put him off. He stands as a "social animal," following only the instincts of enrichment, career, and outer propriety. That which is masculine, fatherly, spiritual, or intellectual remains unmanifest in him. For him, life only begins when death is a hair's-breadth away, and it is only his death throes that pull him from the state of apathy, or anesthesia, in which he has spent the better part of his forty-five-year existence.

For Tolstoy, childhood is life's fullest focal point. I. I.'s son is the one here closest to childhood, but he, too, is presented as lifeless; an alienation effect, moreover, arises in the writer's very gaze, which locks in on only that which is most stereotypical. "[There] appeared the little figure of Ivan Ilyich's schoolboy son, who looked terribly like him. He was a little Ivan Ilyich, as Petr Ivanovich remembered him from law school. His eyes were tearful and such as are found in impure boys of thirteen or fourteen" (46). Of everything that may be said of the boy, the only thing noted is that he is a schoolboy and is already impure, i.e., an accessory to the vice through which 99% of teenagers pass. To the very end of the novella, Tolstoy shows the boy no mercy. "After him a little schoolboy crept in inconspicuously, in a new uniform, the poor lad, wearing gloves, and with terrible blue circles under his eyes, the meaning of which Ivan Ilyich knew. He had always pitied his son" (81). This is roughly the same way that Gogol depicts Manilov's children, Femistoklius and Alkid: they are still small but already resemble mannequins. We don't even know for certain what I. I's son's name is: Vasya or Volodya—apparently Tolstoy could not be bothered to check: "He said farewell to us a quarter of an hour before he died, and also asked that Volodya be taken away" (chapter 1; 44). "Apart from Gerasim, it seemed to Ivan Ilyich that Vasya alone understood and pitied him" (chapter 7; 81).

It should be noted that the device of defamiliarization, which Viktor Shklovsky considered highly characteristic of Tolstoy, is most often used by the writer for a totally different purpose than the one ascribed to it by the theoretician. "[A]rt exists that one may recover the sensation of life; it exists to make one feel things, to make the stone *stony*" ("Art as Technique").[4] However, in Tolstoy, defamiliarization is mostly used not to restore the sensation of life but, to the contrary, to deaden, to pull to pieces what is normally perceived as alive and whole. The very examples cited by Shklovsky attest to the fact that in Tolstoy, defamiliarization is a *deadening* rather than an enlivening of an object; if such an object is indeed "remove[d] … from the automatism of perception,"[5] then this is done solely to demonstrate its mechanicism, senselessness, and lifelessness.

> The dead body of Serpukhovskoy, which had walked about the earth eating and drinking, was put under ground much later. Neither his skin, nor his flesh, nor his bones, were of any use. Just as for the last twenty years his body that had walked the earth had been a great burden to everybody, so the putting away of that body was again an additional trouble to people.[6] ("Strider" ["Kholstomer"])

> The essence of the service consisted in the supposition that the bits of bread cut up by the priest and put into the wine, when manipulated and prayed over a certain way, turned into the flesh and blood of God. These manipulations consisted in the priest, hampered by the gold cloth sack he had on, regularly lifting and holding up his arms, and

---

4 Shklovsky, "Art as Technique," 12.
5 Ibid., 13.
6 Tolstoy, *The Devil and Other Stories*, 160.

then sinking to his knees and kissing the table and all that was on it.[7] (*Resurrection* [*Voskresenie*])

Here, as in his articles against the Church, Tolstoy depicts religious rituals by strikingly defamiliarizing them, steadily reifying and deadening that which its participants perceive as living, as the source of any life.

For Shklovsky, defamiliarization and automatism are polar opposites. "And so life is reckoned as nothing. Habitualization devours works, clothes, furniture, one's wife, and the fear of war."[8] But in Tolstoy, it is precisely defamiliarization that works as a method of automatization, of rendering soulless that which is usually perceived as full of meaning, feeling, and dignity.

In taking a stand against the syllogisms of common sense that efface human individuality, Tolstoy in fact corroborates them using their same manner of representation. I. I. recalls a syllogism he was taught in school: "Caius is a man, men are mortal, therefore Caius is mortal" (70). He had always felt this had not applied to him. Caius is a person in general, but I. I. is not some generic person but "had always been quite, quite separate from all other beings; he was Vanya, with mama, with papa, with Mitya and Volodya, with toys, the coachman, with a nanny, then with Katenka. … [H]ad [Caius] been in love like that?" (70).

There is no room in a syllogism for such a particular being, one not subject to the general rules of logic, and who thus cannot die. But the paradox is that we only hear of this particular being I. I. when he ponders a syllogism; in everything else, I. I. is presented precisely as an average being, like the great majority of persons of his circle, insofar as he has once and for all taken on their values and does his best to stand out from them as little as possible. I. I., as Tolstoy represents him, *is* Caius, an updated Caius of the nineteenth century, an incarnation of the court official in the abstract. Such a *caius*, a common as opposed to proper noun, is entirely capable of dying, because he does not live; his individual characteristics are declaratively asserted but exist at a remove from artistic portrayal.

---

7   Tolstoy, *Resurrection*, 147.
8   Shklovsky, "Art as Technique," 12.

The Defamiliarization of Lev Tolstoy 165

This being has never become a personality, and so death essentially changes nothing in him.

The forcible nature of the artistic operation Tolstoy has performed on his character is particularly clear if we juxtapose I. I. with the person he is based on, Ivan Il'ich Mechnikov, a prosecutor of the Tula District Court who died on 2 July 1881. T. A. Kuzminskaia recalls that "during Mechnikov's stay at Iasnaia Poliana, Lev Nikolaevich was riveted by him, sensing, with his artistic intuition, that this was an extraordinary person." She adds: "He is an intelligent and original person. ... No wonder Levochka so esteemed him, and after a long discussion with him ... when Mechnikov had been with us at Iasnaia, said of him: 'Smart, very smart.'"[9] The great biologist Il'ia Il'ich Mechnikov, who devoted his life to the struggle against aging and death, wrote: "I was present during the final minutes of my older brother's life (his name was Ivan Il'ich—his death served as the theme for Tolstoy's famous novella *The Death of Ivan Ilyich*). My forty-five-year-old brother, sensing the approach of his death from sepsis, maintained the full clarity of his great mind."[10]

There are no traces of the "extraordinary person" or "great mind" to be found in the figure of I. I. Everything is done so as to turn Ivan Il'ich Mechnikov into an I. I. who is as average as possible, an incarnation of the commonplace, *das Man*, a subject of impersonal constructs. In order to demonstrate his magnificent art of "tearing off all and any masks," Tolstoy must himself first mold these masks, and only then reveal their emptiness.

"In the morning, when he saw the footman, then his wife, then his daughter, then the doctor—their every movement, their every word confirmed the terrible truth revealed to him that night. In them he saw himself, all that he had lived by, and saw clearly that it was all not right, that it was all a terrible, vast deception concealing both life and death" (86). But what this deception consists of, and how life without deception should be—this we never find out. Of course, the wife and the daughter and the doctor each pursue their own aims (prosperity, marriage, entertainment, the maintenance of one's reputation), but neither are they alien

---

9   Kuzminskaia, *Moia zhizn' doma i v Iasnoi Poliane*, 445–46.
10 Mechnikov, *Etiudy optimizma*, 264.

to compassion for the patient, nor the desire to actively help him, nor the sorrowful, nagging feeling of the impossibility of saving him. Everyone behaves like a human being; they are all imperfect, but they do their best to be kind, supportive, and compassionate. This is that flicker, that faint glimmer of life that in his growing aloofness I. I. does not wish to notice around him. Perhaps it is I. I.'s disease itself, his fear of death, that keeps him from seeing what is human in the people around him and turns them into social marionettes? But this society's customs do include compassion, mutual aid, and active love: one of I. I.'s "soulless" coworkers, Petr Ivanovich, even experiences a feeling of shame, because compassion for the deceased does not keep him from thinking with pleasure about playing a game of vint. This too is human—being ashamed of one's imperfection. Yes, people pretend to be better than they really are, but this pretense is a sign of civilization, which gradually creates a facemask: the ability to dissimulate coexists with the aspiration to overcome such dissimulation. Would it really be better if people did not pretend, did not seek out any forms of propriety?

Suppose the dying I. I., retreating further and further into his own illness, perceives life, his own and that of those around him, as a "terrible, vast deception." But then, the author himself proposes no other, more charitable view. The more judgmentally I. I. looks upon those around him, and the greater his disgust with their life, so full of extraneous interests, hence false—the closer and more sympathetic he becomes to the author. It is as if Tolstoy himself, following his character's lead, is so sick with the fear of death that all people seem lifeless to him.

"Court is in session!... Here is that court!" (85). Thus does I. I. imagine his lot upon falling under the power of a fatal illness. Having always sat in judgment of others, he learns for the first time what it is to be judged. But then, Tolstoy too, who finds all things "judiciary" repugnant, takes it upon himself to judge I. I. himself and his circle—and in this role he may very well be even more merciless than his character had been when going about his prosecuting. I. I. "never misused this power of his; on the contrary, he tried to soften its expression" (50). Tolstoy's power over his characters is limitless, and he is inclined not to soften it but to make it more severe, subjecting to his irrevocable tribunal a doctor who merely wishes to keep his patient calm, a daughter who has the bad luck to receive a marriage proposal when her father is ill.

It is only at the very end, a few hours before death, that I. I. begins to understand that there is something in his life that may yet be rectified—and he begins to experience pity, not for himself, but for his wife who is looking upon him despairingly, and his son who is kissing his hand. "He was sorry for them, he had to act so that it was not painful for them. To deliver them and deliver himself from these sufferings. 'How good and how simple,' he thought" (91). And then for the first time in long months, his pain eases, as does his fear: "There was no more fear because there was no more death. Instead of death there was light. 'So that's it!' he suddenly said aloud. 'What joy!'" (ibid.)

As soon as I. I. is reconciled with the weak, incomplete, but genuine life taking place around him, his fear of death disappears. And when someone standing over him says, "It's finished," he gives his own meaning to this word. "'Death is finished,' he said to himself. 'It is no more'" (ibid.). And it is only after this that he "stretches out and dies," i.e., departs now not into death but what is beyond it, its absence—into an existence unknown to him.

This means that the novella's title is *doubly* deceptive. It is about how I. I. had been dying while he lived, and about how he comes alive a little bit while he is dying. This enlivening takes up only a single page, the novella's last, roughly one one-hundredth of its length. But such an ending lends the whole affair a sense of reconciliation with the very life it has doggedly debunked. The author, together with his main character, ceases to be a judge, and thereby overcomes the fear of death. True, such an ending for the novella comes across as hasty, as ostentatiously kindly parting words to a character whose author has made him suffer so much, and taken to such physical and mental agony, that he cannot refuse him one final gesture of mercy.

b. "Alesha-the-Pot"

In his later years, Lev Tolstoy famously demanded of art that it be, first of all, simple, and second, that it be edifying, with a clear moral meaning. The story "Alesha-the-Pot" meets the first goal: it is written in a vernacular comprehensible even to the very young. But what about edification? What is the story's meaning and the author's intent?

This is a rare case in which a short story encompasses not a single episode or event but a whole life—and thus approaches the genre of hagiography. But while a saint's life emphasizes that everything that is happening is ultra-significant and "foreordained from above," in Tolstoy, to the contrary, everything is random, and the genre of hagiography is once more defamiliarized, as if turned inside out. The story begins with an accident: Alesha's mother sends him on an errand with a pot of milk, and he trips and breaks the pot. Hence the derisive nickname unbefitting a canonical saint. And the story ends with an accident: the clerk sends Alesha to clear snow from the roof, he slips and falls, is badly hurt, and dies. The result is a meaning-making repetition: "His mother sent him [to take a] pot of milk"—"the clerk sent him to clear the snow off the roof" (369, 372). Alesha is twice-*sent* and twice-*fallen*.

But whose envoy is he, and why is chance so significant in his life and death? He is obedient, never "talks back," and only does what he is asked or ordered. He is always running errands, and without the slightest hesitation agrees to carry out whatever is requested of him, even as he neglects his own needs: "He ate breakfast on the move, and he rarely managed to eat dinner with the rest of them" (370).

He dies just as humbly, believing as he does "that, as it is good here, provided you obey and do not hurt anyone, so it will be good there" (373). It would seem that we could apply to Alesha the precept: "Blessed are the poor in spirit: for theirs is the kingdom of heaven" (Matthew 5:3). Alesha not only has no material possessions, he does not even have any assets in the form of words, knowledge, or standing in society. Only once has he been able, with the kopecks given him as tips on holidays, to save two rubles and buy himself a knitted jacket, but, like a "bright patch," this underscores his penury all the more. He never gets angry at anyone, never judges, never accuses. Although he is ordered about mercilessly, he responds to every wish with a meek smile, and so to him the precept "blessed are the meek" (Matthew 5:5) is also applicable. Alesha "wanted to stand up but could not and began to smile.... 'It hurts everywhere, but never mind'" (373). What is this smile about? About how he, a young man, cannot do anything with himself, cannot get up and work: he is inviting us to laugh at him, at such ineptitude. He hides nothing, has no "dark side," no pretense or dissimulation: "Blessed are the pure in heart: for they shall see God" (Matthew 5:8). Alesha is "blessed" in all three of these senses, and though it "hurts everywhere" after he falls from the roof, and his suffering lasts three days, spiritually, death is not hard for him. Tolstoy finds a strange verb to describe it: "to be surprised." People usually resist death, meeting it with fear and torment, but Alesha is only surprised. "He spoke little. Only asked to drink and kept being surprised at something. He got surprised at something, stretched out, and died" (373). Surprise indicates the acceptance of something incomprehensible, unknown.

The name Alesha immediately calls to mind Aleksei, the man of God (AKA Alexius of Rome), one of the most beloved of saints in Byzantium and old Russia, the very image of Christian patience and humility. According to legend, he left his parents' home on the eve of what was to be his wedding day, spent seventeen years living on the steps of the Church of the Virgin in Edessa, and another seventeen years back in Rome as a beggar taken in but unrecognized by his own parents. Key moments in Aleksei's hagiography intersect with those of Tolstoy's story. Alesha has a fiancée but renounces her; he is a "holy unmercenary," laboring without recompense (his father receives all of his pay); and in a certain sense he goes unrecognized, insofar as his patience and humility earn him no reward, nor even gratitude from his father or any of the persons he so zealously serves. This is a sort of worldly saint, a saint without a church, or even without any verbal prayer. "He did not know any prayers; what his mother had taught him, he had forgotten; but he still prayed in the morning and in the evening—prayed with his hands, crossing himself" (370). He may be said to pray also via his deeds, because these are all for the benefit and aid of others.

The meaning of his nickname may be explained by the image of clayware in Paul's epistle to the Corinthians: "But we have this treasure in earthen vessels, that the excellency of the power may be of God, and not of us" (2 Corinthians 4:7). Thus is Alesha nothing but an earthen vessel, fragile and nondescript. And his life is just as easily shattered as the pot he dropped as a child.

But has this earthen vessel ever contained any sort of treasure—or only a readiness to be shattered, its spirit never ripening into a personality, never becoming a free will and identity? If Alesha is poor in the name of the spirit, then of what sort? Spirit means struggling with oneself, with one's givenness, whereas Alesha goes along with his own passive inclinations, his kindly nature. Alesha gives the impression of subjection, unconsciousness, lifelessness, as if he is acting in his sleep, or a wind-up person, flapping his arms, running, bustling about, never managing nor even being capable of realizing what he is doing, of making a conscious choice or applying his own free will.

> In winter Alyosha got up before dawn, split wood, swept the yard, then fed the cow, the horse, and watered them. Then he stoked the stove, cleaned the master's boots and clothes, prepared samovars, cleaned them, then either the clerk called him to take out the wares or the cook ordered him to knead dough or scrub pots. Then they sent him to town now with a message, now for the master's daughter at school, now for lamp oil for the old woman. (369–70)

This whole life, to put it in contemporary terms, is a "clip show"—minor fragments of other people's lives, needs, commands, and whims.

This is why, unlike a spiritually uplifting hagiographic life, it leaves so melancholy an impression—that of, not just a lack of enlightenment, but downtroddenness. In order truly to give of oneself, one must first become someone, but Alesha has not managed to become anyone, nor even shown any interest in doing so. He has no will to being, just a sort of amiable apathy, or rather an indifferent acceptance.

Is he capable of loving? Even when, once, a desire of his own does arise—to marry the cook, Ustin'ia—he readily renounces it. For the first and only time, he "felt ... that another person needed him, not his work, but him himself" (370–71). But the merchant and his wife are against this "foolishness," since then the cook would have a child; and they tell Alesha's father, who tells him. "When the father finished, Alesha smiled. 'Well, it can be given up'" (372).

So easily does he renounce his own will. Nor does he offer a word of objection when his father calls Ustin'ia a "slut." Not for a moment does he have the urge to stand up for his love. True, the same day, answering the merchant's wife's question as to whether he has "dropped this foolishness of [his]": "'Seems I have,' said Alyosha, and he laughed and all at once wept" (372). This is the only willfulness in his whole life: weeping over an unfulfilled love. But later, when he is dying, Alesha is glad that he obediently gave up on the idea of marrying. "Thank you, Ustyusha, for pitying me. You see, it's better that they told us not to get married, otherwise it would have come to nothing. Now it's all for the best" (373).

Perhaps it is Pavel Florensky who, unbeknownst to himself, has given the profoundest truth about Alesha-the-Pot, when he says, not of Tolstoy's character, but the collective significance of the very name Aleksei,

> Aleksei ... is invariably conceived as leaning against someone or something, but if he were not thus externally moored in place, he would inevitably be carried off who knows where by who knows what winds. There is something ontologically sickly about him: he is unadapted to an independent existence in the world. ... In his most supreme revelation, Aleksei is a holy fool. ... In this defenselessness and sickliness, holy foolishness/deformity[11] are to some extent matched by signs of a certain wretchedness: either a lisp, or a stutter, or lameness, or pallor, or muteness, and so on.[12]

Interestingly, Tolstoy himself was dissatisfied with this story. "I was working on 'Alesha,'" completely bad. I dropped it."[13] In this he contradicts Blok, who, to the contrary, raved over the story: "A most ingenious thing I just read, Tolstoy, 'Alesha-the-Pot.'"[14] Perhaps it was just what Tolstoy didn't like about his own story that so captivated Blok, who had a decadent's rapturous adoration for the kindly *muzhik*. As Tolstoy himself possessed a far better knowledge of this *muzhik*, he felt that this

---

11 Florensky plays on the shared etymology of *iurodstvo* ("holy foolishness") and *urodstvo* ("deformity")—trans.
12 Florenskii, *Imena*, 8.
13 Tolstoi, *Polnoe sobranie sochinenii*, 55:125.
14 Blok, *Dnevnik A. Bloka: 1911–1913*, 37.

tender portrait ultimately rang hollow. Not coincidentally, Alesha differs sharply from the actual *muzhik* he was based on—a worker who lived at Lev Tolstoy's Iasnaia Poliana. T. A. Kuzminskaia writes of him the following:

> The cook's helper and caretaker was the quasi-idiot "Alesha-the-Pot," who for some reason was so poeticized that when I read about him, I didn't recognize our deformed holy fool[15] Alesha-the-Pot. But, as far as I can remember, he was quiet and harmless, always doing what he was told, without a murmur.[16]

It is understandable why Tolstoy, having brought the story to a formal ending, "dropped" it, that is, declined to apply any artistic finishing touches. The "quasi-idiot" is too glaring in Alesha—he obediently carries out anyone's will because he has none of his own. The clearer Alesha's image gets, the more obvious it becomes that such sermonizing on simpleness and unreasoning humility goes against the conception of Christianity as an active, conscious love of people, a love that does not come down to obedience and humility but represents a means to remake the personality, to self-transform. Alesha never does become a personality, and his uncomplaining gratification of the self-interested and petty everyday needs of his masters can in no way stand as an exemplar of Christian behavior; to the contrary, it serves to justify a rapacious and consumeristic attitude toward life. Alesha may be an innocent, mute sacrifice, but he is hardly some hero of asceticism. In holding up Alesha's humility as a model of worthy behavior, Tolstoy is in effect consecrating the sort of oppression he otherwise made war on as a Christian.

Indeed, even death for Alesha becomes the perfect expression of the meaning of his life, that of spineless submission to the laws of worldly being. Alesha is submerged in the very automatism of existence that Tolstoy sought to rouse people from with his preaching. And if in *The Death of Ivan Ilyich* Tolstoy, denouncing the automatism of upper-class

---

15   Kuzminskaia makes the same pun (*iurodivogo i urodlivogo*) described in note 11—trans.
16   Kuzminskaia, *Moia zhizn' doma i v Iasnoi Poliane*, 2:53.

being, passes over that life without regard for its spiritual or mental content, in "Alesha-the-Pot" he reduces lower-class life to the same sort of automatism, but now tries to pass it off as Christian virtue.

In *The Death of Ivan Ilyich*, Tolstoy nevertheless finds an artistic solution, leading I. I. to a crisis and momentary contact with the sort of life that is not subject to death's power. "Alesha-the-Pot" has no such resolution: the automatism of obedience is presented as the highest virtue; there is no hint of any possible crisis or spiritual renewal. While I. I.'s life has resembled death, and the approach of death returns him to real life, Alesha's death is essentially no different from his whole previous life, suffused with the same obedience and abdication of personal will.

In both cases it is clear that what Tolstoy is telling us in his works is something entirely different from what he was trying to say.

c. Happy and Unhappy Families: *Anna Karenina*

The third and final experiment with the defamiliarization of Tolstoy presented here has to do not with a novella or story but just a single phrase—granted, one that is key to an entire novel. *Anna Karenina* opens with what is likely Tolstoy's most famous pronouncement: "All happy families are alike; each unhappy family is unhappy in its own way."[17] This is widely quoted and accepted as a view undoubtedly held by Tolstoy himself. It has always struck me as controversial, and I have even had trouble remembering whether it was the happy or unhappy families that are alike—so reversible are the statement's two parts. For that matter, does the novel itself corroborate this statement? Does it not, rather, do the opposite? After all, the main thing in family happiness is love, a feeling rare enough in itself, and if *mutual* love is stipulated, then doubly rare, which Tolstoy and his characters clearly understand:

> Levin took this occasion to convey to Yegor his thought that the main thing in marriage was love, and that with love one was always happy, because happiness exists only in oneself. (401)

---

17 Tolstoy, *Anna Karenina*. Further citations in the text are to this translation.

People differ more in love than in antipathy (estrangement, indifference), because it is precisely love that reveals what is most "one's own" in a person, their singularity. The same is true of happiness, to which love is fundamental. How can happy families resemble one another if people who love are, thanks to this love, so unalike? "[H]appiness exists only in oneself." This is incidentally why it is so much harder to depict happiness than misfortune and hardship: it is not a wholesale item but rather custom-made.

The main refutation of the novel's opening sentence is the novel itself. There is only one happy family in *Anna Karenina*, that of Levin and Kitty, and it is this one that is really unlike any other. By contrast, the families that are experiencing rifts, the Karenins and Oblonskys, resemble one another, and share a common pattern: betrayal, jealousy, cooling, desperation, arguments, self-isolation, loneliness, the attempt to forgive and forget… With the Karenins and Oblonskys, a parallel plot plays out; the difference is simply in tonality: tragic in the former vs. comic-banal in the latter. But the Levin and Kitty plot remains in a class by itself, and is not reflected in anyone's mirrors. Could it be that, in beginning his novel as he does (on the similarity of happy families), and ending it as he does (with the distinctness of the book's only happy family), Tolstoy himself did not understand this?

He understood this perfectly well, at least in this passage on Levin:

> He thought that his engagement would have nothing in common with others, that the ordinary conditions of engagement would spoil his particular happiness; but it ended with him doing the same things as others, and his happiness was only increased by it and became more and more special, the like of which had never been known and never would be. (407)

That's just it: a person does the same thing as others, but his happiness is a particular one, "the like of which has never been known." What, then—is Tolstoy contradicting himself with the novel's opening sentence?

> Levin had been married for three months. He was happy, but not at all in the way he had expected. At every step he found disenchantment

with his old dream and a new, unexpected enchantment. He was happy, but, having entered upon family life, he saw at every step that it was not what he had imagined. (479)

Is Tolstoy again contradicting himself? Levin's happiness is not only unlike that of other people but does not even resemble his own notions of happiness. Isn't this too many contradictions? Or should we instead take the opening sentence itself as a mockery, although many readers take it at face value? Tolstoy "tosses out" a thought that is easy to fall for, and then step by step, episode by episode, defamiliarizes it, "dismantles" it.

But for that matter, most readers also take Pushkin's "Blessed is he who was young in his youth" seriously, and this is much easier to recognize as sarcasm. This line is quoted on the Internet almost 100,000 times, nearly always approvingly, as if it were a belief held by the author himself with which the reader wholeheartedly concurs. Even in a dictionary, the expression's meaning is explained thus: "Every age has its opportunities and limitations, and happy is the person who in old age does not aspire to make up for the opportunities missed in youth, insofar as this person has in his own time managed to live through and experience everything to the fullest."[18] But upon reaching the line that blessed is he who "at thirty is advantageously married," the attentive reader will wonder: just what does Pushkin mean? Perhaps he is making fun of this "Blessed is he who in his youth" business, this apologia of commonplace thinking and conformism?

But in Pushkin, the transition from enthusiasm to sarcasm is too obvious, coming as it does within a single stanza, whereas in Tolstoy it is spread across a whole novel. The irony of the opening sentence goes unnoticed because it emerges slowly in this narrative of two unhappy families and one happy one. And if most people have not read this one Onegin stanza all the way through, or more precisely, have not *thought* it all the way though, that goes all the more for Tolstoy's novel. But then, to sense Tolstoy's sardonicism, it is essentially enough just to make it to the

---

18   "Slovoborg"—http://www.slovoborg.su/definition/блажен+кто+смолоду+был+молод.

first episode, which begins with a no less famous phrase: "All was confusion in the Oblonskys' house" (1). Stiva himself is perfectly aware: "There's something trivial, banal, in courting one's own governess!" (3–4). And later, after the scene with Dolly: "'And what trivial shouting,' he said to himself, remembering her cry and the words 'scoundrel' and 'mistress.' 'And the maids may have heard! Terribly trivial, terribly!'" (13).

"Trivial, banal." Is such triviality supposed to attest that every unhappy family is unhappy in its own way, and not in a manner utterly typical? Can such "wisdom" really be taken as an expression of the author's own thought? Isn't it time we realized that the opening sentence contradicts the meaning of the novel, that happiness as it appears in *Anna Karenina* is far more singular, surprising, incredible, and one-of-a-kind than all the utterly trivial family woes with their predictable outcomes?

The opening sentence's ironic relationship with the novel does not necessarily mean that Tolstoy is intentionally playing a trick on the reader. That initial maxim is intonationally neutral: the thought is neither clearly corroborated nor refuted but proposed for further testing, and perhaps to be disproved. It is a moral-philosophical maxim of the sort La Rochefoucauld or La Bruyère might have uttered. Such a sententious comment would have been at home in a high-society drawingroom. At worst, it could be the thought of Stiva Oblonsky himself, a phrase from his internal monologue, an ironic prelude to the scene of his family life in ruins.

Stiva simultaneously regrets what has happened and tries to console himself: yes, he says, it's trivial, but in every unhappy family it happens in its own way.

However, upon being tested by the plot, this thought does not hold up. It gradually becomes clear that this is no monologic assertion by Tolstoy but rather the novel's disputation with its own opening line, an example of "someone else's word" (Bakhtin's *chuzhoe slovo*) in authorial speech—or in any case, of such a word being defamiliarized by the author in the course of a novel.

***

The Defamiliarization of Lev Tolstoy 177

Criticism that defamiliarizes an author carries on his defamiliarizing work, directing it at literature itself. A work is interpreted as bizarre, biased, one-sided, sometimes even as a manifestation of obsession or madness. Such treatment does a minor writer in, but in the case of a major writer, it resurrects him from the inertia of a rotely deferential reception. Before this technique became well known as "defamiliarization," its theoretician Viktor Shklovsky called it "resurrection" ("The Resurrection of the Word"). Hence it is clear that this is not at all a matter of formalism, which Shklovsky helped to pioneer, but of the profoundly meaningful purpose of art: "to resurrect things—to restore a person's experience of the world."[19]

This chapter could thus have justly been called "Resurrecting Lev Tolstoy." Resurrection is possible only after death, and must be based on it. First, a great writer lives, and his work enlivens readers, wakes them up and stirs them. Then the writer begins to be perceived as a sort of gold reserve, a canon in which he congeals and dies. Writers may only be revived by pulling them down from this pedestal, uncovering the faultiness of their methods, the cruelty of their errors, etc.

In a letter to the critic N. N. Strakhov, Tolstoy remarked: "Everything seems just about ready to write, to perform my earthly obligation; but something is lacking: the impulse of faith in myself, in the importance of the work; the energy of error is lacking, the earthly elemental energy that you can't just make up."[20] Why does Tolstoy use the word "error" here approvingly? It is akin to "defamiliarization": deviating from the truth or habit, we reinforce in ourselves the fresh, elemental feeling of life. We need the energy of error, of injustice, even of the trampling of the truth, so as to engage our gaze, and not to be bored by the truth but shaken by it. A writer makes a sacrifice of the self for the reader's sake, rouses the thinking, the passionate disapproval thereof—even at the price of being wrong. And it is the critic's job to rouse once more this energy even in hopelessly classic texts.

---

19   Shklovskii, *Voskreshenie slova*, 1.
20   Letter of 6 April 1878; http://rvb.ru/tolstoy/01text/vol_17_18/vol_18/0697.htm

3 | Soviet Heroics and the Oedipus Complex

> Does this sound like incest? But after all, that's just what it is: man,
> born of the earth, makes her fruitful with his labor.
> Maksim Gorky, "On M. M. Prishvin."[1]

a. "Big Brother": Between Freud and Orwell

In his works *Totem and Taboo* (1912) and *Mass Psychology and Analysis of the "I"* (1921), Sigmund Freud describes a model of social upheaval based on an act of patricide—the killing of the leader by his sons in the "primal horde." "A process like the removal of the primal father by the band of brothers must have left ineradicable traces in the history of mankind"[2]—such is the psychoanalytic subtext of revolutions and subsequent totalitarian regimes. The father imposes limitations on the instincts of the sons, and they, conspiring, kill him. Power is transferred to the Older, or Big, Brother—a glorification familiar to us from Orwell's book *1984* that may very well hark directly back to the terminology of Freud. And indeed, the overthrow of the tsar caused the people, for centuries having been faithful to "autocracy-Orthodoxy," to feel an exultant sense of liberation... And at the same time—the profoundest dread, seemingly from nowhere but in reality, from the devastation this wrought upon the ego-ideal, which now had no one to identify with; for the ego-ideal, according to Freud, is the introjected image of the Father.

Of course, the soul did not pine so much for "the little father tsar" (*tsar'-batiushka*) as for the Heavenly Father who was cast down at the same time by the common fraternal will. The social patricide is a

---

1 Some of the wording in this section, and such renderings as "godlet" for *bozhen'ka* and "full-blown man" for *materyi chelovechishche*, draw on Anesa Miller-Pogacar's translation of Mikhail Epstein, *After the Future: The Paradoxes of Postmodernism and Contemporary Russian Culture*, from which this epigraph is quoted (184)—trans.
2 Freud, *Totem and Taboo*, 200.

counterpart of the religious one. The killer brethren, orphaned, now immediately required an Older Brother who would take the place of the father and fill the space of the ego-ideal, without which neither the individual nor society is able to live. Among the brothers there commenced the cruelest struggle for the title of Eldest. "Big brothers" began to replace one another according to seniority, destroying their rival brothers along the way. The very notion of "fraternity" became dubious in the absence of the Father—like a reminder of him who ought to be forgotten.

It was precisely the feeling of guilt before the murdered Father that induced such a furious faith in the new father, that led the people to offer him their ever-increasing sacrifices. From the standpoint of Marxism, the so-called "cult of personality" (*kul't lichnosti*) is merely a deviation from the immutable laws of history. From the psychoanalytic standpoint, to the contrary, the cult of the "older brother" is inevitable in societies that have undergone the revolutionary event of patricide. Moreover, all of this had been expressed well before the spread of the "older brothers" cult in communist Russia, fascist Italy, and Nazi Germany. In this case Freud, despite not making any predictions, had foresight—which Marx, who made many predictions, alas did not.

As Marxism developed and was embodied in practice, it accumulated a number of deviations, at first seemingly insignificant, that permitted certain adjustments in the interest of its creative development. Now socialism in one country, now the cult of personality, now the *non*-absolute (*non*-) immiseration of the proletariat in capitalist countries, now economic backwardness, the growth of alcoholism, and the flourishing of "religious holdovers" in countries with "mature and developed socialism," etc. Every theory has its critical mass of flaws; when enough of them pile up, it turns into a pseudo-theory. In a country led astray by Marxism, Freudianism has the attraction of being a broader alternative theory, one capable of explaining not only the things that contradict Marxism but Marxism itself.

b. The Mythological Basis of Materialism

The philosophical basis of the Marxist-Leninist worldview is materialism. The mythological basis of materialism, in turn, is the cult of Mother Nature, the veneration of the maternal element of being.

One often encounters the viewpoint that materialism was grafted onto Russian philosophy from without, that Russians are by nature the furthest thing from materialists—that perceiving the world as a distinct reality is alien to them, as is the sobriety of Western Europe, its aspiration to rely on objective laws that operate regardless of desire and will. However, materialism should not be confused with rationalism or empiricism. Materialism comes from a conviction as to the primacy and rightness of nature, its maternal claim on humanity and humanity's duty before Mother Nature. Indeed, materialism meant this and nothing else to its philosophical founders. Here is Friedrich Engels's most famous definition: "Those who asserted the primacy of spirit to nature ... comprised the camp of idealism. The others, who regarded nature as primary, belong to the various schools of materialism."[3] Vladimir Lenin puts it roughly the same way in "Materialism and Empirio-Criticism": materialism is the "recognition of the objective reality of the external world and the laws of external nature"; the "necessity of nature is primary, while human will and consciousness is secondary."[4]

That a doctrine confessing the maternity and primacy of nature should be called "materialism" is hardly accidental. "Mother" (in Russian, *mat'*) and "matter" (*materiia*) share an etymology not just in Russian but in Latin as well, as attested in Lucretius's long philosophical poem *On the Nature of Things*. (The Latin *materia* most likely comes from *mater*, "mother," "source," "origin.") Matter is the maternal, generative element of being, while God is the masculine and paternal. The initial basis of such a concept is the ancient cult of the earth as the maternal element and the sun as the paternal: as if the sun's rays, bearing a current of energy, impregnate the earth's womb, which all vegetable life sprouts from. V. N. Toporov reminds us of materialism's mythopoetic subtext: "The connection between matter and mother noted by Plato responds to a profound reality of the mythopoetic consciousness that is frequently reflected both in language and in mythical images proper. Suffice it to recall the classic example: the Latin *materia*

---

3 Engels, *Ludwig Feuerbach and the Outcome of German Classical Philosophy*, 21.
4 Lenin, *Sochineniia*, 14:176–77.

('matter') etc. and *mater* ('mother'; cf. also *matrix*). The Slavic data is equally convincing. ... To a certain degree, the relationship between Moist Mother Earth [*mat'-syraia zemlia*] and the Sky-Father (among Slavs and in many other traditions) may be seen as a remote source of the Platonic relationship between matter ('mother') and idea/form ('father')."[5]

Thus it is not just the root of the word "materialism" but the very essence of this concept that expresses a veneration of the maternal in the image of nature as bringing all that lives into the world. Russian thought, moreover, even religious thought, particularly asserts the specifically material-cosmic nature of creation. In Losev's definition, "Russian philosophy is first and foremost sharply and unconditionally *ontological*. ... This ontologism, however, unlike in the West, accentuates matter, something characteristic of it since mystical antiquity. The very idea of divinity as it developed in the Russian Church foregrounds elements of corporeality (e.g., the doctrine of "Sophia," the "wisdom of God"), which P. Florensky sees as particular to Russian as opposed to Byzantine Orthodoxy.... In his investigation of the origins of Christianity, Vladimir Solov'ev refers to 'religious materialism,' the 'idea of holy corporeality.'"[6]

The religious attitude toward corporeality is seen also in Russian sophiology, the doctrine of the sacredness of the flesh and the feminine principle of creation, of wisdom as God's female companion, who has been with him as an artist and "helpmeet" since the world was made. But in twentieth-century Russia, sophiology as the veneration of immaculate, virginal, chaste femininity was vanquished by Marxist-Leninist materialism, which made every effort to counter the paternal and heavenly-spiritual principle of creation with the material-maternal.

c. Militant Atheism and the Oedipus Complex

The Leninist model of materialism is a fully conscious and consistent negation of God, that is, in mythological terms, a refusal to venerate the paternal principle, and a favoring of the maternal in its stead.

---

5 Toporov, *Issledovaniia po etimologii i semantike*, 1:62.
6 Losev, "Osnovnye osobennosti russkoi filosofii," 509.

This "militant materialism" is so bound up with "scientific atheism," to use Lenin's terms, that any religion is declared to be necrophilia. As Lenin wrote, outraged by Gorky's concessions to god-building: "Any godlet [*bozhen'ka*] means necrophilia;[7] it could be the purest little godlet you please, the most ideal, not one that is sought out, but 'built'—it doesn't matter."[8] Any alert psychoanalyst would see such militant materialism, with its opprobrium for the "godlet," as a manifestation of the Oedipus complex.

Of primary significance is Lenin's desire to engage in some mocking baby-talk, dubbing God a "godlet," turning him from a Father into a little kid, and thereby ridding himself of a rival in the love-struggle for the mother. Thus does a child fantasize about changing places with his father. It is instructive to juxtapose two of Lenin's neologisms in which the diminutive suffix *-en'k* and the augmentative suffix *-ishche* appear antonymous not just grammatically but in terms of worldview: on the one hand, the derisive "godlet" (*bozhen'ka*), on the other, the somewhat crude, awestruck *chelovechishche*. "What a great big full-blown man!" (*Kakoi materyi chelovechishche!*)—Lenin's famous characterization of Lev Tolstoy, cited in Gorky's essay "V. I. Lenin," is frequently quoted as an example of Lenin's "active" or "militant" humanism. The inclusion of the epithet *materyi* ("adult," "full-grown"), which derives from the root *mat'* ("mother") and signifies the highest degree of sexual maturity, also points to the psychoanalytic subtext of Leninist materialism. In the competition for the mother, the son imagines himself a "great big full-blown man," and the father, an impotent "godlet."

As partnered with atheism, materialism is nothing other than a subconscious projection of the Oedipus complex, only elevated to the level of a "philosophical doctrine"—the son's urge to take the mother away from the Father, having killed him or declared him dead, which is why loving such a father is "necrophilia." Indeed, in a single phrase,

---

7 Lenin uses *trupolozhestvo*, a term more imagistic (hence cruder) than the more clinical-sounding *nekrofiliia*—trans.
8 Lenin to Gorky, 13 or 14 November 1913. Marx, Engels, and Lenin, *O religii*, 242. Lenin refers to "god-seeking" and "god-building," various trends of non-traditional religious consciousness in prerevolutionary Russia.

Lenin demonstrates two sorts of reprisals to be taken against the Father: turning him into a child, and turning him into a corpse. Such is the aspiration of the "great big full-blown man" who rebels against the Father so that he might take possession of Mother Nature for himself.

The Oedipus complex is not limited solely to the framework of individual-family relations, as Freud indicates:

> The endeavour of the son to put himself in place of the father god appeared with greater and greater distinctness. With the introduction of agriculture the importance of the son in the patriarchal family increased. He was emboldened to give new expression to his incestuous libido which found symbolic satisfaction in laboring over mother earth.[9]

The cult of matter, or of the mother-earthly principle as opposed to the heavenly-fatherly one—this is in essence not even a philosophy but a mythology, in which subconscious desires come to light and are realized in the form of collective fantasies. But the psychoanalytic interpretation of materialism does not stop there: it also explains a paradox that cannot be explained from the standpoint of Marxism itself. Why did a consistently materialistic interpretation of nature and history lead to such unprecedented human violence thereupon? The primacy of matter would seem to have been proclaimed, but so much contempt did the "planned economy" and "ideological approach" evince for the laws of matter that matter itself began to diminish and disintegrate. Fields ceased to be fertile; the shelves of grocery stores went empty. Pasternak in *Doctor Zhivago* describes the winter of 1917–18, which saw the first glaring appearance of the revolution's tendency to devour reality itself, leaving ideas in its stead: "They had to prepare for the cold, stock up on food, firewood. *But in the days of the triumph of materialism, matter turned into a concept*, food and firewood were replaced by the provision and fuel question" (emphasis mine).[10]

---

9 Freud, *Totem and Taboo*, 196.
10 Pasternak, *Doctor Zhivago*, 162–63.

And so it continued till the very end of the Soviet period: in 1982, the year Leonid Brezhnev died, and at the very height of "developed socialism," a country that was incapable of feeding itself adopted a state-sponsored "Provision Program."

Psychoanalysis explains this precisely via the logic of the Oedipus complex: after all, the son desires to kill the father, not at all as some theoretical annunciation of his unisexual origin from his mother, but in order to possess her. Thus materialism-atheism does not get rid of God the Father for the sake of Mother Nature's triumph but for the sake of triumphing over her. The son becomes master and spouse—such is the incestuous implication of materialist civilization.

Of course, it is no secret to medical science and genetics what sort of fruit is born of the union of mother and son. The innumerable pathologies to be found in this clinic of materialist civilization include pathoeconomics, pathosociology, pathopedagogy, pathoaesthetics, patholinguistics, etc. Violence against one's native nature, the desolation of her life-giving womb... Constant miscarriages, crops ruined where they stand due to negligence, the ravaging of rich underground deposits. Violence against one's own people, their segregation into classes so as to sic them on one another. The destruction of the memory of the Father, of the memory of that fecund, peacemaking love of Spirit and the earth that is expressed in the very concept of "peasantry"—a union of Christian faith with the activity of working the land. (The Russian *krestianin*, "peasant," derives from *khristianin*, "a Christian.") Violence against language, its use as a bayonet for the class offensive: words mechanistically composed from stumps and particles: "Komsomol," "kolkhoz," "partkom"... Such are the consequences of this epoch-making incest.

Perhaps the only solid monument left by this epoch of militant materialism will be the underground palaces of the metro—the Metropolitan [*Metropoliten*], to use its full Russian title, which one is tempted to call our *Matro*polis, the city of the Mother. It was precisely in the mid-1930s, when the mass godlessness campaign was at its peak, and temples to the Heavenly Father were being destroyed all over the country, that new, upside-down temples began to be erected in their stead, like some revelation of materialism's conquest. Asserting the triumph of Earth power, they were constructed of the finest underground rock in the womb of the earth herself. There was nothing of the kind in Western countries, where the metro was simply a means of transportation. The new mission of the underworld was proclaimed at the opening of the Moscow metro in 1935 by L. M. Kaganovich, who had presided over its construction and in whose honor it was named. "The Moscow metro goes far beyond the usual conception of a technical installation. Our metro symbolizes the new socialist society that is being constructed. ... The delegates of the Congress of Councils and Congress of Kolkhoz Workers have thus seen the metro, as they descend below the earth into its stations, as the embodiment of their own immediate future, ... the embodiment of their strength, their power" (Kaganovich, "The Victory of the Metro is the Victory of Socialism").[11]

Underground palaces were built in the USSR not simply to be used for transportation but also for the sake of "transcendent" beauty. These were sanctuaries or temples to the new faith, complete with their own icons and frescoes depicting events from sacred Soviet history. Sublime leaders surrounded by the reverent masses; stern men and women, workers and peasants, armed and ready to defend the gains of the revolution; representatives of all nations feasting at a common table set with Georgian wine, Moldavian apples, Ukrainian cherries, and other fruits of fraternal friendship and abundance. Such are the icons and frescoes of the new materialist faith that consecrate the womb of the earth.

The destruction of the fatherly temples and the creation of maternal ones was essentially a single process, at least insofar as slabs of stone removed from demolished churches were used to build the upside-down churches of the underworld. In particular, a considerable part of the

---

11 "Pobeda metropolitena—pobeda sotsializma." Available electronically: http://www.metro.ru/library/kak_my_stroili_metro/105/. According to the sculptor A. Burganov, author of several compositions on stations of the Moscow metro: "The country had not yet cooled down from the devastations of revolution and war, but suddenly we were in a rush to get underground so as to put all our strength into building fantastic palaces under the earth. For us, the metro was never a means of transportation; it was a new religion, into which we directed the raging energy of the people" (Burganov, "Derev'ia v skolz'iashchem potoke sveta").

Revolution Square station (the firstborn of the Matropolis) was constructed of stone taken from the Danilov monastery upon its dismantling.

d. The Call of the Underworld: The Erotics of the Worker's Blow

In his book *Poetry of the Worker's Blow* (*Poeziia rabochego udara*, 1918), the proletarian poet and thinker Aleksei Gastev had already prophesied this new turn of civilization from the heavenly to the subterranean. Here is a passage from a chapter characteristically titled "We Have Encroached" ("My posiagnuli"):

> We won't strain toward those pathetic heights known as the sky. The sky is a creation of idle, lay-about, lazy and timid people.
> We will dash below!
> Away we will go, we will burrow into the depths, we will pierce them with a thousand lines of steel. ... For long years we will go away from the sky, from the sun, from the twinkling of stars, and pour into the earth: she into us, and we in her.
> We will go into the earth by thousands, we will go in by millions, we will pour in as an ocean of people! And from there we will not come back, we will never come back. ... There we will perish and bury ourselves in the insatiable rush and the laboring blow.
> Born of the earth, we will return to her, as was said of old; but the earth will be transformed. ... When she can bear no more and rends her steel armor, in an ecstasy of labor's outburst, she will birth new beings, whose name will no longer be man.[12]

Such is the frenzied erotics of labor: man's penetration of the womb that birthed him. "Born of the earth, we will return to her"—this is the formula of Oedipal desire. The passage is technically about labor, but Gastev's whole vocabulary is pregnant with openly erotic metaphors that recall images of sexual intercourse in such candid authors

---

12 Gastev, *Poeziia rabochego udara*, 139–40. Most of this passage is quoted from the translation of Anesa Miller-Pogacar.

as Gastev's contemporaries D. H. Lawrence and Henry Miller: "We will burrow into the depths, we will pierce them ... we will lay bare the chasms ... in an outburst of ecstasy." Materialism, with its disgust for the sky and frenzied love of the earth, reveals here its incestuous underside.[13]

Images of labor in "proletarian" literature are generally suffused with a highly specific eroticism, one rendered all the more piquant because in the naïve consciousness of these authors and their characters, it is entirely repressed by the heroic pathos of struggle and creation. This peculiar combination of conscious heroics and latent eroticism may be named using the centaur-word "eroics" (heroics + erotics). It is heard full-force in the classic socialist-realist Boris Gorbatov, who hymns the labor of mining. Here is a description of the work of the coal miner Viktor Abrosimov, one of the main characters of Gorbatov's novel *Donbass* and the unfinished novel *Before the War* (*Pered voinoi*):

> He got down on his knees before the wall of coal and switched on his hammer. *A familiar tremor of joy rolled over his hands and then through his whole body.* ... And maybe it was because the air in the hammer was *good, supple, and strong*; maybe because *his dream had come true*, and the whole coal face *lay submissively before him*—there was room for a miner *to really let himself go*—and ... was enticing him, luring him; but suddenly Viktor Abrosimov felt *his muscles fill with a daring, hitherto unknown force; his heart was consumed with bold courage, and he believed that he would be able to do everything, to overcome everything, and to achieve everything this night.*[14] (Emphasis mine)

---

13 For more on the connection between labor and eros in Soviet civilization, see my essay "Blud truda"; an English-language version, "Labor of Lust: Erotic Metaphors of Soviet Civilization," may be found in *After the Future: The Paradoxes of Postmodernism and Contemporary Russian Culture*, 164–87.

14 Cited from Brovman, *Trud. Geroi. Literatura: Ocherki i razmyshleniia o russkoi sovetskoi khudozhestvennoi proze*, 146. In discussing this scene, the critic goes on portraying the very same naiveté: "The reader cannot help feeling a sensation of involvement in Viktor's labor, so vivid and physically palpable is this description" (ibid). "Physically palpable," indeed.

One gets the impression that the author copied this scene from a pulp novel or some passionate "decadence" of the early twentieth century, changed *deva* ("maiden") to *lava* ("coal face or panel," "longwall") and the male hammer to a mechanical-pneumatic one, and passed off this quasi-porn as a tempestuous scene of inspired labor. As with Gastev, Gorbatov's "poetry of the worker's blow" is aimed at the depths of Mother Earth, where under cover of eternal night a son may celebrate the rite of taking possession of his progenitrix: "he would be able to do everything, to overcome everything, and to achieve everything this night."

In general, the miner is the most archetypal, the most glorified figure in the Soviet ideological pantheon. Why did these "children" and "sovereigns" of the underworld so stir the communist imagination? Couldn't it be because they were the first to overthrow the Heavenly Father, the sun-tyrant—and settle themselves deep in the womb of Mother Nature? One of the first and strongest revolutionary unions was organized, after all, by the "Carbonari"—members of a secret society of "coal diggers" that had its own complex hierarchy and symbolism (probably an offshoot of the Freemasons). In particular, they made a ritual of burning charcoal (hence their name). The Soviet cult of the miner harks back to this revolutionary caste of the Carbonari, the "black bones" (*chernaia kost'*) or commoners who threw down the gauntlet to the "white bones" and blue blood of aristocrats, the sons of light and air.[15]

"Labor and only labor makes a person great!" The main proclaimer of this Soviet maxim, Gorky, is considered to have been the first, already at the dawn of the twentieth century, to introduce the proletarian hero into literature, in the figure of the worker Nil in the drama *The Petty Bourgeoisie* (*Meshchane*, also translated as *The Philistines*; 1901). What does work mean for Nil? This is expressed in the scene between Nil and Tat'iana Bessemenova, who is in love with him and who is trying in vain to hasten the development of their relationship:

Tat'iana: You don't pay enough attention.
Nil: To what?

---

15 On the mythology of the miner's underworld, see my "Podzemnye khramy i ugol'nyi vek" ("Underground Temples and the Age of Coal").

Tat′iana: To people... To me, for instance.
Nil: To you?... Well...
[Tat′iana makes a move toward him.]
Nil [not noticing]: You know, I really love forging. In front of you there's this red, shapeless mass, angry and burning... It's such a pleasure to beat it with a hammer... It's alive, supple. And smashing away at it with strong blows, you make it into whatever you need.
Tat′iana: You have to be strong for that.
Nil: And skillful.[16]

We are faced once again with the poetry of the "worker's blow" full-force: the "eroics" of the hammer, which is even imprinted on the Soviet coat of arms. In general, the smith is the second-most important figure in the pantheon after the miner, apparently because he too is armed with a hammer and deals with the deposits of the earth; he has a direct connection with the earth through his iron. Did Gorky realize how comically ambiguous is this love scene that is simultaneously a loveless one, or rather, a scene of another, fetishistic form of love? Is the author himself making fun of Nil, or unconsciously prompting the reader to do so? Or perhaps this bold substitution is exactly what Gorky admires about Nil: "beating this red, shapeless mass with a hammer," when this is precisely what a woman wants from him... The meaning of the "worker's credo" that Nil gives in response to Tat′iana's love-call is as clear as an "I'm in love with someone else": he is the passionate hammersmith of another flesh, an iron one; his pleasure lies in the use of a *different* hammer to beat a red-hot mass.

On the one hand, this is asceticism, a renunciation of fleshly pleasure; on the other, it is a new eroticism, where the coal- and ore-flesh of Mother Nature has a stronger attraction than the flesh of a woman. Osip Mandel′shtam sums up this new fire raging in the blood of a whole epoch in a single line: "There's a lechery of labor [*blud truda*], and it's gotten in our blood."[17] "Lechery of labor," because all sons have

---

16 Gor′kii, *Sobranie sochinenii v vos′mi tomakh*, 8:32.
17 From Mandel′shtam's poem "Midnight in Moscow. A luxuriantly Buddhist summer" ("Polnoch′ v Moskve. Roskoshno buddiiskoe leto," 1931); this rendering cited from Cavanagh, *Osip Mandelstam and the Modernist Creation of Tradition*, 239.

the same Mother Earth and, penetrating her, they share a common womb. *Homo Sovieticus* is a hard worker, he labors readily, and a lot, but his love of labor seems rushed, promiscuous, incestuous. In this ardent passion for labor there is something sneakily desperate and almost perverse. Hence the "genetic" degeneration of the products of labor, which may be surmised from the traces of ubiquitous deformity on the faces of cities and villages, from the ruts and potholes on the body of the worn-out earth, whose son takes by force what she does not wish to give him.

It is interesting to compare this "eroics" of socialist labor with Gogol's eroticism-patriotism complex (see in part 1, "The Motherland-Witch: The Irony of Style and Nikolai Gogol"). Gogol has the aerial-acoustic erotics of the open expanse, which is pierced by Chichikov's troika; love-longing is diffused in the air, in song and sound, and is connected with the sensation of flight or fast riding (we might also recall the blacksmith Vakula, who flies aboard a devil, as does Khoma aboard a young witch). The erotics of socialist realism is aimed not at the expanses of the air but the strata of the earth, at burning-hot coal or tempered steel; it is incarnate not in flight but in extracting coal or forging iron, i.e., once again, focused on the maternal body of the earth.

We find the erotic-patriotic theme taking a new turn in Vladimir Sorokin's novel *Blue Lard* (*Goluboe salo*, 1999), which deals with the sect of the "earth-fuckers" (*zemleeby*). Constituting a mystical satire on "ero-to-patriots," these are lovers and *lovers* of their native land, who literally fornicate with it, that is, penetrate it not with plow or pickaxe or hammer but their own manhood: "The black earth of Chernigov and the clays of Polesie. ... six times a day did I release my semen therein, with tears of grace and an inconsolable whooping, and upon getting up, I kissed the sites of copulation with a heartfelt wailing, for so sweet and fuckable are those lands, to the point of a spiritual heartburn." "Our Land is neither soft nor crumbly; she is stern, cold, and rocky, and she will not allow just any man's dick into her. Thus have remained so few of us, while the weak-dicked have fled to the warm lands that are accessible to all. Our Land may be rocky, but is strong in love: whosoever's dick she allows inside her is replete with her love forever."[18] Here we clearly see the difference between Soviet eroto-communists and post-Soviet eroto-patriots: the former had sought to penetrate deep into the womb of the earth, to excavate foundation pits in her and build underground metro-palaces. The latter squirm along her surface, hurriedly exhausting themselves, lacking the hardness to penetrate her or fill her from within. At the same time, it is apparent that the communist experience has left its trace on this new, post-Soviet cohort of "earth-copulators." Nothing remains in them of Gogol's aerial erotics, which even in its demonic incarnations is aimed at the open expanse receding into the heavenly heights. The erotics of the new mother/matter-worshippers is directed entirely toward the earth, and toward its most palpable layer at that, the part of it nearest the surface, without any attempt to drill through, to dig, to pave the way to the womb of the underworld.

e. Materialism as Rooted in *Mat* (Mother-Based Profanity)

Viewed as a philosophical-political mythology, materialism is self-conceived in the soil of any national culture, from its most ancient pagan strata. Once more do we wonder: was Russian society really saddled with materialist ideas from without? Whence did they come to Russia? From German chemists and physiologists, the "vulgar" materialists Karl Vogt, Ludwig Büchner, and Jacob Moleschott by way of Chernyshevsky and Pisarev? From the German founders of dialectical materialism, Marx and Engels, by way of Plekhanov and Lenin? Or may materialism's roots be found, rather, in the vehement profanity itself with which the founder of the Soviet state cussed out all the German professors, practically inviting them to go fornicate with their own mothers? Couldn't this whole grandiose materialist idea, which was given three cheers by Russian society's lower classes after October, be traced to the favorite expression of these lower classes, to that almost automatic invective that bursts forth—in season and out, apposite or no—as a way to express one's worldview?

---

18 Sorokin, *Goluboe salo*, 153, 154.

If matter is Mother Nature, then the profanity of *mat* or *matershchina*[19] is tantamount to depriving the mother of her lawful and only spouse, the Father, and turning her into a whore. The basic formula of this profanity ("fuck your mother") may signify, among its various historically changing meanings, commanding a son to enter the womb of his own mother. According to Boris Uspensky, there are three main cussword variants that differ by verb form: the first- and third-person singular (*eb*, "fuck"); the imperative (*ebi*, "go fuck"); and the infinitive (*eti*, "to fuck"). Our interpretation of *mat* as an incestuous curse relates to the imperative and to some extent the infinitive. In his research on Russian obscenities, Uspensky demonstrates that the primary expression of profanity/*mat* is connected to the "myth of the sacral marriage of Heaven and Earth, the marriage that results in the fertilization of the Earth. At this level, the *mat*-expression's subject must be understood as the Sky God or Thunderer, and its object as Mother Earth."[20] According to Uspensky, the transition of the *mat*-expression to the category of blasphemous invective suggests a role-reversal: the Sky Father or Thunderer is replaced by his adversary, the dog, who becomes the subject of the action expressed by the verb "fuck." In the subsequent historical evolution of *mat*, Mother Earth is replaced by the mother of one's interlocutor, and her cohabitant is now the speaker himself, or, as hinted by the grammar of the imperative, the interlocutor, who is being told to go to his own mother's womb. This is corroborated in the folkloric legend Uspensky cites on the origin of swearing, which is connected here to incest: "Every person has three mothers: one's own mother, and two great mothers: the mother who is the moist earth and the Holy Virgin Mother of God. The devil confused a certain man, who as a result murdered his own father and married his own mother. Ever since then, people have used swear words, mentioning in their profanity the name of the mother; ever since, this degeneracy has spread throughout the land."[21]

---

19 These words may signify "profanity" in general; but they specifically connote the sort involving use of the word "mother"—trans.
20 Uspenskii, "Mifologicheskii aspekt russkoi ekspressivnoi frazeologii," 103.
21 Ibid., 68. It should be specified that Uspensky himself does not see incestuous motifs as central to profane expressions.

As is well known, profanity is highly characteristic of the Russian language, and defines the speech behavior and way of thinking of nearly the majority of speakers. A custom had existed in old Rus that in the early eighteenth century Ivan Pososhkov described in an outraged epistle to Metropolitan Stefan Iavorsky: teaching an infant practically still in its swaddling-clothes how to swear. Parents themselves taught their offspring to *bliakat'*, i.e., to use profanity, specifically by calling someone *bliad'*, a "whore": "mama shit mama whore whore" (*mama, kaka mama blia blia*), and as the child's speech developed, he would receive a complete course in cussing. "Among our people, an insane custom is being observed. Though I have not been to other countries, even so I would not expect to find such foul customs anywhere. Is this not a crazy business when, even before an infant has learned how to ask for food, parents are giving him his first training in profanity and concomitant sin?... When the infant begins to swear using the word 'whore,' the father and mother are delighted, and make the infant call them whores, and call strangers whores, and so on without cease. ... You can hear it throughout our country—on the roads, in the marketplace, at meals, and especially ... in churches—all manner of profanity and blasphemy and all sorts of obscene ranting."[22]

Of course, there's a great distance between this language that parents teach infants to use toward themselves and others and, on the other hand, profane notions of a matter-mother that may be ravished by her sons; but this interval is nevertheless psychologically easy to traverse. Dmitrii Pisarev expressed the conviction that "[n]o philosophy in the world takes root in the Russian mind so firmly and so easily as modern healthy and fresh materialism."[23] And indeed, materialism caught on in Russia with uncommon ease—but hardly because Russia was particularly disposed toward the scientific or scientistic "Bazarovian" materialism this ideologue of the "thinking proletariat" had such hopes for. Materialism corresponded to the intuitions of that archaism of the soil, that pagan chthonism that had lasted longer in agrarian Russia than in other European cultures.

---

22 Sreznevskii, *Sborniki pisem I. T. Pososhkova k mitropolitu Stefanu Iavorskomu*, 11–14.
23 Cited from Losev, *Filosofiia. Mifologiia. Kul'tura*, 509.

The mother-based profanity of *mat* is a worldview in itself, an elemental mass materialism in which the cult of the mother, combined with hostility toward the heavenly Thunderer-Father, becomes its own opposite, a blasphemy against the mother. As Uspensky observes: "In Slavic paganism, the cult of the Moist Mother Earth is directly connected with the cult of the enemy of the Thunder God."[24] In other words, the cults of Mother Earth and of her "whelp," the dog, develop in parallel, supplanting the cult of her heavenly husband. Profanity is a verbal expression of the conviction that the Father does not exist; there is only matter, and she is to be fertilized by her sons. Profanity is not just the underside but the unofficial essence of materialism. The first step toward materialism is the glorification of the mother over the Father ("matter is primary"), the second is the total denial of the Father ("there is no God"), and the third is the mother's belonging to her son as a husband ("fuck your mother"). Thus does materialism come round to swearing.

Seeking out the historical roots of Bolshevism, the philosopher and theologian Sergei Bulgakov found them unexpectedly in the Russian people's ambivalent attitude toward Mother Nature, toward Mother Earth. On the one hand, the earth is revered and deified in the pagan manner; on the other, through the magic of mother-based profanity, she becomes the object of violence perpetrated by her own son.

> If we look for the roots of the revolution in the past, then they are quite apparent: Bolshevism was born of *mat* swearing [*maternaia rugan'*], in fact it is essentially the desecration of all manner of motherhood, in the ecclesiastical and historical senses. Words are a force to be reckoned with; they have a mystical, even incantation-like power. And one shudders to think what dark cloud has come to hang over Russia—there it is, the people's Smerdiakovism![25]

In Russian, *mat*, or "telling someone to fuck off with reference to his own mother," has the same root as *mat'* ("mother") and *materiia*

---

24 Uspenskii, "Mifologicheskii aspekt russkoi ekspressivnoi frazeologii," 73.
25 Bulgakov, "Na piru bogov," 594.

("matter"), and the transitive verb *materit'* ("to cuss someone out using the word 'mother'") corresponds to the intransitive *materet'* ("to mature" or "grow to full size"). It is no accident that all these meanings are closely bound up with one another in the language. They come from the same complex of incest, although as civilization develops, these meanings diverge along different levels, from the obscene to the scientistic. But their connection may at times be observed in puns, which express how "jokes are related to the unconscious" (to use the title of Freud's work). In the late 1920s and early 1930s, a pun was making the rounds among the more ironic members of the Soviet intellectual elite: the Party higher-ups adore dialectical materialism (*dialekticheskii materializm*), whereas the masses prefer the *mat* dialect (*maternyi dialekt*). If you think about it, this joke implies not a contrast between materialism and profanity (*materializm, matershchina*) but their unexpected convergence. In the way they treat mother-matter, the Party and the people are indeed united, and that which is expressed in the language of philosophy as "believing in the primacy of matter" is the same thing as, in the lower-class vernacular, telling someone to fuck off with reference to his own mother.

Society's lower classes, especially criminal underworld elements, to a certain extent constitute a sediment of the most ancient formations, a remembrance of prehistory, its first layer, and the least affected by civilization. Is this not the source of the felon's strange attachment (more asserted than proven) to his own mother, despite being bereft of all the gains of humanity: his only intelligible motto, "I will never forget my dear mother!," goes hand in hand with his favorite incestuous greeting *mat' tvoiu* ("[fuck] your mother"). Is not the whole of Soviet materialism simply a scientistic dressing-up of *mat*, of the primal incest drive experienced by the infantile-primitive soul? At which point materialism reveals its essence as a *philosophical profanity* that has as much reverence for matter as a son who makes sexual use of his mother. The Party officially recognized common criminals as "socially proximate," as opposed to political prisoners, who were "enemies of the people"—is it surprising that such a party should have sworn and pledged allegiance to materialism?

f. Mother-Worshippers and Incestors

Marxism teaches that the coming communist society will represent a rebirth, at the highest technological level, of the classless structure of primordial communism. If this avant-garde/reactionary idea is taken seriously, then shouldn't we expect also a rebirth, in this new iteration of communism, of the ancient practice of incest, at least as the ideology of a direct marriage between Mother Nature and her human progeny?

It is well known that in the course of supplanting wildness, civilization imposes a ban on incest because that practice leads to the degeneration of offspring. The USSR would seem to be the first example of a civilization built on spiritual incest.

It is hardly accidental that the Bible of this new world was Gorky's novel *Mother* (*Mat'*). The father spends his days off making the rounds in taverns and starting fights. Wild and impetuous, he strikes fear into people, and will stand up to a crowd all by himself. But one day he raises his hand against his fourteen-year-old son.

> But Pavel grasped a heavy hammer, and said curtly:
> "Don't touch me."
> "What!" demand his father, bending over the tall, slim figure of his son like a shadow on a birch tree.
> "Enough!" said Pavel. "I am not going to give myself up any more."
> [A]nd he waved the hammer.[26]

Again, as in Gorky's *Petty Bourgeoisie* and Gorbatov's *Donbass*, we are faced with a *hammer*—the weapon of the proletariat. But while in those works, the hammer smashes into a panel of coal, a supple, red-hot mass, here is laid bare not just its erotic but its directly Oedipal meaning. Pavel threatens his father with a hammer, and the father, folding his "shaggy hands" (7) behind his back, is forced to yield to his son. To yield *the mother*.

---

26 Gorky, *Mother*, 7. Further citations in the text are to this translation.

Shortly after this he said to his wife:
"Don't ask me for money anymore. Pasha will feed you now."
"And you will drink up everything?" she ventured to ask.
"None of your business, you louse! I'll get myself a mistress."²⁷

And so Pavel has used his hammer to overpower his father, take his mother away from him, and push him to seek out a mistress as a replacement. This domestic tyrant of a father soon dies—thus does the author settle accounts with faith in the Father, so as to make room for the son next to the mother. Now *he* will provide her with food, fill her heart and mind with his convictions, and take the lead with her. The whole subsequent content of the novel, in spite of, or rather because of its revolutionary message, discloses the growing intimacy of a mother and her son.

Here they are left alone together, and what is this, if not a son's bold attempt to possess, and a mother's meek readiness to give herself up?

> She listened to him eagerly and awestruck. His eyes burned with a beautiful radiance.... "What joys did you know?" he asked. "What sort of a past can you recall?"... It was sweet to her to see that his blue eyes, always so serious and stern, now glowed with warmth, softly.... He took her hand and pressed it firmly in his. The word "mother" pronounced by him with feverish emphasis, and that clasp of the hand so new and strange, moved her.... And with a look of affectionate warmth, which seemed to embrace his firm, well-shaped body, she [spoke] hastily, and in a low voice." (16–18)

Here Maksim Gorky has produced a practically Turgenevian scene, complete with a "strange clasp" and "feverish emphasis," with a "he" and a "she" and an awkward passion flaring up between them. It's just more crude than in Turgenev, and more importantly, the "he" and "she" are a son and his mother. "It's magnificent—the mother and son side by side" (390), as Soviet citizens knew by rote from their school days, never sensing the

---

27 Ibid., 7, but the last sentence quoted here is absent from the translation; cited from Gor'kii, *Sobranie sochinenii v vos'mi tomakh*, 5:8.

strange overtones of these ecstatic words. And they'd written essays about how the mother was brimming with the thoughts and deeds of her son, how under the influence of Pavel, she straightened her posture, becoming younger in soul and body.

Gorky subsequently revealed the secret of his worldview. As often happens with erotically dangerous, "repressed" matters, this came in the form of a reference to another writer, the naturalist and Earth-seer Mikhail Prishvin, in whose writings he discovers and warmly approves the spirit of all-encompassing incest with Mother Nature.

> This sense of the earth as one's own flesh comes through to me with amazing clarity in your books, O husband and son of the great mother. Does this sound like incest? But after all, that's just what it is: man, born of the earth, makes her fruitful with his labor.[28]

What is subconsciously contained in the figure of Pavel Vlasov is here expressed outright: Pavel is the "husband and son of the great mother," which lends this figure an archetypal depth. Gorky realizes that what he is saying "sounds like incest," but insofar as in the 1930s this is already an archetype of a new civilization, the shamefulness of admitting this disappears; to the contrary, one is proud of man for fulfilling this role. Toil is here conceived not as a form of obedience to the Father, nor a curse as punishment for the original sin, but precisely as the poignant joy of copulation with Mother Nature.

Nor is it a coincidence that *Mother*, this "very necessary" book, as Lenin put it, was written right after the defeat of the first Russian revolution, in 1906–07—almost simultaneously with Lenin's treatise "Materialism and Empirio-Criticism" (1908), which tries to prove scientifically what *Mother* shows artistically: that matter is utterly independent of the heavenly father and any paternal principle, and an incomparably better fate awaits both Mother and Matter should they ally themselves with their revolutionary sons, the transformers of the heaven and the earth.

---

28 Gor'kii, "O M. M. Prishvine." (This article is written in the form of an open letter to the writer.)

It is curious to trace how Lenin's philosophical convictions are bound up with his predilections in the sphere of the glaringly gendered Russian language. He dismisses and ridicules masculine-gendered concepts like "God," "spirit," "sign," "symbol," and "hieroglyph," declaring them to be imaginary or at best secondary, while investing his philosophical hopes invariably in words of feminine gender: "matter," "reality," "truth," "given" (*dannost'*), "nature." Moreover, for Lenin nature is of course not simply a wife or fiancée, a man's "intended," but precisely the mother who gives him life. He devotes a whole polemical chapter to this—"Did Nature Exist Before Man?"—where this mother/matter-worshipper fulminates against those empirio-monists who held that the "central member" (to use Avenarius's term), i.e., the human subject, man, has a merely conjugal relationship with the reality around him. These theoreticians proceeded from the conception of a "principal coordination," which posits a correlation between man and the environment he perceives with his senses, a mutual determinability of their characteristics; whereas Lenin insists that man is begotten of this environment, and only then enters into relations with it. Hence the famous formulation by which matter is rendered unto man: "Matter is a philosophical category denoting the objective reality that is given to man via his senses."[29] In all these feminine-gendered words[30] we hear the rustling of a "grammatical skirt."

Thus, in the grim years of "reaction," i.e., the defeat of the sons by the father-tsar, the Oedipal philosophy was being vengefully laid in the foundation of the postrevolutionary future. The subsequent development of this complex may be seen in the famous words of the agronomist I. V. Michurin, who specialized in the cross-breeding of plants and became an icon of Soviet militant-materialist ideology: "We cannot await favors from nature, our task is to take them from her."[31] To take from Mother Nature those favors she herself is hardly disposed to grant us...

---

29 Lenin, *Sochineniia*, 14:17.
30 The Russian nouns *materiia*, *kategoriia*, and *real'nost'* are feminine, and feminine adjectival forms are used to agree with the latter two here—trans.
31 Michurin, *Itogi shestidesiatiletnikh rabot po vyvedeniiu novykh sortov plodovykh rastenii*, 11.

The abovementioned L. M. Kaganovich gives a dramatic picture of the resistance nature put up against the builders of the metro. Earth herself resisted the "earth-lovers'" impudent penetration of her womb, by which they hoped to deploy a "symbol of the new socialist society being built." "We struggled with nature, we struggled with Moscow's poor soil. Moscow's geology turned out to be prerevolutionary, an old-regime geology (laughter), it had no sympathy for the Bolsheviks, and was against us. You drill into what seems like dry rock, but suddenly it starts to tighten up and get inundated, and there's quicksand."[32] Once again the language of Soviet ideology reveals the underlying motivation of the "worker's blow." Madam Nature, an aristocrat by origin, resisted the Bolsheviks, but, venturesome sons that they were, they prevailed upon their "old-regime" mom ...

Instead of the fiery Prometheus that served as an allegory of the revolution for its Marxist prophets, we find a different, Freudian figure: blind Oedipus.

---

[32] Kaganovich, "Pobeda metropolitena—pobeda sotsializma."

PART IV

Being as Nothingness

1 | A Farewell to Objects, or, the Nabokovian in Nabokov

> My life is one big farewell to objects.
> Nabokov, "In Memory of L. I. Shigaev"[1]

> The living flesh is full of shadows or specters... But sweetest of all is to depart from them, remembering nothing.
> Ol'ga Sedakova, "In Memory of Nabokov."[2]

Three approaches to literature and art may be conventionally singled out: 1) the purely theoretical approach, which has to do with general terms like "genre," "composition," "plot," etc.; 2) the purely historical, focused on concrete individuals with proper names: Pushkin, Gogol, Tolstoy, Nabokov; 3) and lastly, the *aesthetic proper* approach, which takes proper names as its point of departure, removing them from the realm of the biographically specific and turning them into generalizing terms: the Pushkinian, Gogolian, Tolstoyan, Nabokovian... It is precisely this *unique-universal* quality that we love, intuiting and recognizing it in works of literature and art. Although these categories refer to individual qualities, they have general significance and cannot be reduced to their namesakes. The Pushkinian (*pushkinskoe*) is not identical to Pushkin; its meaning is broader and narrower at the same time. The phenomenon of Pushkin is broader than the Pushkinian because one can find in Pushkin something Derzhavinian or Zhukovskian. But the Pushkinian is also broader than Pushkin and can be found in Mandel'shtam or Nabokov.

---

1 Nabokov, *Sobranie sochinenii v chetyrekh tomakh*, 4:351.
2 https://rustih.ru/olga-sedakova-stansy-chetvertye-pamyati-nabokova/

These aesthetic categories derived from proper names have some advantage over general concepts when applied to concrete authors. The discrepancy between abstract concepts and individual works is an inevitable evil of literary studies; this gap between the theory and its subject, however, can be bridged using concepts immanent to authors' names. These intermediate categories, quasi-terms and quasi-names, do not impose a general concept on an author's creation but derive this concept from the uniqueness of his or her personality.

It is not my intention here to speak of Nabokov per se in some general literary terms. Rather I will regard the "Nabokovian" (*nabokovskoe*) as a principal category of Russian aesthetics and literary metaphysics. Nabokov is an individual; the Nabokovian is a unique concept that encompasses a multitude of phenomena. Along with the Pushkinian and the Gogolian, the Tolstoyan and the Dostoevskian, it possesses an enormous clarifying capacity.

Doesn't it seem to us at times that "the expanse of a free novel" and "the magical crystal" (*Eugene Onegin*) reveal the Nabokovian in Pushkin? Indeed, Pushkin, Turgenev, Bunin, Mandel'shtam, Andrei Bely, and Andrei Bitov—they all contain the Nabokovian. Nabokov himself, of course, does as well; or rather, more so than any other. For this reason, he is of special interest to those who love all that is Nabokovian in life and literature.

It is rare to find someone possessed of so many Nabokovian pearls as Nabokov himself, even in the most commonplace phrases where no claim is laid to any specific imagery. For example, consider the beginning of "Spring in Fialta" ("Vesna v Fial'te"), both the story and the collection: "Spring in Fialta is cloudy and dull."[3] What appears to be Nabokovian here, aside from the fact that this sentence has issued from Nabokov's pen? Don't you feel, however, a special pearly nuance of the Nabokovian spring and its charming autumnal sluggishness? The "violet" (*fioletovyi*) color of the very name Fialta in combination with the cloudiness—what a delicate gamut of silvery-pearly tones, a palely diffused light, that is reflected in the epithet "Fialta ... cloudy!" What about the wonderfully whimsical combination "spring ... dull"—this epithet weakens, as if by a soothing gesture,

---

3 Nabokov, *The Stories of Vladimir Nabokov*, 413.

the intense and almost sickly energy of spring that is strengthened by that very exotic name "Fialta"! But would the two epithets have arisen side by side if not for the assonance, like the crunching of footfalls in melting snow, of the suffix *chn*? *Vesna v Fial'te obla**chn**a i sku**chn**a*—you suddenly find yourself in a damp, transparent, Nabokovian springtime world, as one quality dissolves into the other: Fialta melts in a cloud, spring dissolves in boredom. Thus, this world is already filled with the pellucid presence of something *other*, for which there is no direct name.

If Nabokov were inclined to hymn this otherworld, we would be dealing with metaphysics, symbolism, and the reaping of words specifically comprehensible to you and me. But Nabokov's style is free of that strong bias of super-significance that unites the mystic and the ideologue, the symbolist and the socialist realist. His style invariably lays hold of a thing seemingly on the verge of presence; the thing leans in one direction or another, listing, almost disappearing, and finally emitting some sort of diffuse reflection.

In Russian, Nabokov (*na boku*) literally means "on its side," "leaning sideways" (perhaps the closest English approximation would be "Sideman"). The name itself seems to contain the formula of his style and conveys the magic of this bending, this slanting movement of all things: not straight but askew, like a ray of light at sunset. Thus, the sum of all Nabokovian works turns out to be the justification of this magical surname, which is the first and most important word uttered about the writer, pinpointing him, and setting the path for his own words.

The first word to significantly impress upon the consciousness of an individual is his or her own name. Should the individual grow to become a writer, all his artistic self-expression becomes a modification of this name, which is his way of assimilating the world, of "pushkinizing" or "nabokovizing" it. Thus we can understand:

the lightness of Pushkin (like "feather-fuzz [*pukh*] from Aeolus's lips";[4] a "light, cheery name," as Blok put it);

---

4 Pushkin, *Sobranie sochinenii v 10 tomakh*, 4:8.

the teasing-doubling of Gogol, with his mirror-magic and absurd self-repetition of his characters (Akaky Akakievich, Chichikov, and Bobchinsky/Dobchinsky);

the austerity of Nekrasov, who introduced the aesthetic of the nakedly prosaic—the "homely" (*nekrasivoe*) or unembellished (*nepriukrashennoe*)—to Russian poetry;

the hulking unwieldiness of Tolstoy ("fat," *tolstii*);

the overstated self-awareness of Dostoevsky's characters, so preoccupied with human dignity (*dostoinstvo*);

the melodious, lilting tone of Vladimir Solov'ev (the "nightingale," *solovei*);

the "encapsulated" restraint of Chekhov (*chekhol*, a "case" or "cover");

the bitter vagrancies illuminated by Maksim Peshkov-Gorky ("on foot," *peshkom*, and "bitter," *gor'kii*);

the evocative signaling of Maiakovsky (*maiak*, a "beacon" or "lighthouse");

and the wistful clarity of Esenin ("autumn," *osen'*; "clear," *iasnyi*).

Or let us recall "the hiss / Of foaming goblets and the pale-blue flame / Of punch" from *The Bronze Horseman*. The sound imagery of this phrase is often admired, but remarkable here is also the *name* imagery:

> Шипенье пенистых бокалов
> И пунша пламень голубой.

The name "Pushkin," the letter-combination *p-sh-n*, is inscribed in **shipen'e** ("hiss") and **punsh** ("punch"), and resounds in other words as well: **penistyi** ("foaming"), **plamen'** ("flame"), **goluboi** (*g* being the voiced equivalent of *k*; and *b* of *p*).

The feeling of a word starts to grow in a writer from the sound of his own name, which eventually turns into a system of stylistic means, enveloping the whole universe. The name is a super-word that reverberates in a host of other words; it leads to the renaming of things, which echo back such that the whole language resounds in harmony with the namer's name itself. A writer is precisely a master of names; he writes first and foremost "in his own name"; he enchants the world with this

A Farewell to Objects, or, the Nabokovian in Nabokov 207

magic sound. The writer's goal is to prove that the universe could be given his own name.[5]

Nabokov sharply formulated his principle of "side vision" in the novel *The Gift* (*Dar*). The protagonist Fedor Godunov-Cherdyntsev, Nabokov's *alter ego*, is a sophisticated aristocratic poet who writes a critical essay on Chernyshevsky, the father of Russian revolutionary realism. For him, Chernyshevsky is an example of a rectilinear, plebeian mind that neglects nuances and recognizes only the utilitarian view of things. A genuine artist, according to Nabokov, sees all things in a slanted perspective and in oblique cases:

> Like words, things also have their [grammatical] cases. Chernyshevski saw everything in the nominative. Actually, of course, any genuinely new trend is a knight's move, a change of shadows, a shift that displaces the mirror.[6]

Here I would cite several phrases from Nabokov's earlier stories that reveal something inevitably Nabokovian about them.

> Far away, in a watery vista between the jagged edges of pale bluish houses, which have tottered up from their knees to climb the slope.... ("Spring in Fialta")[7]

> Occasionally, in the middle of a conversation her name would be mentioned, and she would run down the steps of a chance sentence, without turning her head. ("Spring in Fialta")[8]

> And in the same way as the luminosity of the water and its every throb pass through a medusa, so everything traversed his inner being, and

---

5 We might propose an experiment to verify this hypothesis: counting up the frequency with which Pushkin uses the letters *p*, *sh*, *k*, and *n*, or Nabokov uses *n*, *b*, *k*, *v*; and compare with the average use in Russian as a whole. Such a check would probably not take much time using computers.
6 Nabokov, *The Gift*, 219.
7 Nabokov, *The Stories of Vladimir Nabokov*, 413.
8 Ibid., 424.

that sense of fluidity became transfigured into something like second sight. As he lay flat on his couch, he felt carried sideways by the flow of shadows and, simultaneously, he escorted distant foot-passengers, and visualized ... the sidewalk's surface right under his eyes (with the exhaustive accuracy of a dog's sight). ("Torpid Smoke" ["Tiazhelyi dym"])[9]

It would seem that all of this deals with different things—but the reader, the Nabokov lover, comprehends with a sixth sense the particular, always askance, "sidelong" Nabokovian vision of this world. Examples abound: a girl runs down the small stairs of a chance sentence, paintings shine obliquely, homes arduously arise from their knees, the tilt of a chair is seen through matted glass, and a person is borne sideways by the current of shadows.

To be sure, this bending is not always spatial; it can be visual, auditory, psychological, or situational—or just a routine case of displacement, when a thing is situated in a sideways plane. Such an item may be reflected in something; it may fall somewhere or cast its reflection and disappear unnoticeably, leaving only a shadow. Nabokov is masterfully consistent in this overlap of different projections of an object, and these projections generally reshuffle the object's existence, reducing the bulk of it to naught.

This tendency may be seen even in Nabokovian titles, which merit particular study themselves. *Bend Sinister* is an explicit example: the phrase signifies the reversal of an insignia on a coat of arms. "Torpid Smoke" or *Pale Fire*—the meaning of one word effaces the meaning of the other. The "smoke" is "torpid"; according to the word order in the title, it has already settled to the earth but then rises to the sky, producing two flowing currents above and below that keep it in the vacillating middle, or more precisely, moving sideways; this smoke has a waddling gait. These and other Nabokovian titles, such as *Laughter in the Dark* and *Camera Obscura*, are not oxymorons of the "burning snow" type, in which juxtapositions collide head-on; here there is no collision but rather a

---

9 Ibid., 397.

blending or a sidelong bend. The two signs, "pale" and "fire," do not initiate a juxtaposition but rather dilute one another. This is the same tilting that permeates all syntactical couplings and lexical links.

We grasp all this Nabokovism even in just a single sentence from "Torpid Smoke":

> Out of the depths of the adjacent parlor, separated from his room by sliding doors (through the blind, rippled glass of which was diffused the ripply shine of the lamp there, while lower down, there showed through, as if in deep water, the hazily dark slope of a chair placed thus due to the doors' inclination to slowly, shudderingly disperse), one could hear, from time to time, an indistinct, taciturn conversation.

> Из глубины соседней гостиной, отделенной от его комнаты раздвижными дверьми (сквозь слепое, зыбкое стекло которых горел рассыпанный по зыби блеск тамошней лампы, а пониже сквозил, как в глубокой воде, расплывчато-темный прислон стула, ставимого так ввиду поползновения дверей медленно, с содроганиями, разъезжаться), слышался по временам невнятный, малословный разговор.[10]

This sentence alone contains perhaps a dozen instances of self-erasure. The parentheses (after which it barely recovers) constitute a graphic equivalent of doors that slide in opposite directions. It is difficult to catch both ends of the sliding doors with outstretched arms, just as it is difficult to catch both ends of the sliding phrase with one's consciousness. This slipping from one's grasp is the characteristic trait of Nabokov.

The parlor in this description is separated by glass doors from the room where the narrator and main character are located.

The glass of the doors is "blind" (matted, apparently) and "rippled" (*zybkoe*); it does not let light through but casts it back.

The light from a lamp similarly spills forth and shines with a watery ripple.

---

10 Nabokov, *Sobranie sochinenii v chetyrekh tomakh*, 4:340.

A bit lower, to the side of this washed-out spot, the reflection of the chair shows through.

Not even of the chair but rather its particular leaning, its "slope," to the side, toward something else.

And this leaning is itself "hazily dark."

And it is reflected "as if in deep water."

And this chair stands in the way of the doors—something is always running into something else from the side, distorting the line of movement or vision.

And these doors themselves have a propensity to slide somewhere in different directions, to slip away from themselves.

And even the conversation itself, its sound carried from the parlor, is heard only for a while, and then "disperses" like the doors.

And this indistinct talk is itself vague and oblique, with an omission of meaning and words.

In this one sentence, there are so many deviations or peripheral distractions—perhaps the attentive reader will discover more—that they disclose a certain peculiarity of Nabokovian stylistic thinking. What does such a sentence add to the reader's perception of reality? It makes it feel unreal. Each thing is shunted to the side in a verbal dissolve, evanescing in something else; and the world, even as it is described in great detail, disappears in proportion to its description.

Each object manifests itself as a disappearance, as if on the verge of loss or death. Here I would cite the beginning of John Shade's poem from *Pale Fire*:

> I was the shadow of the waxwing slain
> By the false azure in the windowpane;
> I was the smudge of ashen fluff—and I
> Lived on, flew on, in the reflected sky.[11]

Nabokov's own stylistic peculiarities are condensed to some extent in the writing of his hero-poet. "I," the most immediate reality that

---

11 Nabokov, *Pale Fire*, 7.

A Farewell to Objects, or, the Nabokovian in Nabokov 211

I have, appears as a shadow cast by a dead bird, killed by the illusion of the mirror's lying azure. Reality reveals in itself a double or triple illusion that is capable of endless proliferation. What could be more weightless and phantasmal than fluff that is also akin to ash? But here only a smudge of this fluff is taken, a shadow of a shadow, the nonexistence of nonexistence. One could measure Nabokovian illusoriness by such strict ontological units as "one disappearance," "two disappearances," and so forth. Details do not add up to this world; rather, it is as if they were subtracted from it.

What remains? Nabokov himself answers: "an illusory perspective, a graphic mirage, captivating in its transparency and emptiness."[12] The morbid spirit of this mirage is not frightful—unlike in the case of Gogol, that great expert on "dead souls." Rather, its illusiveness is captivating. Gogolian detail is *underscored* by its absurdity, its protruding thingness, as with the famous wheel discussed separately from the carriage in the beginning of *Dead Souls*. Conversely, Nabokovian detail is *crossed out* with a swift, slanting gesture, upon which it turns into part of the mirage.[13] The Nabokovian style is a soft eraser, effacing the outlines of objects, so as to bring the substance of absent reality, or the blank paper on which the author works, into sharper resolution.

The last example is from "The Visit to the Museum" ("Poseshchenie muzeia"):

> [B]eyond were visible still other halls, with the oblique sheen of large paintings, full of storm clouds, among which floated the delicate idols of religious art in blue and pink vestments; and all this resolved itself in an abrupt turbulence of misty draperies.[14]

> [Д]алее открывались еще и еще залы, косо лоснились полотна широких картин, полные грозовых облаков, среди которых плавали в синих и розовых ризах нежные идолы религиозной

---

12 Nabokov, *Sobranie sochinenii v chetyrekh tomakh*, 4:340.
13 Epstein plays on *podcherknuta* ("underscored") vs. *perecherknuto* ("crossed out")—trans.
14 Nabokov, *The Stories of Vladimir Nabokov*, 283.

живописи, и все это разрешалось внезапным волнением туманных завес.[15]

The canvases in the museum have an "oblique sheen" or "shine slantwise" (*koso losniatsia*). The common component of both these words is *os'*, which in Russian means "axis" and is associated with "revolving." The entire artistic view is revolving around the objects' axis. While shining slantwise, the paintings are also full of "floating" storm-clouds; they are simultaneously washed out, that is, from within and from without, dissolving in the light of the cloudiness and in the luster they themselves reflect. The canvas's reality is itself lost in these two cross-reflections, and beyond it is revealed something more nebulous still, even by comparison with clouds—"delicate idols" "floating" in the delicate-hued raiment of "vestments."[16] Moreover, "all this resolved itself in an abrupt turbulence of misty draperies." This may not be Nabokov's best phrase, but it is perhaps one of the most Nabokovian. Each of the key words here signifies, in exemplary fashion, the same process of turbulent dissolution: "abrupt" is a distraction in time, "turbulence" in space, "misty" in lighting, and "draperies" is itself the substance of swaying; and all of these are different methods of designating the blurring and erasure of reality.

Tolstoy said that the most important thing in art is *chut'-chut'*, "the tiniest bit." Is it not because "the tiniest bit" is the essential object and spirit of Nabokov's creation that he is perceived as a model and mentor of pure artistry? His rare, unique flair in Russian literature extends to the very limit of this "tiniest bit." *Chut'-chut'* in Russian is the imperative mood of "feeling" (*chuiat'*). Thus it is the very will of the Russian language that we feel more deeply about what follows *chut'-chut'*: "a tiny bit" of a scent (*chut'-chut' zapakha*) means the imperative to have a keener sense of smell, and the same is implied by *chut'-chut'* of a breeze, *chut'-chut'* of the soul's presence in this world.

Nabokov's love for *chu't-chut'* led him to hate all great ideas and missions of art that were provoked by its alleged social, political, psychological,

---

15 Nabokov, *Sobranie sochinenii v chetyrekh tomakh*, 4:357.
16 Epstein plays on the shared etymology of *oblako* ("cloud") and *oblachenie* ("raiment")—trans.

and religious functions. Literature, for Nabokov, must not take too much upon itself, for its eternal love is what is small and meek, the fuzziness of the world, which loses one feature after another as they are crossed out by the flowing, slanted Nabokovian handwriting.

Nabokov is a genius of disappearances, not just a grandmaster, as John Updike called him in the well-known article "Grandmaster Nabokov," but a great master of the end-game. This determines his marvelous and irreplaceable affinity with Russian culture, which is chiefly a culture of the end, the insight into the final mystery and culmination of all things. Surfacing from these depths come the themes "Nabokov and Chaadaev," "Nabokov and Vladimir Solov'ev," "Nabokov and Berdiaev," "Nabokov and the Apocalypse," "Nabokov and Revolution."

As Chaadaev had occasion to lament, Russia has not often surprised the world with creative discoveries or positive newness. "Not a single useful thought has sprouted in the barren soil of our country, not a single great truth put forth from our midst."[17] Isn't this lack of "originality" a prerequisite for a different art—the art of dissolution and decomposition? Not knowing how to start, it is as if Russia had found her mission in the completion of all those beginnings that she had assimilated from abroad, from the "Varangians" to the "Greeks." Upon entering Russia, everything foreign will gradually diminish to nothing and bend into nonexistence, becoming phantasmal and empty. Nature herself attracts by her fading, "farewell" or valedictory beauty (*proshchal'naia krasa*)—these words of Pushkin's are quintessentially Nabokovian.

Any entity in Russia constitutes its own farewell: civilization is a farewell to civilization, freedom is a farewell to freedom, revolution a farewell to revolution, life a farewell to life. This does not mean that Russia is contrary to civilization or to life, functioning as their negation—that would imply that Russia has another fixed essence: "barbarity" or "death." Rather, Russia is a farewell to all these objects and essences that are seen long after they disappear into the Nabokovian darkling haze. This is an appropriate answer to those who consider Nabokov too Western, not Russian enough:

---

17   Chaadaev, *Sochineniia*, 32.

where else do things scatter irreversibly and illusively as they do in Russia, as she does herself?

The Nabokovian is the art of the farewell. Because of this, in the entire post-Soviet epoch, when Russia is not beginning anything new but is again and again saying goodbye to her past, Nabokov suggests essential words that translate the political and economic disembodiment of reality into the poetic dimension. "Everything was as it should be: grey tints, the sleep of substance, matter dematerialized" ("The Visit to the Museum").[18] For the Nabokovian hero, this endless museum, a collection of sleepy and increasingly phantasmal things, turns out to be his elusive native land, Russia.

---

18 Nabokov, *The Stories of Vladimir Nabokov*, 278.

2 | The Secret of Being and Nonbeing in Vladimir Nabokov[1]

According to the most widespread conceptions of the nature of being, God created the world out of nothing. Such is the worldview of Plato and the Neoplatonists and of Judeo-Christian and Muslim theology. But it remains the greatest mystery exactly how something may come from nothingness. As the philosopher Sergei Bulgakov remarks: "For what reason and why this emanation of the world takes place from the single Nothing, there can be no answer, and we will not find it in Plotinus's doctrine."[2]

In its creative daring, literature at times proposes the sort of solutions to cosmic mysteries that would never be ventured by theology, bound as it is by the dogmas of faith, nor by philosophy, which is subject to the supremacy of reason.

"The nothingness within everything" is one of the metaphysical leitmotifs of Vladimir Nabokov, who thus engages in a kind of dialogue not only with Western philosophy and theology but with the traditions of Buddhist thought, as well as concepts from modern cosmology.

a. The Chain of Negations. Omnipresent "Nonnons"

Nabokov comes closest to this theme in his final Russian-language work, the story "Ultima Thule."[3] The ancients conceived of Ultima Thule as

---

1 I would like to thank Prof. Gennady Barabtarlo for his profound comments and advice, which I found very useful in working on this chapter.
2 Bulgakov, *Unfading Light: Contemplations and Speculations*, 163.
3 To be more exact, "Ultima Thule" is the first of two chapters of Nabokov's unfinished novel *Solus Rex* (1939–40). The author writes in a preface to the subsequent English-language publication: "Perhaps, had I finished my book, readers would not have been left wondering about a few things: was Falter a quack? Was he a true seer? Was he a medium whom the narrator's dead wife might have been using to come through with the blurry outline of a phrase which her husband did or did not recognize?"

the edge of the world, a quasimythical island country in northernmost Europe. Metaphorically, it means the limit of all creation, beyond which humanity is vouchsafed no glimpse.

The story's main character, Falter, is an ordinary businessman who is suddenly struck by the solution to the riddle of all creation. Having experienced a revelation of something inconceivable, he lets loose a harrowing cry, and seems to lose all human feelings, will, and interest in existing. The psychiatrist who has come to treat his strange malady hears the gist of the revelation, and dies on the spot of heart failure.

What did Falter figure out? And, having learned his secret, would it be possible not just to remain alive but to preserve one's feelings of love, faith, and goodwill, and to be even more solidly affirmed therein?

If we follow the logic of the deliberately confused explanations that the story's narrator, the artist Sineusov, manages to elicit from Falter, then his revelation may be formulated thus: the world consists of a multitude of concrete things, and each of them may become a point of departure for understanding the whole. But at the point of arrival, this Everything turns into Nothingness. We live in a world that does not exist, just as we ourselves do not—which is precisely why it seems to exist to us.

Falter's insight pertains directly to nonbeing, as witness the parable with which he explains his revelation:

> In a country of honest men a yawl was moored at the shore, and it did not belong to anyone; but no one knew that it did not belong to anyone; and its assumed appurtenance to someone rendered it invisible to all. I happened to get into it.[4]

Here, reality—the yawl's belonging to someone—stands as merely a transitional moment between two negations: the yawl does not belong to

---

(Nabokov, *The Stories of Vladimir Nabokov*, 667–68). We will never know the answers to these questions. However, the fact that Nabokov published "Ultima Thule" as a standalone story (in 1942) entitles us to treat it as a finished work.

4 Nabokov, *The Stories of Vladimir Nabokov*, 514. Further citations in the text are to this edition.

The Secret of Being and Nonbeing in Vladimir Nabokov 217

anyone, and no one pays it any attention. Falter happens to get into this skiff of nonbeing, and so has solved the riddle of a dual negation.

Another of Falter's hints as to the secret revealed to him:

> If you are looking [for an object] under a chair or under the shadow of a chair, and the object cannot be in that place, because it happens to be somewhere else, then the question of there existing a chair or its shadow has nothing whatever to do with the game. To say that perhaps the chair exists but the object is not there is the same as saying that perhaps the object is there but the chair does not exist, which means that you end up again in the circle so dear to human thought. (517)

Both these parables, albeit aimed more at concealing than revealing a secret, follow a uniform logic. An object is defined through its absence, through the various forms of its nonbeing: its not belonging, not being seen, not being found. And even if the object does turn up, then this comes at the price of the disappearance of another object. We think it isn't where we were looking for it, whereas the place it was supposed to be located is itself absent. Both the "yawl" and the "object" are unrealities, defined only negatively, through that which they are "not." It is not even important what Falter says but rather how he prattles on, creating a picture of a universe consisting of iridescent voids, of "somewhere elses," where the things one needs allegedly migrate to—and where they are also impossible to find.

Such voids, non-phenomena formed by the negation of other phenomena, may be referred to using the Nabokovism "nonnon" (*netka*). In *Invitation to a Beheading* (*Priglashenie na kazn'*), Cincinnatus's mother Cecilia C. describes non-things that took on the appearance of real things when reflected in a non-mirror.

> [T]here were objects called "*nonnons*"... and, you see, a special mirror came with them, not just crooked, but completely distorted. You couldn't make out anything of it, it was all gaps and jumble, and made no sense to the eye—yet the crookedness was no ordinary one, but calculated in just such a way as to.... [Y]ou would have a crazy mirror like

that and a whole collection of different "*nonnons*," absolutely absurd objects, shapeless, mottled, pockmarked, knobby things, like some kind of fossils—but the mirror, which completely distorted ordinary objects, now, you see, got real food, that is, when you placed one of these incomprehensible, monstrous objects so that it was reflected in the incomprehensible, monstrous mirror, a marvelous thing happened: minus by minus equaled plus, everything was fine, and the shapeless speckledness became in the mirror a wonderful, sensible image; flowers, a ship, a person, a landscape.[5]

In the distorted mirror, the "nonnon" looks like a full-fledged thing, but this is only the overlay of two negations, which yields a positive. "Minus by minus equaled plus." However, it is hard not to see, behind each such "plus," the "minuses" that make it up, i.e., the infinite proliferation of "nonnons" from which every object we perceive is created—from which we ourselves are created. In everything that exists there is only an assemblage of mutual negations: it is precisely the multitude of "not-nesses" and negations that binds everything together. Every thing is only a means by which one "not" relates to another. One gets the sense of an infinitely multiple world of phantoms, who are real to one another but who in their totality amount to zero.

It would come as no surprise if our cosmos, this expanding universe, which contains many planets, stars, galaxies, and galaxy-clusters, also turned out to be nonexistent as a whole. Well-known in physics is the academician M. A. Markov's theory that "due to the great gravitational mass defect, the total mass of a closed universe is equal to zero."[6] A mass defect is formed by gravitational interactions within the universe, by the forces of attraction and repulsion that expand the universe from within and at the same time reduce its total mass to zero as far as the outside observer is concerned. Our universe, if it is closed, as a whole represents nothingness; and if it is quasiclosed, it has the dimensions of an elementary particle. And conversely, well-known elementary particles may

---

5 Nabokov, *Invitation to a Beheading*, 135–36. Further citations in the text are to this edition.
6 Markov, *O prirode materii*, 142.

contain whole universes, with agglomerations of galaxies, stars, black holes, etc. The universe seems nonexistent or vanishingly small to the outside observer, which is what the main character of Nabokov's story becomes at the moment of his epiphany: an outsider to all that exists, even an other-sider, like a denizen of the next world.

As Falter puts it:

> Logical reasoning may be a most convenient means of mental communication for covering short distances, but the curvature of the earth, alas, is reflected even in logic: an ideally rational progression of thought will finally bring you back to the point of departure ... aware of the simplicity of genius, with a delightful sensation that you have embraced truth, while actually you have merely embraced your own self. Why set out on that journey, then? (513)

Some positive movement—the acquisition of knowledge, meaning, a point—may be realized on only a limited patch of being (of civilization, language), but when you make a full circle and come back to your point of depature, then the fullness of the truth you have grasped turns to nothingness.

b. "A Series of Hinged Lids"

Falter's epiphany extends absolutely to all that exists, and even such a concept as God enjoys no privilege in the picture of the world revealed to him. Falter is for that matter indifferent as to where to begin the argument, what pathways lead to the revelation of the secret:

> What, then, would you say about a Truth with a capital T that comprises in itself the explanation and the proof of all possible mental affirmations?... How can I answer you whether God exists when the matter under discussion is perhaps sweet peas or a soccer linesman's flag? You are looking in the wrong place and in the wrong way, *cher monsieur*, that is all the answer I can give you.... By means of ornate language and grammatical trickery [you are] merely disguising the expected *non* as an expected *oui*. At the moment all I do is deny. (515, 518)

Insofar as this is a matter of negations, the chain of them might begin with whatever you please. Let's begin, as Falter proposes, not with God but with *sweet peas*; let them be the primary essence of the universe, its central element. If *sweetness* exists, then clearly, by way of contrast, there must also be bitterness, or else the concept of "sweet" would lack definition. A limit is placed on bitterness, in turn, by saltiness, and on the latter by sourness. But taste is only one of the senses, and its limit is delineated via a correspondence with smells, sounds, and colors. Thus is the whole wealth of the sensorily perceived world introduced into the universe.

The second element of this primary essence is *peas*. These are defined by their relationship to other plants of the legume family: kidney beans, soy, clover, acacia, etc. The legume family is in turn defined by its differences from other families: the cereal, umbel, hyacinth, laurel, walnut, etc. families. Further, plants are defined by their relationship to minerals and animals, animals by their relationship to the human being, etc. In relation to the human being, the part of such a "not" is played by spirits, angels, and finally God, the purest of the apophatic conceptions that have no appearance or manifestation, the "super-NOT."

Of course, one could also construct the universe starting with God, then ushering in all that is *not* Him via the negation that defines Him, now in a not ascending but cascading progression: universe, Earth, human being, animals ... finally getting all the way down to sweet peas. For Falter it does not matter what one begins and concludes with, because the Whole that we thus receive consists only of negations. NOT rules the world. So that sweet peas might be that which they are, the universe must contain all that is NOT sweet peas, that is, *non*-sweet and *non*-pea in the whole variety of their manifold "nots," negations, distinctions, othernesses. The universe is nothing but this totality of negations, with countless negatives for every positive. "Not" is always infinitely prevalent in the structure of creation. For peas alone there are innumerable non-peas, and peas themselves are defined as the infinite totality of negations of that which they are not.

The only positive moment in this whole world-formation would seem to be the first point of exit from nonbeing. This touches off a chain reaction: not-A, not-not-A, etc. This is apparently what happened in the beginning of our world, which physics describes as the Big Bang and the

Bible as "In the beginning God created the heaven and the earth." Here commenced the division of all the forms and varieties of existence: light and darkness, day and night, water and dry land, plants and animals, men and women, the tree of life and the tree of the knowledge of good and evil, etc. This A, the first *not-nothingness* from which everything came to be, is called the "Supreme Beginning," "First Cause," "Super-Cause," "Creator," "Logos," "First Word," "Alpha," "Absolute," etc. According to the Bible, the first crack in nonbeing came between the heaven and the earth. The primary element in the myths of various peoples is water, a mountain, fire, a volcano, an earthquake, etc. This same role could also be played by the distinction between peas and kidney beans, between sweet and bitter, round and oblong, angular and straight. Once the chain reaction of "not-nesses" is begun (earth is not heaven, water is not dry land, a circle is not a square), this reaction may—right away or gradually, but with the same inevitability—encompass all being as a whole. When dominos stand one after another, forming a system that is, however big, closed and circular, then whichever one we knock down first, all the rest will fall. Everything is Nothingness, and, being located inside Everything as a small portion thereof, we nevertheless cannot but sense its vexed nonbeingness, which extends to us ourselves. "I" am not-you, not-him, not-them... But they are all not-I. Such is the "series of hinged lids," as Falter calls his solution to the riddle of "Everything."

c. Physical Vacuum and the Buddhist Nirvana

Falter's "insane" theory echoes modern physics's notion of a vacuum that lies at the foundation of the whole world of material phenomena. "The subtleties and unexpected properties of the quantum vacuum elevated it to play a leading role in fundamental physics in the mid-1970s. Since then its position has become increasingly wide-ranging and pivotal," notes John Barrow in a book tellingly titled *The Book of Nothing: Vacuums, Voids, and the Latest Ideas about the Origins of the Universe* (230).

The vacuum's key property is its instability, which makes the rise of substance "from nothing" possible. In and of itself, the space of the vacuum has no matter, but virtual particles, i.e., particles that are principally unobservable, are constantly arising and disappearing in it.

The unstable vacuum is even capable of spawning whole universes—according to the familiar conception, this is how the Big Bang occurred. If God created the universe from nothing, then this "material" is still perceptible at its base. The vacuum is also said to experience fluctuation, that is, random and temporary deviations from the zero value of all physical quantities contained therein. Hence the concept in physics of the "vacuum foam," that is, the multitude of bubbles as if effervescing (fluctuating) on the surface of the vacuum. From these quantum bulges, in the process of their stretching, their "inflation," universes are constantly being born, including our own.[7] As the American physicist Edward Tryon puts it: "Our Universe is a fluctuation of the vacuum.... The spontaneous temporary emergence of particles from a vacuum is called a vacuum fluctuation, and is utterly commonplace in quantum field theory."[8] "These vacuum fluctuations will eventually lead to the aggregation of matter into galaxies and stars, around which planets can form and life can evolve," explains Barrow, concluding with the paradox that "[w]ithout the vacuum the book of life would have only blank pages."[9]

But how does the vacuum's instability correspond to its nature—void, nonbeing? If a vacuum is an absence of particles, then the instability of a vacuum is a temporary *absence of absence itself*. Thus both a vacuum and its instability have at base a certain overall "not" that explains the rise of something from nothing, of particles from a vacuum. It is as if the vacuum makes a vacuum of itself, as if the void self-voids and nothingness *nihilates* itself—forming something different from itself, and ultimately a whole expanding universe. Insofar as a vacuum contains nothing but nothingness, then the "not" is directed at itself, and thereby produces

---

7 According to the American physicist Andrei Linde, one of the founders of the cosmic inflation theory, the process by which universes are born of vacuum foam is chaotic and infinite, i.e., it never ceases. Some quantum bubbles stretch to the size of universes, housing galaxy-clusters; and some dematerialize, "bursting" at the moment of their birth and returning to the vacuum. See http://wsyachina.narod.ru/astronomy/universe_5.html; and also L. M. Gindilis's work *Cosmology and Worldview*: http://svitk.ru/004_book_book/12b/2614_gindiliskosmologiya.php.
8 Tryon, "Is the Universe a Vacuum Fluctuation?," 222.
9 Barrow, *The Book of Nothing: Vacuums, Voids, and the Latest Ideas about the Origins of the Universe*, 245.

something, just as minus times minus equals plus. Here it would be germane to quote Semen Frank: "[T]his '*not*' is directed *at* '*not*' *itself*. The truly boundless power of negation consists in the fact that it retains its force *even when it is directed at itself*, at the element that constitutes it."[10]

This self-negation of "not" gives rise to all concrete objects and relations, whose being may be defined as a double nonbeing, a non-nonbeing. There is an interesting parallel in the mathematical relationship of zero to itself. According to the rules of arithmetic, division by zero is forbidden, but an exception is made for dividing zero itself by zero. The meaning of the operation 0/0 is considered "undefined," and such a problem has an infinite number of solutions, that is, the result is every real number.[11] In just the same way, relating nothingness to itself may be considered to result in the whole multitude of extant things.

Nothingness is infinitely divisible, and may comprise the most complex structures within itself, even as it remains nothing. Such is precisely the existentially slackened state of the world we observe around us, and in our own selves. Instead of beauty, *non-ugliness*; instead of good, *non-badness*. Instead of love, *non-enmity*. Non-nonbeing does not have the fullness of reality—it is rather an "*unstable unreality*." As S. N. Bulgakov puts it: "everything simultaneously is and is not, begins and ends, arises in nonbeing and submerges in it, *comes to be*."[12] This ontological slackness and indeterminacy, "neither this nor that"—the "precariousness and shakiness" of creation—is a sign of its having arisen from nothing.

This accords well with the world as depicted in Buddhism. According to the prominent Buddhologist F. I. Shcherbatskoi:

> The elements of existence ... disappear as soon as they appear, in order to be followed the next moment by another momentary existence. ...

---

10 Frank, *The Unknowable: An Ontological Introduction to the Philosophy of Religion*, 78. Frank means that the "unknowable" is an affirmative concept; it contains a dual negation, insofar as knowledge itself, "knowing," operates via distinguishing negations: "this is not that."
11 Vygodskii, *Spravochnik po elementarnoi matematike*, 83. Another way to demonstrate the same thing: dividing zero by any number is known to result in zero; it follows that dividing zero by zero results in any number.
12 Bulgakov, *Unfading Light: Contemplations and Speculations*, 191.

> Disappearance is the very essence of existence; what does not disappear does not exist. ...[13] The picture of the world that appeared to the spiritual gaze of the Buddha was thus an infinite number of separate fleeting essences abiding in a state of beginningless turmoil, but gradually bound for tranquility and the absolute destruction of all that is living, when its elements are brought one after the other to total peace. This ideal has received many names; among them, nirvana has been the most suitable to express the concept of annihilation.[14]

There is something to stumble upon here, just as Falter has suddenly stumbled amid his smooth life-path. In English, Falter's name refers to stumbling, hesitating, wavering.[15] If the Buddha is the awakened one, then Falter is the one who has stumbled. Buddha came to understand the illusory nature of the world and the path to liberation from attachments and suffering, the path to nirvana. Falter does not get so far, he merely stumbles upon the world's illusoriness and discovers the secret of "not." Or it may be said that already in this world he has experienced a vulgar-esoteric, aborted form of nirvana, from which he has fallen back into being. This is why it is as if his skeleton and soul have been removed, why "one need not expect from him any of the human feelings common in everyday life" (511).

We ephemeral beings subconsciously suspect our own "notness." When this vague consciousness suddenly becomes fully clear—that's when you'll hear the sort of harrowing cry that shakes the nighttime quiet of the little hotel where Falter is staying. He has come here, let us note, "having passed a hygienic evening in a small bordello on the Boulevard de la Mutualité," returning to his room "clear of head and light of loin" (506). Such a voiding of physical being, the cessation of the "will to reproduce,"

---

13 Scherbatskoi, *The Central Conception of Buddhism and the Meaning of the Word "Dharma,"* 37–38.
14 Shcherbatskoi, *Izbrannye trudy po buddizmu*, 202.
15 In German, *Falter* means "butterfly," which may be seen as hinting at the metamorphosis of this character, whose new insight renders him as if having gained a new life, like a butterfly in its reincarnatory succession. But the English subtext of this name should also be taken into account. In fact, these two interpretations do not contradict one another; we may think, that is, of the flitting of a "faltering butterfly."

has purified his mind and all of a sudden clearly represented to him the truth that being is illusory, that there is no he, no Falter in the sense he has formerly perceived himself as existing. Likely contributing to this is also "the news, recently received ... of the death of a half-sister, whose image had long since wilted in his memory" (506).

It's no wonder that the first person to whom Falter entrusts this secret, a cheerful and inquisitive doctor, meets the same fate—sudden death. This is why Falter refuses to answer Sineusov's questions directly, and instead plays a cat-and-mouse game with him, now opening a window just a crack on his secret, now hiding it.

d. The Secret of the Afterlife

Falter emphasizes that the question of whether God exists has no bearing on his discovery, which is rather such that it "comprises in itself the explanation and the proof of all possible mental affirmations," and "every thought about its practical significance automatically, by its very nature, grades into the whole series of hinged lids" (515–16). It is a matter of some sort of universal relation, one that connects this world and the next. The artist Sineusov inquires about this in the hope of learning the fate of his deceased wife: is there at least "something" there, or is there "nothing"? There are two opposing positions with regard to the afterlife. Either it exists, and in it we may find our near and dear ones once again; or it does not exist, in which case our near and dear ones, having departed this life, are found only in us, in our memory. Sineusov is torn between these two suppositions: he would like to believe that his deceased wife has gone on to some other state of being, but he is ready to admit that he himself constitutes her final existence in this world. The truth that Falter reveals a bit of but Sineusov cannot grasp consists in the fact that there is no difference whatsoever between these two hypotheses. But not at all because there, beyond the grave, we find eternal life; but because here too, in this world, being is suffused with illusoriness. There is only nonbeing, populated with being's phantoms, and if these phantoms pass from one world to another, this does not change their essence but, to the contrary, corroborates their spectrality.

The fact that these worlds are mutually interpenetrable is confirmed as Falter repeats the words that Sineusov's wife said to the artist before her death, to him alone, unknowable to anyone else:

> ([Y]ou were already confined to your bed and unable to speak, but would write me funny trifles with colored chalk on a slate—for instance, that the things you liked most in life were "verse, wildflowers, and foreign currency.") (510)

This is Sineusov addressing his wife in his thoughts, remembering the final days spent with her; the parentheses underscore the triviality and randomness of this memory fragment, which Falter subsequently frames within his omniscience, his discovery of "everything." He tells Sineusov:

> One can believe in the poetry of a wildflower or the power of money, but neither belief predetermines faith in homeopathy or in the necessity to exterminate antelope on the islands of Lake Victoria Nyanza. (515)

Also in passing, as if in a concessive clause, Falter reveals his knowledge of what Sineusov's wife said before dying. "Verse, wildflowers, and foreign currency," "the poetry of a wildflower or the power of money."

But how does he know? Has he visited the other world and "ferreted" this information out of a denizen of the afterlife? Or are all three objects part of the "series of hinged lids," lids that open, that is, with the very same key that fits everything? Indeed, verse and wildflowers are connected via a banal "poetic" association, while foreign money is contrasted with them twice, because money is by its nature an antipoetry, whereas foreignness makes it less practical and closer to poetry, introduces an aspect of disinterest, like the Kantian criterion for beauty. A line of triple negations is formed: not—not—not. High culture (poetry)—nature (wildflowers)—low culture (money)—high culture (foreignness). Or: the poetry of signs (verse)—the poetry of nature (wildflowers)—the prose of signs (money)—the poetry of this prose (foreignness).

Sineusov does not understand Falter, does not even catch the direct hint—the repetition of his wife's words. He therefore conceives of the

The Secret of Being and Nonbeing in Vladimir Nabokov

relationship of the two worlds in the banal manner of an agnostic or atheist: while he lives, his dead wife lives in and through him.

> Most terrifying of all is the thought that, inasmuch as you glow henceforth within me, I must safeguard my life. My transitory bodily frame is perhaps the only guarantee of your ideal existence: when I vanish, it will vanish as well. Alas, with a pauper's passion I am doomed to use physical nature in order to finish recounting you to myself, and then to rely on my own ellipsis.... (522)

Falter apparently considers the hereafter no less real than the here, but only because this life is just as unreal as is the afterlife; and so these two nonbeings communicate like two vessels.

> Having learned what I have—if this can be called learning—I received a key to absolutely all the doors and treasure chests in the world; only I have no need to use it, since every thought about its practical significance automatically, by its very nature, grades into the whole series of hinged lids. (515)

The "hinged lids" in Nabokov's story are a series of negations that lay bare the secret that being is a manifold nonbeing. While the treasure chests are closed, we imagine that it is precisely in them that being conceals its secret. But suddenly, up come the lids, and it becomes clear that there is nothing in these treasure chests, or to be more exact, they contain the most mysterious thing of all: nothingness itself.

3 | Andrei Platonov between Nonbeing and Resurrection

Here I will analyze Andrei Platonov's artistic philosophy by way of juxtaposition with two thinkers: his compatriot Nikolai Fedorov and contemporary Martin Heidegger. Despite the widespread view of Platonov as a "Fedorovian," one who carried on the resurrectionary project of the "Common Cause," there is a still more profound basis to associate him with the Heideggerian existential ontology of being and nothingness. The point is of course not that Platonov was a "Heideggerian"; one could just as easily characterize Heidegger as a "Platonovian." Their principal works—*Chevengur* (1927–28) and *Being and Time* (1927)—were written almost simultaneously, even as the writer and thinker remained utterly unaware of one another till the end of their lives. It is precisely the absence of any mutual influence that lends a particular significance to their encounter in the space of artistic-philosophical bilingualism and Russo-German cultural dialogue.

Naturally, the goal is not to translate Andrei Platonov into the language of Heideggerian philosophy or to translate Martin Heidegger into the language of Platonovian prose but rather to find a commonality in their creative intuitions, which came to maturity in European culture in the latter half of the 1920s. Framing the issue this way is all the more appropriate because among all twentieth-century Russian writers, Platonov is the most metaphysical in his artistic aspirations, just as Heidegger is the most poetic and linguocentric of twentieth-century German thinkers.

a. Russian Literature and German Philosophy

The mutual attraction between German philosophy and Russian literature took hold already in the nineteenth century. This was due to the fact that the two nations, which were opening pathways for one another to

Andrei Platonov between Nonbeing and Resurrection

an unknown world beyond—for Russians, Germans pointed the way to Europe; for Germans, Russia led to Asia—expressed themselves in different ways: Germans, primarily through philosophy, Russians in literature. The two hundred years of German philosophy from Kant to Heidegger were as decisive for the fate and self-definition of German culture as the century from Pushkin to Platonov was for Russia. Conceptual thinking influences all of German culture: in it, even literature, from Goethe to Thomas Mann and Hermann Hesse, is philosophical through and through; while in Russia, even philosophy is thoroughly literary, and has most often appeared in the form of essay-writing and criticism (from the Slavophiles to Rozanov and Shestov). The systematic/conceptual and intuitive/figurative elements that predominate in the consciousness of these peoples has defined their primary contribution to the various fields of creative activity.

How exactly did German philosophy and Russian literature influence one another in the nineteenth century? Where were the main points of their attraction and repulsion? For German philosophy, from Kant all the way to Heidegger, the decisive question has been that of the relationship between being and thinking. Kant drew a clear line between these spheres, rescinding the naïve, precritical status by which they had been merged, and marked out the middle ground of the theory of knowledge, epistemology, which mediates between ontology, the science of being, and psychology, the science of the soul. Proceeding from this distinction, post-Kantian philosophy has done its best to overcome it, reducing Kant's dualistic system to a monism of a particular type—the oneness of thinking or the oneness of being. The two extremes in this process are represented by Hegel and Nietzsche: for the former, all existence in its unfolding is nothing but the incarnation of the self-developing Absolute Idea, whereas for Nietzsche, to the contrary, all thought, from logic to morality, is part of the sphere of life's self-affirmation, an instrument of the will to power.

Nineteenth-century Russian literature had its own primary question, one that was struggled over from Pushkin to Tolstoy. This was the issue of the individual and the people, or of "oneself and others." This question was first posed by Pushkin, who has played virtually the same foundational role in Russian literature as Kant in German philosophy.

Pushkin drew a distinction between two truths, those of the individual and history, the person and the state, asserting that each is undeniable in its own proper sphere. The whole pathos of *The Bronze Horseman* and *The Captain's Daughter* (*Kapitanskaia dochka*) lies in the coexistence and irreducibility of these two truths: Peter and Evgenii, Pugachev and Grinev. Before Pushkin, all Russian literature bore a sort of precritical, prereflective character, equating the aims of the individual and the laws of society in a naïve, Enlightenment-style manner. Instead of the individual and the people, Lomonosov, Derzhavin, and Fonvizin feature the citizen and the state, who naturally coincide in their rational-enlightened premises and aims. True, already we find Radishchev putting forward the category of the people, and Karamzin, that of the individual, but these are still clearly not distinct nor opposed to one another: their correlation harbors no problem, they exist each in and for themselves.

Just as Kant did for German philosophy, Pushkin divested Russian literature of its precritical innocence. Significantly, both Kant and Pushkin came from traditions of the French Enlightenment (Kant more from Rousseau, Pushkin more from Voltaire); overcoming the optimistic illusions and rationalist dogmatism of this legacy, they thereby became the spiritual pioneers of nineteenth-century culture. Both had a profound involvement with the experience of the French Revolution, which, having incarnated the philosophical and literary precepts of the Enlightenment, served to debunk and reject them once and for all. It was precisely the French Revolution that revealed the fatal mismatch and incongruity between the needs of the individual and the aims of society, and it did so in two ways: offering the individual to society as a blood sacrifice thereto (Robespierre), and elevating the individual to an unprecedented height over society (Napoleon). Robespierre is the revolutionary Enlightenment's negative lesson; Napoleon is the cornerstone of the new romantic and imperialist doctrine. It might be said that the French Revolution, in the persons of Robespierre and Napoleon, struck the very same blow against prereflective, dogmatically naïve *politics* that Kant did against dogmatic *philosophy* in Germany and Pushkin against dogmatic *literature* in Russia. Where Harmony was once presumed to reign, now stood Antinomy. The famous Kantian antinomies (for instance, that of universal causality and inherent freedom) are merely a philosophical variety of the antinomism also manifest in politics (with the greatest "revolutionary" freedom leading to the greatest despotism).

French politics, German philosophy, Russian literature—upon entering the nineteenth century each nation, in accordance with its tendencies and predilections, crossed a boundary separating the critical epoch from the precritical, reflection from naiveté. The nonreflective identification, presumed self-evident, of individual and body politic, thinking and being, the person and the people, was rent asunder, and at the focal point of the schism, in order that it might now be consciously overcome, the greatest efforts of Russian literature and German philosophy were marshaled.

b. The Nonbeing within Being

We shall now touch upon the most significant stage for the two national traditions, that in which, having experienced its rupture with being, thought tries to find a way back into the bosom thereof, supposing itself to be a means for being's self-revelation. Here we encounter two figures, Martin Heidegger and Nikolai Fedorov, who are as congenial a match in their national-cultural contexts as Kant and Pushkin.

Heidegger's thinking exposes nonbeing to human questioning. Nothingness is the breach through which existence may be glimpsed.

> Only because the nothing is manifest in the ground of Dasein can the total strangeness of beings overwhelm us. Only when the strangeness of beings oppresses us does it arouse and evoke wonder. Only on the ground of wonder—the manifestness of the nothing—does the "why?" loom before us. Only because the "why" is possible as such can we in a definite way inquire into grounds and ground things. ... The question of the nothing puts us, the questioners, ourselves in question. It is a metaphysical question. ... Going beyond being occurs in the essence of Dasein. But this going beyond is metaphysics itself.[1]

---

1 Heidegger, "What Is Metaphysics?," 95–96.

The prose of Andrei Platonov is deeply metaphysical in precisely this Heideggerian sense. In his works, the tormenting strangeness of existence that gives rise to wonder and questioning lies in the sensation of Nothingness. Consider one of Platonov's main metaphysician-characters, the folk philosopher Voshchev in *The Foundation Pit* (*Kotlovan*):

> Right until evening, Voshchev walked silently around the town, as though waiting for the world to become a matter of common knowledge. But nothing in the world got any clearer to him, and he could feel in the dark of his own body a quiet place where there was nothing at all, though nothing prevented anything starting there. Like someone living in absence, Voshchev did his walking straight past people, sensing the gathering strength of his grieving mind.[2]

Every thinking person in Platonov carefully harbors within themself this "quiet place where there [is] nothing at all" but from which emerges a wonder at the world and an interrogation as to everything that exists. Only when this precious Nothingness is lost does the world become "a matter of common knowledge," and a person homogenized, a "one of the," a part of the "allness," the faceless and nameless human multitude (the Heideggerian *Man*). But for Voshchev, unlike for this *Man*, the world remains "unclear"; he lives as if in absentia, observing his life from the side, and goes "past" people without becoming one of them. Platonov even has a particular metaphorical term for this *in absentia* observer dwelling inside a person: the "eunuch of the soul":

> But inside a person there also lives a little spectator—he takes part neither in actions nor in suffering—he is always cool-headed and the same. His job is to see and be a witness, but he does not have the right to vote in the person's life, and why he exists all by himself is unknown. This corner of a person's consciousness is illuminated day and night, like a doorman's post in a big building. Round the clock sits this wakeful doorman in the lobby of a person, he knows

---

2 Platonov, *The Foundation Pit*, 8–9. Further citations in the text are to this translation.

all the residents of his building, but not a single resident asks the doorman's advice as to their own affairs. The residents come and go, while the doorman-observer follows them with his eyes. ... He existed as if like a person's dead brother. ... This is the eunuch of a person's soul.[3] (*Chevengur*)

Within a person, Nothingness exists as if it were one's "dead brother"; without, it exists first and foremost as death. Which in Platonov is palpable even when it is not the matter at hand—in the form of some sort of hopelessness and melancholy permeating every living creature that is doomed to die. It is specifically due to this all-encompassing feeling of mortality that Platonov's prose becomes metaphysical in the sense of "going beyond existence" in its physical givenness.

Accordingly, Platonov's attitude toward death, toward Nothingness, cannot be interpreted as entirely negative. It is *impossible* to overcome and annihilate Nothingness, for it itself is "nihilating," as Heidegger puts it; but neither *should* it be annihilated, insofar as it harbors the possibility of a wondering and grateful attitude toward the extant. According to Heidegger, Nothingness is the very "openness" and "transparence" of being; it thus emerges as a philosophical questioning, an artistic creation, and an evaluative human attitude toward existence. Without Nothingness, we would neither know nor contemplate existence but would merely abide in it.

c. Between Martin Heidegger and Nikolai Fedorov

In his attention to the meaning of existence as generated from the mystery of Nothingness, Platonov is closer to Heidegger than to Fedorov, whose conscious follower he is sometimes considered to be. It would be erroneous to reduce Platonov's thinking on death, or more precisely his thinking *from* death (for Nothingness is not the object but rather the source of such thinking), to the tenet of universal resurrection that suffuses Fedorov's philosophy.

---

3 Platonov, *Sobranie sochinenii v 5-i tomakh*, 2:76–77.

In her research on Platonov, the philosopher Svetlana Semenova, the leading contemporary interpreter and continuer of Fedorovian ideas, seeks proof of Platonov's reliance on, even discipleship to, Fedorov. The natural world in Platonov is boring and melancholy because death inexorably devours it—and only the release from this predator's claws, to be brought about by the coming technology, shall save humanity, opening as it does the prospect of universal resurrection.

> Only this future victory is capable of redeeming everything. Or else what is the point of all our technological might, all the miracles of conquering the celestial abysses?... The refusal to accept the situation of "orphanhood" produced by death; the aspiration to meet again in the future, to work toward transforming the afflicted natural world into a new, immortal state of being—these are the main discoveries of [Platonov's] "idea of life."[4]

In part, this does accurately describe Platonov, especially in his earlier pieces and journalism, where technology indeed stands as, unlike organic matter, a "beautiful new world" that provides humanity with tools to master the forces of mortal, deadening nature. But this would be far more applicable, for example, to Vladimir Maiakovsky, for whom nature is an "unperfected thing," and a person is by vocation an engineer and designer, a struggler and creator. Thus does Maiakovsky envision, in the finale of his long narrative poem *About That* (*Pro eto*), "shining, towering through the centuries—the workshop of human resurrections,"[5] in which a future chemist resurrects Maiakovsky himself. It might be said that Maiakovsky has coarsened and narrowed the meaning of Fedorov, reducing his metaphysical and aesthetic aim, the victory over death, to the scientific-technical achievement of earthly immortality. But the point is that in Fedorov himself, conquering death means precisely returning to *this* life: the resurrected fathers join ranks with the resurrecting sons, replenishing humanity's labor army in its

---

4 Semenova, *Preodolenie tragedii: "Vechnye voprosy" literatury*, 339, 374.
5 Trans. cited from Triolet, *Mayakovsky, Russian Poet*, 43.

struggle against mortal nature. Fedorov's hope for resurrection forfeits its metaphysical depth, projected as it is on the flat plane of physical doing. Nothingness, or death, ceases to be a source of mystery, and turns into an object of mastery, susceptible to technical operations. One might sardonically imagine a soul that has flown off, now frolicking in the groves of paradise as the angels sing—and suddenly, through the zeal of some well-meaning descendant, it is ripped from this splendor, resurrected as a bearded ancestor to once more cultivate the earth by the sweat of his brow.

Deprived of its mortal profundity, life forfeits also its creative element, turning into a repository or warehouse, a grandiose museum where the remains of the dead are preserved until they may be fully resurrected at the hands of their descendants. The profundity and unpredictability of creative work is only possible when disappearance is profound and irrevocable. Fedorov's utopia is noble in its moral impetus but chilling in terms of its practical consequences; espousing the resurrection of the dead, it would turn the world of the living into a museum-cemetery. The idea of immortalizing a person in their own flesh is essentially just as unidimensional (albeit fantastic-utopian) as the atheist conception of a person being immortal in their deeds ("so as, dying, to be incarnate in steamships, lines of poetry, and other long-lived matters," as Maiakovsky has it in "To Comrade Nette, Steamship and Man" ["Tovarishchu Nette—parokhodu i cheloveku"]).[6]

Fully executed, Fedorov's project allows for no radical otherness, no realm of being that would be independent of human will. "When all the alterations in the world shall be defined by rational will, when all the conditions on which man depends shall be made his implements and apparatus, then shall he be free; that is, the project of resurrection is also a project of liberation."[7] In Fedorov, however, this "liberation" comes at a great cost: the tethering of humanity to the earth, the renunciation of other worlds, connecting with which grants a person freedom from this world. What Osip Mandel'shtam says of the Russian Revolution could be applied

---

6 Maiakovskii, *Stikhotvoreniia: Kniga vtoraia*, 192.
7 Fedorov, *Sochineniia*, 29.

to Fedorov's utopia: "the earth has cost us ten heavens"[8] ("Freedom's Twilight" ["Sumerki svobody," 1918])—in order to take charge of the earth, to effect its labor and social conquest, we had to disavow ten heavens, that is, spiritual quests and discoveries. The world of the earth is socially active and technically equipped but bereft of mystery and a sense of what lies beyond.

Pertinent here are the words of Dostoevsky's elder Zosima: "Much on earth is concealed from us, but in place of it we have been granted a secret, mysterious sense of our living bond with the other world, with the higher heavenly world, and the roots of our thoughts and feelings are not here but in other worlds. ... God took seeds from other worlds and sowed them on this earth, and raised up his garden; and everything that could sprout sprouted, but lives and grows only through its sense of being in touch with other mysterious worlds" (320). If we recall the epigraph to *The Brothers Karamazov* (*Brat'ia Karamazovy*) from the Gospel of John (12:24), a key to the whole novel, then it becomes clear that this garden may arise only from seeds that fall and die in the earth. "Verily, verily I say unto you: Except a corn of wheat fall into the ground and die, it abideth alone; but if it die, it bringeth forth much fruit" (John 12:24). Only a seed that has died may bear fruit. This is precisely why the roots of our thoughts and feelings lie in other worlds: suffering and dying in one yields sprouts in another. Such, in its simplest essence, is the novel's answer to the question posed by the rebel Ivan: why do the innocent suffer and perish? The question remains unanswered unless one grants the existence of other worlds where that which has been sown in this world sprouts. In recognizing the profound meaning of death and the mystery of the Other, the non-Christians Platonov and Heidegger are closer to the Christian Dostoevsky than is the Christian Fedorov.

There is no doubt that Platonov evinces a number of typically Fedorovian aspirations, but in his work the riddle of death remains unsolved and unsolvable. For Platonov, death is both that which must be conquered (in this he is a Fedorovian, a technicist and Proletcultist)

---

8 Mandel'shtam, *Kamen'*, 129.

and that which, in its invincibility, forms the forbidding, mysterious, forbearing world of human life that has departed, destination unknown.

> Fomin's feeling for Aphrodite was humble enough to be satisfied even by the fact that she had breathed here once upon a time, and the air of her birthplace still held the diffused warmth of her mouth and the weak fragrance of her body that had disappeared—for there is no destruction in the whole world that leaves no trace behind.
> "Good-bye, Aphrodite! I can feel you now only in my memories, but I still want to see you, alive and whole!" ...
> [Fomin's] heart, schooled now in patience, would be able to stand, perhaps, even eternal separation, and could preserve its faithfulness and its feeling of affection until the end of his existence.[9]

This passage from "Aphrodite" ("Afrodita") is undoubtedly one of the most "Fedorovian" moments to be found in Platonov, but it also evinces a substantive difference in the two worldviews. Her "footprints," the "ashes" of things she had touched, the "diffused warmth of her mouth" and the "weak fragrance of her body that had disappeared"—all of this is a transient world in which Fomin abides with his love, devotion, and forbearance. Were it not for mortality, how would Fomin's heart have become "schooled ... in patience," and how would he "preserve ... faithfulness" to his lost love? Life would be bereft of its most precious feelings, which are born precisely of being-toward-death: sorrow and hope, faith and forbearance, suffering and surmounting... And the mysteriousness inherent to the best works of Platonov.

According to Heidegger, truth always abides between openness and concealment; it belongs in part to mystery.

> The essence of truth, i.e., unconcealment, is ruled throughout by a denial. This denial, however, is neither a defect nor a fault—as if truth were a pure unconcealment that has rid itself of everything concealed.

---

9 Platonov, *The Fierce and Beautiful World: Stories*, 244.

> If truth could accomplish this, it would no longer be itself. *Denial, by way of the twofold concealing, belongs to the essence of truth as unconcealment.*[10]

Fedorov's world, like the world of Maiakovsky, does not know this double "concealment" of truth, does not recognize mysteries—only secrets that people will sooner or later figure out entirely. The world consists of two chambers, for the living and the dead; between them is a door that no key has yet been found to match. But it is theoretically possible (and feasible in the future) to open this door, to find, behind it, the very same deceased just as they were in life (unchanged, as if they had been kept in cold storage), and transfer them to the other chamber, where they awaken and recommence their earthly toil. This is roughly how resurrection is according to Fedorov: it emerges from the technical capabilities and societal aims of this world, and does not allow for some other life or the will of those dwelling therein, which might resist the measures taken by the resurrectors, or, to the contrary, might be so miraculous as to far outstrip them.

Platonov's world is suffused with mystery in particular because he accepts that human existence is at base insurmountably temporary. This aligns him with Heidegger, for whom, beginning with *Being and Time*, death is not something that may be overcome through certain technological efforts or thanks to some immortal essences. Existence "temporalizes in time," and death, as the unannihilatable Nothingness, lends existence a meaningfulness and mystery. Both in Heidegger and Platonov, the human being is not the creator or struggler that he is in Fedorov and Maiakovsky but rather an attentive listener and experiencer, a sensitive "shepherd of being." He is within being rather than outside it, and so does not try to reorganize it, but merely illuminates and makes sense of it from within. He goes the same way as being like a shepherd going along with his flock. This existence within that which exists is the particular contribution of Heidegger to philosophical thought and of Platonov to the structure of artistic discourse.

---

10 Heidegger, "The Origin of the Work of Art," 31.

d. A Strange Language: On the Other Side of Subject and Object

The enigma of Platonov's artistic peculiarity is famously manifest specifically in his language. Here too he echoes Heidegger, for whom language is the home of being, the site of truth's disclosure. The harkening to being is manifest in the fact that language harkens to its own roots, reveals its own first meanings. Heidegger finds significance in the primordial meanings of words, hence his constant etymologizing as a way of retaining the existential amid semantic conventions and the arbitrariness of verbal signs.

Platonov's style is largely alien to etymologizing, for, as the language of an artist, it is bound to correspond to the variety of the world of objects. How then may one be faithful to being, listening to it attentively, if language is not derived from its existential, root depths? Platonov achieves this via a peculiar mix of lexical and grammatical structures, owing to which a word does not so much name a thing as partake in its existence. Hence the characteristic irregularity of Platonov's language, which allows it to take root in being, not etymologically, but structurally. Here I will cite several such "irregularities" to illustrate how they "redirect" thinking toward being. Not one of these phrases bears any generalization in and of itself; they are purely narrative, and the thought here lies in the very means of its verbal expression.

The first example is from the story "The Third Son" ("Tretii syn"): "[T]he mother had not endured living long."[11] Usually the verb *vyterepet'* ("to endure") corresponds to some concrete phenomenon that negatively affects a person, who, for instance, "could not endure a separation, could not endure pain or violence." This verb typically goes with a noun, that is, a part of speech signifying an object (to not be able to endure *what*?). But in Platonov it is used not with a concrete phenomenon but with a whole life, signified moreover not with a noun but a verb, that is, it qualifies a process, a duration: she had not endured *to live long*. The result is that "endurance" loses its objectness; it becomes a characteristic of life itself in its length and self-enduring.

---

11 Platonov, *Soul and Other Stories*, 153.

Let us compare this word usage of Platonov's with what we find in his contemporary Nikolai Ostrovsky, celebrated as a "socialist realist": "Life … is given to [man] to live but once. He must live so … that, dying, he can say: all my life, all my strength were given to the finest cause in all the world—the fight for the liberation of mankind."[12] We won't go into the ideological meaning of this sentence; of interest here is rather its grammar, the use of the word "life." Life "is given" to a person—this verb already presupposes the objectness of life. It "must" be lived such that—the objectness becomes more acute, for now there is talk of how life is best put to use. Finally, it concludes with roughly the same thing Maiakovsky says in "To Comrade Nette, Steamship and Man": the goal of life is to remain after it, in earthly matters ("dying, he can say"). In Ostrovsky, being is taken as something subservient to a person, who is a creator and struggler; something he can and must use according to his will. Not so in Platonov: being is not objectified by a subject who may use it as he sees fit ("lived such that"). Being encompasses a person and is undergone thereby. A person does not wield life as a tool, but rather, life involves a person, "beingizes" them within itself.

This is similar to how the verb "to live" is used in another "strange" sentence: "Frosya awoke; it was still light in the world and it was necessary to get up and live."[13] Here we might expect a concrete verb: to "go to work," "make lunch," etc. Usually "to live" is not used as a verb of purpose, for life is implicitly understood to be self-evidently given, the basis upon which all manner of goals are set. Here, though, it is life itself that forms the goal, and one ascends to it: "get up to live"—such is the conceptual turn taken by Platonov's phrase.

In Platonov, "to exist" is not a formal or abstract concept, nor the overall prerequisite for everything (as in the proposition that, naturally, if someone eats or walks, they exist). Existence is a particular action, one that has been thrown into time and space, and that demands, like any other action, constant effort and conceptualization. "'To what purpose do you walk about and exist here?' asked one

---

12 Ostrovsky, *How the Steel Was Tempered*, 73. Further citations in the text are to this translation.
13 Platonov, *Soul and Other Stories*, 201.

man, whose beard was growing weakly because of exhaustion" (*The Foundation Pit*, 191). Here, "to exist" does not mean simply "to be" (as opposed to "not to be") but rather to occupy some position, to extend in space and "temporalize" in time, to displace other existences or snugly coalesce with them. Thus does Voshchev not simply go down the road but walk, "surrounded by universal enduring existence" (5), i.e., rocks, grass, wind, etc. He "live[s] through the substance of existence" (191; one of the most characteristic and oft-cited of Platonov's word combinations).

"She had no wish to spend time on anything except her feeling of love" ("Fro").[14] Here too is a particular Platonovian irregularity: "to spend time on" a "feeling of love." "To spend time" usually applies to something concrete, some activity or occupation, but not to a feeling, which is thought of as somehow removed from time. As a result of this shift, "the feeling of love" is temporalized, transferred from the abstractness of the psyche or ideal to the duration of being.

"'No,' said Frosya, 'I shall stay here and miss my husband.'"[15] "Miss" (*skuchat'*) is used here in some almost ancient, primordial sense, like the action of *kukovanie* ("cuckooing," or "bewailing") or *plach* ("lamentation"); *skuka* ("boredom") derives etymologically from the same onomatopoetic *ku* in the word *kukushka* ("cuckoo"); and the ancient verb *kukati* meant "to mourn" or "bewail." In Platonov, it does not signify an internal state or subjective feeling but a distinct activity, to which a person knowingly gives over some portion of their time. Whereas in the first two examples above (with the verb "to live"), we saw the objectness of the concept "life" removed, and life rendered whole, an end unto itself, here we find the removal of the accustomed subjectness of such concepts as a "feeling of love" and "to miss." Taken out of the sphere of the psychic or ideal, they acquire the solidity and definiteness of activities, deeds elapsing in time.

---

14 Ibid., 197.
15 Ibid., 189.

Endurance dragged on wearily in the world, as if everything living found itself somewhere in the middle of time and its own movement; its beginning had been forgotten by everyone, its end was unknown, and nothing remained but a direction. ... And so Voshchev disappeared down the only open road." (*The Foundation Pit*, 65–66)

What is being described is all-encompassing existential temporality—the precariousness of every subsequent second, the absence of firm, "eternal" essences that might define some undoubted permanence and meaningfulness of existence.

Platonov's usage of words is peculiar in that it abolishes the subject/object duality characteristic of both everyday and scientific language. These odd turns of phrase cast objects and feelings alike into the duration of "temporalizing" being, depriving them of material and ideal discreteness, immersing them in something viscous and elastic. "We had a cow. While she lived, my mother, my father and I all ate milk from her."[16] This statement from Platonov's story "The Cow" ("Korova") is ascribed to a child, and thus seems to express, with a vividness multiplied by this character, the author's shifting of customary perception. For one thing, an utterly superfluous subordinate clause seems to be added: "while she lived"—clearly, after all, you cannot get milk from a dead cow. Without this clause, the text would retain all its informational content but would lose the main thing: the cow's life in its duration, in which people, too, are implicated. And the second discursive "unevenness" here: "ate milk from her" instead of "drank her milk." Platonov creates the image of the cow as having an "open being," in a downright Heideggerian sense: they ate "*from* her." "Ate" instead of the more obvious "drank" here also implies a fleshliness, a solidity of this milk, like a continuation or outpouring of the cow's flesh. The "superfluous" subordinate clause and the odd construction "ate milk from her," then, turn out to be Platonov's way of representing the self-expanding basis of being, which is not appropriated from without by a subject but as it were itself emanates "from" itself. Thus is the world perceived by a little boy who has not yet lost his rootedness in being, has

---

16 Ibid., 259.

not yet turned into a "subject"—and the author perceives the world in just the same way.

e. The Boring Void and Deathening

Nearly every Platonov character is in the grip of a certain feeling, describing which would seem to condense all the peculiarities and "oddities" of Platonov's style. This is the strange, ponderous sensation of the world's emptiness, into which the lonesome human being is cast. It might be said that the "eunuch of the soul" does not dwell only inside a person but also in the nature that surrounds one, which thus becomes like one's "dead brother." This dead brother cannot be resurrected, because the void cannot be eradicated from the nature of space, and keeps it open and habitable for humanity. The most varied characters—from a cow to a scholar, from a fascist army officer to the village boy Vasia, from Dzhemal', a nomad in the Turkmen desert, to Bertrand Perry, an English engineer—in Platonov's works, all that lives, at times even trees and inanimate objects like rocks and sand, is suffused with a sense of the tedious, vacuous prolongedness of life. This is described by Heidegger, who speaks of the "total strangeness of being" that originates from our immersion in Nothingness:

> [Zarrin-Tadzh] looked with curiosity into the empty light of the Turkmen plains, dull as a child's death, and did not understand why people lived here.[17] ("Takyr")

> Around the road watchman's house stretched level, empty fields which over the summer had borne themselves out and fallen silent, and were now mown down, deserted and dull.[18] ("The Cow")

> At that sorrowful moment of his life, Fomin looked at the sky; above were the dark clouds of autumn, driven by gloomy bad weather; it was dull there, and there was no sympathy for man, because all nature, though it is big, is all alone, knowing nothing but itself.[19] ("Aphrodite")

---

17 Platonov, *Izbrannye proizvedeniia: Rasskazy, 1934–1950*, 9.
18 Ibid., 351.
19 Ibid., 303.

In Platonov, Nothingness is always palpable as boredom, as the void that gapes from the depths of the extant—but that in so doing allows it to be manifest. It has long been recognized that the world in Platonov is remarkably barren and sparse; what is left is only existence as such in its dragging endlessness and incomprehensible destination. The most "Platonovian" characters are the unknowing and the non-having. One of them (the "loner" in *The Origin of a Craftsman* [*Proiskhozhdenie mastera*]) manages to die "without having ever harmed nature in any way."[20] This voidness, this "foundation-pitness" of being is filled with constant considerations regarding the future, the rational organization of people so as jointly to attain the meaning of life—to which Platonov's characters aspire precisely because they are bereft of all of this.

However, despite the widespread opinion as to the "mass" and "collective" nature of the Platonovian person, this person, even if he belongs to a commune (such characters in *Chevengur* and *The Foundation Pit* as Aleksandr Dvanov, Kopenkin, Voshchev, and Prushevsky), is usually depicted in a state of solitude, "lonerism," and "orphanhood." Their being elapses in the void of the world, which lacks the sort of solid material, technical, or intellectual modality that might lend existence meaning. This existence requires tremendous strength on the part of Platonov's characters, because it is not guaranteed by any order; every moment it emanates from the depths of its own nothingness and runs the risk of rupture: not just dying but entering into death, "deathening." This rupture itself does not so much halt the person as take him or her back into nothingness, into that very void of pure duration. Much as Platonov's characters do not simply live but beingize, performing the enormous and lengthy labor of existence, so do they enter into the condition of death, they *deathen* (*smertstvuiut*).

Thus is Aleksandr Dvanov immersed in death on the last page of *Chevengur*—stepping into the lake, into the depths of his motherland—the resting place, he thinks, of his father.

> And there was there for Alexander a close, inseparable place where could be anticipated the return of [the] eternal friendship of blood

---

20 Platonov, *The Portable Platonov*, 26.

which once the father had divided in his body for his son. Dvanov urged Proletarian Strength into the water, until it reached the horse's chest. Then, not saying farewell to the horse, continuing his own life, Dvanov got from the saddle into the water himself. He sought that same road along which once his father had passed in his curiosity about death.[21]

Aleksandr does not die but rather "continues his life" in death, returning through his blood to his father's blood, following in his father's footsteps, drawing ever closer to him, "because Aleksandr "remained ever and the same, bearing the same ... still undestroyed ... warming traces of his father's existence."[22]

"To deathen" is not the same thing as "to die," that is, to reach the end of one's life, disappear. While "to die" is to submit to the effect of death, and "to kill" is to become its cause or culprit, "to deathen" means to depart from this subject/object dualism, to exist-through-death. A *human being* is *mortal*, which means it is bound to both *humanize* and *mortalize itself*, or *deathen*. Strictly speaking, in Platonov's world every thing essentially "thingifies" in and out of itself. What is living lives, flowers flower, grass *grassens*, the earth *earthens*, the mortal *mortalizes itself* or *deathens*, that is, de-objectifies itself in action, as if turning its name into a verb, into a method of being. Heidegger's method of etymologizing, extracting from the depths of a given word-root all the new derivatives that clarify it, is essential for Platonov as well—not in terms of vocabulary but style of thinking. "To deathen" is to turn death from an object ("he met his death") or subject ("death overtook him") into the predicate of the existence of that which is mortal. The Platonovian person just as fully "deathens" in death as beingizes in being.

***

Nikolai Fedorov and Martin Heidegger may be regarded as the two philosophical poles in Andrei Platonov's creative quest. His formation as an artist and thinker is tantamount to movement from Fedorov to Heidegger. The early Platonov hymns the technological might of humanity,

---

21 Platonov, *Chevengur* (Olcott trans.), 332.
22 Ibid.

which, armed with faith in communism, was to conquer death on a planetary scale. The resurrection of the dead—that is the common goal of the social and scientific revolution. The mature Platonov comes to the realization that death lies deeper, at the very wellsprings of being, and is thus not subject to technological capabilities or social transformations. The "eunuch of the soul" is inseparable from a person's being as a person; it abides within everyone just as Nothingness itself abides at the core of being. To represent this Nothingness in the spirit of Nikolai Fedorov, as a force solely inimical to humanity and due to be overcome technologically, would be to fail to understand humanity's deep-rootedness in this Nothingness, from which grows the openness of being and the human capacity to contemplate, make sense of, and articulate it. Without reference to Nothingness, one can explain neither the existential anguish nor the everyday heroism of the individual, who performs the labor of being with every breath and movement, with the doggedness and patience to live. Death is also a labor; it does not come easy to a person, "free of charge," but requires bravery, determination, and humility. Deathening is the life that is constantly tested by death, by the emergence from and return to Nothingness. One cannot defeat Nothingness or oust it from being. One may only pass through life in the company of one's own death, harboring it within oneself like a "dead brother" who is an outsider to all, and for just that reason is doomed to conscious and forbearing participation in being.

f. Nabokov and Platonov: A Metaphysical Dispute

Nabokov and Platonov, writers born the same year (1899), seem to represent two poles of twentieth-century Russian literature. They are customarily contrasted according to a whole host of criteria: elitism—*narodnost'* (the quality of being "of the people"); aristocracy—the proletariat; individualism—collectivism; conservatism—revolutionary spirit; a refined idealism—elemental materialism; reflection—organicism; aestheticism—realism; contemplation—labor; nature—technology; ethereality—earthiness; etc. However, a profound metaphysical resonance exists between Nabokov and Platonov in their conceptions of life and death, waking and dreaming.

Andrei Platonov between Nonbeing and Resurrection

The theme of the nonbeing within being has deep significance for both, but they approach it from different directions. For Platonov, this is the primordial condition of a person's being in an empty, dull world, where one is to prolong an existence that is not backed up by meaning. This is the "eunuch of the soul" and "dead brother" inside every being. In Nabokov, the intuition of nonbeing appears to such poetic natures as Cincinnatus (*Invitation to a Beheading*) at the pinnacle of existence, at moments of exceptional insight, amid the most subtle reflection. Life appears somehow alien, and ultimately gives way like cardboard scenery falling apart, or a funhouse mirror smashed to pieces. This sensation of the world as a mirage in Nabokov is a vestige of the symbolists' intuition of *dvoemirie*, the conception of dual existence or parallel worlds. For Platonov, to the contrary, the void gapes within the world and constitutes its most real feature. Hence the labor of existing, which is persistent, onerous, and lacking any clear meaning. Nabokov has a *gnostic* perception of nothingness, Platonov an *existential* one. The gnostic comes to understand the world at large as false, as a prison one has been locked up in by the insidious demiurge—and yearns for the real world. At the base of *this* world, he senses, like Cincinnatus, a falsehood and nonbeingfulness.

> All around there was a strange confusion. Through the headsman's still swinging hips the railing showed. ... The spectators were quite transparent, and quite useless, and they all kept surging and moving away—only the back rows, being painted rows, remained in place. (222)

There is a parallel in Nabokov to Platonov's "eunuch of the soul" or "dead brother": the spiritual double who lives inside Cincinnatus and is ever less involved with the outside world. "[A]n additional Cincinnatus" (15) speaks for him; he is followed by his "phantom"; "the real Cincinnatus" (193) tries to keep his composure, even as the weak Cincinnatus fears everything. At the end of the novel, already during the execution, "one Cincinnatus" is preoccupied with the countdown, while "the other Cincinnatus" (222) goes off to join beings like himself. Particularly illustrative is the episode in which Cincinnatus removes his clothing, then his head, collarbones, and rib cage; "he took off his arms like gauntlets and threw them in a corner." "What was left of him gradually dissolved, hardly coloring the air" (32). Thus is manifest the deep nothingness within a person, which both allows him to perceive the surrounding world as solid and material, and at the same time to outgrow it and open a portal to another world, a mysterious *beyond*. For good reason does Vera Nabokov remark, in her preface to a posthumous collection of her husband's verse (1979), that his primary theme is *potustoronnost'* ("the hereafter" or "otherworldliness"), which spurred the appearance of numerous studies of Nabokov's "otherworlds."

One could hardly apply the term "otherworldly," however, to Platonov. It is precisely where the two authors come closest to one another that the difference between them appears so striking. Indeed, while in Nabokov at times we glimpse the faint outline of a liberating otherworld, Platonov is concentrated entirely on this world—except that it stands as a kingdom of the dead. Not a realm beyond the grave or tomb, that is, but precisely a sepulchral one, a tomb-realm—it is hardly accidental that Platonov's "foundation pit" itself turns into an enormous grave, where peasants from neighboring villages bring their makeshift coffins to inter themselves at the base of the future edifice of communism, which is fated to go unfinished. Nor is Platonov's "dead brother" anything like Cincinnatus's internal double, who is capable of freeing himself from his bodily shell and entering a world of his brethren ("amidst the dust, and the falling things, and the flapping scenery, Cincinnatus made his way in that direction where, to judge by the voices, stood beings akin to him," 223). Platonov's "dead brother" has nowhere to go; he is doomed to remain in this world and contemplate its melancholy emptiness. Thus are the gnostic terms and images so characteristic for Nabokov—"specter," "sham," "illusion," "unreality," "phantom," "translucent," "transparency"—absent from Platonov. This is not his worldview, not his lexicon. Platonov has: "melancholy," "boredom," "emptiness/void" (*pustota*), "desertedness," "yearning," "forbearance," "persistence," "inescapable time" (*neizbyvnoe vremia*). This is an existentialist lexicon.

The authors converge in the theme of dreaming, and at the same time differ in its interpretation. According to Platonov, "[t]here is no transition

Andrei Platonov between Nonbeing and Resurrection 249

from clear consciousness to dreaming: the exact same life continues in sleep, only in a bared form."[23] Dreaming does not hinder the characters' actions: these are sleeping warriors, who do not perceive the world as real but persistently act in it, battling, toiling, building a new life. "The loner's surprise merely shifted from one object to another, changing nothing in his consciousness."[24] This is a rapid (eye movement) sleep, active and at times heroic, albeit incapable of changing the nature of being. The dream does not differ from waking reality; there is no basic presumption of reality, just as there is no subsequent demystification thereof.

Nabokov, to the contrary, tries to pinpoint the moment when his characters realize themselves or the world to be "dreaming": "'We're living in a fine dream,' he said to her softly. 'Now I understand everything.' He looked about him and saw the table and the faces of people sitting there, their reflection in the samovar—in a special samovarian perspective—and added with tremendous relief: 'So this too is a dream? These people are a dream? Well, well.'"[25] Nabokov's characters suddenly sense that they have been transported to the dream state by some alien sorcery; that the being they have perceived as waking reality is in fact a tissue of dreams. This is a passive, hypnotic, captivating dream—but hence also the possibility of waking up. Platonov's characters are denied this opportunity: for them there is only one world, in which dream is indistinguishable from waking. They live almost unconsciously, as if asleep, whereas Nabokov's characters are capable of *perceiving* their being as a dream, and thus of waking up. What is essential for Nabokov is the effort of the psyche: the hero tries to awaken, and is even capable of seeing himself sleeping, from the side; he can perceive his own spectrality.

The main character of the story "The Visit to the Museum" finds himself in a museum that houses a portrait he has been seeking, that of a friend's grandfather from St. Petersburg. The magic of that faraway life, inserted into this provincial little French town, suddenly pulls him in and whisks him back to the portrait's homeland, only now it is not Petersburg but modern Leningrad.

---

23   Platonov, *Chevengur* (Olcott trans.), 131.
24   Platonov, *The Portable Platonov*, 24.
25   Nabokov, *The Defense*, 133.

> "No, no, in a minute I shall wake up," I said aloud, and, trembling, my heart pounding, I turned, walked on, stopped again. ... [A]nd already I knew, irrevocably, where I was. Alas, it was not the Russia I remembered, but the factual Russia of today, forbidden to me, hopelessly slavish, and hopelessly my own native land. A semiphantom in a light foreign suit, I stood on the impassive snow of an October night, somewhere on the Moyka or the Fontanka Canal, or perhaps on the Obvodny.... Oh, how many times in my sleep I had experienced a similar sensation! Now, though, it was reality.[26]

Here we see Nabokov's beloved word (semi-)"phantom" and the juxtaposition of dream and reality. The surrounding world is perceived as a dream, and at the same time is recognized as such, which stands as a sign of awakening.

Let us sum up. What makes Platonov akin to Heidegger is what separates him not just from Fedorov but also from Nabokov. Platonov and Heidegger perceive Nothingness existentially, Fedorov perceives it theurgically, and Nabokov, gnostically. For Fedorov, the goal is to conquer death and annihilate Nothingness itself—a problem to be solved by technology and theurgy. Using its own resources, humanity solves a problem proposed or even imposed on it by God, and thereby itself becomes like unto God, gains the power to resurrect its ancestors, and is virtually immortal. Platonov and Heidegger see the inescapability of this Nothingness that is cast into the world, that illuminates it from within and spurs the interrogation and contemplation of being. For Nabokov, meanwhile, the world itself may be cognized as nothingness, an illusoriness that, upon some epiphany or miraculous circumstance, is dispelled via conscious effort and will. "Nothingness" in this case is not the final reality, but rather the lifting of that "hinged lid," the unmasking of this world's spectrality, beyond which is revealed the reality of another order, one we cannot fathom.

---

26 Nabokov, *The Stories of Vladimir Nabokov*, 284–85.

4 | Dream and Battle: Oblomov, Korchagin, Kopenkin

The dualism of Russian literature, the explosive interaction of its metaphysical extremes, has already been spoken of on numerous occasions in this book. Ivan Goncharov's Oblomov and Nikolai Ostrovsky's Korchagin, to give another example, are two figures who would seem to be as removed from one another as Bashmachkin and Myshkin.[1] What could a starry-eyed gentleman lay-abed and an unbending warrior of the revolution have in common? But, as paradoxical as it may seem, Oblomov and Korchagin represent two facets of a single Russian (arche)type that is developed in full in the works of Andrei Platonov. A suitable term for this favorite Platonovian type, the warrior-dreamer, might be a portmanteau of the two characters' names: Oblomagin. In this oxymoron of a name we have a key to solving the riddle of Russian culture's intense bipolarity.

a. Oblomovka and Chevengur

Among outstanding features of the Russian character, *Oblomovshchina* (i.e., civic and occupational lethargy) and *Korchaginshchina* (warlike determination and aggressiveness) have always strangely coexisted. How may the country be understood in the unity of two of its countenances, that of the wistful sybarite and the merciless (toward himself and others) enthusiast? We have long since learned to recognize the Oblomovian in ourselves: this is the non-sensation of reality, the tendency to wave practical matters away, to indulge all inertia and stasis. But on the other hand, it is impossible to imagine Russia without her Korchagin, with his fierce

---

[1] Nikolai Ostrovsky (1904–36) was a Red Army fighter, a participant of the Russian Civil War and of socialist construction. His novel *How the Steel Was Tempered* (*Kak zakalialas' stal'*) is considered one of the most influential works of communist literature.

squint and his finger on a cocked trigger. Even having been knocked down, laid low by illness, he is able to stand up straight, "[grip] the helm firmly with both hands," "burst ... steel bonds," and "return to the fighting ranks ... armed with a new weapon," so that his "bayonet [too] will take its place in the attacking columns" (*How the Steel Was Tempered*, 2:223, 242, 225).

The secret of this kinship is revealed by the most quintessential of grassroots writers, Andrei Platonov. The famine-stricken and resolute characters of his *Chevengur*, who construct a commune whose main worker is to be the sun, and they its equal and idle freeloaders—what is this but a remarkable hybrid of Korchaginian enthusiasm and Oblomovian sybaritism? The Chevengurians are ready to perform unheard-of feats of valor so that the common man, having thrown off the yoke of the masters who had forced him to labor, might do nothing, and carefreely vegetate in the sun. How much energy is expended—for the sake of the revolutionary abolition of all manner of effort! The result is universal idleness, people stepping over fallen wattle fences to visit one another, picking grass as if it were manna. The Chevengurian commune, where the main workers are plants and the good ol' sun, while people are utterly inconspicuous and inanimate, hardly budging in their sloth and hunger—this all reminds us not so much of Campanella's City of the Sun as the sleepy realm of Oblomovka. People are tucked away here and there amid the abundance of the natural expanse; space stretches purely and smoothly from the limpid heavens to the depths of the earth, scarcely interrupted by the membrane of vanity and mold known as "civilization." The only difference is that Oblomovka's tranquility and stupor is that of satiety, Chevengur's, of hunger. But just as over-satiety and emaciation may equally lead to the extinguishment of life-energy, so as a positive and negative do the two idylls, manorial and communard, coincide in their contours. It is as if a negative taken in the mid-nineteenth century were developed eighty years later:

> All was quiet and sleepy in the village. The mute huts stood wide open, and there was not a soul to be seen. ... Entering a hut, in vain would you call out. Dead silence would be the reply. ... It was

Dream and Battle: Oblomov, Korchagin, Kopenkin 253

an all-encompassing, invincible sleep, the spitting image of death. Everything was dead, except for all the snoring coming in every tone and tune and from every corner. Occasionally, someone would lift his head in his sleep and look around blankly, in surprise, in both directions, and turn over on his side or, without opening his eyes, spit half-asleep—smacking his lips or muttering under his breath—and fall back to sleep.[2]

How could we not recognize Chevengur here!

There was no communism in Chevengur on the surface; it probably lay hidden in people—Dvanov did not see it anywhere—the steppe was deserted and lonely, while near the houses, the rest sat sleepily. ... The rest went to bed early. ... they wished to exhaust the time more quickly in sleep. ... Chevengur woke up late; its inhabitants were resting after centuries of oppression and could not catch up on their rest. ... The houses stood extinct; they had been abandoned forever not only by the semi-bourgies but by the petty livestock as well.[3] There were not even any cows anywhere. Life had renounced Chevengur and gone off to die in the weeds of the steppe. ... All the Bolsheviks of Chevengur were already lying on straw on the floor, muttering and smiling in unconscious dreams.[4]

What was the point of the raging battles, the blood spilled, the streaming banners? So that one might enter the kingdom of dreams at full gallop, dreams even more wakeless than those of Oblomovka. "The revolution had won dreams for Chevengur county."[5] At least the inhabitants of Oblomovka engage in toil, so as to have plenty of giblets and meat pie; but they are not fond of it: "They endured labor as a punishment laid upon our forefathers in times gone by, but they could not love it, and where there was the chance always avoided it, finding this both possible and proper" (128). The Chevengurians found a more decisive

---

2 Goncharov, *Oblomov*, 108, 118. Further citations in the text are to this translation.
3 Platonov, *Sobranie sochinenii v 5-i tomakh*, 2:240, 256, 162, 191.
4 Platonov, *Chevengur* (Olcott trans.), 205, 222.
5 Platonov, *Sobranie sochinenii v 5-i tomakh*, 2:162.

way out: having overthrown the masters, they do away with the bad habit of labor altogether, limiting their needs to flowers and grasses of the steppe, albeit in this ensuring themselves unlimited satisfaction:

> [I]n Chevengur the sole sun worked for all ... for in Chevengur the sun had been declared the world-wide proletarian. ... [L]abor was declared once and for all to be a survival of greed and animal exploitative voluptuousness, because labor encourages the formation of property, and property [encourages] oppression. However the sun released normal rations which are completely adequate for people to live on, and any increase of those rations through deliberate human labor goes to feed the bonfire of class warfare, since it creates a surplus of dangerous objects. ... The overgrown steppe ... was an International of grass and flowers, and thus all [the poor] were guaranteed abundant food without the interference of labor and exploitation.[6]

It was probably worth it to have done some fighting to guarantee such "abundant food" for the rest of one's life and for generations to come; but the main achievement is that communist ideal to which the residents of Oblomovka have aspired in vain: they do not know how to put an end to the masters and the circumstances that compel one to toil. Such a life, rearranged on right principles, has all the sufficient and necessary features of death, and puts an end to any sort of antagonism. "These good people [of Oblomovka] understood life as nothing other than an ideal of tranquility and inaction, which was disturbed from time to time by various unpleasant coincidences, such as illnesses, losses, quarrels, and, oh yes, labor" (128). In the society of the future that the Chevengurians are building, this ideal will be realized without hindrance, because the main obstacle, labor, will fall away as a result of the struggle. This will also bring an end to quarrels—there will be nothing to quarrel over; and losses—there will be nothing to lose. Sleep and food, food and sleep—such is the image of happiness for the residents of Oblomovka and Chevengur, the difference being that in the latter, people eat less and sleep more.

---

6 Platonov, *Chevengur* (Olcott trans.), 171, 223.

Here is how Platonov's characters dream: "You'll eat your fill of lamb fat, and then you just lay yourselves down and sleep!... And at dinner you can steam yourself [with] borscht, then swallow a bit of meat, and then some kasha, then blintzes. ... [T]hen you feel like going straight to bed. Not bad!"[7] To realize this bold dream, you have to do some work with your hands, like the good people of Oblomovka, where "concern over food was the principal and most vital concern" (116). There was much concern, but then the food was much better: "What calves were fattened there for the annual holidays! What fowl were raised! How many subtle considerations and how much work and care went into looking after those birds!... And so, until midday, all was bustle and care, and all was filled with this remarkable life, as packed as an anthill" (116).

But then, after midday, the fussing ceases, and life becomes unremarkable and soundless. "Dead silence reigned in the house. ... It was the hour of the universal postprandial nap" (117). The Chevengurians have gotten rid of this superfluous bothersome interval between dreamings: they have no fatted calves, and even the petty livestock has abandoned them, but on the other hand there is nothing to keep them from making use of nature's gratis bounty. They do not eat as well as they dream, but they sleep even better than the residents of Oblomovka dream. "The proletariat ... barely" had to "budge its exhausted powers"[8] to fully attain the Oblomovka "ideal of tranquility and inaction." Historical progress thus follows a line of increasing dreaming, so that the whole of meager reality might be transferred thereto.

At the same time, moral progress too is ensured by material conditions. There are no thieves to be found in Oblomovka, but it is ripe for them; given the residents' lethargy, it would be no challenge to clean them out—whereas in Chevengur they are already "clean." "It would be easy to steal them blind ... had there been any thieves roaming the area" of Oblomovka (118). Replacing "thieves" with "things" would result in yet another transition from one century to the next.

---

7   Ibid., 80.
8   Ibid., 225.

All that remains for the Chevengurians are the "communist Saturdays"[9] as holidays of labor—but this is precisely so that all labor, without remainder, should transition to idleness;[10] so that toil would amount to the observance of a particular ritual, lacking any directly productive purpose, as Chepurnyi explains: "That's not toil, that's the communist Saturdays!... [O]n these communist Saturdays, there's no production of property whatsoever. ... You think I'd allow that? All that happens is the voluntary spoilage of the petty-bourgeois legacy."[11]

Now it is clear why in the Soviet tradition from the very "great beginning,"[12] the "communist Saturday" typically meant moving logs, piling firewood, tidying up the schoolyard. Such is the archetype of this work, which transfers an object from place to place without adding any of that dangerous bourgeois "surplus value." We had the image etched in us from childhood: the leader of the world proletariat carries a log on his shoulder, consciously not towering over the anthill of the toiling masses. And so the Chevengurians, having used the week to catch up on their sleep, on Saturdays drag wattle fences from house to house, joyfully strewing the road with some of the oppressors' "legacy."

b. Warrior-Dreamers

And so, the upshot of the great battles has been to burn the oppressors themselves in the "bonfire of class warfare" along with what they accumulated, so that the Saturday of idle labor should be followed by a week of non-doing,[13] and profits and losses done away; so that one might "sleep and feel no danger."[14] Goncharov's "invincible sleep, the spitting image of death" becomes even more "spitting" in Platonov, now not very much like but identical to death: "inside [the] hut a peasant was lying in an empty

---

9   The *subbotnik* (from *subbota*, "Saturday"), a day of officially encouraged volunteer labor on public projects—trans.
10 "Holiday" in Russian, *prazdnik*, is etymologically an "idle" day—trans.
11 Platonov, *Sobranie sochinenii v 5-i tomakh*, 161.
12 Epstein plays on the title of Lenin's 1919 pamphlet *A Great Beginning*, which among other things lauds the "communist Saturdays"—trans.
13 Epstein plays on the fact that "week" (*nedelia*) in Russian is literally "non-doing" (*ne-delia*); *nedelia* was originally the Slavic name for Sunday, the day you don't work—trans.
14 Platonov, *Chevengur* (Olcott trans.), 199.

Dream and Battle: Oblomov, Korchagin, Kopenkin 257

coffin, closing his eyes at the least sound as if he had passed away. ... From out of all his own benighted powers the peasant was trying to stop the inner beating of life, but long years of momentum made life unable to come to an end in him" (*The Foundation Pit*, 90-91). This is the rest to which the people have been led by the socially restless among them: class conflict is the prologue to eternal sleep.

But it is not just in its outcome but its very outset that the Chevengurians' activity resembles rapid eye movement sleep, when the sleeper's face and hands nervously twitch from inner exertion. This is the way Kopenkin, Chevengur's communist knight, lives. For him, the commune itself is a reflection of a loftier goal: he seeks the remains of Rosa Luxemburg, which he would press himself to, make a low obeisance before; he would wreak vengeance upon world capital for its destruction of the fiery woman who embodied the temptation of revolt, the supreme splendor and rampancy of the world proletariat's forces.[15] This Platonic revolutionary erotics pulls him across Russia on his heavy Rocinante, Proletarian Strength. Everywhere, in the forests and steppes, in valleys and hills, he tracks his Lady of the Rose, his Dulcinea. In terms of genre, *Chevengur* is a chivalric novel, with all the requisite reveries and heroic feats.

As seen in epics through the ages (Ariosto's Roland, Torquato Tasso's Rinaldo), militancy and daydreaming are hardly mutually exclusive. The true warrior, stern and merciless, is easily swayed by the charms of a dream. Whom did the Saracens fear most of all, just as the bourgies fear Kopenkin?—why, the pale and gloomy knight, entirely consumed by his vision of the Holy Virgin. Let us recall Pushkin's "poor knight," who had a "single vision, unfathomable to the mind."[16] "'Rosa!' Kopenkin sighed and grew envious of the clouds that flowed off in the direction of Germany."[17] A warrior is a person of fate, and dreams are manifestations of fate. That which is sent from above—success, a

---

15 Rosa Luxemburg (1871-1919), renowned Polish-German revolutionary of whom Kopenkin knows only her name and the fact of her execution/martyrdom.
16 "There lived a poor knight" ("Zhil na svete rytsar' bednyi"). Pushkin, *Sobranie sochinenii v 10 tomakh*, 2:248.
17 Platonov, *Chevengur* (Olcott trans.), 84.

portent, a foreordaining—everything appears to the warrior in dreams. Thus do Achilles and his fellow Achaeans learn the dispensations of the gods in dreams. Everything civilian and industrial that one may obtain in the world by toil—all this is despised by the true warrior no less than Oblomov. Give such persons chainmail or a bathrobe, anything but the civilian's unsightly suit, which affords the body neither epic-heroic sweep nor domestic ease.

Toil is the main link that is lost between dreaming and battling, which is why the two are so directly connected in Russian life. And if the war is over, finding himself in everyday labors may be more than the recent warrior can bear. For some the tragedy is not falling dead in a field but taking their seat peacefully in an office chair. We may recall Aleksei Tolstoy's "The Viper" ("Gadiuka") and her revulsion at civilian life: this example of an Amazon is even more vivid than that of the knight, all the more striking when traditionally "inherent" female domesticity is forever tainted by the adrenaline-fueled "thrill of battle."

As Platonov discloses of the soul of the Chevengurian Kirei, "He was growing bored of living without war, with only a single conquest."[18] True, no victory precludes further fighting with the defeated; is this not the reason that the class struggle necessarily intensifies once the class victory is already achieved? First you annihilate the enemy right in front of you, then the one off to the side; first every Tom, Dick, and Harry, then your own fellow-traveler; then you end up with, and put an end to, yourself. And so to curtail this whole rigmarole of drawn-out battle, why not just soar right to one's ultimate happiness and, like the Chevengurians, "exhaust the time more quickly in sleep"?

"Battle is eternal—peace is but a dream"—thus does Aleksandr Blok divine the dream-basis of battle itself in "On the Field of Kulikovo" ("Na pole Kulikovom"). We could add: "Dreams are eternal, and battle is but a dream." In dreams everything is incredible and astonishing, like in battle, and right away the soul gets everything it asks for.

The fact that Oblomovian idleness is in no way incompatible with Korchaginian militancy, but to the contrary presupposes it, is manifest

---

18 Platonov, *Sobranie sochinenii v 5-i tomakh*, 2:235.

already in the figure of Il'ia Muromets, who is both our first Oblomov and our first Korchagin. Il'ia sits idly on the stove a full thirty-three years so as then to gallop and frolic in the open field to his heart's content. It may not be accidental that Oblomov's given name is Il'ia; his patronymic is Il'ia as well, and Muromets would be a fitting father for him. Out of the epic-heroic past, the name Il'ia comes bearing some trace of drowsy indolence.

This is where such far-flung branchings of Russian literature, Oblomov and Korchagin, intermesh. And they coalesce once more in the writings of Andrei Platonov, where these two motifs, lying on the stove and mortal combat, are represented not by different characters but merge in the strange, enchanted state of a knight dreaming during battle itself, as if frozen in mid-gallop, and galloping in one's sleep, to boot. The very lack, on the part of the people, of capitalist-accumulative instincts, as manifest in their penchant for sleep, dissipation, oblivion—this is exactly what makes the man of the people a fearless warrior, ever eager to get away from miserly cares and fall in under a bullet-riddled banner. Kopenkin and lance-bearers like him ("Kopenkin" may be derived from *kop'e*, "lance") know no fear; they have no concern even for their own flesh—which after all is just a "bourgeois comfort" knit of proteins and fat and all the other "surplus value" of the organism. This is where the antipathy toward fat people comes from—the sense that such persons harbor their capital in their sides and bulges, whereas the proletarian is to expend their body for the good of society, even to the point of disappearing. There is nothing to worry about, nothing to lose; we have accumulated nothing in this trifling life, and so are ever ready for the next. Sleep is desired; dying is fun.

This errantry of the soul in the borderlands between life and death is well conveyed in Boris Pasternak's poem "Fairy Tale" ("Skazka"), about a wondrous knight who frees a beauty from her captivity to a dragon. Recalling the folkloric plot about St. George the Victorious, the poet gives it a strange turn, so as to tell a truth about his own time. The warrior conquers the dragon, just as he is supposed to, but then he himself, and the soul-beauty that he has freed, sink into an unmoving torpor. There is no such plot-twist in folkloric songs of brave Egor (the traditional Russian name for St. George). What manner of unlikely victory is this, and at what cost does it come, if the death that has been vanquished nevertheless still holds the warrior and the damsel in the thrall of an all-vanquishing sleep?

> Steed and dragon body
> Lie there on the sand.
> The rider is unconscious,
> And the maiden stunned. ...
>
> Yet their hearts keep beating.
> And now she, and now he
> Tries to awaken fully,
> And then falls back to sleep.[19]

This is already not just a fairy tale but history. The poem is dated 1953:[20] the dragon was dying, but the rescued beauty, and the warrior-savior himself, were sinking into oblivion, their souls meeting in the kingdom of dreams.

> Tightly shut eyelids.
> Lofty heights. Clouds.
> Waters. Fords. Rivers.
> Years and centuries.[21]

The poem's conclusion begins and ends with this repeated stanza. Who is it that slumbers so regally? Past whose closed eyes do whole worlds and centuries flow? This is the soul of the very people languishing in the thrall of "sleep and oblivion." And it is impossible to make out in this "Fairy Tale": does the liberator fall asleep from "the loss of so much blood" and "failing ... strength,"[22] or is he himself only a dream-figment of the sleeping damsel? This is either a post-battle sleep, or battling in one's sleep.

---

19 Pasternak, *Doctor Zhivago*, 477–78.
20 The original autograph of the poem comes in Pasternak's letter to Nina Tabidze of 29 October 1953.
21 Pasternak, *Doctor Zhivago*, 478.
22 Ibid.

Dream and Battle: Oblomov, Korchagin, Kopenkin

The year 1953. And prior to that, eight years of oblivion after four years of battle. And centuries of alternating battles and dreams.

c. Oblomagin: Bipolarity in Russian Culture

For centuries, Russian culture has suffered a bipolar disorder, not in the narrow psychological but rather cultural-historical sense. In this, the manic element was predominant in the ruling classes, at the pinnacle of politics and culture, while the popular masses were steeped in the depressive state, reflected in the dejected, dreary songs of the people, in their melancholy and grievances, and most of all in their boundless indifference to everything.

The manic personality type appears most glaringly in people of prominence; indeed, it has been the power of manias and phobias that has brought such persons to the fore—the despots and revolutionaries of various generations. These are the persistent and vehement monomaniacs, who like Lermontov's lyric persona have known "the power of a single thought, a single but ardent passion." All these people, even amid the greatness of their nature and genius, have the "prejudice of the favorite thought," an obsession that pushes all other ideas aside. It is as if reality itself were so unsteady and malleable, so indifferent, that only an extreme constriction of all effort—a form of monomania or monesthesia—may endow it with meaning and purpose.

Any society contains some proportion of socially active individuals seeking to saddle all their countrymen and the world at large with their idée fixe. But it is Russian society that has proved to be the most defenseless before these extreme types. Usually they are forced into marginal groups, some minor underground like the "red brigades" or esoteric totalitarian sects; but in Russia, such an underground comes to power and starts setting the terms of the country's political and intellectual life. One such "brigade" and "sect" famously managed to seize the country and determine the fate of humanity for most of the twentieth century. This may be connected with Russian statehood itself, its particular type—the necessity of assimilating such an enormous geographic and multiethnic space. This is no place for moderate ideas and actions; you need a very strong push, frenetic and furious energy, if you want an idea to take hold and catch on. Which came first: the frenetic personality, or the pliancy of the space, its readiness to give way and absorb? It would be hard to say. A mania takes hold of a whole person, putting the entirety of their spiritual and physical forces at the service of a single particular and finite goal. Such a person is terribly broad at the base, the intake point of fantastic energy, and extremely narrow at the point of its application. This manic tendency combines two opposite concepts: party-mindedness (*partiinost'*), which derives from the Latin *pars*, "part," and totalitarianism, from the Latin *totus*, "whole." The mania is total in its pretensions, and party-minded at the point of application; here the particular and the total complement one another. "Pars pro toto," "the part instead of the whole"—that is the mania's formula. Insofar as a person becomes bigger than himself in mania, outgrows the scale of the human—to that very extent does he become smaller than himself as an integrated personality. Thus does he feature the striking combination of breadth of heart with mental sloth. Dilated pupils staring fixedly at a single point, tunnel vision—this is the emblem of mania.

Taken as a whole, this type is depressive and manic at the same time, and Oblomov and Korchagin are two stages of a single social psychosis that goes from manic agitation to depressive dejection and back. A person of this makeup, with this sleepy-warrior's soul, may be designated as OBLOMAGIN. There is no such character in any work of Russian literature, and yet his spirit hovers, not just over the country's writings, but over its whole historical fate. On rare occasions he may even show up as a coherent figure, in the works of such writers as Nikolai Leskov and Andrei Platonov, who reveal in their characters the great power of the deed, which operates, however, as if in dreams rather than waking. The "enchanted wanderer" Ivan Sever'ianovich Fliagin; all those characters from *Chevengur* and *The Foundation Pit*: Aleksandr and Prokofii Dvanov, Kopenkin, Chepurnyi, Chiklin, Voshchev, etc. They do battle, they run both rampant and amok, but all in some sort of magic slumber, as if without moving their hands, as if fettered, enchanted, numbed by their own strength. This connection between epic heroism (*bogatyrstvo*) and quiescence is foreordained, as has been noted, in figures from the Russian sagas, the *byliny*—not just Il'ia Muromets but Sviatogor too. Taking his mighty strides along his native

Dream and Battle: Oblomov, Korchagin, Kopenkin 263

ground, this giant sinks therein with his whole bulk, so that he is rooted to the spot: his very power renders him powerless. He reaches for a saddle bag, but it won't be lifted, won't move, won't budge: "But then he sank knee-deep into the earth, and from his face there streamed not tears, but blood. Where he sank, he could not rise; and that was the end of him."[23]

Of course, there is a whole chasm separating Korchagin standing guard and Oblomov lounging on a couch. However, national consciousness and culture always seek out the mediation of extremes. And here emerges just such an intermediary character: Kopenkin, who stands Korchagin-like and reclines Oblomov-like, furiously uprooting the past, even as he is fast asleep on its wreckage. Kopenkin with equal ease fits into two seemingly incongruous sets: Chapaev-Nagul'nov-Korchagin, and Manilov-Oblomov-Satin. In him the most opposite figures—Platon Karataev and Sergeant Prishibeev; Rakhmetov and Khlestakov; a *muzhik* providing for two generals, and a general unable to provide for himself; a work-horse and a show-pony—exchange glances and instantly recognize one another: "Kopenkin paid no attention to the taste of the bread. He ate without zest, slept without fear of dreams, lived according to the most direct path, in no way yielding to his body.... He fought precisely, quickly, on the fly and his horse, unconsciously saving his feelings for future hopes and action."[24] Like an enchanted wanderer, he is alien to himself, does not sense his own body and actions, which accomplish themselves for him while his mind is occupied with the melancholy of "monotonous memories of Rosa Luxemburg."[25]

Kopenkin is a variant of this ubiquitous but elusive Oblomagin. You catch a glimpse of him everywhere, but as a whole he slips away. Oblomagin is a generalized myth-character, of whom writers most typically grasp particular features. And while classic Russian literature was most fond of the upper-class depressive type (the "superfluous man," from Onegin to Oblomov), Soviet literature foregrounds the lower-class manic type, from Chapaev to Korchagin, as heroes of the civil war and socialist construction. In reality the distribution of types is more often the reverse:

---

23 Joffe, "Svyatogór," 185.
24 Platonov, *Chevengur* (Olcott trans.), 92, 109.
25 Ibid., 109.

the upper classes are active, the lower, passive—but literature likes to play upon contrasts, to depict the lethargic nobleman and the mischievous *muzhik*. Is this not why it was precisely in the works of Platonov, in the late 1920s-early 1930s, that this type was portrayed so vividly as a cohesive whole? The upper crust had been overthrown. The lower classes that took its place now infused their age-old quiescence with a military zeal: they fought the way they slept; and the dreams they had—about the gratuitous and the common—were such that the soul yearned for the final, decisive battle.

But the cohesiveness of this type was prepared and verified by history well before the Soviet period, in the very interaction of its two components. One can find aspects of Oblomagin in the character of the most prominent personalities, like the feverish changeover of manic-depressive states. Cheerless melancholy alternates with fantastic dreams; hence the remarkable, "spasmodic" view of Russian writers of themselves and their country. In his first "Philosophical Letter" (published in 1836), Chaadaev complains that "we have given the world nothing, and have taken nothing from it... We have produced nothing worthwhile for the general welfare of people."[26] Whereas in his "Apology of a Madman" (1837), he defines Russia's higher purpose as compared with other peoples: "to contemplate and judge the world from the full height of thought."[27] Or consider Gogol's vision of Russia: "[T]hose barren spaces themselves that cast a melancholy upon my soul enraptured me with the great vastness of their space, their broad arena for action."[28] Contemplating one and the same space, the soul is "suddenly" transformed, falling now into melancholy, now into rapture.

It is not necessary for the features of Oblomov and Korchagin to coexist in a single person, but they are all too capable of doing so in the character of society itself. Some are in the grip of mania, others suffer depression, and the more maniacal the former, the more depressive the latter. A single manic type like Ivan the Terrible is enough to drive a whole people into a long-term depression. On the other hand, the

---

26 Chaadaev, *Sochineniia*, 25.
27 Ibid., 150.
28 Gogol', *Vybrannie mesta iz perepiski s druz'iami*, 245.

Dream and Battle: Oblomov, Korchagin, Kopenkin 265

lethargy of the masses gives rise to a constellation of frenetic awakeners ready to shake the soul right out of the people, if only to get the snoozing body politic to flip over on its other side, usually the left one (Bakunin, Nechaev, Tkachev, Lenin, etc.). The only difference between a revolutionary and a tyrant is that the former's manic phase stems from the longstanding depression of the people, while the latter's manic phase is what caused that depression. Then again, it would be absurd to consult a psychiatrist as to which came first; bipolarity presumes the congruence of both poles. In just the same way, a historian can hardly hope to determine whether it is the people's inertness that makes the leaders obsessive, or the rampaging of the higher-ups that makes the lower classes lie low and petrify.

It is not just socio-psychological layers that stratify in two but also historical periods. In some periods, manic impulses predominate: sweeping reforms, revolutions, coups, initiatives, leaps, when the past is knocked over in one epic-heroic blow—and, sniffing the call of the future, the whirlwind-steeds impatiently take the bit between their teeth. Let us consider a few symptoms from a medical textbook—do these not perfectly match the portrait of social life of the Soviet 1920s-30s?

> Elevated moods ... the excessive urge to act. ... Superficial reasoning, an optimistic attitude toward one's present and future. The patients are in an excellent frame of mind, they feel an extraordinary vigor, an onrush of energy, and fatigue is the furthest thing from them. ... Now they undertake a great multitude of matters, never seeing any one of them through to the end; now they spend money unthinkingly, erratically, making unnecessary purchases; at work they interfere in the affairs of their coworkers and superiors. The patients are extremely voluble, talking without cease, to the point of hoarseness; and they sing and recite verse. Ideation is often saltatory. ... Intonation is typically histrionic and full of pathos. It is typical for the patients to overestimate their own personalities ... [and experience] delusions of grandeur.[29]

---

29 Snezhnevskii, *Spravochnik po psikhiatrii*, 56.

This is not just a description of the manic phases of the life of society but also of a persistent manner of thinking on the part of its leading strata, who by the nature of their service exist in a state of what Dostoevsky called "administrative ecstasy." Undertaking everything at once, butting into other people's business, impetuously making histrionic speeches, ascribing historic meaning to one's actions—it is hardly necessary to indicate particular persons here; this is a composite portrait of "the activist."

But then follows a period of stagnation, decline, standstill, when all that remains of the people's fate is a drearily lingering trace of the past.

> An oppressive, hopeless melancholy is observed.... Everything around is perceived in a gloomy light; impressions that formerly afforded pleasure now seem to make no sense, to have lost their relevance. The past is seen as a chain of errors. Old offenses, misfortunes, incorrect actions bubble up exaggeratedly in the memory. The present and future appear gloomy and hopeless. The patients become motionless, spending days at a time in the same pose, sitting with the head lowered, or lying in bed; their movements are extremely slow, and facial expression is mournful. The urge to act is absent.[30]

Such are the depressive periods which, according to the general rule of the disease's course, occur in Russian history, too, far more frequently than the manic ones. But at the same time, this also describes particular social layers and the persistent mode of their existence: melancholic and monotonous, without any internal impulse to act.

Oscillation of this sort occurs in the history of every country, but rarely does it attain such an amplitude, with such spikes and valleys. Of course, inasmuch as this is a matter of society, such a bipolarity is not a medical issue but a metaphysical one; it is the binary nature of the cultural-historical model itself, in its unhealthy, at times self-destructive expression.

Vasilii Kliuchevskii explained this sociocultural peculiarity via the alternation in Russia of a brief and strenuous summer harvest—when in the space

---

30 Ibid., 59.

of a few weeks, the fate of the crops is decided, and a whole year's worth of energy is combusted—and a long winter hibernation, when time seems to stop in one's heated house, at one's drunken table, on a soft featherbed.

> Thus did the Great Russian become habituated to an extraordinary short-term exertion of his forces, accustomed to working quickly, feverishly, and efficiently, and then resting for the duration of the enforced idleness of autumn and winter. Not a single people in Europe is capable of the sort of short-term exertion the Great Russian can make; but neither would we find anywhere in Europe, it seems, the sort of unaccustomedness to steady, moderate, and deliberate labor as in that same Great Russia.[31]

Without question, climate is a fundamental component of social psychology and mythology. But literary myth goes farther, setting a path for social development, and including ever newer historical components... It is the great task of a writer to give proper names to national myth—of which "Oblomov" and "Korchagin" are the most significant.

---

31 Kliuchevskii, *Sochineniia v 9 t.*, 315.

PART V

The Silence of the Word

1 | Language and Silence as Forms of Being

a. Quietude and Silence

Silence is usually interpreted as the absence of words, and contrasted with speech. Ludwig Wittgenstein concludes his *Tractatus Logico-Philosophicus* with the famous aphorism: "Whereof one cannot speak, thereof one must be silent" ("Wovon man nicht sprechen kann, darüber muß man schweigen").[1] Silence begins where speech ends. This reflects logical positivism's characteristic urge to separate observable "atomic" facts and provable, "verifiable" propositions from the realm of so-called metaphysical mysteries. Logically consistent assertions cannot be made regarding the latter, and so they should be passed over in silence.

But is it really true that silence and the word are mutually exclusive? The very construction of Wittgenstein's aphorism, the parallelism of its parts, constitutes a paradox, combining as it does silence and speaking, and thereby casting doubt on what the author means to say. "*Whereof* one cannot speak, *thereof* one must be silent." This means that silence and speech *share a common topic*. It is precisely the impossibility of speaking *about something* that makes keeping silent *about the very same thing* possible. Silence gets its theme, already singled out and articulated, from conversation, and silence becomes the form of this theme's further development, its extraverbal pronouncement. If it weren't for conversation, there would be no silence; there would be nothing to be silent *about*.

Silence, *molchanie* in Russian, should be differentiated from the quietude of stillness (*tishina*), the natural state of soundlessness in the absence of speech. In Russian, you can "keep silent" about something (*molchat' o chem-to*), but you cannot be still (*tikhii*) about it. The absence of sounds in a still winter landscape has neither topic nor author, whereas silence

---

1 Wittgenstein, *Tractatus Logico-Philosophicus*, 189, 188.

presupposes the possibility or ability of speech; it is both thematic and authorial. The difference is succinctly expressed by Mikhail Bakhtin: "In quietude nothing makes a sound (or something does not make a sound); in silence nobody speaks (or somebody does not speak). Silence is possible only in the human world (and only for a person)."[2]

The linguistic analysis of N. D. Arutiunova attests to the same distinction: "the verb *molchat'* [to be or keep silent] ... presupposes the possibility of performing a speech act."[3] It would not normally be said of a mute person or a foreigner who does not speak a given language that they "keep silent"; this predicate only pertains to one capable of speaking, which means that silence itself belongs to the virtual realm of language. The choice between speech and non-speech is a covert act of speech.

The distinction of quietude and silence is the foundation of Leonid Andreev's story "Silence" ("Molchanie"): after a priest's daughter commits suicide, all the stillness that exists in the world turns, for her father, into a silence looming over and haunting him, insofar as it expresses the daughter's unwillingness to answer the question of why she chose to die by throwing herself under a train. "From the day of the funeral, a silence befell the little house. This was not stillness, for stillness is merely the absence of sounds, while this was silence, when those who are silent would seem to be able to speak, but do not want to." And later, when he visits his daughter's grave, Father Ignatii "sensed the profound, incomparable stillness that holds sway in cemeteries when there is no wind and the dead foliage does not rustle. And the thought occurred to Father Ignatii once more that this was not stillness but silence. It spilled over to the cemetery's brick walls themselves, climbed oppressively over them, and flooded the city. And there was no end to it except there, in the gray, stubbornly and persistently silent eyes"—the eyes of his deceased daughter, who the night before her suicide refused to answer her parents' questions as to what was tormenting her.[4]

Although externally and acoustically, silence is identical to quietude, and signifies an absence of sound, structurally silence is far closer to

---

2 Bakhtin, *Speech Genres and Other Late Essays*, 133.
3 Arutiunova, "Fenomen molchaniia," 418.
4 Andreev, *Izbrannoe*, 82, 87.

conversation; in both, consciousness is intentionally directed at something. As Husserl says, consciousness is always "consciousness-of-something." Silence is also a form of consciousness, a method of articulating it, and takes its rightful place among other such forms: to think about x, to speak about, ask about, write about, be silent about x. People in love may speak about their love, or they may be silent about it. Already in antiquity did the Greek mystic and neo-Pythagorean Apollonius of Tyana express the same thought regarding silence's "wordness" and meaning-fullness: "silence also is a logos."[5]

We might rephrase the concluding aphorism of Wittgenstein's *Tractatus* thus: "Whereof one cannot speak, thereof neither can one be silent, for one can only be silent of that whereof one can speak." Or, to make the formulation as concise as possible: "One is silent of the same thing whereof one speaks." If something cannot be spoken of, it abides in quietude rather than silence, like a non-topic, a "not-about."

Hence the tendency to perceive the quietude reaching us from the past as an intentional silence about something, even as the very questions passed over "in silence" by the past are themselves often raised precisely by the present. Twentieth-century Russian thinkers, for instance, write with poignancy and perplexity of the "silence" of ancient Rus, but most likely this was simply the quietude of the premodern, preliterary age. It was only after the Petrine reforms loosened Russia's tongue, bestowed upon her the new intentionality of educated, high-society conversation and belles-lettres, that the pre-Petrine period came to be perceived as silent. As Georgii Florovsky remarks in his *Pathways of Russian Theology* (1937): "The transition from the agitated and often loquacious Byzantium to the quiet, silent Rus is amazing for the historian. ... This quality of unexpressedness, of going unsaid, often seems morbid."[6] Georgii Fedotov writes of the same thing in his article "The Tragedy of Old Russian Holiness" (1931): "Amid the poverty of its educational means, Old Rus is remarkable for the muteness of expression of what is most profound and holy in its

---

5 Cited from Brown, *Love's Body*, 256.
6 Florovskii, *Puti russkogo bogosloviia*, 1, 503.

religious experience."[7] Verbal epochs, and especially epochs as verbose as the Russian twentieth century, conceive of quiet times as silent; they ascribe to these periods their own intention to speak, at the same time finding in them no embodiment of this intention whatsoever.

b. The Word as Being

Thus word and silence, even given their whole opposition, are born from the same intentional-notional field, and can become convertible. At times a situation arises in which "words say nothing," while "silence says everything," or where "words speak of the same thing whereof silence is silent." The Russian icon *St. John the Theologian in Silence* (early eighteenth century) may serve as a symbol of this tradition.[8] Here we see the apostle John with his left hand opening his own Gospel: "In the beginning was the Word, and the Word was with God, and the Word was God. The same was in the beginning with God. All things were made by him." John the Theologian's right hand is raised to his lips, as if he is making the sign for silence.

At first glance, the meanings of these gestures are directly opposed: one hand opens "the Word," the other exhorts that it be withheld. But the point is that at the supreme level, the word and silence are interchangeable: what John speaks of in his writing is just what he keeps silent about with his lips. When silence and word speak of one and the same thing, what is said acquires a dual significance.[9] It is precisely because "the Word was

---

7 Fedotov, *Sud'ba i grekhi Rossii: Izbrannye stat'i po filosofii russkoi istorii i kul'tury*, 1:307.
8 This icon is in the collection of the Irkutsk Art Museum. My observations on it are based on the reproduction published by the Irkutsk section of the Russian Cultural Fund (VRIB "Soiuzreklamkul'tura," 1990).
   The Gospel of John is widely considered the most cryptic and esoteric of the Gospels, which is exactly why it has a mystical connection with Russian Orthodoxy, along the same line of symbolic correspondences by which the succession of ecclesiastical power associates the apostle Peter with Catholicism, and the freedom of theological investigation associates the apostle Paul with Protestantism.
9 The written word generally presupposes the silence of its audience, which is precisely why writing is subject to interpretation, such that a reader might later enounce its hidden meaning.

God" that it requires silence, and is pronounced in silence. "The Almighty speaks in the language of quietude." (F. Glinka).

Hence the *umnoe delanie* ("mental action" or "wisdom-act") fundamental to Eastern Christian mysticism and asceticism: the constant internal utterance of a prayer so as to bring the mind to a state of total wordlessness. Hesychasm (literally "wordlessness"), the doctrine that arose among the monks of Athos in the fourteenth century, is essentially a discipline of falling-silent-through-speaking, that is, through the pronouncement of that internal prayerful Word, which is being itself, and which precludes external speech, the action of the tongue. The Word, through which "all things were made," apparently itself constitutes being. It does not communicate something located beyond the word; it is not informative but formative. Henceforth we will distinguish these two functions of the word, the *formative* and *informative*. The Word/Logos by which God created the world according to the book of Genesis is a formative word: "And God said, Let there be light: and there was light" (1:3); "And God said, Let the waters under the heaven be gathered together unto one place, and let the dry land appear: and it was so" (1:9). The word that "God said" does not communicate something about light or water or land, as would be the case if these already existed, but itself creates all these elements of the universe, just like the Word/Logos mentioned in the beginning of the Gospel of John. But when man first starts to use the word, on human lips it acquires a different function, that of naming. God brings unto man every creature He has made in order "to see what he would call them: and whatsoever Adam called every living creature, that was the name thereof. And Adam gave names to all cattle, and to the fowl of the air, and to every beast of the field" (2:19–20). The beings named by man exist independently of these names. The Word of God creates the world; humanity's word communicates about the world.

It is clear that in the context of these biblical conceptions, human language bears a primarily informative function, a naming or nominative one; it communicates about the world that lies beyond the bounds of language. But one must not deny language also its formative function, which emerges with particular clarity in the "sacred tongue" in which humanity addresses God and itself seems to become like unto God. Such is the language of spells and prayers, whose purpose is not to give information about some sort of phenomena but to call forth the phenomena themselves.

c. The Beingfulness of the Russian Word

A peculiarity of the Russian language highlighted by numerous writers and thinkers is its formative orientation, or "beingfulness" (*bytiistvennost'*). An unequivocal explanation for this characteristic of Russian is hardly to be found; but it is useful to keep in mind that in its written form, it arose from the very beginning as a "sacred tongue," as a language for translating the Bible. The creators of Slavonic literacy Cyril and Methodius were, after all, missionaries bringing the word of God to pagan peoples. According to Lomonosov, "this richness [of the Russian language] was especially acquired conjointly with the Greek Christian law, when church books were translated into Slavonic for the glorification of God."[10] It is possible that this primordial connection with Greek—and not the Greek vernacular but the language of Holy Scripture—may explain in part the Russian language's "innate" proclivity for religious rites: it was intended for the purpose of "glorifying God." The language does not communicate about being but itself is being.

Osip Mandel'shtam may have put it best:

> Russian is a Hellenistic language. As a result of a number of historical conditions, the vital forces of Hellenic culture, having ceded the West to Latin influences and having tarried for a while in childless Byzantium, rushed headlong into the bosom of Russian speech. ... *That is why Russian became the resonant, speaking flesh it is today* [emphasis mine]. ... The life of the Russian language in Russian historical reality outweighs all other facts in the abundance of its properties, in the abundance of its being. Such abundance appears to all the other phenomena of Russian life as but an inaccessible outer limit. The Hellenistic nature of the Russian language can be identified with its [beingfulness[11]].

---

10 Lomonosov, "Predislovie o pol'ze knig tserkovnykh v rossiiskom iazyke," 16.
11 Mandel'shtam offers the coinage *bytiistvennost'*, which I would prefer to render with the corresponding coinage "beingfulness"—M.E.

The word in its Hellenistic conception is active flesh consummated in the event. ... No language resists more strongly than Russian the tendency toward naming and utilitarian application. Russian nominalism, that is, the idea of the reality of the word as such, breathes life into the spirit of our language.[12]

The Russian language resists the nominative and communicative purpose because real life takes place not outside it, in what is named and communicated, but in it itself—Russian is beingful (*bytiistven*), or beingizes (*bytiistvuet*), at the expense of all other kinds of being. Language is the only fleshly, palpable reality that in Russia is surrounded by a sea of less-real things. This is why literature, or more precisely, literariness and verbality (not just belles-lettres), is the basis of all Russian history. Contrary to Chaadaev's belief that Russia did not belong to the historical circle of peoples, Mandel'shtam asserts that "[s]o highly organized, so organic a language is not merely a door into history, but is history itself."[13] In Russia what is historic is only the language; other phenomena are at most half-beingful, or not beingful at all. Things want to be named and communicated, but language lives its own life; it is a thing unto itself, the only thing substantial enough for national self-consciousness to prop itself against. "In days of doubt, in days of burdensome contemplation of the fate of my motherland—you alone are my rock and pillar, O great, powerful, truthful, and free Russian language!" (Turgenev).[14] Such a tradition of "language-faith" and "language-worship" culminated in early twentieth-century Russia in the religious movement of *imiaslavie* (lit. "name-glorifying," and sometimes referred to as *onomatodoxy*), which was taken up by such major Russian thinkers of the time as Pavel Florensky, Sergei Bulgakov, and Aleksei Losev. According to the movement's founder, the schema-monk Ilarion, "God himself is present in the name of God, in all His being and with all His infinite attributes."[15] Sergei

---

12 Mandelstam, "On the Nature of the Word," 75.
13 Ibid., 76.
14 Turgenev, *Polnoe sobranie sochinenii i pisem v 30 t.*, 10:172.
15 Ilarion, *Na gorakh Kavkaza: Beseda dvukh startsev podvizhnikov o vnutrennem edinenii s Gospodom nashikh serdets cherez molitvu Iisus Khristovu*.

Bulgakov underscored the specifically formative, or perhaps magical, function of the word: "The creative 'let there be' lies in the mystery of naming, which is the mystery of language itself."[16]

This creative "let there be," pronounced, like on the first day of creation, over an earth that is "without form, and void," over the "darkness" of "the deep," constitutes the underlying foundation of the word and verbality in Russia, where all other foundations prove shaky and unstable. Hence the word's repetitiveness and incantatory quality, its urge to fill up empty space with itself—and hence, also, the impression of its strange muteness, its weak connection to what is signified. "Russian nominalism" results in the excess of the language's "resonant, speaking flesh" and the deficiency of its naming and utilitarian properties, behind which is revealed a semantic void. When the word fully becomes being, it is already not saying anything; silently it is full of its own being, as a self-sustaining object: semiotics becomes ontology. Its physical sound is tantamount to semantic soundlessness. The Word-Being is uttered in silence precisely because it communicates nothing but rather manifests itself.

Hence, at the lower levels of the life of the Russian language, such phenomena as Dostoevsky's Foma Opiskin and Saltykov-Shchedrin's Iudushka Golovlev, the endless garlanding and weaving of sophisticated, "soul-rotting" verbiage. Iudushka's interlocutors fester in exhaustion before the senselessness of his flowery, smarmy speech. And at the language's highest levels—Gogol, Dostoevsky, and Mandel'shtam himself, for whom language is indeed "resonant, speaking flesh"—the word grows from its roots, gets overgrown with prefixes and suffixes, puts on the weight of self-sufficient being. It is not reduced to a conventional sign or designative instrumentality; it is itself what it means. For example, in speaking of the "beingfulness of the Russian word," Mandel'shtam might have backed up this thesis with the word "beingfulness" (*bytiistvennost'*) itself. The word grows in an accretion of rings, like a tree-trunk from an original root. What is *bytiistvennost'*? Where is it; what is it in? There it is, in the word itself. First we have the root, the verb *byt'* ("to be"), from which grows the noun *bytie* ("being"), where the action becomes already an independent

---

16 Bulgakov, *Filosofiia imeni*, 73.

Language and Silence as Forms of Being 279

phenomenon. Then the word acquires the suffix -*stv*, transitioning either into the abstract noun *bytiistvo* or the embryo of the verb *bytiistvovat'*, "to beingize," that is, not just "to be," but "to be being itself," "to have the property of being." This property is further augmented with the suffix -*enn*, unfolding into the adjective *bytiistvennyi* ("beingful"), to which in turn, in the final iteration, is accreted the suffix -*ost'*, by which the word becomes a noun once more—one that subsumes "to be" in all its subsequently unfolding properties of action, phenomenon, and attribute (verb, noun, adjective). So, what is *bytiistvennost'*? It is the fullness of being as being, the ability of something not just to be but to be being itself. The word is compact but nevertheless excessive in its suffixial excrescences. It does not convey meaning but manifests *bytiistvennost'* in its very makeup. In English it would be something like "beingfulness" or even "beingfulousness" (four suffixes)—a word that is, in English, hardly conceivable. This is a case of a single word being wordy. Amid all the excessiveness of its derivational components, one senses a certain inner muteness: the word does not communicate but precisely *bytiistvuet*, beingizes.

2 | The Ideology and Magic of the Word: Anton Chekhov, Daniil Kharms, and Vladimir Sorokin

Let us recall Gogol's frequently anthologized comments in *Dead Souls* on the Russian word's ability to be apt, to adhere so firmly to a person that there is no unsticking it:

> Strongly do the Russian folk express themselves!... [L]ively and pert Russian wit ... does not fish for a word in its pockets, does not brood on it like a hen on her chicks, but pastes it on at once, like a passport, for eternal wear, and there is no point in adding [anything] later. ... There is no word so sweeping, so pert, so bursting from beneath the very heart, so ebullient and vibrant with life, as an aptly spoken Russian word. (123)

Indeed, the word sticks to a person so firmly that it lives in their stead. If Pliushkin is "patchy," then he will die as "the patchy one" (122). Gogol delights in this: if the people "bestow a little word on someone, it will go with him and his posterity for generations, and he will drag it with him into the service, and into retirement, and to Petersburg, and to the ends of the earth. And no matter how clever you are in ennobling your nickname later, ... nothing will help" (123). This is a grassroots manifestation of what Mandel'shtam calls the "beingfulness" of the Russian word, which might also be called semantic vampirism—the word eats away at the object, taking its place, and drains the object's life.

The Russian language's very "aptness," its ability to sweepingly pin nicknames on things that never come off, later became a reliable tool of Soviet ideology. Indeed, the whole ideology constituted a system of "apt words," or cliché nicknames: if you're talking about Nicholas I, then it's "Nikolai Palkin" (Nicholas the Stick); if Nicholas II, then "Nicholas the Bloody"; if tsarist Russia, then the "prison-house of peoples"; if the Party, then "the mind, honor, and conscience of our epoch"; if writers, then "engineers of human souls"; if Trotsky, then "Iudushka" (little Judas) and "the hireling of the world bourgeoisie"; if Lenin, then "the most human human being." Indeed, even the proper names in this case were originally pseudonyms—Lenin, Stalin, Trotsky—that caught on and never came off. For that matter, any unit of the ideological lexicon—*udarnik* (a shock worker), *kulak* (a wealthy peasant farmer), *patriot*, *kosmopolit* (a cosmopolitan)—was akin to an alias, insofar as it did not simply name an object but saddled it with an evaluation, conjuring it to "be!" or "don't be!" For good reason does Maiakovsky constantly compare the word to a weapon, equating his pen to a bayonet—nullifying, that is, the language's informational function, and exalting its formativity, its weaponization. Ideology is the language of spells and curses, a verbal sorcery that entirely fulfilled its purpose and transformed the world at large, or more precisely, turned it into a figment. Lev Shestov directly associated the ideological "dictatorship of the word" under Bolshevism with vestigial magic. Revolutionary Russia

> believes in the magic effect of the word. Strange as it may seem, the Bolsheviks, even as they fanatically espouse materialism, are in fact the most naïve of idealists. The real conditions of human life do not exist for them. They are convinced that the word has a supernatural force. Everything is done through the word—you just have to put your faith in the word, fearlessly and boldly. And they have done so. Decrees rain down by the thousands.... And never have words been so drearily monotonous, never have they corresponded so little to reality.[1]

Words grow dull and lose their edge because, being unable to creatively transform reality, they have at the same time forgotten how to reflect

---

1 Shestov, "Chto takoe russkii bol'shevizm?," 49.

it; they are formatively impotent and informationally void. As Joseph Brodsky remarks in his afterword to Platonov's *The Foundation Pit*:

> Platonov subordinated himself to the language of the epoch, having seen in it such abysses. ... But in Platonov's case this was a matter of ... a writer's dependence on the synthetic (or, more precisely, non-analytic) essence of the Russian language itself, which ... gives rise to concepts utterly devoid of any real content. ... Platonov speaks of a nation that has in a sense fallen victim to its own language; or to be more exact, he speaks of the language itself, which has proved capable of spawning a fictitious world and has fallen into grammatical dependence on it. I tend to think therefore that Platonov is untranslatable, and, in a sense, so much the better for the language into which he cannot be translated.[2]

The Russian language's synthetic structure is manifest, in particular, in that the substantive meaning of a word and its evaluative one, semantics and pragmatics, prove inseparable.[3] Contrasting the Russian and French languages in his *Comparative Lexicology*, Vladimir Gak concludes: "Neutral French words have Russian equivalents with markedly negative or positive expressive connotations. ... A single stylistically neutral French word quite often has a parallel in several Russian words of varying stylistic qualities (negative, positive, neutral)."[4] For example, the French word *entente* has no expressive connotation but may be conveyed in Russian only by several words with different evaluative meanings: the positive

---

2 Brodskii, *Sochineniia*, 50, 51.
3 Usually synthetic languages like Russian are contrasted with analytic languages like English or French according to the fusion or demarcation of semantics and syntax. In a synthetic language, grammatical and lexical meanings are expressed as a single lexical unit, whereas in analytic languages they are expressed separately. For example, the Russian word *bratu* contains the lexical meaning *brat* ("brother") and the grammatical meaning (recourse, directedness) of the dative case. In English, these two meanings are expressed analytically, using two lexical units, the noun "brother" and the preposition "to." One could further expand the distinction of synthetic and analytic structure to the relationship in a given language of semantics and pragmatics, that is, substantive-nominative and expressive-evaluative meanings, denotations and connotations.
4 Gak, *Sopostavitel'naia leksikologiia*, 99.

soglasie ("accord"), the negative *sgovor* ("cahoots"), the neutral *soglashenie* ("agreement"). The French *fameux* has at least three Russian equivalents: the positive *znamenityi* ("renowned"), the negative *preslovutyi* ("notorious"), and the neutral *izvestnyi* ("famous," "well-known"). Here again we see the evaluative component embedded in the lexical meaning of the Russian word, whereas in French this component must constitute a separate lexical unit.

Such "apt words" or word-labels as these potential parallels of *entente*: *sgovor* ("cahoots") or *sborishche* ("bunch"); such "apt" alternate pairs as *spodvizhnik* ("fellow-fighter") or *posobnik* ("accomplice"), *miroliubie* ("love of peace") or *primirenchestvo* ("appeasement"), *soglasie* ("accord") or *soglashatel'stvo* ("appeasing")—these words do not so much name a phenomenon as cast spells on it, performing the magic trick of its rise or fall, commanding it to be or not to be. A word that subordinates semantics to pragmatics—that's what a spell is. "Lenin" is a word-spell, because it not only indicates the individual Vladimir Ul'ianov but in the pragmatics of the Soviet language ascribes to him such characteristics as "leader of all workers," "supreme genius," and "the most human human being." *Kulak* is a word-spell: it not only indicates a well-off peasant but also demands that this person be annihilated. The words "internationalist" and "cosmopolitan" (*kosmopolit*), or "patriot" and "chauvinist," are "synthetic" as well; they indicate one and the same phenomenon, only giving it two different aliases, acting as a love spell and a breakup spell respectively. An ideologeme is an "apt word" at the service of power. However much Chamberlain and his policies changed, he will never be free of the nickname "watchdog of reaction"; just as Dmitrii Shepilov will always be "Shepilov, who joined them."[5] These nicknames are repeated eternally; their muttering completely drowns out the object itself, which is thought of only under a definite label, an evaluative sticker.[6]

---

5 From official condemnations of the late 1950s "Anti-Party Group," which invariably named the primary conspirators and then "Shepilov, who joined them."
6 For more on the ideological word, see the chapter "Relativistic Patterns in Totalitarian Thinking: The Linguistic Games of Soviet Ideology" in my *After the Future: The Paradoxes of Postmodernism and Contemporary Russian Culture*.

As Lenin wrote: "We are reproached with stubbornly 'hammering home' the same slogans. We take this reproach as a compliment. ... We must repeat ourselves millions and billions of times."[7] Soviet ideology made hundred-percent use of the language's ability to talk an object into a state of enchantment;[8] to affix to it a nickname that endless repetition lends the appearance or sound of being. This is why the word "seethes and trembles" so vampirically: the object's life has been drained into it, while the object itself has faded and died.

Pavel Florensky, in the spirit of the Russian philosophy of the name, defended the magical function of the word as its most significant, proposing that it can utterly preclude the cognitive or communicative function. "The magically powerful word does not necessarily require, at least not at the lower levels of magic, an individual-personal exertion of will, nor even a clear consciousness of its meaning." He cites an example: "The witch-healer [*znakharka*] who whispers hexes and incantations whose precise meaning she does not understand, or the clergyman who reads prayers that contain certain words even he is not sure of. ... Contact has been established between the word and the individual, and the main thing is done: the rest will take care of itself, by virtue of the fact that the word itself is a living organism, with its own structure and its own energies."[9]

Under the influence of such magic, a person becomes possessed by the word, repeating it endlessly without realizing its meaning. Like a shaman or dervish, the word spins on its acoustic axis, turning, to use the expression of the Russian *budetliane* (futurists), into a "self-woven" or "self-spun" word (*samovitoe slovo*). It was not only politicians but also artists—futurists, conceptualists—who deployed this "transsensical" or "transrational" property (*zaumnost'*) of the word, which is used as a nonsensical but supposedly salvific magic formula. This is why, for instance, in the stories and novels of Vladimir Sorokin, the key device involves

---

7   Cited from Galkovskii's *Endless Dead End* (*Beskonechnyi tupik*, 491).
8   Epstein alludes to the connection in Russian between "casting a spell" on someone and "wearing them out with speech" or "talking their head off," both of which actions may be expressed by *zagovorit'*, which for that matter may also mean "to begin speaking"; even as a *zagovor* is a "conspiracy." Speech has a nefarious power—trans.
9   Florenskii, "Magichnost' slova," 273.

taking some emphatically correct, wise, and ideologically freighted word and turning it into a mantra, whereupon an action that is boringly correct, tedious, and consistent suddenly collapses, transitioning into some sort of monstrous and nonsensical ritual.

Sorokin's story "The Geologists" ("Geologi") features a "business" conversation on the difficult situation the eponymous characters find themselves in—are they to take the trouble to preserve the samples they have obtained, or go in search of comrades who have gotten lost? The style and intrigue are entirely worthy of the best examples of socialist realism. "What are we supposed to do, abandon our friends in an avalanche zone and just clear out?!" A long argument takes place, playing on every cliché of the "problem" or "production" story. Finally, at the request of his junior comrades, the most experienced geologist, Ivan Timofeevich, expresses his authoritative opinion:

> "Upon evaluating the current situation, it seems to me that we must simply wranch the gremlet a bit." In the silence that followed, Alekseev nodded. An expression of rapture ran across his face: "Indeed, you're right... I should have known..."[10]

A choir of geologists now repeats after their magician-mentor:

> "Prax, prax, prax the snotsmitter."
> "Prax, prax, prax, hafhaired ladigig."[11]

Sorokin in this story replicates a certain ritual meant to solve a professional problem, much as, in works of socialist realism, analogous problems were solved by the ritual of the party meeting or politburo session, as well as by the repeated pronunciation of mantras like "the party and the people are united," "cadres decide everything," "death to the enemies of the people," and the like.

---

10 Sorokin, *Pervyi subbotnik*, 30. Here and in other translations from Sorokin, English equivalents like "wranch the gremlet" are offered to approximate the transsensical words used in the original—trans.
11 Ibid.

In another Sorokin story, "A Session of the Factory Committee" ("Zasedanie zavkoma"), an issue is discussed at extraordinary length: what to do with the slacking worker Viktor Piskunov, who is not fulfilling his quota, comes to work drunk, is rude to supervisors... There is a proliferation of phrases like "We are, after all, the factory committee! The factory committee of the labor union, comrades! Labor unions are the forge of communism! Lenin himself said so!" This is the Soviet ritual of the collective reprimand of a colleague. Among those taking part is a local policeman, who advises the offender to listen more often to classical music, insofar as it "ennobles a person." "Bach, Beethoven, Mozart, Shostakovich, Prokof'ev." Again great names ring out, becoming, in the context of the ideological chastisement of a factory worker by a policeman, mantras and incantations absurdly detached from what they signify.[12] Then the policeman excuses himself—it is time for him to go to a musical rehearsal—and disappears behind the door, only to appear therefrom a minute later with a "savage, inhuman roar." "'Ch ... ch ... choply ... choply,' he bellowed, shaking his head and opening his mouth wide."[13]

Prorubono, the quasisensical word rendered here as "choply," sounds like *prorubleno* ("cut through") and *prorabotano*, the Russian term (lit. "worked over") for being collectively reprimanded thus— as if in oratorical ardor, under ideological pressure, the sound might spread a bit, and the comrade will be set straight... But at this point the meeting's other participants go into a frenzy, shouting out "choply" and other adverbial glossolalia[14]—piercely (*proboino*), gorely (*probodelo*), slaughterly (*uboino*), drawly (*vytiagono*), drainly (*slivo*), farshly (*nashpigo*), stuffly (*nabivo*), cramly (*napikho*). At the same time, they perform corresponding ritualistic actions: they pierce the

---

12 In the ancient Hindu tradition, the *mantra* (Sanskrit, "verse" or "incantation") was a magic formula for invoking the gods, frequently transmitted from teacher to pupil.
13 Sorokin, *Pervyi subbotnik*, 52.
14 Glossolalia (from the Greek *glossa*, "tongue," and *lalia*, "chatter," "prattle") is the production of nonsensical sound combinations that preserve certain characteristics of coherent speech (division into words, into syllables, etc.).

body of the factory cleaning lady with a pipe, drain her blood, stuff her with maggots, etc.

> "Farshly! Stuffly!" bellowed the policeman.
> "Cramly the maggotry! Cramly the maggotry!" cried Simakova…
> "Cramly the maggotry," repeated Starukhin. "Cramly…"
> "Cramly in accordance with the operational flow diagram produced on a state basis and diminified after value engineering per the third quarter," muttered Urgan.[15]

Urgan is still in the thrall of production jargon, cramming it with new magic formulas as if not noticing the switch. Indeed, there is no switch, because "operational flow diagram," "value engineering," "third quarter"—in Sovietese, these are the same sort of incantations as "stuffly" and "choply." Or "Bach" and "Beethoven."

In Sorokin we observe how an ideological word, screwed to the extreme of tightness, breaks off into conspiracy and sorcery. Familiar and seemingly intelligible ideologemes turn into horrifying glossolalia bearing that same worked-over-and-chopped meaning. Thus are manifest and sharpened the absurdist forms of magic inherent even in everyday words, which loop upon themselves, communicating nothing, merely droning on incantingly, reproducing their own beingness.[16]

a. The Word-Figment: Daniil Kharms and Anton Chekhov

An even more drastic turn in the relationship between word and being is possible; this is when the relationship comes to a halt entirely, when words turn into pure figments whose sole function is to mean nothing, even as they sound like or acoustically imitate a speech act. Sound creates the illusion of safety, insofar as it manifests the being of an other, whereas silence is perceived as concealment, a hidden threat.

---

15 Sorokin, *Pervyi subbotnik*, 53.
16 "Conspiracy" here is *zagovor*; "droning on incantingly" is *zagovarivaiut*; see note 8—trans.

> We cannot bear strained silence—
> The imperfection of souls is a shame, after all!
> The reciter showed up perplexed,
> And was greeted cheerfully: "Go ahead!"
> (Mandel'shtam, 1912)

> Мы напряженного молчанья не выносим—
> Несовершенство душ обидно, наконец!
> И в замешательстве уж объявился чтец,
> И радостно его приветствовали: просим![17]

The audience is happy to listen to the reciter not so much due to the meaning of his words as the soothingness of his smoothly flowing speech. In the Soviet period this healing property of speech began to be used for the exact opposite purpose: to commit a sort of "mid-conversation murder." All the firing-squad campaigns of the 1930s-50s were accompanied by a continuous "recitation," the incessant ideological noise of the loudspeakers that were so popular, impressing upon people that they were safe. The state conversed with them, recited articles, poetry, weather bulletins, putting so much effort into correct speech—this must have meant that the state cared about them, was protecting them. But it was killing people, looking them right in the eye clearly and lucidly, in mid-sentence, amid some smooth turn of phrase. Thus, for instance, in Daniil Kharms's little story "Grigor'ev and Semenov":

> Grigor'ev (*hitting Semenov in the mug*): So, winter is here! Time to light the stoves. What do you think?
> Semenov: I think, if one gives your comment serious consideration, that it is perhaps indeed time to light the stove.
> Grigor'ev (*hitting Semenov in the mug*): What do you think, will winter this year be cold or warm?
> Semenov: Well, seeing as the summer was rainy, winter will be cold. If summer is rainy, winter is always cold.

---

17 Mandel'shtam, *Sobranie sochinenii v 2 t.*, 1:87.

Grigor'ev (*hitting Semenov in the mug*): As for me, I'm never cold.

And so on, all the way to the denouement:

Grigor'ev (*hitting Semenov in the mug with his heel*): Go ahead and talk, talk! We'll listen.
Semenov (*falling on his back*): Ouch![18]

Analyzing Kharms's story, the writer Dmitrii Galkovsky remarks that the Russian language "turns communication into bludgeoning and murder. The Russian language is a language of executioners and victims. ... Such a savage, creepy 'dialogue' would be absolutely impossible either in the West or the East. For one thing, the beating would take place in silence."[19] One would have to agree with this. The point is that in this story, the word bears no relation to the deed at all, it goes its own way, curving away from the action. It is semantically empty, communicating nothing, which makes it easy to step away both from the topic of conversation and from the beating that is taking place during it. Why is Grigor'ev discussing the weather with Semenov? Is he mocking him? Is he trying to calm his runaway nerves? No psychological explanations would help here; for that matter, such would hardly be applicable to a Kharmsian character, an entity that is bereft of personality. This is not a matter of the psychology of an individual but the semiotics of speech. The topic of the weather is not random here only in the sense that it is the most random of all possible topics: a conversation about the weather is the most ritualized, semantically null form of social interaction there is. As soon as a bit of what is happening breaks into the conversation—Semenov's "ouch!"—the conversation is over then and there. The communicative or informational function, even if what is expressed is simply an interjection of pain, undermines the conversation, which cannot bear such an insult to its abstract, fictitious essence.

---

18 Kharms, *O iavleniiakh i sushchestvovaniiakh*, 248–49.
19 Galkovskii, *Beskonechnyi tupik*, 65, 66.

Kharms is merely taking to an extreme something mapped out by Chekhov: the gap between speech and events. In *Uncle Vania* (*Diadia Vania*), for instance, Astrov says to Voinitsky:

> The weather is not too bad today, my dear Ivan Petrovich. It was overcast in the morning, as though it were going to rain, but now it's sunny. It must be admitted that the autumn has turned out very fine ... and the winter corn is quite promising. ... The only thing is—the days are getting short.[20]

Chekhov's intonation directly anticipates that of Kharms, because in mockingly pronouncing these ritual phrases about the weather, Astrov is in essence doing to Voinitsky just what Grigor'ev is to Semenov, punching him in his mug. We have here a scene of the cruelest moral bludgeoning, insofar as Voinitsky, who is in love with Elena Andreevna, has just discovered her in the embrace of Astrov, whose comments on the weather sound, for him, murderous. What is happening is signified by a parenthetical remark: "Voinitsky [*wiping his face*]: What? Oh, yes ... very well" (162). He is wiping his face because he has just received a punch in the mug—and the conversation is going on about "the weather." Kharms's story is essentially a hyperbolic parody of this main Chekhovian device of having speech curve away from action.

Here it is apparent that the power of Chekhov, like that of Kharms, lies not at all in subtext. The fact that a conversation is being used in effect to muffle the sound of a man's beating does not make the conversation itself any more profound or significant, or laden with particular meanings. It is not a matter of the word's undercurrent or semantic saturation but just the opposite, its absence of meaning, which is a mockery. Word and action diverge radically; the two have nothing in common. A word may be banal and superficial, as may an action. Neither a beating, nor still less a conversation about the weather, contain any profundity whatsoever. If actions and words backed one another up, the impression made would simply be feeble and flat. But this is a matter of combining two banalities

---

20 Chekhov, *Plays*, 162. Further citations in the text are to this translation.

that have almost nothing in common: a conversation about one thing, and an action about something else. The result is precisely a dual banality, which seems to harbor something within it, in the gap between speech and action—but there is absolutely nothing there; this two-layered "nothingness" gives speech and action the illusion of voluminousness. Chekhov is a master of creating dual banality and thereby dispelling the impression of banality. Two banalities performed simultaneously are too much for ordinary perception, which tries to conjoin them by some profundity. What is heard most in Chekhov's plays is thus, as in the stories of Kharms, the silence of the word itself.

b. Three Literary Episodes: The Silence within and around the Word

Here we should pause to consider three famous episodes of silence in Russian literature: 1) the mute scene with which Gogol's *The Inspector General* concludes; 2) the silence with which Christ responds to the monologue of the Grand Inquisitor in *The Brothers Karamazov*; and 3) the mute scene in Chekhov's *Cherry Orchard* (*Vishnevyi sad*). Different as these episodes are, it may be noted that in each case, silence is preceded by logorrhea.

In Gogol, this comes in the form of lines delivered by Bobchinsky and Dobchinsky, the town's most vapid and tireless chatterboxes. It was they who had earlier brought the "news" about the inspector general, spawning this grandiose figment, which they now disown just as doggedly.

> Bobchinsky: I swear, it wasn't me, it was Petr Ivanovich.
> Dobchinsky: No, Petr Ivanovich, after all, you were the first to…
> Bobchinsky: Not at all, the first was you.[21]

It is at this moment that a gendarme appears with the news that the actual government inspector has arrived, after which comes the mute scene.

In Dostoevsky, the monologue of the Grand Inquisitor, who speaks for the "intelligent spirit, the spirit of … non-being" (251), similarly receives no verbal follow-up on the part of his interlocutor. Christ answers

---

21 Gogol', *Polnoe sobranie sochinenii v 14 tomakh*, 4:95.

every accusation with silence, and a wordless kiss upon the bloodless lips of his accuser, his betrayer, the new Judas, who serves not Christ but the one who tempted him in the wilderness. Christ's kiss here repeats Judas's kiss from the Gospels but inverts its meaning. The Grand Inquisitor's apostasy, which is expressed via the word, can only be answered with love, which transcends words. "Though I speak with the tongues of men and of angels, but have not love, I have become sounding brass or a clanging cymbal" (1 Corinthians 13:1). In the face of Christ's silence, the Grand Inquisitor's entire speech suddenly turns out to be just such a sound or clanging. Christ's kiss in turn places a seal upon lying lips, restoring the dignity of silence thereto. It has a dual meaning, being the cessation of speech and an answer to speech.

In Chekhov, it is Gaev, the most verbose of *The Cherry Orchard*'s windbags, who spouts profusely prior to a mute scene. The more he speaks, the more a muteness accumulates around him, soon to be discharged by some strange, otherworldly sound.

> Gayev [*in a subdued voice, as if reciting a poem*]: Oh, glorious Nature, shining with eternal light, so beautiful, yet so indifferent to our fate ... you, whom we call Mother, uniting in yourself both life and death, you live and you destroy...
> Varya [*imploringly*]: Uncle, dear!
> Anya: You're starting again, uncle!...
> Gayev: I'll keep quiet, I'll keep quiet.
> [*They all sit deep in thought; the silence is only broken by the subdued muttering of Firs. Suddenly a distant sound is heard, coming as if out of the sky, like the sound of a string snapping, slowly and sadly dying away.*] (277)

As soon as Gaev falls silent, nature gets her own "word" in. The alarmed vacationers treat this strange sound just as they would a word, trying to fathom its source and meaning. "[A] lift cable in one the mines" far away "must have broken" (277), or it was the cry of a heron or the screech of an owl, or a sign of misfortune. Ranevskaia trembles, tears come to Anya's eyes. Chekhov's characters keep silent about the main thing, because they sense the helplessness of any sort of speech—and the sound of a string snapping becomes speech.

In all three episodes, in Gogol, Dostoevsky, and Chekhov, it is precisely when the human word reaches an excess that its deficiency is revealed. The word does not so much name an object as hush it up, get it to fall silent. Wordlessness builds up in words themselves, like the unsaidness of a meaning that has been deafened by words. Ultimately an oppressive silence reigns—this is when the phantoms of muffled, talked-to-death topics surround the words and begin to impose a loud, deafening silence about themselves. Out of the mouths of the Bobchinskys and Dobchinskys, of Gaev and the Grand Inquisitor, the word does not name anything but cries out its own self. This is not Logos as Lord and King but Logos as Pretender. And when the real sovereign shows up—the government inspector in Gogol, Christ in Dostoevsky, nature in Chekhov—he or it proves to be a silent Logos. Silence comes like retribution upon the False Word, like the unmasking of its imposture.

Two diametrically opposed opinions may be heard regarding Russian culture: 1) It is a taciturn, diffident, vestal culture, one that guards its innermost meaning, blushing at the thought of voicing or exposing it; and 2) It is exceptionally garrulous, given to exhausting blather, a culture in which words take the place of deeds.

Both these opinions are essentially valid, and they reinforce rather than refute one another. The two features of Russian culture—taciturnity and garrulousness—are interconnected. And this is not simply an antinomy, where both contrary positions are true. Silence itself grows and gathers strength in the process of speaking, and garrulousness itself comes from the tension and ineffability of silence. Silence grows along with speech; words stoke it. Russian verbality is remarkable in that it exposes its own deep wordlessness; it is loudly, tenaciously silent, concealing this silence behind an abundance of words. It is along these lines that the artist and theoretician of conceptualism Il'ia Kabakov analyzes the three writers mentioned above, Gogol, Dostoevsky, and Chekhov:

> [There exists a] neurosis in our great literature, in the minds and nerves and memories of each one of us—the neurosis of incessant talk, the

preference for verbal self-realization, for the incessant, unflagging, raging sea of words ... washing all before it. ... [I]t is generally known that the great mass of the text of [Dostoevsky's] books is made up of interminable, unremitting debates. ... We can say that these debates are not about something fundamental but more than anything else they are debates debating debates. The novels contain short debates, long debates, and garlands and chains of debates of monstrous length. Every reader of these novels is familiar with the feeling that the thread has been lost ... the basic idea is gone ... drawn into the process itself, into the multidirectional references, digressions, relationships, supplementary and subsidiary explanations of previous references, and so on. ... [This may be] compared with the interminable stupor of an inquest or the interminable torture of clerical work or a nightmare where the loops of one "relation" become entangled in the loops of another "declaration" forming a nauseating "relation to the relation"—from which not one of the characters can extricate himself. ... [T]his vicious circle of judgements and opinions does have its limit, and the limit is the void. In Chekhov we meet the same thing, the same theme. Here the characters do not live, they talk. ... The primary feeling of emptiness embraces all the words, deeds, and actions of all the characters—almost spatially. The emptiness is behind everyone, behind everything that happens to them—but they talk nonetheless. They talk so as to fill up this emptiness, so that the void will not appear with them on the stage, so that they will not disappear into the noiselessly resounding awfulness of the void. They must talk, they must weave an unbroken net from words, phrases, and opinions which even *from the very beginning have been devoid of sense.*[22] (Emphasis mine)

Kabakov is in effect referring to what Mandel'shtam solemnly proclaims the beingfulness of the Russian word. "The life of the Russian language in Russian historical reality outweighs all other facts in the abundance of its properties, in the abundance of its being." But this also means that one "must talk" without cease, "weave an unbroken net" of words, hold being

---

22 Kabakov, *Das Leben der Fliegen/The Life of Flies/Zhizn' mukh*, 242, 248–49.

The Ideology and Magic of the Word 295

on the tip of one's tongue; to fall silent means to vanish, die, not be. "I speak, therefore I am"; I hear myself, thus, I am. Speaking is the only way to "enchant,"[23] to exorcise the void of the world around us, whose wordlessness in response to this endless speech becomes all the more ominous.

Pascal writes of the horror of the human being, a speaking being, in the face of a universe that is mute. "The eternal silence of these infinite spaces fills me with dread."[24] No other country in the world has space like that of Russia, and nowhere is the silence of space so loud, so dread-inducing for speakers, who are impelled to speak ever more quickly and loudly, attempting to drown out their fear with the audibility of their own verbal being. But the more they speak, the more they are surrounded by an oppressive silence.

---

23 On this word *zagovorit'*, see note 8—trans.
24 Pascal, *Pensées*, 66.

3 | The Russian Code of Silence: Politics and Mysticism

a. The Eternal Quiet

The people's age-old silence, seemingly uninterrupted since the days of Old Rus, produces the sort of semantic tension that among the intelligentsia bursts forth in a torrent of words and leads to the "literature-centrism" of Russian civilization. Such is the social stratification of these two poles in Russian culture: the verbosity of the intelligentsia and the silence of the people. The former's surplus of words is the flip side of their absence among the latter.

> In the capitals, noise; the orators fulminate,
> A verbal war rages,
> But out there in the depths of Russia,
> There is the eternal quiet.
> (N. A. Nekrasov)

> В столицах шум, гремят витии,
> Кипит словесная война,
> А там, во глубине России,
> —Там вековая тишина.[1]

The contrast indicated by Nekrasov makes us wonder: are Russian oratory and Russian quietude mutually conditioned? Could this be why such noise is made in the capitals—to drown out the country's strained silence;

---

1 Nekrasov, *Polnoe sobranie stikhotvorenii*, 58.

to take those who keep silent, and turn them, if not into talkers, at least into listeners?

Russia's "eternal quiet" would seem to be just what allows every word to reverberate resoundingly, even a word that is whispered—so covetously do the ears latch onto it—whereas in the West, with its centuries-long tradition of openness, it is nearly impossible to be heard. The philosopher V. V. Bibikhin comments:

> Those who have taken up the word talk and talk incessantly in the people's ears, conjuring with the word. ... But they are only able to talk because they are silently and patiently listened to. Not every people is capable of such a thing. The thinker and the poet sense it: in this expanse, the word resounds; the space is such that in it the word is audible. The fact that such a space exists is an event of world history.[2]

Indeed, in a silent country, the word reverberates loud and far. But what is louder still, even more audible, is the silence itself. The speaker gets no reply to his words, as if they have fallen into a deep well from which not even the sound of falling escapes. "The people are silent" (Pushkin); "Rus, where are you racing to? Give answer! She gives no answer" (Gogol, *Dead Souls*, 284). This theme is nearly as traditional in Russian literature as that of the prophet who burns people's hearts with his words. The prophet suddenly finds himself in a society of the mute, or possibly even deaf. Consider Nekrasov's famous "Elegy" ("Elegiia," 1874), the one that proclaims: "I have dedicated my lyre to my people." What is the people's response?

> And loud is my canticle!.. The vales and fields chime in
> And the distant mountains send the reply of their echo,
> And the forest responds... Nature pays me heed,
> But they of whom I sing in the evening quiet,
> To whom the poet's reverie is dedicated,—
> Alas! they do not heed, and give no answer.

---

2   Bibikhin, *Iazyk filosofii*, 379.

…И песнь моя громка!.. Ей вторят долы, нивы
И эхо дальних гор ей шлет свои отзывы,
И лес откликнулся… Природа внемлет мне,
Но тот, о ком пою в вечерней тишине,
Кому посвящены мечтания поэта,—
Увы! не внемлет он—и не дает ответа.³

Nearly a century later, Evgenii Evtushenko writes the poem "Dolgie kriki" (1963; translated as "A Far Cry"), in which the poet, standing on one side of a river, shouts to the other side, the location of "the people" (*narod*), trying in vain to get a response from a ferryman. But there is only a dead quiet on the other side:

A hut is drowsing on the opposite bank.
A horse looms white against the dark meadow.
I call loudly and fire shot after shot
But I cannot wake a soul.

……………………………………

As for the peasants who sleep as though ploughing,
breathing heavily, they sleep at their leisure,
they don't hear my voice, any more than
the rustle of the pines and the noise of the rushes.⁴

Дремлет избушка на том берегу.
Лошадь белеет на темном лугу.
Криком кричу и стреляю, стреляю,
а разбудить никого не могу.

……………………………………

И для крестьян, что, устало дыша,
спят, словно пашут, спят не спеша,
так же неслышен мой голос, как будто
шелесты сосен и шум камыша.⁵

---

3 Nekrasov, *Polnoe sobranie stikhotvorenii*, 203.
4 Yevtushenko, *The City of Yes and the City of No, and Other Poems*, 45.
5 https://www.litmir.me/br/?b=224463.

"They do not heed, and give no answer." "They don't hear my voice." One starts to doubt Bibikhin's thought that in Russia anyone who takes up the word is "silently and patiently listened to." Clearly, people are silent, but do they listen? And if they do listen, do they hear? And if they hear, do they understand? Russian discourse, with its "far cries" addressed to the people, is just what enables the people's answering quietude to be heard, and insofar as this quiet resounds precisely in response to the word, it is thus perceived as silence.

The Soviet period, with its endless eruption of "correct" words directed at the people, also sought to rely on literary classics, but this only intensified the effect of the resounding silence that came in response. In Platonov's *Chevengur*, the communist Simon Serbinov, tasked with restructuring the life of the rural masses, reads aloud from Gleb Uspensky in "reading huts."[6] "The muzhiks lived on silently, while Serbinov drove further into the depths of the soviets"[7]—probably in order to dekulakize, exile, and eliminate the enemies of the people. This is already prescribed by the Russian code of silence. If it is easier to kill to the accompaniment of a conversation on the weather or belle-lettres, then life, sensing this hostility of the word's meaning, takes shelter in silence.

One more example. While in Nekrasov and Evtushenko, it is a poet that the people do not heed, Dmitrii Prigov has a poem in which the people are addressed by a simple woman of the people:

> Along the waves, the waves of ether
> Having lost her outward appearance
> The cattlewoman Glaphyra
> Speaks with the country...
>
> And the country hears all from afar
> Unseen, as if across a river
> But it keeps silent, and breathes loudly
> Like some enormous beast.

---

6 *Izby-chital'ni*, rural reading rooms organized as part of the anti-illiteracy campaign.
7 Platonov, *Chevengur* (Olcott trans.), 287–88.

По волнам, волнам эфира
Потерявши внешний вид
Скотоводница Глафира
Со страною говорит…

…А страна вдали все слышит
Не видна, как за рекой
Но молчит и шумно дышит
Как огромный зверь какой.

"In this expanse, the word resounds," says Bibikhin. Yes, but it does so nervously: it cringes and cracks wise, teases and puts on airs, because it turns out to be unanswered. No dialogue takes hold; the word turns into the inner monologue of the speaker. To speak = to hear oneself. I hear myself, therefore I am. The word suffers from agoraphobia, Pascal's dread before the "eternal silence of these infinite spaces." Silence and quiet have something kingly about them, while amid this expanse, the word senses that it is a pretender.

What enables the word to resound so loudly is just what ultimately drowns it out, turns it into white noise. Whereof one can speak, thereof can one also be silent. Everything said recedes into silence; all that is left is summed up by Dmitrii Merezhkovsky thus: "Life has departed into the wordless depths. Nowadays what is written is more meaningful than what is printed; what is said is more meaningful than what is written; and finally, what is kept silent about is more meaningful than what is said."[8]

Such is the nature of Russian negativity: whatever is said immediately becomes petty, is brushed aside as secondary. Tiutchev's "the spoken thought is a lie" is the Russian code of silence. And the more significant the writer, the more mysterious seems the silence emanating therefrom. Dostoevsky concludes his speech on Pushkin thus: "Pushkin died in the full flower of his creative development, and unquestionably he took some great secret with him to his grave. And so now we must puzzle out this secret without him."[9] Merezhkovsky titles an article on Vladimir

---

8 Merezhkovskii, *Izbrannoe*, 543.
9 Dostoevsky, *A Writer's Diary*, 505.

Solov'ev "The Mute Prophet," because when it comes to the main thing, the "impending onslaught of subterranean forces ... Vladimir Solov'ev himself says nothing, or speaks, not with words, but by waving his hands and making signs, like a person who is mute. Yes, mute, despite the ten volumes of his works."[10] And so, "let us hope that more attentive criticism shall someday solve the mystery of his prophetic muteness."[11] What Merezhkovsky admires about Chekhov is that he never butted into the noisy talk of eternity and the meaning of existence but laughed it all off, and in general, "kept a sacred silence about what is sacred."[12] Pushkin and Solov'ev and Chekhov all appear speechless, despite the abundance of what they say, the many volumes of their collected works.

And even Rozanov, who created a new, totalistic kind of literature... In Rozanov, especially in his final diaries, everyday life itself—the life in which people usually keep silent, perform work, are idle, have children, and deal with trifles—became literature. The result was that this most prolific of writers devalued the language, undermined the status of literary discourse, spoiling it with an excess of words. After Rozanov, Russian literature could scarcely catch its breath: mouths made to open, lips moved—but there was nothing to say, the oxygen had run out. A quiet quickly grew around Rozanov's verbal experiment, a menacing zone of silence, the language's Soviet gulag. After Rozanov, who managed to speak about everything and from every point of view, the only intelligible words were military orders and Central Committee edicts. But even Rozanov himself, having said so much, in effect said nothing, and hardly anyone attempting to translate him into more information-oriented language would understand what, after all, he meant to express, whether

---

10 Merezhkovskii, *V tikhom omute: Stat'i i issledovaniia raznykh let*, 118–19.
11 Ibid., 126.
12 "I was young; I was in a hurry for answers to questions of the meaning of existence, of God, of eternity. And I posed these questions to Chekhov in his capacity as a teacher of life. But with him, everything came down to anecdotes and jokes.... I was irritated, almost offended: here I was asking him about eternity, and he's telling me about some bumpkin.... We had to gab as much as we did, sin as much as we did, with the forty-nine sacred words, in order to understand how right he was to keep silent about what is sacred.... What a joy, what sanctity it is to keep silent about what is sacred" (ibid., 49–50).

in particular lines or in the totality of his statements. Even Rozanov's most fervent contemporary admirer, Dmitrii Galkovsky, who has written a thousand-page introduction to Rozanov's works in the form of the novel/self-commentary *The Endless Dead End* (*Beskonechnyi tupik*), grants that "the content of Rozanov's book is tantamount to zero. He really did SAY NOTHING, and departed this world a great silent Sam [*velikim molchunom*]."[13] For that matter, Galkovsky himself, in surrounding that certain primordial "nothingness" of his book with rows of multilayered commentary, with "relations to the relation" (to borrow Kabakov's phrase cited above), is consciously boiling down the content to absolute zero, to the "endless dead end." In a self-review included in the book, he writes: "The reader is a test-subject; the Great Lonely ocean presents him with a whole series of phantoms it has spawned, which, squealing, grimacing, and sticking out their tongues, herd the reader into the endless dead end of the final silence."[14]

b. Two Silences: Political and Mystical

What would be a typical attitude toward silence in Russia? The Russian sayings and proverbs cited by Vladimir Dal' are mutually contradictory. Some positive sayings on silence (most of which feature a proverbial rhyming lost in translation):

> The word is silver, silence is golden.
> Whoever is silent does not sin.
> The wise man is silent while the fool grumbles.
> A good silence is better than a bad grumbling.
> You'll never offend anyone with silence.
> Whoever keeps silent is a teacher to two.

And some that censure it:

> You can't be right by being silent.
> A firm silence answers nothing.

---

13 Galkovskii, *Beskonechnyi tupik*, 323.
14 Ibid., 677.

He is as silent as a tree stump.
He is as silent as the dead, as the lifeless.
To play mum, play the silent one (*igrat' v molchanku*).
It's not the barking dog that bites, but the silent one wagging its tail.

This seems to be a matter of two different silences: a wise and humble one, and a dead or menacing one.

Such a dual perception of the meaning of silence is hardly limited to folkloric culture. On the one hand, there exists a mistrust of silence as a form of timeserving, from Griboedov's Molchalin—whose name derives from *molchanie* ("silence"), and who dares not "have his own opinion," and so "shall reach the well-known ranks, / For nowadays they love the *wordless*"[15] (emphasis in original)—all the way up to the famous song by Aleksandr Galich: "All the silent Sams have become bosses, / Because silence is golden." Naturally, Galich's ironic injunction to "[k]eep silent, and you'll wind up a winner. / Keep silent, keep silent, keep silent!" sounds entirely different from when Tiutchev bids us in "Silentium" to "be silent, hide yourself, and conceal / Your feelings and your dreams."

For Tiutchev, silence has to do with the most profound mystery of the soul, that which must remain unspoken; it is the opposite of the word, which is a lie. For Galich, silence has to do with supporting the authorities, who suppress the right to free speech; it is the opposite of truth and openness/ *glasnost'*. Even the words expressing these two types of silence may be divided into two groups. The Tiutchevian group, the mystical one, includes *bezmolvie* ("wordlessness," "hush," etc.), *nemota* ("muteness"), and *umolkanie* ("going silent, trailing off"); the Galich group, the political one, has *umalchivat'* ("to conceal"), *zamalchivat'* ("to sidestep or suppress"), *promolchat'* ("to not say anything [out of fear]"), and *pomalkivat'* ("to keep quiet, mum about").

Nor is this duality of "silence" unique to Russian culture. Both concepts are in circulation in the West, in each case among nonconformists. One of them is expressed in Susan Sontag's book *Against Interpretation* (1966) and her article "The Aesthetics of Silence" (1969), and in Roland

---

15 Griboedov, *Gore ot uma*, 49.

Barthes's book *The Pleasure of the Text* (1973): "Bliss is unspeakable"[16] (Barthes); "more extended and more thorough description of form would [provoke] silence"[17] (Sontag). At the same time, Sontag notes that "the art of our time is noisy with appeals for silence"[18]—a reproach that could be leveled against Tiutchev and all those who loudly and eloquently stand up for silence. "Quiet, orators! The floor is yours [lit., "your word"—trans.], Comrade Mauser"—thus does Maiakovsky quite oratorically adjure revolutionary sailors. The most consistent positive conception of silence appears in silence itself—in the silence of anchorites, hermits, mystics.

The other, negative conception of silence has a political meaning. From this point of view, silence signifies not a mystical deepening but political oppression: it is the result of particular voices being *suppressed*, ousted from a culture. Those who have been silenced must find their voice, rend the mantle of wordlessness that surrounds them in a politically unidimensional society.

Clearly, silence itself comes in two varieties, political and mystical. If free speech is every citizen's sacred right, then silence signifies enslavement, oppression, submissiveness. In this case silence is interpreted as a quietude leveling the human being with the wordless creature, the animal. Culture is the realm of semiotic conduct: unlike animals, human beings are meant to express their thoughts and feelings verbally. But neither can the level of the "political animal"—openness/*glasnost'*, debate, eloquence—accommodate the whole person. Just as the word separates the human being from the stillness of nature, from the wordlessness of the wild, so does the ability to be silent place them over the word, above politics and culture. This is not a preverbal but a *transverbal* silence, one that, like the abovementioned icon *St. John the Theologian in Silence*, houses the entirety of the Word not uttered. We are summoned to this silence by sages and poets. The Guanzi: "The sound of the unspoken word is louder than the peal of thunder or the pounding of drums." Dmitrii

---

16 Barthes, *The Pleasure of the Text*, 21.
17 Sontag, *A Susan Sontag Reader*, 102.
18 Ibid., 187.

Venevitinov: "Blessed is he who was a poet while keeping silent."[19] Heidegger: "[T]he person who is silent ... can develop an understanding more authentically than the person who never runs out of words."[20]

In Griboedov and Galich, the prevailing approach is the political one: in the face of lowly, backward, subservient, cowardly muteness, the voice and openness (*glasnost'* is literally "voiceness") constitute a breakthrough, the realization of one's human dignity. For Tiutchev, and subsequently for Mandel'shtam, with their philosophical-mystical worldview, silence is the breakthrough, rending the verbal and cultural mantle that envelops the speaking animal. This is a birth into a higher, mysterious world where the human encounters the divine and is silent, insofar as one may perceive and pronounce the divine word only through the entirety of one's own silence.

> May my lips attain
> The primordial muteness,
> Like a crystal-clear sound
> Immaculate since birth![21]
> (Mandel'shtam, "Silentium")

> Да обретут мои уста
> Первоначальную немоту,
> Как кристаллическую ноту,
> Что от рождения чиста![22]

Clearly this muteness, "immaculate since birth," is of a different nature than the muffling of speech mentioned in another Mandel'shtam poem: "We live without feeling our country beneath us, / Our speeches can't be heard from ten steps away."[23]

---

19 An ecumenical selection of comments on silence may be found in Perry, *A Treasury of Traditional Wisdom*, 987–93. On the mysticism of silence in Byzantine culture, see Averintsev, *Poetika rannevizantiiskoi literatury*, 55–56.
20 Heidegger, *Being and Time*, 159.
21 Mandelshtam, *Selected Poems*, 6.
22 Mandel'shtam, *Kamen'*, 19.
23 Trans. cited from Shrayer, *An Anthology of Jewish-Russian Literature: Two Centuries of Dual Identity in Prose and Poetry*, 676.

The question is whether the preverbal silence inherent to slavery may express or symbolize the supraverbal silence characteristic of wisdom. The peculiarity of the Russian tradition is its confusion, intentional or otherwise, of these two varieties of silence, its tendency to interpret political silence as mystical; the suppressed, "Griboedovian" silence as the profound "Tiutchevian" one. The silence of submission and the silence of mystery are perceived as a single meaningful silence. The individual or the people keep silent because they are not permitted to speak, their mouths are shut up, their word is not provided for by society's structure, they are denied the right to self-expression. But great is the temptation to interpret this closed mouth as the result of one's own finger intentionally pressed to one's lips, as a sign of keeping silent about the most essential and sacred depths of being and belief.

It is entirely clear, for instance, that in the 1930s-50s, the silence of the Russian thinkers who remained in Russia was politically enforced. Florensky, Losev, Bakhtin, Golosovker, and others, might-have-beens whose names we don't know, fell silent for a long time or forever because they were forced to fall silent. But when a speaking and thinking being is silent, even an enforced silence begins to be perceived as a word. The thinkers just mentioned, moreover, kept a *dual* silence: first, because they did not say what they wanted to say; and second, because they did not say what was wished to be heard from them. This silence thus represented a combination of submission to the state's barring of free speech with resistance to the state's demand for an obedient word. Soviet Russia saw the rise of a new type of silence hardly known to prerevolutionary Russia: the *bold silence* that signals dissent, as expressed in Solzhenitsyn's exhortation "to live not by lies." If one cannot speak freely, then one can still freely be silent, one can refuse to be a yes-man or cheerleader. Between the free silence of the sage and the submissive silence of the slave lies the silence of the semi-free person.

Hence the attempts to interpret a political silence as a mystical one, for instance, by V. V. Bibikhin. "The twentieth century has had decades of silence in Russian thought. This is a speaking silence. A new thought cannot begin in us unless we first listen attentively to the silence of the twentieth century. … What if that silence was a message? Of what, then, does it speak?"[24]

---

24   Bibikhin, *Iazyk filosofii*, 36.

Such is the tradition of interpreting the "eternal quiet," in which one can see both the people's downtroddenness and submission, and its wisdom and eschewing of vanities. Such is the tradition of Russian Orthodoxy, which was silent both because it supported the powers that be and because the virtue of humility predisposes toward silence. Orthodoxy's not-of-this-worldness seemed to combine the sacred duty and the everyday self-interest of silence, asceticism and conformism, with the one easily reencoded into the system of the other.

c. The Formative, Informative, and Fictive Word: The Self-Devouring of Language

As has already been mentioned, researchers speak of the quietude of pre-Petrine Russia, of the strange muteness of the Russian people. In *The Russian Idea*, Nikolai Berdiaev refers to the "thoughtlessness and voicelessness of pre-Petrine Rus."[25] As Georgii Florovsky remarks in *Pathways of Russian Theology*: "The Russian spirit was not manifest in verbal and mental works."[26] Chaadaev even sees this stamp of silence, or rather, of muteness, not so much inexpressibility as inexpressiveness, on his countrymen's faces: "So many times when in foreign lands, especially in the south, where faces are so animated and expressive, I have compared the faces of my fellow countrymen with the faces of local inhabitants, and I have been shocked at this muteness of our expressions."[27]

In the post-Petrine period comes the time of verbal exaltation, an excess of speech, and one that trends upward: the nineteenth century is more voluble than the eighteenth, and the twentieth century explodes in some sort of unimaginable abundance of words. But, strange as it may seem, this whole spewing and spinning of words produces the impression of muteness, that is, of speech that drowns itself out and turns into a form of silence. In the 1840s, as *raznochintsy* (persons of miscellaneous rank) like Belinsky and Chernyshevsky entered the culture, the "aristocratic" French language begins to go out of circulation, even as the Russian language absorbs a great number of foreign words, especially political

---

25 Berdiaev, *Russkaia ideia: Osnovnye problemy russkoi mysli XIX veka i nachala XX*, 8.
26 Florovskii, *Puti russkogo bogosloviia*, 1:503.
27 Chaadaev, *Sochineniia*, 23.

terms: "socialism," "bourgeoisie," "progress," "reaction," "solidarity," "exploitation," "emancipation," "obscurantism," and other words that formed the backbone of revolutionary-democratic—and later, Soviet—phraseology.[28] From this time on, Russian culture falls into a verbal trance, a frenzy, a rampant flagellantism and braggadocio;[29] it whips itself with words, many of them foreign and barely understood but sonorous and correct; it whirls about and squats like a shaman trying to chant away society's pain, droning and beating his tambourine. Words are used not to convey messages, as a means of communication, but as incantations. *Progress, intelligentsia, reason. The people, Russia, salvation. The proletariat, dictatorship, communism.* In the Buddhist East one falls into a silent trance; Russian culture, a talking one. But insofar as speech is used precisely as an incantation, resounding as an end unto itself, it falls into silence, ceases to be heard, just as the loud watchwords and slogans repeated hourly on Soviet radio ceased to be heard. This silence returns us to the stillness of pre-Petrine, "Asiatic" Russia, but now on the level of speech incessantly droning and drowning itself out.

Dmitrii Galkovsky observes that the Russian language is "prone to the ailment of nonsense."[30] But this ailment stems from its affinity for *supersense*, where a word does not communicate a fact (the informative function of speech, according to Wittgenstein) but exists in its own right as the "creative 'let there be'" (the formative function of speech, according to Sergei Bulgakov). Speech's formative function is just what creates a zone of silence amid the verbal squall. Informational speech communicates exactly as much as it communicates; it does not accumulate silence within itself. The Russian word turns out to be formatively excessive and at the same time informationally deficient; it spins around itself, bearing an empty vortex of meaning.

Three word levels may be identified: the *holy word*, the *meaning word*, and mere verbiage, or the *empty word*. At the supreme level, the word is being or the creation of being, and may be pronounced in silence. At the middle

---

28 See Sorokin, *Razvitie slovarnogo sostava russkovo literaturnogo iazyka 50–90 godov 19-go veka*, 30, 31.
29 Epstein plays on the similar-sounding *khlystovshchina* (flagellantism) and *khlestakovshchina* (boasting à la Khlestakov, main character of Gogol's *The Inspector General*)—trans.
30 Galkovskii, *Beskonechnyi tupik*, 417.

level, the word communicates about being, its signification corresponds to reality; it conveys a fact and acquires a meaning. At the lowest level, the word neither contains being nor communicates about it; it is bereft of meaning, and although it sounds full-fledged, it nevertheless harbors a muteness. The peculiarity of the word in Russian culture is that it skips between the highest and lowest levels, bypassing the middle. Eschewing the "human," informative function, and seeking all at once to assume a "divine" function, the word turns into a magical or ideological incantation, and ultimately into a pure figment, a series of sounds that mean nothing. When the formative word issues from human lips and imitates the act of divine creation, the "let there be," without the support of an informational, cognitive-communicative act, such a word becomes destructive, deformative, insofar as it is indifferent to the reality of its object, merely subjecting it to the magical mission. The holy word turns into the empty word, supersense into nonsense, because the middle word-level—the word as sign, as communication—cannot be sustained. Speechlessness turns out to be the underside of Russian verbality.

The physiologist Ivan Pavlov, analyzing how humans differ from animals in creating language—the "second signal system"[31]—nevertheless considered that amid his countrymen, the development of this system had gone too far. "The Russian mind is not tethered to facts. It loves words more, and operates through them. ... Russian thought does not apply the critical method at all, that is, in no way does it verify the meaning of a word, does not go behind the scenes of a word, does not like to look at genuine reality. We are not students of life but collectors of words. ... Beautiful verbal gymnastics, verbal pyrotechnics. ... We are mainly interested in words, operating through them and paying little heed to reality."[32] The modern prose-writer Viacheslav P'etsukh calls Academician Pavlov's opinion of his own people "frightening," but is nevertheless forced to agree with it. "Indeed, when a Russian espouses a word, it's good and horrifying at the same time."[33] It is good if the word shapes

---

31 Is it not this theory of Pavlov's, incidentally, from which Soviet semioticians and structuralists got the notion of languages of culture as "secondary modeling systems," a term arising at the turn of the 1950s-60s with obvious pretensions to materialist, "Pavlovist" reliability? In that case it would be more precise to call culture a "third signal system," insofar as the second signal system is natural language.
32 Pavlov, "Ob ume voobshche, o russkom ume v chastnosti," 15–16.
33 Selivanova, "Interv'iu s Viacheslavom P'etsukhom," 2.

being, horrifying if it turns being into a figment. Serving as a hedge against such a verbal fall from the supreme, ontological level to the lower, destructive one is the middle level, that of the informative word, which does not alter or supplant being but, to the extent possible, faithfully attests to it.

This is why it is so important for a word to anchor its meaning at the informative level, and only from there to rise to the formative one. Otherwise it invariably falls to the fictive level, and then, losing both its formative and informative fullness, the word turns into a frantic sound, surrounded by the loud silence of God, the people, and nature.

Such is the fate of the Russian language even in the hands of a Dostoevsky. As Mikhail Bakhtin emphasizes, "the main object of his representation is the word itself... Dostoevsky's works are a word about a word addressed to a word."[34] But this self-directedness of the word may be understood not only in the positive sense of a dialogue of different consciousnesses but also as an instance of the language's closedness and self-stupefaction. Joseph Brodsky saw in Dostoevsky an "omnivorous voracity of language: one fine day, neither God, nor man, reality, guilt, death, eternity, nor Salvation is enough for it, and then it pounces upon itself."[35] This means that language begins to talk about itself, overflow with itself, answer a "relation with a relation," make reference to reference—and trails off into silence, collapses on itself. In its place is left a black hole, the "eternal quiet" in the depths of Russia.

What is this quiet that sounds especially loud when the orators of the capitals try to outshout it? What is this silence about—or is this a quiet about nothing? And if it is a silence, then what kind—that of the sage or the slave? Does it harbor some sort of word, or only the absence of words? Would it be possible to speak on behalf of this silence, or is it indifferent to words, lending them a resonance and muffling them in equal measure? If the latter, the entirety of Russia's dazzling discourse starts to resemble Tiutchev's comparison of flashes of heat lightning to a conversation of deaf-mute demons. The mute word in a deaf quiet.

---

34 Bakhtin, *Problems of Dostoevsky's Poetics*, 266.
35 Brodskii, *Sochineniia*, 4:183.

PART VI

Madness and Reason

1 | Methods of Madness and Madness as a Method: Poets and Philosophers[1]

This chapter is about two kinds of madness, poetic and philosophical, or ecstatic and doctrinal. I will explore madness as a cultural symbol rather than as a medical fact, the poetics and metaphysics of madness rather than its clinical aspect. I will try to show the connection between madness and the tendencies of the creative mind, to characterize a method of critical reading founded on the hypothesis of an author's madness, and then to trace briefly the *self-critical* side of this method.

Madness (*bezumie*) is a language. Culture expresses itself in this language as eloquently as it does in the language of reason (*razum*). If we consider lack of reason to be one state, and reason itself to be another, then madness, which is the loss of reason, is a third, *post-rational* state. As was discussed in part 5, soundlessness or quiet do exist in nature, but silence is characteristic only of beings capable of speech. Similarly, thoughtlessness or absence of thought exists in nature, but madness is characteristic only of beings capable of thought and reason. Madness exists in approximately the same relationship to the mind as that of silence to speech. Although externally, in an acoustic sense, silence is the same thing as quiet and merely signifies a lack of sounds, structurally silence is much closer to conversation: both are *about* something and have the property of intentionality, in the Husserlian sense. As Edmund Husserl has said, consciousness is always "consciousness *about*" something. Madness is also a form of consciousness, a means of its articulation, and can take its rightful place among other forms: thinking about…, speaking about…, writing about…, being silent about…, being mad about. … Lovers can speak about but they can also be silent about their love. If it weren't for

---

[1] This chapter was translated by Angela Brintlinger.

conversation, there would be no silence; there would be nothing to be silent *about*. In the same way, if it weren't for reason, there would be no madness; there would be nothing to be mad about.

This is especially applicable to those madmen and silent men who were once brilliant in thought and word. They have the right to be questioned: *about what* are they being silent, *about what* are they mad? Through their creative work they have already entered that field of "*aboutness*," intentionality, from which there is no exit. Meaning fills all breaks, pauses, and hiatuses in this field just as pauses and spaces fill language, absorbing its utmost, otherwise inexpressible meaning. Just as war is the continuation of politics through other means, so too is madness the life of the mind (*um*), continued through other means.[2]

It is this question, "about what?," that hovers over the madness of Friedrich Nietzsche, whose own philosophy justified madness generally and thus anticipated his own illness. "Almost everywhere it was madness which prepared the way for the new idea."[3] In Nietzsche's case, didn't this mean that the opposite was also true: new ideas prepared the way for madness?

a. Hölderlin and Batiushkov

The Muses sell us talent at a dear price!
Konstantin Batiushkov
As though in heavenly captivity cowering...
Friedrich Hölderlin

---

2 Translator's note: The Russian words related to mind, reason, and madness are all connected etymologically and will have great relevance throughout this chapter. A short glossary may be of use. *Um* is "mind"; "reason" is *rázum*; and "madness" is *bezúmie*, literally "without mind." Other related terms include *poloúmie*, which here is rendered as "half-witted state" or "half-wittedness"—etymologically it is derived either from *polu* ("half") or *polyi* ("empty"), in the latter case literally meaning "empty-minded"; *záum*, or "trans-sense," a kind of language invented by futurist poets in the early twentieth century; *sumasshéstvie*, or "madness," literally "having gone out of one's mind" (also *soití s umá*, "to go out of one's mind"). Epstein has coined the terms "mad-making" (*obezúmlivanie*) and "driving-mad" (*sumasvedénie*), as well as the final related term, *inoúmie*—"othermindedness"—for the purpose of his argument in this chapter.
3 Nietzsche, *Daybreak: Thoughts on the Prejudices of Morality*, 13–14.

Methods of Madness and Madness as a Method 315

There are two victims—or two heroes—of poetic madness who in their striking resemblance permit us to delineate more clearly the general rule, the connection between madness and the poetic tendency of the mind itself: Friedrich Hölderlin and Konstantin Batiushkov.

Hölderlin (1770–1843) and Batiushkov (1787–1855) were virtual contemporaries, the German only seventeen years older than the Russian. They both belonged to the era which has received the name of romanticism. Both were great poets, but they spent their lives in the shadow of even greater ones: Goethe and Pushkin. And how similar were their fates!

Both men lived in the light of consciousness, in the muses' good graces, for exactly half of their earthly lives. Batiushkov lived for sixty-eight years: thirty-four as a poet and thirty-four as an "idiot." Hölderlin's life was also split in two and just as equally, as if someone's relentlessly strict calculation was at work: he lived seventy-two years, the first half (thirty-six) as a dreamer, a traveler, and a lover, and the second (also thirty-six) as a homebody, the most gentle of fools. The two spent the remainder of their lives on the periphery, in provincial Tübingen and Vologda respectively. How terrible it must have been to return from the glitter of cultured capital cities to the remote estates of their ancestors, bringing with them only their darkened reason, to deteriorate in the same remote spot where they had been born.

The middle of life… Dante wrote that "in most lives I believe it is attained between the thirtieth and fortieth year, and I believe that in those whose nature is perfect it is attained in the thirty-fifth year."[4] He himself, upon reaching the age of thirty-five, experienced the horror of spiritual eclipse:

> Along the journey of our life half way,
> I found myself again in a dark wood
> Wherein the straight road no longer lay.
> Ah, tongue can never make it understood:

---

[4] Dante, "The Convivio," book 4, chapter 23, translated by Richard Lansing, www.dante.ilt.columbia.edu.

> So harsh and dense and savage to traverse
> That fear returns in thinking on that wood.[5]

What is this gloomy, dense forest? Is it not that fit of insanity, that shady slope of life, that awaits those who ascended life's peak of creativity on the sunny slope? The higher the mountain, the darker the shadow. But even if Dante had visions that darkened his reason, he still emerged, guided upwards by the classically lucid Virgil to the victorious, decisive world of the "crystal sky" and "heavenly rose." But Batiushkov and Hölderlin, who also chose the ancients as their mentors, in the middle of their lives got lost in the gloomy forest, and were never able to find their way out of it.

In thinking about why such a punishment befell Hölderlin and Batiushkov, one sees that it was not only in their madness that they were alike. Indeed, their very intellectual tendencies were similar. How they loved Greece and Italy, how they gave themselves up to those times of long ago! It seems that among poets of the new era there were none as frenzied and self-sacrificing in their love of southern climes and the pagan beauties found there:

> Oh fate, give my sorrowful heart
> A place to rest in the land of Anacreon
> In a small home
> Among the sacred heroes of Marathon!
> Oh, my poem, be the last tear
> On the road to the sacred border!
> Parcae, send me death,—
> I belong to the kingdom of the dead.
> ("Greece"[6])

Hölderlin never travelled to Greece, but the soul of his poetry hovered over it, far afield from his German body. Isn't such a separation from the self dangerous? Doesn't it in fact signify a kind of death in life? "I belong to the kingdom of the dead," Hölderlin wrote. His soul, which for

---

5 Dante, *The Divine Comedy: Hell, Purgatory, Heaven*, 5.
6 Hölderlin, "Griechenland," http://www.textlog.de/17772.html

so long had chased after Hellenic specters, finally broke away and flew off to return no more. Who among the German poets did not strive "thither, thither" (dahin! dahin!), to the region of almond groves and holy oaks...? But probably only Hölderlin chose to stay there. Is his madness not the result of this secret decision?

True, in the last years before his illness he praised Germany tirelessly, as if he felt the oncoming gloom and ruin of his soul and was rushing to lessen his sin through a belated union with a vital homeland:

> And backward now my soul shall not escape
> To you, the vanished, whom I love too much.
> To look upon your beautiful brows, as though
> They were unchanged, I am afraid, for deadly
> And scarcely permitted it is to awaken the dead.
> ("Germania"[7])

Knowing the subsequent fate of the poet, one cannot help but shiver in reading these lines. In them is a last attempt to shake off a contemplative torpidity and to arouse in a simple, crudely contemporary life the dying quivering of a soul that has felt too late its captivity to the other, its confinement in its own temple as if in a prison. How else can we interpret the poet's superstitious horror upon observing the Hellenic gods—"the dead"—when upon waking them he himself is rooted to the spot?

> What is it that
> To the ancient, the happy shores
> Binds me, so that I love them
> Still more than my own homeland?
> For as though in heavenly
> Captivity cowering, in flaming air
> I am where the stones tell Apollo walked
> In the guise of a king...
> ("The Only One"[8])

---

7 https://books.google.co.uk/books?id=HuwecCR6oDQC&pg=PA209&lpg=PA209&dq
8 https://books.google.co.uk/books?id=HuwecCR6oDQC&pg=PA239&lpg=PA239&dq

318   Madness and Reason

Thus in vain did Hölderlin try to acknowledge and weaken the pull of the blessed banks that were about to chain him forever and take away his mind, a mind that had voluntarily chosen the "captivity" of foreign skies. Isn't madness a punishment for this betrayal of *his own*, of the real, for the rapture that pulled his soul from its earthly roots? Indeed, madness is not even punishment, but rather this rapture itself—frozen, stopped, continued into limitlessness.

From Batiushkov we have the same impulse:

> Dear friend, my angel! let us hide ourselves
> Where gentle waves wash Tauride
> And Phoebus's rays shine lovingly
> On the holy places of ancient Greece.
> We there, cast out by fate,
> Equal in unhappiness, equal in love,
> Beneath the sweet sky of a southern country
> Shall forget to shed tears about our cruel lot.
> ("Tauride")

> Друг милый, ангел мой! сокроемся туда,
> Где волны кроткие Тавриду омывают
> И Фебовы лучи с любовью озаряют
> Им древней Греции священные места.
> Мы там, отверженные роком,
> Равны несчастием, любовию равны,
> Под небом сладостным полуденной страны
> Забудем слезы лить о жребии жестоком…
> ("Таврида"⁹)

Batiushkov's "southern country," in contrast to Hölderlin's, was more often Italy than Hellas. Tibullus, Petrarch, Ariosto, and Tasso were nearer to him than Homer, Anacreon, and Pindar, but ringing in these names, too, we hear the very same fidelity to foreign lands and tongues. "As few

---

9 http://rvb.ru/batyushkov/0stihi/01opyt/01eleg/034.htm.

Slavic words as possible"—thus he expressed his poetic credo. In one of his letters he jokingly calls Russia "the land of cranberries and whortleberries," and upon leaving the country in 1818 he wrote: "I am hurrying to Rome, though I am unworthy even to look at it!" If through poetry Vasilii Zhukovsky strove to reach something other—something eternal, supernatural, unearthly—with which the soul might comfort itself, then Batiushkov strove for something foreign and of another time, through which the soul might separate from itself. Batiushkov suffered from the deep anguish of an "accidental" northerner, and he tried to become a true "Italian," although he did so in Russian. At the same time Batiushkov, like Hölderlin, wrote many patriotic poems longing for his homeland, but from far away, from the refuge he had found further west and south—beyond the Nieman, the Rhine, the Rhône…—beneath a "delightful sky," where the light of divinity shone more brightly. This divinity was simultaneously master of the sky and patron of the arts. Hölderlin more often called him Apollo, while Batiushkov called him Phoebus.

And yet these Mediterranean dreamers were to spend their last decades dwelling in the backwaters of Russia and Germany. It was as if fate was pointing its finger: here is your lawful place; you didn't care to embrace it with your soul, so you'll have to remain here as a soulless body. When Mikhail Pogodin visited Batiushkov in 1830, he was left with this impression: "He lies there virtually motionless. Wild glances. Sometimes he'll wave an arm or squeeze some wax. My Lord! Where are his intellect and sensibility? He's only a body, barely alive."[10]

What is the main symptom of madness? I'll refer to Mandel'stam's definition: "Tell me, what in a madman makes the most terrible impression of madness for you? The widened pupils—because they are unseeing, not focused on anything in particular, empty. The mad speeches—because in addressing you, the madman does not take you into account, as if he does not wish to acknowledge your very existence, as if he's absolutely uninterested in you. In the main we fear in the madman that eerie absolute indifference that he displays to us."[11]

---

10 Cited from Barsukov, *Zhizn' i trudy M. P. Pogodina*, 3:36.
11 Mandel'shtam, *Sobranie sochinenii v 4 tomakh*, 1:182.

Hölderlin and Batiushkov's widened pupils were directed at antiquity and the Mediterranean; they looked at their own surroundings with unseeing eyes. "It was precisely the loss of dialogic contact that marked the ailing Hölderlin's behavior in Tübingen. He had difficulty both asking questions and listening to them; even his old acquaintances ... found conversation with him to be 'too eerie'. ... Hölderlin's late poetic monologues exclude any hint of the act of speech itself ... of actual participation in discourse," notes Roman Jakobson, who conducted a thorough study of Hölderlin's poetry of the mad period.[12]

The same is reported by Batiushkov's doctor, Anton Dietrich. In his crazed state Batiushkov "spoke in Italian and recalled in his imagination several lovely episodes of Tasso's 'Jerusalem Delivered,' which he discussed with himself aloud and loudly. ... It was impossible to enter into a discussion with him, to start a conversation. ... The patient ... had separated himself from the world, insofar as life in the world presupposes discourse."[13] In 1828 the already hopelessly ill Batiushkov was brought back from Sonnenstein, where he spent four years with no sign of improvement at Dr. Pirnits's psychiatric institution, to Moscow, where he entered into Dr. Dietrich's care. Along the way, Dietrich reports, "Batiushkov began to speak Italian with himself, either in prose or in some short rhymed verses, but completely incoherently, and among other things, in a meek, touching voice and with an expression of passionate anguish on his face, eyes fixed on the sky, he declared: 'Oh homeland of Dante, homeland of Ariosto, homeland of Tasso! Oh my beloved homeland!' He pronounced these last words with such a noble, dignified expression that I was shaken to the depths of my soul" (493).

In this episode of already *clinical* Italomania, it is clearly visible that Batiushkov's insanity was a paralyzed version of his poetic intellect, which had finally broken the connection with surrounding reality. As a matter of fact, Dr. Dietrich, who treated Batiushkov for about a year and a half and left extraordinarily perceptive and conscientious notes about his condition—"On the Illness of the Russian Nobleman and his Imperial Majesty's Court Councilor Sir Konstantin Batiushkov"—came to the same conclusion. Here is his diagnosis: "The essence of Batiushkov's mental

---

12 Jakobson, "Vzgliad na 'Vid' Gel'derlina," 374.
13 Cited from Maikov, *Batiushkov, ego zhizn' i sochineniia*, 494, 500. Further citations of Dietrich's report in the text are to this edition.

illness lies in the limitless dominance of the power of imagination (*imaginatio*) over the other powers of his mind. As a result they are all slowed and suppressed, so that the intellect is in no condition to recognize the absurdity and groundlessness of those thoughts and images that parade before him in an endless colorful sequence. ... He lives only through dreams, through daydreams" (504).[14]

As we see, in Dr. Dietrich's evaluation, madness was inextricably linked to his patient's powers of imagination. Here we might recall the lines from Pushkin's "God grant that I not lose my mind":

> In flaming frenzy would I sing,
> Forget myself within a haze
> Of shapeless, wondrous dreams.[15]

> Я пел бы в пламенном бреду,
> Я забывался бы в чаду
> Нестройных, чудных грез.[16]

As is known, Pushkin visited the sick Batiushkov in 1830, and it is likely that his impressions, along with the reports of Dr. Dietrich, with whom Pushkin was acquainted, served as an impetus for this poem, written in 1833. Certain points in the poem clearly correlate with episodes from the

---

14 This is not to say that excess of imagination and poetic "otherworldliness" were the reasons for Batiushkov or Hölderlin's mental illness. It is possible, on the contrary, that it was precisely the progressive illness that set their lyrical poetry in this direction. Generally speaking, the relationship between madness and creative work is probably not built on causality but rather on participation and incompatibility. Creative work is impossible without *a certain* madness and is simultaneously incompatible with *total* madness. "The pained soul is healed by poetry" (Evgenii Baratynsky). But where illness reigns, there is no room for poetry either. In examining the madness of Nietzsche, van Gogh, and Artaud, Michel Foucault concludes that "madness is the absolute break with the work of art. ... Artaud's oeuvre experiences its own absence in madness. ... *Where there is a work of art, there is no madness*" (Foucault, *Madness and Civilization: A History of Insanity in the Age of Reason*, 287, 288–89; emphasis in original). The silence of mad poets is filled with meaning in relation to their prior speech, but by itself it presents a soul-wrenching emptiness.

15 Pushkin, *Pushkin Threefold: Narrative, Lyric, Polemic, and Ribald Verse. The Originals with Linear and Metric Translations*, 253–55. Further citations of Pushkin in the text are to Walter Arndt's translations in this edition.

16 Russian quotations of this poem are cited from Pushkin, *Sobranie sochinenii v 10 tomakh*, 2:384.

mad Batiushkov's journey as described by Dietrich. Here are three examples of such correspondence:

> During every bout of feverish excitement he becomes very strong. (492)

> And strong were I, and free were I... (255)
> И силен, волен был бы я...

> Once he asked me to let him leave the carriage to walk about in the woods. (493)

> Were they to leave me
> At liberty, how eagerly would I
> Make for the darkling wood! (255)

> Когда б оставили меня
> На воле, как бы резво я
> Пустился в темный лес!

> With an expression of passionate anguish on his face, eyes fixed on the sky... (493)

> And I would gaze, with gladness filled,
> Into the empty skies. (255)

> И я глядел бы, счастья полн,
> В пустые небеса.

b. Two Half-Witted States: Poetic and Philosophical

Madness has been identified with mental illness since the eighteenth century and, as a rule, belongs to the world of doctors and psychiatrists. But it was not always so. Beginning with Plato, madness (*mania*) was considered to be the highest achievement of the human soul, a rising above the limitations of reason. "[M]ania proceeding from divinity is more beautiful than prudence which proceeds from men."[17]

In *The Phaedrus* Plato distinguishes three kinds of madness: prophetic, prayerful, and poetic. About the last he writes:

> [T]he third species is a possession and mania descending from the Muses, which receiving a soul tender and solitary, rouses and agitates it with Bacchic fury, according to odes and other species of poetry; in consequence of which, by adorning the infinite actions of antiquity, it becomes the means of instructing posterity. But he who approaches to the poetic gates without the mania of the Muses, persuading himself that he can become a poet, in a manner perfectly sufficient from art alone, will, both as to himself and his poetry, be imperfect; since the poetry which is produced by prudence vanishes before that which is the progeny of mania.[18]

Madness in this Platonic sense is not the loss of reason but rather liberation from its captivity. Hölderlin belongs to this tradition of poetic madness, indeed quite consciously so. Hölderlin's thought, which so tragically came to pass in his fate, was that "holy madness is the highest manifestation of humanity."[19] In the same way, Martin Heidegger subsequently found Hölderlin's insanity to be a consequence of his poetic illuminations. "Excessive brightness drove the poet into darkness."[20]

Poetic madness, first described by Plato, has been studied at length in the history of culture, and the very expression "poetic madness" has become a common term. This is the madness of frenzy, ecstasy, the free effusion of the most wild images and fantasies. It was the threatening specter of this very madness that hovered over Pushkin as well.

> And I would hark my fill of waves,
> And I would gaze, with gladness filled,
> Into empty skies;

---

17 Plato, *The Works of Plato*, 3:319.
18 Ibid.
19 Hölderlin, *Sämtliche Werke*, 16:414.
20 Heidegger, *Elucidations of Hölderlin's Poetry*, 62.

And strong were I, and free were I,
Like to the whirlwind gashing fields,
[And] breaking forests down. (255)

И я б заслушивался волн,
И я глядел бы, счастья полн,
В пустые небеса;
И силен, волен был бы я,
Как вихорь, роющий поля,
Ломающий леса.

But there is also a madness of another order, which does not soar above reason but falls into step behind it. Both the delirium of *irrationality* and the delirium of *hyperrationality* exist. The prefix "hyper" in this case means not merely a strong but an excessive degree of rationality (the same meaning that occurs in such words as "hypertonia," "hypertrophy," "hyperinflation," "hyperbole"...). Beyond measure—this is the quality of excess that, overstepping a boundary, turns into its own opposite. *Hyperrationality* is just such a super-rationality, an obsession with rules, principles, the laws of reason, which turns into its opposite—madness.

In other words, madness can be a deviation from reason, but it can also be a manifestation of a lack of deviation. Polonius, as we know, concludes about Hamlet, "Though this be madness, yet there is method in't" (*Hamlet*, act 2, scene 2). The opposite would also be true: not only does madness have its own method, but absolute devotion to a method is indicative of madness. We might invert Polonius thus: "Though this be method, yet there is madness in't."

As Pascal noted, "there is nothing so conformable to reason as [this] disavowal of reason."[21] Reason that trusts itself completely, tyrannically holding sway over the individual—this is already madness. As we know, two main threats to society exist: anarchy and tyranny, the collapse of government power or, on the contrary, a power which becomes absolute and

---

21 Pascal, *Pensées: Notes on Religion and Other Subjects*, 100.

the repressive apparatus that accompanies such power. In just the same way reason, as a system of fundamental concepts and functions of thought, can be defeated by an illness of anarchy— *ecstatic madness*, or by an illness of totalitarianism—*doctrinal madness*. Coherence and mobility are two complementary qualities of any living system, including that of reason. When one of these qualities is lost, reason falls into a madness either of *incoherence*, or of *immobility*. Circularity of reason, its concentration on one immobile point, is no less fraught with madness than *unbalance* of reason, which wanders without direction. What is more mad: a chaotic dance of images, an orgy of imagination, or an organ of reason stuck on one super-valued idea? These two halves of madness, two half-witted states, deserve one another. The very concept of "half-wittedness" means that a person retains only half of his brain—either an immobile cluster of ideas or their incoherent racing.

This *other* half-wittedness can be called philosophical, if we use the opposition of poetry and philosophy put forward by Plato. Poetry is a world of intoxicating, illusory images, while philosophy is a world of eternal, identifiable ideas. If poetic madness undermines the foundations of strict morality, a crime for which poets have been exiled from their countries, then *the madness of philosophers directs the government itself*, and this is the madness not of anarchy but of ideocracy, the madness of immutable, inexorable ideas in the name of which rulers tend their rational flock. We might call this form of madness *noostasis* (from the Greek *noos*, "intellect, reason," and *sta*, the root of *histanai*, "to stay motionless"). The term *stasis* comes from physiology, where it signifies an embolism of the vessels, an anomaly whereby the flow of liquid (for example blood) slows or comes to a stop. *Noostasis* is a delay of the intellect, an embolism, so to speak, of the vessels of the brain, not in a physiological but rather a psychological and intellectual sense. In such a case *noostasis* is the opposite of *ekstasis* (from the same root: Greek *ekstasis*, *ex* + *stasis*, from *histanai*).

If Plato was the philosopher who discovered poetic madness, then Jonathan Swift was the writer who discovered philosophical madness. Here is the description of this illness from his *A Tale of a Tub* (1704), from the ninth section, titled "A Digression Concerning the Original, the Use and Improvement of Madness in a Commonwealth":

> Let us next examine the great Introducers of new Schemes in Philosophy, and search till we can find, from what Faculty of the Soul the Disposition arises in mortal Man, of taking it into his Head, to advance new Systems with such an eager Zeal, in things agreed on all hands impossible to be known.... Because, it is plain, that several of the chief among them, both *Antient* and *Modern*, were usually mistaken by their Adversaries, and indeed, by all, except their own Followers, to have been Persons Crazed, or out of their Wits, having generally proceeded in the common Course of their Words and Actions, by a Method very different from the vulgar Dictates of *unrefined* Reason: agreeing for the most Part in their several Models, with their present undoubted Successors in the *Academy* of *Modern Bedlam*. ... Of this Kind were *Epicurus, Diogenes, Apollonius, Lucretius, Paracelsus, Des Cartes,* and others; who, if they were now in the World, tied fast, and separate from their Followers, would in this our undistinguishing Age, incur manifest Danger of *Phlebotomy*, and *Whips*, and *Chains*, and *dark Chambers*, and *Straw*.[22]

Further, Swift sarcastically lays out Epicurus's and Descartes's systems as "Conceptions, for which the Narrowness of our Mother-Tongue has not yet assigned any other Name, besides that of *Madness* or *Phrenzy*."[23] And he concludes: "Then has this *Madness* been the Parent of all those mighty Revolutions, that have happened in *Empire*, in *Philosophy*, and in *Religion*."[24] For Swift there is no specific difference between a philosophical system, a government dictatorship, and military aggression, since at their foundation lies a kind of "fury" of thought. According to Swift's fantastic physiology, this "fury" is created by a surplus of pressure and a darkening action of the vapors of the brain. "Of such great Emolument, is a Tincture of this *Vapour*, which the World calls *Madness*, that without its Help the World would ... be deprived of those two great Blessings, *Conquests* and *Systems*."[25] In other words, it is as if Swift has turned the thought of Shakespeare's Polonius inside

---

22 Swift, *The Basic Writings of Jonathan Swift*, 89.
23 Ibid., 89.
24 Ibid., 91.
25 Ibid., 90.

out, finding madness in the "inventors of new systems" precisely because of the indisputable and rash methodicalness of their thinking.

Scientists, researchers, thinkers, philosophers, politicians, ideologues, and transformers of society are more inclined toward this *methodological* kind of madness than poets, musicians, and artists, since searching for and designing methodology is part of the essence of their professions. In fact, any ideological or philosophical "ism" is a minor form of madness. And some "isms," such as those that inspired the Soviet system, are major forms of madness, able to drive entire peoples crazy over the course of long periods of time. A symptom of *noostasis* (the inhibition and stoppage of reason) can be recognized by its persistent effort to trace an enormous variety of phenomena to one all-explaining reason. Plato defined poetic madness with the word *mania*. We can define philosophical madness, which in his senile works, especially in the *Laws*, was not alien to Plato himself, as "monomania."

c. Madness as Method

If in madness we seek the traces of a mind lost, then we can find the potential signs of madness in a mind that is overly imperious and obstinate. From this point of view, every mind of philosophical bent has its own project, its own universe subject to recreation, its Method and Absolute, and thus its own potential for madness. Plato would have lost his mind differently from Aristotle, Hegel differently from Kant... One method of reading great texts is to look for the germs of madness that beyond the texts themselves might have developed into systems of their own. Madness is more methodical than sense, which is continually ready to make logical indulgences and evasions. Madmen know for certain and act decisively. The mistake we often make when we write the word "madness" in Russian (*sumasshestvie*), forgetting the second "s" (i.e. *sumashestvie*) has a logic of its own: the madman parades (*shestvuet*) with all the ceremonious straightforwardness inherent in this action, while the healthy mind dodges, tramps about and shifts from one foot to the other.

Kornei Chukovsky, one of the most astute critics of the early twentieth century, interpreted writers of his time—D. Merezhkovsky, M. Gorky,

L. Andreev, F. Sologub—in a Swiftian manner, precisely as *clever madmen*, the bearers of *idées fixes*. In his view, a person with an excess of intellect often loses his mind as well. For example, Merezhkovsky was obsessed with paired things, with the idea of two abysses, an upper and a lower one. Chukovsky comments:

> For Merezhkovsky, it seems, all things are enchanted, because over the course of those hundreds and hundreds of pages they always, in some completely magical manner, move before us in the same [antithetical] order, fulfilling Merezhkovsky's simple formula. ... Here we see the magnitude of this writer's fetishism.[26]

And about Leonid Andreev, Chukovsky has the following to say:

> In the world he always sees only some little shred, one tiny dust mote, one bit of fluff, although this mote then becomes Ararat, blocking out the sky and the earth and the entire horizon for him. ... This psychology of possession, affliction, is so much a part of Andreev that he endows everyone with it. His heroes are more often than not monomaniacs. ... For example, in the story "The Curse of the Beast," the hero begins by declaring: "Oh city!.. false city... accursed city... My last curse: city!" He then continues to declare the same thing page after page. Never once does he speak of anything else. It is quite clear: this is a maniac. A person seized and tormented by only one image, only one thought, blind and deaf to everything else.[27]

In order to understand a writer, Chukovsky has to *make him mad (obezumit')*, to hypothetically *drive him out of his mind*. Madness becomes for Chukovsky a critical method, a kind of hyperbole of analysis. Or rather, such a method has as its basis simultaneously both hyperbole and hypothesis—a combination of "hyper" and "hypo," exaggeration and underestimation. Certain *idées fixes*, idiosyncrasies, constant obsessive images

---

26 Chukovskii, *Sobranie sochinenii v 6-i tomakh*, 6:200.
27 Ibid., 6:31, 33.

are analyzed in an exaggerated way as characteristics of madness, but the modality of the statement itself is not declarative but rather hypothetical. We might call such a method of reading "mad-making" (*obezúmlivanie*) or "driving-mad" (*sumasvedénie*)—the concentration of a writer's image in the mirror of his potential madness. In this way Chukovsky transformed the pantheon of literary divinities of his time, the dominant influences, into a panopticon of intellectual maniacs and monsters, fanatics of one method or idea.

We can apply the concept of madness as method not only to individual authors but also to entire ideologies, to the ideological preoccupation as such. The method is particularly applicable to totalitarian ideologies, where internal consistency and the all-powerfulness of a single idea are achieved at the cost of its complete conceptual isolation from reality and the practical destruction thereof. Ideocracy is a *philosophical madness* that takes possession of the masses and becomes a material power.[28]

The theme of *ideomania*—ideology as madness—dominates Aleksandr Zinov'ev's book *The Madhouse* (*Zheltyi dom*, 1980).[29] As a junior research scholar at the USSR Academy of Sciences' Moscow Institute of Philosophy, one of Zinov'ev's duties was to work with citizens who suffered from an excess of ideological zeal. The KGB would send the manuscripts of such citizens to the institute for an expert opinion. Authors were divided into two categories: committed Marxists and committed enemies of Marxism.

Here it is essential to note three things: 1) the KGB supposed that psychological deviations occur on philosophical grounds along with metaphysical delusions; 2) the security organs had control of such cases of philosophical lunacy; 3) the USSR Academy of Sciences' Institute of Philosophy was entrusted with diagnosing these lunacies and deciding whether they were purely medical or were ideologically harmful in nature. The KGB's use of philosophical expertise demonstrated an important

---

28 To describe this process of pseudo-philosophical indoctrination, I have suggested the term "intoxophication"—intoxication by "sophia."
29 "Yellow house" (*zheltyi dom*) has been a term used to describe Russian madhouses since their very founding under Catherine the Great.

specificity of the ideocratic state: the certainty that deviations from the mental norm were in one way or another the result of philosophical errors—either deliberate, ideologically dangerous digressions from Marxism, or its involuntary, mentally ill distortion. Such an interlacing of philosophy and psychiatry are characteristic for an ideocratic society. Philosophy is entrusted with expertise on the mental health of the citizenry because the very norms of life of the given society are defined by philosophy.

The experiment of the totalitarian system heightened the sensitivity of its former citizens to any forms of totality, even within the borders of strictly individual, innocently dreamy madness. After all, it is precisely from the heads of the most unrestrained dreamers that the most perfect systems of general slavery emerge. If in *The Madhouse* Zinov'ev presented one form of doctrinaire madness, Soviet Marxism, then the artist Il'ia Kabakov, in his total installations *The Madhouse, or the Institute for Creative Research* (1991) and *The Palace of Projects* (1998), demonstrates a number of systems of thought, both historically genuine and imaginary, each of which contains within itself the "consistency of madness," the broad sweep of its wings eclipsing the sun. In one series he examines the acclaimed philosopher Nikolai Fedorov's project[30] for the resurrection of the dead and their distribution to various star worlds, and, for example, the project of the fictional homemaker E. Lisovskaia from Chkalovsk for the creation of paradise in her apartment.

The Madhouse, or the Institute for Creative Research (1991) consists of an aggregate of projects authored by patients. The treatment involves having the patients freely fulfill their own creative ideas, since it is society's rejection thereof that has caused their psychological breakdown in the first place.

> At the institute there is no separation into "doctor" and "patient," "well" and "sick"—there are instead "authors" and "collaborators," "creators" and their "assistants." Both work diligently and persistently to implement the "projects," pursuing them to a successful result. ...

---

30 Nikolai Fedorov (1829–1903), a Russian Christian philosopher, is considered the founder of the Russian cosmism movement and a precursor of transhumanism. See Part II, ch.2.

Methods of Madness and Madness as a Method 331

> The installation consists of a complex labyrinth of large and small rooms. ... The first room ... is called the "doctor's office" and its walls are covered with numerous instructions and rules. The other twelve rooms into which the viewer can see, in addition to their objects, have explanations on the walls that clearly show when the patient entered the institution, the nature of his "project" and its main idea, and also the attending doctors' opinions about it. The entire installation is illuminated with a bright electric light.[31]

Kabakov invariably puts the word "project" in quotation marks. It signifies both the creative project in which the author of the Institute for Creative Research is engaged and that "peculiarity" with which the madhouse patient is obsessed. A unique characteristic of these "creative deviances" is their systematic character, the fact that they are presented precisely in the form of projects, the kind of doctrine that aspires to save the world and organize human life according to principles of harmony and justice. For example, a project is exhibited in room eleven under the title "Energy should be uniformly distributed." The patient is concerned that in the world, energy is distributed unevenly—in some places there is more of it, and in others less. He has invented the project "universal uniform System"—"a network of sputniks hanging motionless over the entire surface of the Earth and capturing excess energy in certain places so as to transfer it immediately to those regions that have insufficient energy."[32] In order to give a visual sense of his idea, he has created a scale model of it in which an entire chain of drawings of various quality are connected into a whole and hung on the wall—the best and worst of them average out in quality. The *hyperrationality* of these lunacies is reinforced by the fact that the entire space of the "Institute for Creative Research" is lit by "bright electric light," the light of triumphant reason. The power of that reason is also demonstrated by the "numerous instructions and rules" adorning the doctor's office that opens the installation.

---

31 Kabakov, *Sumasshedshii dom, ili Institut kreativnykh issledovanii*, 12–13.
32 Ibid., 166.

It would seem that we have before us a method of humanistic psychotherapy: the patients are treated solicitously, with respect and encouragement for the "value and creativity of each mental illness."[33] On the other hand, Kabakov uses a method of critical *maddening* that allows any system of thought to be interpreted as a "project" (in quotation marks), as a "peculiarity." The more a given idea is rationally grounded, and the wider its proposed range of applicability, the more strongly does its abnormal "hyper" quality stick out. Humanistic psychiatry turns into a hermeneutics of suspicion, a presumption of complete lunacy. If a madhouse can be transformed into an Institute for Creative Research, then the opposite is also true: all kinds of systematic ideas and "creative ideas" can be transformed into divisions of applied psychiatry.

For Kabakov it is essential to demonstrate that the Institute for Creative Research is an open institution where visitors and patients' relatives can be admitted to work out their own "projects":

> Upon visiting the institute the viewer realizes something very important: here any "project," no matter how audacious, strange, or unusual it seems, will meet with understanding, assistance, and recognition. And this situation causes the viewer to pause and ask himself: "Why shouldn't I realize my 'project'? And what might that be, my very own 'project,' sensed within myself since childhood?" In such cases where these questions arise, the institute's administration meets the visitor halfway: in an anterior room of the institute, at a private meeting, in spontaneous discussion, the viewer can receive preliminary information about the potential nature of "his project."[34]

---

33 It is the conviction of the clinic's director Dr. Lublin that "at the basis of any mental illness or trauma lies the elevated and continually active creativity (a productive creative ability) of a person who for various reasons (familial, social, cultural, etc.) is not recognized but rather rejected by the environment in which he is currently immersed" (ibid., 27–28).
34 Ibid., 31.

In other words, the Institute for Creative Research is prepared to open its doors wide to welcome every "project-maker"...

Not excluding the author of the total installations himself. Kabakov emphasizes that his *Palace of Projects* is in turn simply one of the projects, that is to say it has within it a measure of the very madness it is exhibiting to thorough review. This is an interesting paradox even from the standpoint of logic: an aggregate of all projects includes itself as one of its own elements. In the foreword to *The Palace of Projects* (1998), Kabakov stipulates the self-reflective quality of his artistic research: "The meaning of the work which we are presenting—which, of course, also must in turn be considered as a project—is to call attention to a type of ideas and proposals in which one main characteristic dominates: the transformation and improvement of the world."[35]

This means that the same ambivalent, critical-utopian attitude that defines the modality of the entire collection of over-intelligent and half-intelligent projects should be extended to the metaproject of Kabakov himself, this project of *The Palace of Projects*. In a case where an aggregate of lunacies is transformed into an element of itself, we can speak already of a *self-critique* of the creative intellect, bordering on the danger of its own madness.

d. The Self-Critique of Pure Reason

It is possible to apply this method of maddening to oneself, especially if your profession entails methodical thinking, creating a method for your own work. "To madden yourself" is to avoid the opposite, being "maddened." The mind that recognizes the danger of its own madness is in part already delivered from it.

Plato, who laid the foundation of the theory of poetic madness and was himself not immune to philosophical madness in the iron consistency of his *Laws*, also gives an example of this kind of self-critique. In the *Laws* he provides the project of his ideocracy with strict guidelines:

---

35 Kabakov, *Dvorets proektov/The Palace of Projects* (no pagination).

> [The lawgiver] must divide up both the city itself and all the country into the twelve portions.... He must mark off 5,040 allotments.... And he must divide the citizens also into twelve parts, making all the twelve parts as equal as possible in respect of the value of the rest of their property, after a census has been made of all. After this they must also appoint twelve allotments for the twelve gods, and name and consecrate the portion allotted to each god, giving it the name of "phyle" [tribe]. And they must also divide the twelve sections of the city in the same manner as they divided the rest of the country.[36]

And suddenly into this mercilessly rational plan of reordering the world, a nagging note enters: Plato tears himself away from the great deed of his intellect and with a stranger's eyes sees the vanity of this legislation as a dream.

For me the next passage of the *Laws* is the most precious of all:

> But we must by all means notice this,—that all the arrangements now described will never be likely to meet with such favorable conditions that the whole program can be carried out according to plan. This requires that the citizens will raise no objection to such a mode of living together, and will tolerate being restricted for life to fixed and limited amounts of property and to families such as we have stated, and being deprived of gold and of the other things which the lawgiver is clearly obliged by our regulations to forbid, and will submit also to the arrangements he has defined for country and city, with the dwellings set in the center and round the circumference,—almost as if he were telling nothing but dreams, or moulding, so to say, a city and citizens out of wax.[37]

One inadvertently recalls the insane Konstantin Batiushkov: "Sometimes he'll wave an arm or squeeze some wax" (from Pogodin's memoirs). Wax is the most appropriate material for the schemes of such an active and

---

36 Plato, *The Laws*, 383.
37 Ibid., 383–85.

elevated madness. Il'ia Kabakov does exactly the same thing in his "Palace of Projects": he takes the thoughts of daring individuals and seers—ideas meant to be incarnated in cities and states, in transformations on a cosmic scale—and molds them from wax or cuts them out of paper.[38]

The critique of ideology/ideomania that both Swift's satirical pen and Kabakov's conceptual sculpture advance is already present in the precious admission of the lawmaker Plato, the self-critique of philosophical reason. Plato does not speak directly about his madness, but is it not madness to put forth examples of one's own dreams as the highest legislation? Plato's project, as declared in *The Republic* and *Laws*, is in essence a total installation in the style of Kabakov, an introductory section for his "Palace of Projects," the "fashion[ing] from wax [of] a certain city and citizens."

Let us take up the implications of Plato's qualm. In contemplating one's own mind—and what mind can resist such self-analysis?—it is useful to imagine a series of repetitions forming a mirror-perspective of madness. Regarding itself in the mirror of its own madness, of its own infallible method, the mind more easily moves in the direction of healthy tolerance and eclecticism. In other words, every learned person, every intellectual, every creator or distributor of ideas needs *the self-critique of pure reason*, the ability to recognize the curve of his own model of the world before it turns into complete gibberish. It would be useful for all intellectuals, following the example of Plato, to pose themselves the question: if I were to follow the rules of my own discourse and method to their end, would I lose my mind?

* * *

For a person raised in Russian culture, it would be natural to associate this question with the prospect of madness that haunted Pushkin. In the poem "God grant that I not lose my mind," he expresses two of the strongest

---

38 For example, in Kabakov's "Palace of Projects," Fedorov's plan for universal resurrection corresponds to a metal-framed table on which lies a plastic box of dirt "planted" with little white paper cut-outs of "resurrected" people (project 35). Clearly this delimitation in a box plays ironically on the philosophical text on universal resurrection, reducing its prophetic and edifying meanings to the scale of paper dolls.

impulses of creative reason. On the one hand, he feels constrained within his own limits and seeks madness as a celebration of freedom:

> It is not that my reason
> I treasure; not that with it
> I would not gladly part. (255)

> Не то чтоб разумом моим
> Я дорожил, не то чтоб с ним
> Расстаться был не рад.

On the other hand, reason fears madness as an even worse form of bondage:

> But here's the rub: go off your mind
> And men will dread you like the plague,
> [And] straightway lock you up... (255)

> Да вот беда: сойдешь с ума
> И страшен будешь, как чума,
> Как раз тебя запрут...

To part with one's reason, but not irredeemably, *to lose one's mind within the limits of reason itself*, to let it roam, but keep it on a leash: this is the salvatory outcome suggested by Pushkin's "dialectic" of creative madness.

Reason must know *its other*, but it must not become one with it. This *other of reason*, which nonetheless remains under its supervision, might be called *othermindedness*. Between reason and madness there is a place for ecstatic forays and ironic returns, for that entire between-minded zone where reason runs from itself and returns to itself. Othermindedness is *controlled madness*. As in the case of a controlled explosion, one must control madness and not allow the kind of blast that tears off the hand of the "exploder" himself, as has happened numerous times in history (such as the cases of Hölderlin and Nietzsche).

Methods of Madness and Madness as a Method   337

It is precisely othermindedness that characterizes both Plato and Pushkin—the ability to transgress the borders of common sense either doctrinally or ecstatically, while at the same time carefully avoiding the abyss of senselessness. Just as poetic *zaum* (transsensical language) is a means of defamiliarizing language, so is philosophical *othermindedness* a means of defamiliarizing the thought process, of simultaneously arousing and restraining it.[39] Othermindedness is the art of thinking dangerously, the play of reason on the edge of insanity, a game in which the thinker himself is not always able to distinguish defeat from victory.

---

39   *Zaum* is poetic *trans-sense*, language that is supposed to make more sense because it forces the reader to perceive it anew. "Defamilarization" (or "making it strange," *ostranenie*) is the formalists' term for engendering this new perception.

2 | Poetry as Ecstasy and as Interpretation: Boris Pasternak and Osip Mandel'shtam[1]

a. Alien Language: Poetry and Kabbalah

Mikhail Bakhtin's well-known statement that culture is created on the border of cultures is borne out by twentieth-century letters, in which a leading place belongs to writers of non-native origin who have crossbred diverse languages and national traditions. Is Kafka a Czech writer? An Austrian, German, or Jewish one? And Nabokov? Is he a Russophone American or an Anglophone Russian author? Various cultural traditions are interwoven in the complex lacework of his artistic polyglossia. At the very least, the language of twentieth-century art is diglossia—another of Bakhtin's concepts.

In the cases of Boris Pasternak and Osip Mandel'shtam, this diglossia may be grasped even more literally than has been usual, as a conversation in, or even a convergence of, two national languages. One language, Russian, forms the external plane of expression, but the other language belongs to a hidden, biblical plane of internal form and content. It must be deciphered in intricately encoded lines that are at times strange and alien to the Russian ear. Even intuitively, the discourse of Pasternak and Mandel'shtam seems thicker, more gelatinous, more mixed with polyglot elements than does that of their predecessors in Russian poetry. Listen carefully to these lines:

---

1 I am grateful to Ruth Rischin, translator of this chapter, for her assistance in identifying relevant sources and for her editing of subsequent authorial additions and revisions.

Where hair all disheveled, and tucked in your sash
The bud of a tea-rose, intoxicant scent,
As waltzing to glory, you bite on your kerchief
In joking, and torment, with barely a breath.
(Pasternak, "The Substitute"[2])

Чтоб прическу ослабив и чайный и шалый,
Зачаженный бутон заколов за кушак,
Провальсировать к славе, шутя, полушалок
Закусивши, как муку, и еле дыша.
("Заместительница")

I drink the roiled air like a dark water.
Time has been plowed, and the rose was earth.
In a slow whirlpool the heavy tender roses,
Rose heaviness, rose tenderness, are plaited in double wreaths.
(Mandel'shtam, "Heaviness and tenderness—sisters: the same features"[3])

Словно темную воду, я пью помутившийся воздух.
Время вспахано плугом, и роза землею была.
В медленном водовороте тяжелые нежные розы,
Розы тяжесть и нежность в двойные венки заплела!
("Сестры—тяжесть и нежность—одинаковы ваши приметы")

Words are pressed together so closely that there is no breathing space for the sonorous, drawn-out quality of the line and the transparent literal meanings of the words that so captivate us in Pushkin and Nekrasov, Blok and Esenin. The speech of Pasternak and Mandel'shtam proceeds as if against the current of language itself, raising up semantic storms— tearing from their roots the figurative meanings of the words, loosening

---

[2] Pasternak, *My Sister Life and the Zhivago Poems*, 51; further citations in the text will be indicated *MSL*. In this chapter, translations not cited from a previous publication are by Ruth Rischin, with minor emendations.
[3] Mandelstam, *The Selected Poems of Osip Mandelstam*.

and overturning the settled layers of the language that have become caked by the effects of time. The "bud" in a more literal rendering of Pasternak's lines is simultaneously "tea-rose" (*chainyi*), "smoky" (*zachazhennyi*), and "crazed" (*shalyi*)—each epithet being a way to dislodge the meaning of "bud" from its semantic nest. In reading such enigmatic lines as Pasternak's "a smoky, crazed, tea-rose bud" or Mandel'shtam's "time has been plowed, and the rose was earth," it is impossible to relax, to lose oneself in the musical flow: the words must be divined, their meaning guessed at, holding readers taut and tense, sending them from one level of meaning to another. Speech is estranged from language, as if another language were showing through it, making it subject to an intricate polysemic deciphering. In order to understand what has been said—the transferred meanings and allusions that show through the system of references by means of another, as yet unread text—every reader unwittingly becomes an interpreter and a sort of Kabbalist. The result is an "arcanization,"[4] a profusion of meanings and interpretations that render it difficult not only to perform a critical reading but *any* reading of this poetry.

In the writings of these two poets, the figurative overload, the text's "overwhelming burden," exceeds its vocal sostenuto. "As image enters into image and as object intersects object" is Pasternak's formula of his own semantic superabundance. Many linguistic roots are crammed into a single line, as if the respiratory, "vowelled" component of the verse were being forced out by the semantic, "consonantal" component. Per aural unit, more roots are present than is usual in a poem. The word is squeezed into its root, and the root is then squeezed into the dry consonantal sounds that comprise it.

Mandel'shtam wrote: "Poetic speech animates the wandering polysemic root. The multiplier of the root is the consonant, the indicator of its vitality. ... A word multiplies not by its vowels but by its consonants. The consonants are the seed and pledge of a language's posterity. A lessening of linguistic awareness atrophies the feeling for the consonant."[5] In Mandel'shtam's definition, the sonority of the poetic line, sustaining its

---

4 I borrow this term from Moshe Idel, who calls the Kabbalistic Zohar a "comprehensive arcanization of the Bible" (*Absorbing Perfections: Kabbalah and Interpretation*, 218).
5 Mandel'shtam, *Sobranie sochinenii v trekh tomakh*, 2:261

long, mellifluous vowels, is squeezed, so that by the grouping of the consonants, the root meanings come swarming in, overlapping each other. Poetry does not hold a wide-open mouth, affirming its inherent "stupidity," as Pushkin suggested ("poetry must be slightly stupid").[6] On the contrary, poetry presents the diversity of barriers arising on the path of a respiratory element, so as to transform it into a "clattering," "crackling" "whistle"[7]—the tactile tickling of language, the flesh of the consonants. The word is hardened to its semantic skeleton, from which is wrung its vocal sonority.

There is a striking correspondence between Mandel'shtam's poetic preferences and the linguistic flair of his ancestors. In biblical Hebrew, the meaning of a word is defined by the root, which consists exclusively of consonants; to this day, Torah scrolls omit vowels. After the eighth century, vowels were added to guide the pronunciation of texts and clarify the grammatical form of words. This aural minimalism creates the basis for a semantic maximalism. Considering that Hebrew has only twenty-two letters in all, nearly any combination of them proves meaningful; moreover, words whose roots have two or three common consonants turn out to be, as it were, cognates.

This explains the endless potential to interpret each word as a derivative of another: since they all descend from one branching-out root, they all are intertwined in fraternal union around one Paternal name. Hence the Kabbalistic notion of the totality of biblical texts as a paraphrase and a self-disclosure of the one sacred primal word—the inexpressible four-letter name of God. Hence also the interpretive inexhaustibility of each biblical word, which by its own root elements is inscribed in a multitude of other words, and which is interwoven with them through all the twists and nuances of its own meanings.

And so this wandering polysemic consonantal root begins to plough up the rich undersoil of Russian poetry, to incorporate variant vowels and thus luxuriously branch into many verbal formations.

---

6 Pushkin, *Sobranie sochinenii v 10 tomakh*, 9:232.
7 Mandel'shtam, *Sobranie sochinenii v trekh tomakh*, 2:261.

Once surmounting Nature's rigidity,
The hard blue eye penetrated her law,
In the Earth's crust, the bedrock plays the fool,
And a moan bursts from the chest like ore...
(Mandel'shtam, "Octets")

Преодолев затверженность природы,
Голуботвердый глаз проник в ее закон,
В земной коре юродствуют породы,
И как руда из груди рвется стон...
("Восьмистишия")

The words of this fragment from Mandel'shtam's series of octets are offshoots of one consonantal root: **p-r-d**. Sometimes it becomes voiceless (t instead of d), rings out (b instead of p), intermingles with another sporadically arising root, **g-l-z-n** (go*l*ubotverdyi, g*l*az, *z*akon, *z*emnoi), or absorbs into its porous depths the liquid vowels: **o-e-u**—germinating with their help into a multitude of diverse words and meanings. But they are all produced in the poem from one hardy, generative primary root, so that **preodolev** ("surmounting"), *zatverzhennost'* ("rigidity"), **prirody** ("nature"), go*lubotverdyi* ("hard blue"), *iurodstvuiut* ("play the [holy] fool"), **porody** ("bedrock"), *ru*da ("ore"), *gru*di ("chest"), *rvet-sia* ("bursts")—all of these lexical units, pressed together within the poem, turn out to be the resilient offshoots of the same polysemic root, PRD, and of its variant, BRT.

With other poets, of course, consonants also play among themselves, echoing one another, but the difference is one of degree. In the case of Mandel'shtam, this is not simply an instance of alliteration, as when the consonants of two or three words chime; it is, rather, the proliferation of a single root in the guise of different words.

These lines, too, reveal an underlying Hebraic component:

Be the malachite cathedral well-groomed
Or the silvery hillside cherished,

The multilobular barrenness of the bell towers
Is reflected in the cupronickel of the shallows.
("Melchior"[8])

Храмовой в малахите ли холен,
Возлелеян в сребре ль косогор—
Многодольную голь колоколен
Мелководный несет мельхиор...
("Мельхиор")

At the very outset, in its title "Melchior," this early Pasternak poem presents a consonantal root that then wanders from line to line, swelling with vowels and intermingling with other roots. In his analysis of these complex and transsensical lines, Christopher Barnes has noted that "a phonetic rendering demonstrates its dense alliterative patterning derived from the 'key-word.'"[9] "*Khramovoi v malakhite li kholen...*" The entire first stanza is a derivative from the primordial root MLKhR. And while the poem is written in Russian, this persistent grinding down of the consonants "m-l-kh-r" seems to have entered by way of another language. This cluster sounds exotic to the Russian ear, but it is a component of familiar Hebrew words such as *melekh* ("king") and *mal'akh* ("messenger," "angel"). It is as if the young Pasternak's poetry has not yet selected its definitive linguistic channel and has mixed into the viscous Russian syllables an abundance of the non-syllabic, dry substance of Hebrew roots. Hence the remarkable, bilingual resonance of these lines.

In the poetry of Pasternak and Mandel'shtam, vowels can easily be squeezed forth from words whose semantic form consists of consonants. One cannot but recall in this regard Pasternak's well-known definition

---

8 The Russian *mel'khior* and English "melchior" are derived from the French coinage for a particular sort of cupronickel, *maillechort*, named for the two metallurgists who first produced this alloy. There is also a Christian association with the word. In the apocryphal oral tradition, Melchior was one of the Magi who brought gifts to the infant Christ. For a detailed analysis of this poem's historical background, see Malmstad, "Boris Pasternak: The Painter's Eye," in which it is suggested that this poem was inspired by a painting by Aristarkh Lentulov (1878–1943).
9 Barnes, *Boris Pasternak: A Literary Biography.* Vol. 1, *1890–1928,* 168.

of poetry as a sponge, where he polemically counterposes it to the traditional understanding of poetry as a spring or fountain: "Modern poets have imagined art to be like a fountain, whereas it is a sponge. They have decided that art must gush forth, whereas it must suck in and be saturated."[10] This very image of poetry-as-sponge appears in Pasternak's poem "Spring" ("Vesna"):

> Poetry! Be a Greek sponge
> With suckers. Amid sticky swards then
> I'd set you to rest on a wet board
> Of the green bench in the garden.
>
> Grow fluffy frills and farthingales,
> Absorb clouds and ravines,
> And at night, Poetry, I'll squeeze you out
> For the good of the thirsty page.

> Поэзия! Греческой губкой в присосках
> Будь ты, и меж зелени клейкой
> Тебя б положил я на мокрую доску
> Зеленой садовой скамейки.
>
> Расти себе пышные брыжи и фижмы,
> Вбирай облака и овраги,
> А ночью, поэзия, я тебя выжму
> Во здравие жадной бумаги.

From this standpoint, poetry is not the gushing forth of content, nor is it comparable to an eruption of water; like the squeezing of a sponge, it is literally the *ex-pression* of content from form. And the stronger the squeeze, the more "crowded" is the verse line with roots and meanings (to use the terminology of Iurii Tynianov[11])—the more the line is charged

---

10 Pasternak, *Sobranie sochinenii v 5 t.*, 4:367.
11 Iurii Tynianov, Viktor Shklovsky, and Boris Eikhenbaum are the three major representatives of Russian formalism, which became renowned as a school of literary

with poetry. This process of condensation, this pressing of thought from form, is the very reverse of the melodic dimension of poetry—of its "singing" breadth, that expansiveness of a resonant lyric composition, that is so characteristic of Blok's and Esenin's poetry. In another essay, Pasternak defines the poetic image as the squeezing and compressing of the forms of existence, as a precipitate abbreviation: "Figurative language is the stenography of a great individuality, the shorthand of the spirit."[12]

Independently of Pasternak's formulations, the same idea of poetry as a compression or squeezing is developed by Mandel'shtam in his essay "Talking about Dante" (1933). After citing the line from Canto XXXII of the *Inferno*, "*Io premerei di mio concetto il suco* (line 4) ("I would squeeze the juice out of my conception"), Mandel'shtam develops this image into an entire concept of poetic creation—that of the squeezing of form from content. "That is, form is conceived of by [Dante] as something wrung out, not as something that envelops. Thus, strange as it may seem, form is pressed out of the content—the conception—which, as it were, envelops the form."[13] In the writings of Mandel'shtam, as in those of Pasternak, the image arises of poetry-as-sponge, with the one difference that the content from which form is wrung, is itself form. Mandel'shtam attests to this when he writes: "But only if a sponge or rag is wet can anything, no matter what, be wrung from it. We may twist the conception into a veritable braid, but we will not squeeze from it any form, unless it is in itself a form" (ibid.).

We would do well to recall that compression or contraction, *tzimtzum*, is one of the most important terms in Kabbalah, defining the reason and the very potential for the creation of the world. The doctrine

---

theorists in the 1920s. Ensuing from the above discussion, the question might be raised as to what extent the Jewish origin of all three of these theorists influenced the basic concepts of the formal school, in particular, the theory of art as "defamiliarization" (Shklovsky), and the theory of "the crowdedness [or tightness, *tesnota*] of the verse line" (Tynianov). (See Tynianov, *Problema stikhotvornogo iazyka*.) This maximum phonetic and semantic compression of poetic speech can be related not only to Mandel'shtam's theory of form as "squeezed" content but also to the Kabbalistic notion of divine contraction.

12 Pasternak, *Stikhi 1936-1959: Stat'i i vystupleniia*, 194.
13 Mandelstam, "Talking about Dante," 75. Further citations in the text are to this translation.

of *tzimtzum* holds that God condensed or "contracted" His own being so that the universe might come to be. Otherwise, how could the world have come into existence, if at the outset all of space was occupied by the Deity? Isaac Luria (1534–72), who produced perhaps the most influential texts of the Kabbalah, explains Creation as the sacrificial act of God's self-contraction, whereby something other than God, the world outside God, became possible. In other words, God "squeezes" a space for the world from Himself, by means of His own "contraction."

This very act of self-condensation is recreated continuously in Logos, in language as a demiurge, when the world of poetry is "extracted" or "wrung" from it. The packed quality of the Hebrew language, concentrated into consonants alone, is the pledge of its capacity to engender an extended world of meanings. Poetic polysemy, like the moisture in a sponge, is pressed from the porous friable language, through a maximum compression. The image of "the sponge," which seems so audacious and unexpected when applied by Pasternak to poetry, originates in this idea, well known in educated Jewish circles, of compression and squeezing as the primal creative act.

To suggest that the poetic discourse of Pasternak and Mandel'shtam is somewhat alien to the Russian language of its composition disparages neither Russian poetry nor these poets. Poetic speech generally sounds "foreign," and people untutored in it perceive it, even in their native tongue, as an assortment of familiar-sounding but incomprehensible word combinations. Poetry is "an estrangement," "a defamiliarization," to use formalist terminology: the ordinary is made strange, different from itself, and language also estranges itself from commonly accepted speech—it appears as if it were "foreign," and those who do not appreciate poetry take this "gibberish" or "abracadabra" for another language. It may be for this reason that "outsiders" play an important role in Russian letters; this innate non-native quality helps to give ordinary speech poetic tension, to transpose it into another, "foreign" dimension. Viktor Shklovsky writes in his programmatic article "Art as Technique": "According to Aristotle, poetic language must appear strange and wonderful; and, in fact, it is often actually foreign: the Sumerian used by the Assyrians, the Latin of Europe during the Middle

Ages, the Arabisms of the Persians, the old Bulgarian of Russian literature."[14]

Elements of Hebrew in Russian poetry of the twentieth century can fall under the same category of aesthetic "foreignness" that is connected to an author's ethnic origins in a complicated and unpredictable way. Ethnic background in some instances hinders a writer from gaining organic mastery of a given language, but it incites other writers to transcend the limitations of language. Emil Mandel'shtam spoke a limp, leaden Russian, whereas his son, Osip, became one of the greatest Russian poets.

Even those poets who are acknowledged as "the most Russian," as "purely Russian"—Zhukovsky, Pushkin, Lermontov, Nekrasov, Fet, and Akhmatova—are ethnically mixed. They are both insiders and outsiders in relation to the Russian language. The issue in general is not one of belonging to a different tribe but of the intrinsic multiethnicity of culture itself, in which national purity is the exception rather than the rule. And, to use Lomonosov's term, the more "distant" (*dalekovaty*) the images and languages that cross in a national culture, the more significant is that crossing as a phenomenon of world culture.

b. Pasternak, Hasidism, and the Sparks of the Universe

Pasternak and Mandel'shtam are drawn toward each other and invite comparison: their very names, by the exact assonantal rhyme (a-e-a), pull them phonically close. While they may be placed in a single line with other renewers of Russian poetic speech—the shamanist Velimir Khlebnikov, or the Dionysian Viacheslav Ivanov—still, they occupy a special niche in any avant-garde or modernist assemblage. Not their similarity, but precisely the dissimilarity between them, the diametrically opposed forces that set one off against the other, allow us to fathom in their art a single circle of influence.

The impact of the Jewish spiritual tradition on Pasternak and Mandel'shtam reveals itself most clearly at the very point of its split into two streams, each of which has largely nourished them. The split between these two forms of Jewish religious mentality appeared in Russia toward

---

14 Shklovsly, "Art as Technique," 22. Shklovsky refers to Aristotle's *Poetics*, ch. 22.

the close of the eighteenth century, as the countermovements of Hasidism and Talmudism. The interrelatedness of the poetic systems of Pasternak and Mandel'shtam gains bold definition precisely against this background.

For more than a millennium, adherents of the Talmud have proposed that the Jews were scattered by God for their sins; they must weep and pray, study Talmud, and follow the spirit and letter of the Law, for this is the path to the redemption of sins and a return to divine favor. The Hasidim, whose approach may be correlated with that of other charismatic movements such as Sufism in Islam or the Pentecostal sect in Christianity, hold that it is given to the believer to perceive God by the fullness of a rapturous and receptive heart. Hasidism emerged as an existentialist mystical current in East European Jewry, which was especially persecuted and afflicted, hence sensitive to the preaching of the *joyous* knowledge of God.

If the Talmudist submits to comprehending the laws inscribed in Holy Scripture and their commentary by his mind, the Hasid reads them in his heart. The *tzaddik*, or saint of Hasidism, is open to the most minute events of the universe qua expressions of divine inventiveness, in which man is called upon to be a blessed collaborator.[15]

"The more accidental, the more true"—this line of Pasternak's, from the poem "February," might almost be quoted from Hasidic teachings. The more accidental the phenomenon, the more divine its nature, for the divine is what has not been envisioned, what cannot be deduced from general rules, nor reduced to them. The entire spirit of Pasternak's poetry is its quality of the *here-and-now*, of a blessed lightness of being in which nothing is stable, in which the heavy spirits of duty and teaching release the soul, in which "[s]trongest of all is the pull away / The passion for a clean break."[16]

To a certain extent, the Hasidic tradition is close to what in Russia has been the cult of the holy fool (*iurodivyi*): these two charismatic countertrends in Judaism and Christianity correspond to one another.

---

15 Throughout this discussion, Hasidism is to be understood as the spiritual current within East European Jewry of the eighteenth and nineteenth centuries, rather than that of contemporary Hasidism in Israel or the United States.

16 Pasternak, *Doctor Zhivago*, 469.

They revere not the cleric prophesying from the pulpit but the holy fool splattered with mud from a puddle, who lives at one with the entire universe, who does not insulate himself from the world and from the mundane. There may be a temptation to include Pasternak himself in this tradition, if we consider his phrases "I'm more blessed than a saint" ("Marburg") and "Who bids the words of the holy fool to burn?" ("Balashov"); or Stalin's memorable remark that allegedly saved Pasternak from arrest: "Leave this holy fool [*iurodivyi*] alone." But there is too much that separates Pasternak from the Russian concept of divine foolishness.

Pasternak and his lyrical hero have none of the hysterical outbursts, the clowning eccentricities, the stinging insult—nothing of that pathos of negation, the unmasking of the surrounding world so characteristic of the Russian holy fool as a type, with his "sickliness," his affectation of weak-mindedness, and his zealous self-abasement. The heavy, somber flagellation of one's clothing and flesh is similarly absent. In Pasternak, rather, there is a blissful, cheerfully spontaneous, joyously rambling acceptance of reality as vindicated and blessed. "Mastering my adoration / Yet worshipping, I observed: / Here were peasant women and villagers, / Students and locksmiths" ("On Early Trains" ["Na rannikh poezdakh"]). The simple listing induces a poetic trance, because everything in creation is adored and worshipped.

From this follows both the enumerative syntax in Pasternak's writings, recalling the biblical "and ... and ... and," as well as his inclination to break up the world into the tiniest particles, so as to disclose the sacral in each of them—what we might call Pasternak's own "theology of singularity," the vision of divine sparks, so characteristic of Hasidism. In Pasternak's conception, life itself is a torrent, broken up into a myriad of drops, as in "My sister—life—in a flood of spring rain / Has bruised herself blue all around us today" (*MSL*, 14). Or life is perceived as colorful flashes—as arrow-like flights of martins and red-gold wads flying from the dawn aflame: "The dawn will make the candle light up, / Will flare up and shoot a martin. / I burst in with a reminder: / May life be as fresh!"[17]

---

17 Pasternak, *Sobranie sochinenii v 5 t.*, 1:210.

If we attempt to single out figurative units in Pasternak's writings, they seem to be smaller than in the writings of any other Russian poet. They include raindrops, snowflakes, bits of fluff, leaves, branches, sparks, tears, crickets, ants, calyces, spouts, icicles, cloves, corpuscles, needles, stars, diamonds, cufflinks, beads, knuckles, pieces of glass, rosettes. Phenomena are reduced to ultimate fragments of the universe, prefigured by the Pasternakian "almighty god of details"—whose all-merciful powers extend not only to his creatures but to the smallest things of the tangible world:

> You will ask, who commands
> The month of August to be majestic,
> And for whom is nothing too small,
> Who is absorbed in trimming
> A maple leaf
>
> ....
>
> —The almighty god of details,
> The almighty god of love,
>
> ....
>
> And life, like autumn stillness,
> Is deep in detail.
> ("Let us drop words")

> Ты спросишь, кто велит,
> Чтоб август был велик,
> Кому ничто не мелко,
> Кто погружен в отделку
> Кленового листа
>
> ....
>
> – Всесильный бог деталей,
> Всесильный бог любви,
>
> ....
>
> Но жизнь, как тишина
> Осенняя,– подробна.
> ("Давай ронять слова")

Numerous examples of this attitude can be found in Pasternak's poetry:

> And diamonds, darkling, hung about
> The sorrel-beaded grass.
> "So It Was" (*MSL*, 99)

> В траве, на кислице, меж бус
> Брильянты, хмурясь, висли...
> ("Имелось")

> Raindrops heavy as cufflinks
> And the garden dazzles like a river reach,
> Splashed and dripping
> With a million blue tears.
> ("You're in the wind that's testing with a branch")

> У капель—тяжесть запонок,
> И сад слепит, как плес,
> Обрызганный, закапанный
> Мильоном синих слез.
> ("Ты в ветре, веткой пробующем")

> [Summer] hung on in thirst for butterflies
> For stingers and for stains...
> ("Summer") (*MSL*, 90)

> Тянулось в жажде к хоботкам
> И бабочкам и пятнам...
> ("Лето")

> A quartz-covered pathway shimmers and steams,
> All littered with twigs and snails.
> ("The Mirror") (*MSL*, 16)

Струится дорожкой, в сучках и улитках
Мерцающий жаркий кварц.
("Зеркало")

Richness of crumpled daisies in the dew—
Lips and lips in exchange for the stars.
("Resting Oars")

Роскошь крошеной ромашки в росе—
Губы и губы на звезды выменивать!
("Сложа весла")

The human being is broken down into lips, collarbones, elbows, palms, fingers, wrists, joints, vertebrae—into particles of corporeal existence. Sounds, too, are fragmented into "gulps," "lappings," "sobs," or into multi-segmented, repetitive configurations of "trilling," "chirping," "clattering" ...

No sign in the dark but the keen
Of sobs and the lapping of slippers,
These tears and the sighs in between.
("The Weeping Garden") (*MSL*, 15)

Ни признака зги, кроме жутких
Глотков и плескания в шлепанцах
И вздохов и слез в промежутке.
("Плачущий сад")

The more clairvoyant the poet, the more generous to him is "the god of details." To one in a state of illumination, "every trifle living and paying [him] no heed / became augmented in its farewell meaning" ("Marburg").[18] In this trance of noting and enumerating details, Pasternak emerges as

---

18 Ibid., 1:106.

a *tzaddik*, a Hasidic holy man, to whom the grace of God is revealed in the minutest of insignificant things.

Here one may recall the key Hasidic image of "the spark" as the authentic form of God's visible presence in the world. According to Kabbalah, in the process of Creation, the divine light was splintered into sparks that descended to the depths of the lower worlds, in order to deposit in the shells of earthly things the kernels of attraction to the higher worlds. Let us turn again to Isaac Luria, who most directly influenced eighteenth- and nineteenth-century Hasidim. In Luria's version of Kabbalah, we have a thoroughgoing explanation of the process by which the world was created, linking the concept of the "spark" to the idea of "compression" discussed earlier. After God absented Himself from primal space and thereby created the universe outside His Being, the divine light, extending back into this external world, encountered an alien milieu—and the vessels of light were broken. This "breaking of the vessels" is regarded as the very crux of Kabbalah. In consequence of the chaotic and catastrophic dispersion of the divine light, holy sparks came into being, imprisoned in the dark regions of the material world, ever after to seek their liberation and return to their primal source.[19]

The essence of this belief may be seen in the following account taken from Martin Buber's anthology of Hasidic legends and parables: "[Some] serve God with learning and prayer; others, with eating, drinking, and earthly delights, raising all of this to holiness. ... Those of the one sort learn and pray the livelong day and hold themselves far from lowly matters in order to attain to holiness, while the others do not think of themselves but only of delivering the holy sparks which are buried in all things back to God, and they make all lowly things their concern."[20] In a related vein, one commentary on Hasidic tales reads: "It turns out that these transitory, practical, ordinary, immediate, short-term, common, animalistic, vulgar, crude, primitive activities are full of the divine sparks—the emanation of the Almighty Himself. How could this be? The answer lies in the simultaneous cultivation of a vivid imagination bordering on the mystical and a strong faith that God is truly everywhere

---

19 The most authoritative exposition of the foundations of Jewish mysticism, including Kabbalah and its Lurianic variant, may be found in the works of Gershom Sholem. See, for instance, his *Major Trends in Jewish Mysticism* and *Kabbalah*.
20 Buber, *Tales of the Hasidim: The Later Masters*, 53-54.

and therefore can be reached not only through Talmudic and Kabbalistic studies, but even more directly by the ordinary concerns of everyday life."[21]

According to Hasidic teaching, it is not given to these frail sparks of the ordinary either to flare up brightly or to fade in the dark, but only to gleam through the obscurity that enwraps them, filling all objects with the presence of the Divinity, diminished yet preserved. The sin of pride is to see the world as all-radiant; the sin of despondency is to see it as all dark, whereas the tiny spark is the precise measure of the holiness of the world.

Pasternak's oeuvre offers glimpses of these flashings: in raindrops and icicles, in elbows and collarbones, in willow branches and oarlocks, where they appear as the wandering of points of holiness in the circles of matter, as flashes of light in the tiniest portions of everyday actuality. The tzaddik's vocation is to capture these sparks, to transfer them into the human heart, where they may fuse in the warmth of faith. And in Pasternak's poetry, Hasidic through and through, these spiritual sparks swarm unceasing, as if they were flying out of some invisible bonfire so as to coalesce once more in the heart of the poet.

Poetry is "the crackling of crushed icicles"; a garden is "splashed and dripping with a million blue tears"; a forest is "filled with the most meticulous gleams, as if in the tweezers of a watchmaker."[22] Everything is split up into autonomous, luminescent, and resonant particles. The very spirit of Pasternak's poetry is the fanning of these innumerable sparks; they cannot and must not flare up into some kind of "pure flame," which "devours the imperfection of existence" (Pushkin). They must remain sparks, no darker and no lighter than the very smallest light, raindrop, or icicle. God is present, not in the All, but in every fragment of it—unique and separate from any other.

It may be said that the quiver is the state most often experienced by the Pasternakian hero, whose soul is one trembling spark. For instance:

I shuddered. I flared up and burned out. ("Marburg")
Я вздрагивал. Я загорался и гас… ("Марбург")

---

21   Polsky and Wozner, *Everyday Miracles: The Healing Wisdom of Hasidic Stories*, 241–42.
22   Pasternak, *Sobranie sochinenii v 5 t.*, 1:118.

> The nightingales, with a quiver, set their sights.
> ("Here passed the mysterious fingernail of a riddle")

> Соловьи же заводят глаза с содроганьем…
> ("Здесь прошелся загадки таинственный ноготь")

> Overcome by a secret quiver… ("When the Weather Clears")

> Объятый дрожью сокровенной… ("Когда разгуляется")

> I'd lay out a poem like a garden,
> With my every fiber aquiver…
> ("In everything I want to reach")

> Я разбивал бы стих, как сад.
> Всей дрожью жилок…
> ("Во всем мне хочется дойти")

This quiver is the sparking of the spirit through each particle of the universe, the glimmering, twinkling existence of the spark itself that comes into being with the minute, the most sudden of breaths. The quiver is a physiological element of Pasternak's religious ecstasy—an excess of bliss in each trifle, the upsurge of delight and the impossibility of going beyond the limits of one's own corporeality.

Hasidism discloses the holiness of each thing through its "whimsicality" and "randomness," a rejection of the paths of reason and law. Hence Pasternak's perception of nature, which in his poetry plays tricks, behaves eccentrically, goes mad, or discovers in itself a wild, naughty, rambunctious creature. Such is the childishness of all nature—like a mischievous child, it is in the bosom and under the surveillance of the Creator.

> How much courage is needed
> to play forever,
> as the ravines play,
> as the river plays.
> ("Bacchanalia")

> Сколько надо отваги,
> чтоб играть на века,
> как играют овраги,
> как играет река...
> ("Вакханалия")

This play of every drop, every trifle is "courage," a challenge to the universe's grand and persistent ways. This tender, non-offensive wildness is revealed in numerous landscape images: a small stream is "a half-mad gossip"; a river is "the speech of high water—the ravings of being"; a month in summer is "July, an uncombed touslehead"; a thunderstorm is when "moisture runs crazed from one calyx to another"; a nightingale "hung amid the bird-cherry like the mercury of crazed rains. / It held the bark spellbound... the crazed trilling vibrates."[23]

"Maddened," "manic," and "crazed" are characteristic Pasternak words, appropriate to the worldview of the "blessed eccentric" of Hasidic culture, who is "completely off," for whom "everything is haywire," and who is pleasing to God, precisely because he expresses spontaneous joy.

Thus Pasternak mistrusts book wisdom, and he believes that one can sooner extract the spark of holiness from Nature than from books of religious instruction. In yet another poetic teaching, the Moscow quasi-Hasid writes:

> That riding in May the Kamyshinsky line
> And reading the schedule of trains on the way,
> It's grander than scripture and sounds so sublime,
> That you could reread it, enraptured, all day.
> ("My sister—life—in a flood of spring rain") (*MSL*, 14)

> Что в мае, когда поездов расписанье
> Камышинской веткой читаешь в пути,
> Оно грандиозней Святого писанья,
> Хотя его сызнова все перечти.

---

23 Pasternak, *Sobranie sochinenii v 5 t.*, 1:28, 179; 2:37, 89.

("Сестра моя—жизнь и сегодня в разливе")

Here it would be worthwhile to consider Pasternak's view of Christianity, which he often contrasted with Judaism as a religion of the Law. In many ways, however, Pasternak's Christianity is itself of a dreamlike nature. This quality comes through in the philosophical disquisitions in *Doctor Zhivago*, both in the debates of the characters and in the author's speculations. His Christianity grew organically out of the unconscious roots of a Hasidic worldview that is similarly anti-legalistic but that is far more fused with the life of things and nature, and as such, is a driving fresh force, infusing Pasternak's poetry and prose. The interpretation of Christianity in *Doctor Zhivago* seems to be an intellectual projection of what organically lived in Pasternak, as a sensing of God through the sparks of holiness in Nature, in everyday life, in love, in the physical interaction of people and things.

To what in the Gospels did Pasternak feel the greatest affinity? Not its religious revelation, nor its moral instruction, but its depiction of the ordinary, where everything, as it were, is brought down to an illumination of what happens in everyday life. One character states: "It has been considered up to now that the most important thing in the Gospels is the moral pronouncements and rules, but for me the main thing is that Christ speaks in parables from life, clarifying the truth with the light of everyday things."[24]

These words are spoken by Nikolai Nikolaevich Vedeniapin, a former Orthodox priest turned freethinker and writer, to whom Pasternak in his novel entrusted many of his own cherished ideas. But behind the concept of "the priest defrocked at his own request" lurks that of a shtetl wiseman, who rereads one Jewish heresy—Christianity—through the eyes of another—Hasidism. And it turns out that the essence of the Gospel teachings lies not in their soul-saving effect but in their blessing of a mustard seed, a vineyard, flour, millstones, lamps, fish, bread, and oil, in their illuminating for man the holiness that surrounds him in his daily life. The usual practice of the parable—explicating the exalted by means of the

---

24 Pasternak, *Doctor Zhivago*, 37.

ordinary—here is turned upside down: glimmers of light and truth come from the everyday, so that Pasternak sanctifies and even theologizes the life of nature:

> As braziers drop bronzed cinders,
> Beetles drop in the drowsy garden.
> Against me, level with my candle,
> Worlds abloom hang over. ...
> I enter this night
> Like a convert to an unheard-of faith.
> ("As braziers drop bronzed cinders")

> Как бронзовой золой жаровень,
> Жуками сыплет сонный сад.
> Со мной, с моей свечою вровень
> Миры расцветшие висят.
> И как в неслыханную веру,
> Я в эту ночь перехожу...
> ("Как бронзовой золой жаровень")

> Oh freshness, oh, a drop of emerald
> In the branches drunken from the downpour,
> Oh, the uncombed and dreamy disorder,
> Oh, the marvelous trifle of God.
> ("The Garden of Neskuchnoe")

> О свежесть, о капля смарагда
> В упившихся ливнем кистях,
> О сонный начес беспорядка,
> О дивный Божий пустяк!
> ("Нескучный сад")

> Nature, the world, the universe's hiding place,
> Overcome by a secret quiver,
> Weeping for joy,
> I will stay for your long liturgy.

Poetry as Ecstasy and as Interpretation 359

("When the Weather Clears")

Природа, мир, тайник вселенной,
Я службу долгую твою,
Объятый дрожью сокровенной,
В слезах от счастья, отстою.
("Когда разгуляется")

These stanzas, in which night is an unheard-of faith, a drop of rain is a trifle from God, and nature is a prayer service, are worthy of an honored place in Hasidic wisdom. Here the faith is espoused not by the God-Man but by nature and everyday life, with its countless trifles.

Hasidism differs as much from Christian anthropocentrism as it does from pagan cosmocentrism. No image in Pasternak's liturgy for nature turns us back from Christianity to a stylized paganism. Objects are treated not in their overwhelming grandeur but in their diminishing smallness that has been called upon as witness to the power and plenitude of the Creator. Things slip away, melt, twinkle in the wind, flicker, consist of flashes and glimmers. Erasing their own existence in the world, they represent Hasidism as an anti-paganism. Rilke, to whom in many ways Pasternak was indebted, wrote that not a single monk could sufficiently disparage himself to beg comparison with a thing, for a thing is pleasing to God, precisely because it observes a more profound reticence than does a monk; it dwells in abject poverty and selflessly serves all those in need of it.

Man is somewhat more demanding. To view his historical and moral concerns as the center of the universe remains alien to Pasternak, whose intuition is sharpened to the utmost precisely by the play and sparking of essences outside history—by everyday life and nature, by the humble diurnal cycle. Despite some of Pasternak's declarations, both age-old Christian historicism and the newest Marxist historicism were outside his creative interests. Just as parables of everyday life in the Gospels moved him, so did the unsophisticated intertwining of the events of the October Revolution with the most everyday prosaic occurrences. "This unprecedented thing, this miracle of history, this revelation comes bang in the very thick of the ongoing everydayness, with no heed to its course. It begins not from the beginning but from the middle, without choosing the dates beforehand, on the first weekday to come along. ... That's real genius. Only what is greatest can be so inappropriate and untimely."[25] The miracle for Pasternak is marked off by the measure of its matter-of-fact entry into the most trifling circumstances of everyday life.

The sarcastic formula that circulated in the 1930s about Pasternak—the "dacha genius" (*genial'nyi dachnik*)—turns out to be not so very superficial after all, and if cleared of its pejorative connotation, borders on the truth. A country place is the most humble home of man in his world, for there, outside "the larger" world of history, he finds himself amid the surroundings of everyday life and Nature. The country place might have been described as the primordial home of the lyrical Pasternak hero, or as his shtetl,[26] not only in its narrowly ethno-cultural sense, but in its metaphysically humble resonance.

c. Mandel'shtam, Talmudism, and the Textbook of Infinity

The art of Pasternak is diametrically opposed to that of Mandel'shtam, yet within the same cultural circle. Their contemporaries grasped this intuitively. Each poet has been compared to an exotic animal from the Near Eastern world, where the poets' common historical homeland lies. Writing of both poets, Marina Tsvetaeva coins the following comparisons. "Pasternak's physical presence is magnificent. There is something in his face both of the Arab and of his horse: a watchful, tense alertness; and at any moment, utter readiness for flight. And the enormous, steed-like as well, wild, and timid sidewise glance of his eyes."[27] Of Mandel'shtam she states: "The eyes look downward, the head is thrown back. Bearing in mind his long neck, his head is set like a camel's. Three-year-old Andriushka asks, 'Uncle Osia, who pushed your head that way?'"[28] In his reminiscence of the poet, Emil Mindlin similarly depicts Mandel'shtam's "delicate,

---

25 Ibid., 173
26 *Shtetl* (a small town, in Yiddish) in Russian is *mestechko*, literally, "a small place."
27 Tsvetaeva, *Proza*, 354.
28 Tsvetaeva, "Istoriia odnogo posviashcheniia," 322–23.

large, hooked nose and [his] head, with a proud air, independently tossed back."29

Thus Mandel'shtam, in the tilt of his head, has been likened to a camel; Pasternak, on account of his elongated face and the impetuosity of his gait, gestures, words—to an Arabian steed. These are more than merely physiognomic comparisons, although they match the features of both poets. Perhaps even before they begin to create symbols, the poets themselves are symbols.[30] The camel and the Arabian steed might be emblematic of a relationship between these two creative worlds. The difference in the poetic approach of Mandel'shtam and Pasternak is analogous to the contrast between the heavy, measured gait of the camel and the light run of the Arabian race horse. In the structure of their poetic being, Mandel'shtam is as unhurried and solemn as Pasternak is impetuous and restless.

The comparison to a camel may be extended further. Mandel'shtam carries a hump, formed by his posture vis-a-vis world culture—the hump of a man who, for his entire life, has been bent over the world as over a book, leafing through its pages and endlessly rereading it. His is the posture of the Talmudist, bent over the text of the Law, and it is characteristic of all of Mandel'shtam's poetic thought. As we know from his rather caustic reminiscences in the "Judaic Chaos" chapter of *The Noise of Time*, the father of the future poet prepared for the rabbinic profession and studied at a Berlin yeshiva. Then Emil Mandel'shtam forsook the vocation that had been passed down from one Mandel'shtam generation to another, chose a secular profession, and gave up all of his religious interests—preserving only, in his desiccated Russian conversation, in his "tongue-tie and languagelessness, ... the capricious syntax of a Talmudist."[31]

---

29 Mandel'shtam, *Sobranie sochinenii v trekh tomakh*, 2:511.
30 As Pasternak himself remarks in his essay "What Is Man?": "A person attains the maximum greatness when he himself, all his being, his life, his activity have become a paradigm, a symbol." *Sobranie sochinenii v 5 t.*, 4:671.
31 Mandelstam, *The Prose of Osip Mandelstam: The Noise of Time. Theodosia. The Egyptian Stamp*, 90.

The irony of origins and the revenge of the cultural unconscious are, however, evident in the fact that Emil Mandel'shtam's son would go on to become a great Talmudist, making the secular profession of poetry into a distinctive, Talmudic exegesis of the signs of world culture. In Mandel'shtam's writings, all of culture comes forward as a holy book, continually demanding rigorous commentary and deciphering.

More than any of his predecessors in Russian poetry, Mandel'shtam views the world through the prism of a cultural-historical exegesis. "Literary competence" and "poetic competence" are at the foundation of Mandel'shtam's demands on talent. In Dante he honors "a good education"—a "school of the most rapid associations, ... a keyboard promenade along the entire mental horizon of antiquity, ... an orgy of quotations" ("Talking about Dante," 68-69). The allusions present in all great poetry seem to him to be not simple borrowings; they are atmosphere aquiver with the resonant dialogue of times and cultures. Mandel'shtam comments that "a quotation is not an excerpt. A quotation [*tsitata*] is a cicada [*tsikada*]. It is part of its nature never to quiet down. Once having got hold of the air, it does not release it" (69). A quotation is not an alien intrusion into a text but the very nature of the text itself, resonating with the whole reality of signs, with the world of the all-embracing Book.

For Mandel'shtam, the writer is less an original creator—which would hardly coincide with the traditional Jewish view of the Lord as First Creator—and more the translator and interpreter of a primary text. He registers his beloved Dante, whose very name is a byword for the limitless power of the imagination, merely as a pupil and copyist of some primordial text. Dante "is set in motion by everything except fabrication, except inventiveness. Dante and fantasy—why, these are incompatible!... What fantasy is there in him? He writes to dictation, he is a copyist, a translator.... He is bent double in the posture of a scribe who squints in fright at the illuminated original that has been lent him from the prior's library" ("Talking about Dante," 100).

This portrait of Dante is also a self-portrait of Mandel'shtam, "bent double in the posture of a scribe," over the pages of world culture.[32] In one

---

32 Although one can speak of the influence of medieval, monastic culture on Mandel'shtam's representation of art as the copying of texts and their exegesis, this culture itself is of biblical origin. According to Sergei Averintsev, "the early Byzantine

way or another, each line of Mandel'shtam's corresponds to some chapter and page in a literary anthology. Each poem is an inscription on the margins of "The Book," a form of commentary on Homer, Ovid, Dante, Ossian, Edgar Allen Poe, Batiushkov, Pushkin, Baratynsky, Tiutchev, or on some as yet unknown, unearthed, but preexisting primary source.

Mandel'shtam changed the hierarchy of values in Russian poetry. Earlier it was esteemed for an author to be considered "the first"; subsequently it became prestigious to be "the last"—not to open up but to close a theme, having set forth its most capacious interpretation, having transposed it into various languages of culture. In so traditional a sphere of spontaneous inspiration as poetry, "the divine word," Mandel'shtam was the first Russian poet to canonize intentional secondariness. While the word remains divine, the poet serves as its interpreter: he has to transmit it through all registers of meaning, to adapt it to the sensibilities of his own epoch, to lead it into the tangible strata of culture. Rather than the caprice of self-expression, art is the tenacity of reception. "It teaches: Beauty is not the whim of a demigod / but the fierce eyeballing of the plain carpenter" ("The Admiralty").[33]

A similar orientation toward intentional secondariness was prevalent amid the new Russian authors and currents that became well known in the 1980s and 90s: the metarealists, conceptualists, presentists, and polystylists. Hence the constant reproach of them for their "bookishness"— but is this truly a word of censure? They share with Mandel'shtam an understanding of art as a self-consciousness of culture, an exploratory and cumulative work with language. The conceptualists prefer to "recycle" the language of Soviet ideology; the metarealists focus on the languages of

---

metaphoric tradition of 'notation' goes back to the ancient Hebrew and more broadly to Near Eastern culture, the works of which were created 'by scribes and bookmen for scribes and bookmen.'" Herein lies a distinction between the legacies of Near Eastern vs. Greco-Roman antiquity in European culture. At the center of the latter was the free citizen and the orator, but not the scribe: "The visual symbol of a citizen of classical antiquity was not at all the bent-over posture of the scribe, carefully and respectfully entering the Emperor's words or recopying a text of sacred legend, but the free bearing and lively gesticulation of the orator." Averintsev, *Poetika rannevizantiiskoi literatury*, 188, 190, 191.

33 Mandel'shtam, *Sobranie sochinenii v trekh tomakh*, 1:29.

earlier artistic epochs; the presentists utilize the languages of new sciences and technologies.[34] The citational mode, or what is now called intertextuality, is the means by which a text exists amid other texts, or more precisely, absorbs them into itself and recreates the universal scope of styles and codes within the microcosm of a single work. This is the porosity of poetic matter, which does not gush forth from its own depths as an instinctive creativity but which "sucks in and is saturated" by the entire system of world culture.

Thus Mandel'shtam, with his inherently Talmudic mind, has influenced Russian literature in the formation of a growing zone of self-reflectivity—"writing to dictation, copying, transcribing" ("Talking about Dante," 100). This kind of secondariness does not exclude genuine originality but makes it stand out in relief from what has already been accomplished in culture. When artists feel summoned to create "from within," as if "for the first time," the result most often turns out to be sheer banality, the first cliché they hit upon. Pasternak, in one of the entries of Iurii Zhivago, speaks of this seeming artlessness: "Pastoral simplicity has no source in these [present] conditions. Its false artlessness is a literary counterfeit, an artificial mannerism, a phenomenon of a bookish order, picked up not in the countryside but from the bookshelves of academic libraries."[35] When the artist creates a "variation on a theme" while aware of its preceding interpretations, then a new interpretation has a chance to become a genuine discovery in its repulsion from what had been created previously. Conscious reproduction is the path to innovation.

For Mandel'shtam, not just culture but also nature turns out to be an open page, strewn with the inscriptions of brooks and crags. Hence the cosmogony and the cosmography of his "Slate Ode" ("Grifel'naia oda"), which represents the world in the process of being inscribed, "written

---

34 On these trends in contemporary Russian poetry, see my book *After the Future: The Paradoxes of Postmodernism and Contemporary Russian Culture*, 19-50.
35 Pasternak, *Doctor Zhivago*, 435. Considerably earlier, in connection with certain poems of Sergei Esenin, Iurii Tynianov had remarked upon this secondariness of the "naive": "The poet who is revered for his writing from 'the gut' [*nutro*] by those who complain that literature has become a craft (i.e., an art—as if it had not always been that)—this poet discloses that his 'gut' is more literary than 'craft'" (*Arkhaisty i novatory*, 546).

with a milky lead stick." The world has been created by the Word and is written like a Book. All the elements are depicted in terms of schooling: all of nature is a pupil who diligently brings forth piles of scribbles, and who is bent over the notebook of naked rocks and species, cutting into it deep lines. Rocks are "disciples of the running water," while "the plumbline preaches to them, the water instructs them, time hones them"; "memory, are these your voices, instructing, breaking the night?" "I break the night, the burning chalk, to firmly record the moment," and so on. The various elements teach one another, and the universe as a whole learns from a higher law, whose weight is felt in the slightest blade of grass. Causality haunts us even in the fortuitous events that are inevitably hung on the hooks of cause and effect:

> Out of bowls full of pins and pestilence
> Causality's delusions we drink.
> With hooks we touch infinitesimals
> Like the lightest of deaths.
> ("Octets," X[36])

> В игольчатых, чумных бокалах
> Мы пьем наважденье причин,
> Касаемся крючьями малых,
> Как легкая смерть, величин...
> ("Восьмистишия")

All of Mandel'shtam's creativity is, to use his own expression, "the discipleship of worlds." This is a typically rabbinic outlook, in which all that exists has been created for study, with the poet cast as the most diligent and painstaking of pupils. As Mandel'shtam writes: "And I now study the scratched diary of the slate summer." The universe turns out to be a kind of yeshiva, a place where the greatest zeal is demonstrated by seminarians immersed in the study of the law: "And your textbook, infinity, / I read by myself, alone..." ("Octets," XI)

---

36 Mandelstam, *The Poems of Osip Mandelstam*, 37.

Nothing of the kind is to be found in Pasternak. "What is not in Pasternak?" inquires Tsvetaeva. "I listen attentively, and an answer comes: the sense of weight. Weight for him is only another form of action—to be thrown off. You're more likely to see him hurling down an avalanche than sitting in a snow-covered hut awaiting the avalanche's deadly thud."[37]

But the very quality that is absent in Pasternak is paramount in Mandel'shtam:

> To some, winter is arrack and a blue-eyed punch,
> To some, a fragrant wine with cinnamon,
> Some get their salty orders from the brutal stars
> To carry back to smoke-filled huts.[38]

> Кому зима—арак и пунш голубоглазый,
> Кому—душистое с корицею вино,
> Кому—жестоких звезд соленые приказы
> В избушку дымную перенести дано.

Or:
> Prickly stars stared through the matting,
> Hooves beat over frozen keys,[39]

> В плетенку рогожи глядели колючие звезды,
> И били вразрядку копыта по клавишам мерзлым.

Or:
> Yes, I am lying in the earth, moving my lips,
> but every schoolboy will learn my words by heart:[40]

> Пусть я лежу в земле, губами шевеля,
> Но то, что я скажу, запомнит каждый школьник...

---

37 Tsvetaeava, *Proza*, 357.
38 Mandelshtam, *Selected Poems*, 43.
39 Mandelstam, *The Complete Poetry of Osip Emilevich Mandelstam*, 142.
40 Mandelstam, *Poems from Mandelstam*, 98.

Mandel'shtam's place truly is in "a snow-covered hut awaiting the avalanche's deadly thud" (precisely what Tsvetaeva finds incompatible with Pasternak's lyrical sensibility). He lies trampled, in particular, under the weight of the Law, by which man is sentenced, and which he must convey to others, like a lesson.

Whereas Pasternak conceives of the world in images of free play, Mandel'shtam does so in terms of strict law and painstaking learning. Therefore, Mandel'shtam's world is full as well of "unkind burdens," of "petrified elements." Stone, the poet's favorite substance, predominates, because it is so dependably obedient to the law, ever abiding by the will of the Creator.[41] Nearly everything in Mandel'shtam appears in stony or earthen images: "the warmed sand cools down"; "the rose was earth." Elements thicken: "I drink the roiled air like a dark water"; "the heavy steam falls down"; "the deposit of lime in the sick son's blood hardens"; wasps suck not drops of nectar but "the axis of the Earth."[42]

This transition of matter into a solid state, this encumbering of the elements by hardening and darkening, may be the fundamental principle of Mandel'shtam's poetics. It is especially striking that in Mandel'shtam's poetry, air becomes statuesque, more like a tree or a tower than the light gas mixture we breathe. Consider such images as "the translucent forest of the air," "in the transparent air, as in a light-blue Coliseum,"[43] and so on. Mandel'shtam never whips up a blizzard or a snowstorm, dynamic forces that are endemic to the Russian poetic landscape.

If we turn to images of winter in Pasternak and Mandel'shtam, the contrast becomes especially clear. Winter, obviously, exists beyond the scope of either Hasidism or Talmudism, being a phenomenon of a foreign, northern landscape, but here too we find a clear difference in the two poetic worldviews. In Mandel'shtam's poetry, winter is typically hard, like a diamond; it lies on the earth like a heavy ice crust, emitting a sharp, terrifying crunch: "Let the dark people hurry along the snow / Like sheep in a flock, and let the brittle ice crust crunch." Or "everything is

---

41 *Stone* (*Kamen'*) is the title of Mandel'shtam's first book (1913; extended and revised edition, 1915).
42 Mandel'shtam, *Sobranie sochinenii v trekh tomakh*, 1:76, 77, 82, 111, 251.
43 Mandel'shtam, *Sobranie sochinenii v 4 t.*, 1:102.

shaggy—people and objects. / And the hot snow crunches" ("Barely gleams the ghostly scene" ["Chut' mertsaet prizrachnaia stsena"]). Elsewhere, "the white, white snow eats one's eyes painfully"—this snow is impregnated with the whiteness of the fateful stars, fixed and cruel as the law ("To some, winter is arrack and a blue-eyed punch" ["Komu zima—arak i punsh goluboglazyi"]). And in "1 January 1924": "As of old, I respect the fraternity / Of the deep frost and the justice of the pike." The strong frost is both litigation and sentence: a legalistic conception of Nature as humanity's judgment.

In Pasternak, it is just the opposite. Winter is swirling snowflakes: "White little stars in a snowstorm"; "As in summer a swarm of gnats / fly into the flame, / Snowflakes sweep from the yard / up to the windowpane"—there is an impetuous jittering of the most minute airy particles forming soft woven patterns. Winter "knits stockings from snowflakes," descends from heaven "in a patched coat," dangles like "a fringed curtain" — in a word, it enters into the category of "materials from which snowflakes are sewn."

> The snow is falling, and all is in disarray,
> Everything breaks into flight:
> The steps of the black ladder,
> The turning of the crossroads.
>
> Снег идет, и все в смятеньи,
> Все пускается в полет:
> Черной лестницы ступени,
> Перекрестка поворот.

In this movement of winter we sense the rollicking gesture and the gamboling gait of the cheery oddball from Jewish folklore. Finally, if for Mandel'shtam, "the frost of eternity" lies encrusted "in icy diamonds" ("Slower than the snowy beehive" ["Medlitel'nee chem snezhnyi ulei"]), then for Pasternak, "time perhaps passes with the same rapidity" of a blizzard ("It's Snowing" ["Sneg idet"]). These contrasting images of winter illustrate the distinction between Law and caprice, eternity and time, ice

Poetry as Ecstasy and as Interpretation 369

crust and snowflakes, as poetic metaphors corresponding to the Talmudic and Hasidic worldviews respectively.

Both poets are attracted to the Caucasus, the area of their geographic homeland (Russia) that lies closest to their historic homeland (the Land of Israel). This is not, however, the romantics' dream of the Caucasus as some wall rising heavenward; rather, it is an inhabitable, homey land in that region and beyond it, the dim distant vision of an inconceivable "promised Land." Mandel'shtam refers to "the land of Armenia" as "Judea's littler sister."[44]

Even in their attraction to the Caucasus, Pasternak and Mandel'shtam are divided between two "Judeas," two southern poetic homelands, as if they were exemplars of two religious traditions. In every aspect of his poetry, Pasternak gravitates toward Georgia; Mandel'shtam, toward Armenia. One country "plays the prankster" and curls up by its forest trifles, among which "the air breathed and clambered out, necks of hornbeams craned upward" (Pasternak[45]). The other, Armenia, is "the country of ploughed-up stones," the bookish land," "the hollow book with its black blood of baked clay."[46] Georgia turns green, lightly sparkles and froths, like the joy of the Hasid. Armenia becomes sallow and is trodden down into its own dead clay, like the seriousness and heaviness of the Law.

Unlike the impressionistically excitable Pasternak, Mandel'shtam primarily addresses the intellectual level of perception. But this does not mean that he is a philosophical poet in the same sense as were Baratynsky, Tiutchev, or Zabolotsky. Usually we equate the intellectual and the philosophical in literature, without noting a vital difference. The biblical-Talmudic tradition has its sages and the most discriminating of intellects, but not philosophers in the ancient sense associated with the thinkers of antiquity. As is well known, the origin of philosophical knowledge goes back to pagan Greek wisdom, whereas Mandel'shtam, despite his often declared love for Hellenism, is nonetheless closer to the Jewish spiritual tradition.

---

44 Mandel'shtam, *Sobranie sochinenii v trekh tomakh*, 2:183.
45 Pasternak, *Sbornik stikhov*, 210.
46 Mandel'shtam, *Sobranie sochinenii v trekh tomakh*, 1:153, 156.

What is an intellectuality that is alien to the philosophical cast of mind? In Mandel'shtam's writings, we are in the presence not of an abstracting, generalizing reason but of an exquisite, explicating intellect. Mandel'shtam's poetic mind is remote from the philosophical generalizations that we encounter in Baratynsky or Tiutchev. It is remote from meditation, from aphorisms, and from maxims like "A thought expressed is a lie" or "Nature has no inkling of the past" (Tiutchev). Even where Mandel'shtam overtly expresses a general judgment, he gives only a partial, narrow interpretation of a broader phenomenon. Compare, for example, two very similar quatrains about Nature. In Tiutchev we read:

> Nature is a Sphinx. And all the more surely
> Does she destroy Man by her seduction,
> Perhaps she never had
> Any riddle in the first place.

> Природа—Сфинкс. И тем она верней
> Своим искусом губит человека,
> Что, может статься, никакой от века
> Загадки нет и не было у ней.

In Mandel'shtam:

> Nature is that selfsame Rome and is reflected in it.
> Its images of civic might we see
> In the transparent air, as in a light-blue Coliseum,
> In the forum of the fields and the colonnades of groves.

> Природа—тот же Рим, и отразилась в нем.
> Мы видим образы его гражданской мощи
> В прозрачном воздухе, как в цирке голубом,
> На форуме полей и в колоннаде рощи.[47]

---

47 Mandel'shtam, *Sobranie sochinenii v 4 t.*, 1:102.

Poetry as Ecstasy and as Interpretation 371

These statements at first seem to perfectly match in their thematics of nature, in their structure ("Nature is such-and-such"), and in the source of their comparison—the selection of proper nouns from antiquity (Sphinx, Rome). Yet we note a subtle difference. Tiutchev poses the riddle of Nature, while Mandel'shtam describes nature in images of Roman civilization. The Tiutchev poem is a meditation on a philosophical problem: What is Nature? What is its essence? Generalizing speculation of this kind is absent from the Mandel'shtam poem. Rather, it is structured by a transposition from one "language" to another, from the language of nature to that of culture. Here Mandel'shtam is the explicator of nature-as-text, not the philosopher of nature-as-essence.

In this distinction lies the difference between philosophical ratiocination and Talmudic explication. Each type of thinking is concentrated on a process of understanding, but while the philosophical moves from the concrete to the general ("this is that"), the Talmudic is driven from the general to the concrete ("that is manifest through this"). Essence is disclosed only to God; therefore explication must be partial, no more general than what is explainable. The *Natürphilosophie* of Tiutchev's world view is an indication of the general attribute of nature as Sphinx: "She destroys Man by her seduction, / Perhaps she never had / Any riddle in the first place." In Mandel'shtam, on the contrary, Roman civilization is more concrete than nature, which can be translated into the language of "civic might"—into the architectural images of the Coliseum, the Forum, colonnades. This is why the Talmud is more detailed than the Torah that it explicates. The task of the interpreter is not to pronounce the one absolute truth but to expound what has been said about it; not to enter into the secrets of nature but to clarify what is manifest in it.

* * *

A general conclusion is called for. Both poets evoke a Jewish spiritual dimension. Just as Pasternak's poetry is not so much Christian as it is Hasidic, so Mandel'shtam's is not so much philosophical as Talmudic. To be sure, the creativity of Pasternak and Mandel'shtam is attendant upon Christian ethical and classical philosophical traditions. But their divergence from the Christian ethical and classical philosophical traditions bespeaks their (mostly subconscious) affinities with expressions of Jewish spirituality.

In his article "The Fate and Tidings of Osip Mandel'shtam," Sergei Averintsev briefly juxtaposes him with Pasternak in light of the criterion of "abstract vs. concrete." "If we recall the Aristotelian division of characteristics into the essential and accidental, then Pasternak's poetry stands as the steadfast equation of the accidental with the essential, and thus as the apotheosis of the concrete.... By contrast, Mandel'shtam's poetry proceeds via the incremental purging of accidental characteristics from the essential, in this sense carrying on the impulse of symbolism, albeit modifying it greatly."[48] But it seems that the "Aristotelian," or for that matter any logical-binary opposition between the two poets within the framework of philosophical universals or "types of worldview," cannot suffice; such an approach passes over the linguistic and religio-cultural heritage within which they become concretely and historically recognizable.

Finally, what vital cultural principles underlie these two creative intuitions that Pasternak and Mandel'shtam transmitted into Russian culture? Russian Jewry was divided not only spiritually and ideologically but geographically as well. The north was the home of Talmudically educated Baltic Jewry, the "Mitnagdim" (opponents of the Hasidic renewal), who established a stronghold in Vilna.[49] Faithful to rabbinic principles, the Mitnagdim insisted on the teaching of the Book and lifelong erudition, and were staunch advocates of the legalistic path to the cognition of God. In the south, above all in the Ukrainian provinces of Podolia and Volhynia, lived a more densely settled Jewish population, which on account of persecution and suffering was more distant from the traditions of learning and was more inclined to seek God in lightheartedness, through the carefree joys of the humble heart. In this setting, the preaching of the Ba'al Shem Tov, or the "Master of the Great Name" (often known by the acronym, Besht), had great success. For followers of the Ba'al Shem Tov, the law is not inscribed in books once and for all but rather

---

48 Averintsev, *Poety*, 213.
49 As early as 1772, the Vilna Gaon issued a ban against the Hasidim, especially condemning their neglect of Torah study and their irrational belief in the powers of the *tzaddikim*.

is marked in the human heart, as an openness to God and the celebration of every trifle, so as to hint at or indicate His will.

The great Jewish historian Simon Dubnow describes the geographic distribution of these spiritual trends as follows: "In the northwest rabbinic scholasticism reigned supreme, and the caste of scholars, petrified in the ideas of Talmudic Babylonia, was the determining factor in public life.... Matters, however, were different in Podolia, Galicia, Volhynia, and in the whole southwestern region in general. Here the Jewish masses were much further removed from the sources of rabbinic learning, having emancipated themselves from the influence of the Talmudic scholar. While in Lithuania, dry book-learning was inseparable from a godly life, in Podolia and Volhynia it failed to satisfy the religious cravings of the common man. The latter was in need of beliefs easier of understanding and making an appeal to the heart rather than to the mind."[50]

In the north, a more reclusive and contemplative character emerged, whereas the more elemental and open tenor of life in the south may have been a factor in the formation of the spontaneous temper of its residents. In any case, these two movements, coming from the north and the south, reveal the territorial context of the two varieties of Jewish spirituality that penetrated Russian letters. Mandel'shtam's ancestors came from the north—his paternal forebears from Riga, and maternal from Vilna. The family of Pasternak originated in Odessa, in the most southerly area of the geographic entrenchment of Jewish culture in Russia.[51]

The predominance of creative Talmudism in Mandel'shtam and of creative Hasidism in Pasternak may, to a certain degree, be attributed to the spiritual milieu that nourished their ancestors. After all, if these influences of origin and ancient homeland skirt the conscious life and

---

50 Dubnow, *History of the Jews in Russia and Poland from the Earliest Times Until the Present Day*, 1:221–22.
51 Information on the Jewish spiritual traditions of Pasternak's forebears is, unfortunately, very limited. However, the fact that his ancestors settled in southern Ukraine in the mid-eighteenth century, and that his grandfather Osip (father of the artist Leonid Pasternak) was a synagogue cantor, suggest a familiarity on the part of the Pasternak family with Hasidism. Sources describing Pasternak's ethnic and cultural origins include Pasternak, *Zapisi raznykh let*; Barnes, *Boris Pasternak. A Literary Biography*; Fleishman, *Boris Pasternak: The Poet and His Politics*; and Levi, *Boris Pasternak*.

nurturing environment of the individual, they are nevertheless passed along. To cite a well-known example, when Lev Tolstoy's heroine Natasha Rostova finds herself at the country place of her uncle, "the little countess"—who has been taught by a French governess—breaks into a Russian dance. How is a manner of speech or gesture inherited?

The question is as irresolvable as it is clear. In discussing the indigenous roots of poetry, one need go no further than the attestation of the poet himself: "As a little bit of musk fills an entire house, so the least influence of Judaism overflows all of one's life. Oh, what a strong smell that is!"[52] Thus does Mandel'shtam in *The Noise of Time* transmit to the reader his almost unconscious olfactory impression of his "real Jewish house." He makes the point especially strongly in regard to Hebrew, in which he was instructed though he never mastered it. His ears were filled to the brim: "The speech of the father and the speech of the mother—does not our language feed throughout all its long life on the confluence of these two, do they not compose its character?"[53]

These are the elements that contributed to the creative formation of two of the greatest figures in twentieth-century Russian poetry—its Talmudist, Osip Mandel'shtam, and its Hasid, Boris Pasternak.

---

[52] Mandelstam, *The Prose of Osip Mandelstam*, 80.
[53] Ibid., 80, 90.

3 | The Lyric of Idiotic Reason: Folkloric Philosophy in Dmitrii Prigov

> The Karamazovs are not scoundrels, but philosophers, because all real Russians are philosophers.[1]

a. Folkloric Philosophism: The Poetics of Platitude

Philosophy is considered to be the activity of a highly developed consciousness and self-consciousness, one that has risen to the point of systematic conceptions of the universe as a whole. Can there be a *folk philosophy*? Can an uneducated, illiterate person philosophize? As Nikolai Berdiaev wrote: "It is characteristic of the Russian people to philosophize. The illiterate Russian *muzhik* likes to pose questions of a philosophical nature, about the meaning of life, about God, about evil and injustice, about how to bring about the Kingdom of Heaven."[2] The urge to engage in metaphysical generalizations on "the nature of things" is manifest not only at the highest intellectual levels but also in the primary reflective instincts of the unconscious, when one thinks "about everything and nothing." The child who incessantly asks questions about the meaning of everything is more philosophical than an adult specialist in some narrow field of knowledge. This sort of naïve philosophy—it would be more precise to call it "philosophism" or "love of wisdom"—precedes and transcends specialization, and has scarcely been researched.

Dmitrii Aleksandrovich Prigov (1940–2007), the leader of Moscow literary conceptualism of the 1970s–2000s, was probably the most

---

1 The words of Dmitrii Karamazov. Dostoevsky, *The Brothers Karamazov*, 558.
2 Berdiaev, *Russkaia ideia*, 32.

prominent spokesman of this intently naive and "artfully inartful" variety of philosophizing, following certain currents of "folksophy" as represented in Andrei Platonov's prose and OBERIU poetry of the 1920s–30s. In Prigov's verse, the "illiterate," vague philosophism that, as Dostoevsky and Berdiaev note, is generally characteristic of the Russian people, finds an almost folkloric expression, constituting virtually the primary feature of his lyric persona. Granted, this is not so much country as urban folklore: a consciousness that has been "processed" by newspapers, bookstall pulp, and television, with the mix found therein of clichés from all mass ideologies. Prigov's lyrical concepts express those primitive, chaotic movements of the soul, "half-mumblings" already formed for one by the media-environment. Here a rough, gnarled speech, the bearer of the people's unconscious, emerges in the zone of intelligentsia consciousness, which is saturated with all manner of philosophically, ideologically, and theologically conceivable ideas.

As strange as it may sound, Prigov's poetry is in large part a philosophical lyric, rising to the level of a certain metaphysical or theological problem while, however, never ceasing to be part and parcel of the platitudinous consciousness—a sort of "folkloric treatise" or "poetics of platitude." Here are a few such poetic "micro-treatises":

> Do I need a lot in life?
> I barely say a word
> Like a Leibnizian monad
> I fly and buzz something
> To some other monad
> It says to me in response: For God's sake
> Don't buzz

> А много ли мне в жизни надо?—
> Уже и слова не скажу
> Как лейбницевская монада
> Лечу и что-то там жужжу
> Какой-нибудь другой монаде
> Она ж в ответ мне: Бога ради

The Lyric of Idiotic Reason

Не жужжи[3]

The inconspicuous critter of my body
Softly weeps in a little corner
I go ahead and pick her innocent self up
I hold her in my avenging hand
And say with a kindly smile:
Live, my little marmot
I'm your God most high
For the duration of this brief life
Humble thyself!

Моего тела тварь невидная
Тихонько плачет в уголке
Вот я беру ее невинную
Держу в карающей руке
И с доброй говорю улыбкой:
Живи, мой маленький сурок
Вот я тебе всевышний Бог
На время этой жизни краткой
Смирись![4]

Oh, if only there were no snow
The wind didn't howl
And any culprit, like Seneca
Would die voluntarily
In a warm bath, pure, proud—
Lord, what a city of
Paradise that would be!

Ах, кабы не было бы снега
Ветер бы не завывал

---

3 Prigov, *Napisannoe s 1975 po 1989*.
4 Ibid., http://lib.ru/ANEKDOTY/PRIGOW/prigov.txt

> И всяк виновный, как Сенека
> Добровольно б умирал
> В теплой ванне, чистый—гордый—
> Господи, вот был бы город
> Райский!⁵

This is a lively philosophism, so animate it's nearly animal; a philosophism at the level of grumbling, mumbling, and muttering, one that enables us to understand much in the phenomenon of Russian communism, which grew out of the refuse of a primeval, almost unconscious folk love of wisdom. From such profoundly teleological and causal constructions as "life, of course, is"; "does a person really need a lot?"; "but then, after all, I too…" From the point where thinkistry has not yet separated itself from belly-rumbling or scratching the back of one's head.⁶

If we take just Prigov's opening lines, we find in many of them a gut-level meditativeness: these are like philosophical folk prints (*lubok*). "All of life is filled with dangers"; "In the middle of the universe"; "Our life ends"; "On the one hand, the people can be understood"; "The Lord flips the pages of the book of life"; "Freedom threatens us all." On the occasion of a friend's wedding, Prigov advises him to lawfully formalize the bonds of marriage, adducing a profoundly metaphysical argument:

> Such a procedure to formalize
> The living material of love
> Exudes a universal principle:
> What has no form is decay

> Такой порядок оформленья
> Любви материи живой

---

5 http://www.kulichki.com/moshkow/ANEKDOTY/prigow.txt.
6 This deeply pensive unconscious was early and most profoundly expressed by Andrei Platonov, whose characters—Aleksandr Dvanov, Kopenkin, Voshchev—are "exhausted by thought and senselessness" (*The Foundation Pit*, 12).

> В нем дышит принцип мировой:
> Что не оформлено—то тленье[7]

The communist psychology and worldview could probably only arise among a philosophizing people like the Russians or the Chinese, and not a people living according to the concrete advantage of a particular moment in the light of practical reason. Communism is not just communal ownership, general to all, but also the habit of generalizing,[8] of proceeding from the general to the general, weakly mediated by whatever sort of object, which is relegated to the task of merely "illustrating" an idea.

> So I'm about to fry up a chicken
> It's a sin to complain
> But then, I'm not complainin' after all
> What am I, better than everyone else?
> I can't tell you how guilty I feel about it
> Who'd have thunk it, after all:
> The country wasted a whole chicken on my account

> Вот я курицу зажарю
> Жаловаться грех
> Да ведь я ведь и не жалюсь
> Что я—лучше всех?
> Даже совестно, нет силы
> Ведь поди ж ты, на
> Целу курицу сгубила
> на меня страна[9]

The Western bourgeois or proletarian gobbles up a chicken with nary a thought for the whole country that expends this chicken for his personal satiety. The consciousness of the person of the West typically lacks any

---

7 Prigov D. A. *Moskva: virshi na kazhdyi den'*.
8 Epstein plays on the etymological kinship of *obshchestvennaia sobstvennost'* ("public, social, or communal property") and *obobshchat'* ("to generalize")—trans.
9 http://lib.ru/ANEKDOTY/PRIGOW/prigov.txt

such abstract register, and it would "exceed the abilities" of even a great professional philosopher like Bertrand Russell or Ludwig Wittgenstein to scale the heights of such generalization: they are more preoccupied with all manner of linguistic casus, atomic facts, logical paradoxes. Philosophemes like "the living material of love" or a "buzzing monad" would be organically alien to them, because these presuppose not so much the analytic work of the consciousness as the philosophizing unconscious.

Prigov's poetics of "mistily primeval profundity" would seem to come in part from the *Deep Book* or *Dove Book* (*Golubinaia kniga*), the collection of old Russian popular spiritual songs compiled and borne about by pilgrims. It is easy for Dmitrii Aleksandrovich himself to "get into the character" of such a pilgrim, one who has a subliterate depth to him and is excited by simple philosophemes, who chants popular spirituals in a new way. Let us compare the interrogatory stance of Prigov's lyric persona (in this case, an energy customer with an unexpectedly high meter-reading)—

> I discovered a figure on my meter
> Where did it, incomprehensible, come from?
> What power sent it to me?
> Whence did it spring forth?
> Of what fields? What bird?[10]

> На счетчике своем я цифру обнаружил
> Откуда непонятная взялась?
> Какая мне ее прислала власть?
> Откуда выплыла наружу?
> Каких полей? Какая птица?[11]

—with that of the *Deep* or *Dove Book*:

> What did our wide world come from?
> What did the righteous sun come from?

---

10 Prigov plays on the idiom *chto eto za ptitsa*? (lit., "what sort of bird is this?"), a question regarding the type of person or entity one is dealing with.
11 http://lib.ru/ANEKDOTY/PRIGOW/prigov.txt

What did the bright moon come from?
What did the dawn come from?
What did the sunset come from?

От чего зачался наш белый свет?
От чего зачалося солнце праведно?
От чего зачался светел месяц?
От чего зачалася заря утренняя?
От чего зачалася и вечерняя?[12]

Both texts have the intonation of someone overwhelmed by questions about "final things." Of course, in Prigov, the "first thing" perplexing the lyric persona (an extra digit on a meter readout) is entirely prosaic, but this does not keep him from embedding it parodically into the grand style of folk philosophizing.

b. The Stripped Consciousness. A World without a Groove. Allthing and Allbody.

Prigov has a whole long narrative poem about *The Makhrot' of All Rus* (*Makhrot' vseia Rusi*). What "makhrot'" is remains unclear, it is somebody or something, or rather allbody or allthing. (If Russian features such a correlative series of negative, indefinite, and definite pronouns as nowhere—somewhere—everywhere [*nigde, negde, vezde*]; never—sometime—always [*nikogda—nekogda—vsegda*]; no sort of—a certain—any [*nikakoi—nekii—vsiakii*], then according to the same morpho-logic, one should also be able to complete a series thus: nothing—something—allthing [*nichto—nechto—vsechto*]; nobody—somebody—allbody [*nikto—nekto—vsekto*].) It is "makhrot'-grass, from the looks of it, blue; from the inside, red"; it is "beautiful," it is a "holy rat," it stands before Reagan, it appears wherever the lyric persona turns his head, it passes by with its

---

12 Soloshchenko and Prokoshin, *Golubinaia kniga: Russkie narodnye dukhovnye stikhi XI–XIX vv.*, 45. Or compare Prigov's poem about how "[t]he repairman steps out into the winter courtyard / He looks: the courtyard is already a spring one" with the spiritual "Song of Death" (*Golubinaia kniga*, 239).

"feline gait," it "has a gleem [sic¹³] in its little eye and licks its little lips with its little tongue," it is a "great beast," it "floats over our hemisphere," it lurks in a wine cup, it climbs and "whores" its way out of the "stillness and grace."¹⁴

> Tenderly singing, thickly hissing
> Tearing meat to a tatter
> there it is, prophetic real life
> In god's name—the Makhrot'
> Of All Rus.

> Нежно-поющая, густо-шипящая
> Рвущая мясо в лохмоть
> вот она вещая жизнь настоящая
> Именем бога—Махроть
> Всея Руси.

The makhrot' here is roughly equivalent to the hallucinatory demon-sprite (*nedotykomka*) in Fedor Sologub's *The Petty Demon* (*Melkii bes*) or the "norm" in Vladimir Sorokin's novel *The Norm* (*Norma*)—something ubiquitous and elusive, an algebraic symbol, some sort of X to match all verbal equations. But while Sologub endows his demon-sprite with a certain psychological plausibility (i.e., as stemming from Peredonov's maniacal suspiciousness and madness), Sorokin's *norm* and Prigov's *makhrot'* are purely conceptual. This is the concept of a certain abstract essence that is present in everything in an absolutely direct manner, without hiding, without any intermediary. This "allthing" is of roughly the same order as matter in Soviet materialism. What is matter? Everything is matter. Bread is matter, and a field, and a person, and the brain, and a thought, and the state—wherever you poke into, everywhere you hit matter and only matter in all its manifestations. This is a model of a stripped consciousness that takes short cuts, passing all

---

13 Prigov uses the nonstandard *bleznut'* for *blesnut'* ("to shine, gleam")—trans.
14 These and subsequent quotes from *The Makhrot' of All Rus* are cited from http://d-a-prigov.narod.ru/index/0-10.

mediations by, and all distinctions of level; "skips" *from the most concrete thing to the most abstract principle*, exulting in its all-pervasive capacity. Posing vague questions about the final, all-encompassing meaning of everything, it receives the briefest of answers: "everything is matter," or "everything is God," or "everything is the norm." This may be an atheistic or religious consciousness, but it always strips the groove from the screw, that is, completely lays bare the process of generalization; it does not allow for partial, interim, open-ended, "non-philosophical" answers. It is philosophical, or more precisely wisdom-loving, particularly because it has a direct need for "the main thing," allthing—and easily finds it. It languishes in philosophical questioning, but any doubt or melancholy immediately turns into its opposite, the euphoria of a found solution. It asks "childish" questions about the world—"why does a mosquito drink human blood?"; "what does a person live for?"; "why is the earth round?"; etc.—and gives them the shortest answers: because that is how God, or nature, has arranged it; because such is the law of matter; etc. The quest for the omnipresent, all-pervasive X is a reflex not only of Soviet ideology but also of its lawful heir, post-Soviet conspiracy mentality. The difference is that while Soviet ideology's object was the *allthing*, some primordial matter, substance, or law of history—that of conspiracy theory is the *allbody*, some all-powerful subject in history who secretly controls it (but who is, unlike the supernatural subject of religion, a human subject).

Prigov organically combines:

—the *ripped consciousness of the intelligentsia loner*, the superfluous man who is alienated from himself and experiences the indelicacy of the world around him, which he towers over in his thoughts even as he is all the while distressed by its indifference;

—and the *stripped consciousness of the man of the people*, vigorous, maniacally self-confident, as if intoxicated by his knowledge of the key to all mysteries.

The *ripped* consciousness is essentially miserable, eternally at loose ends. It rises above itself, contemplates and criticizes itself, and cannot find solace in itself. This is the extreme of the skeptical, perplexed consciousness described by Hegel in *The Phenomenology of Spirit* as unhappy, "divided within itself."¹⁵ The *stripped* consciousness, to the contrary, is cheerful, even euphorically elevated. It overcomes every disturbance within itself; in a trice it arrives at peremptory solutions.

Whereas the policeman (*militsioner*) existed as an element in the socioprofessional hierarchy of Soviet society, in Prigov this figure becomes the Paliceman (*Militsianer*), that is, he is simultaneously debased to the level of the vernacular and elevated to the honor of capitalization—aloft as some absolute, the universal boss, the watchman of the world order, the demiurge. If the makhrot' is Prigov's allthing, then the Paliceman is his allbody, a universal figure who manifests himself everywhere, answers for everything, and keeps everything under observation and control. Such a dual transformation—simplification and glorification—is what Prigov's device of folk love of wisdom is. An image or word is simultaneously "peopleized" (lowered, simplified) and "wisdomized" (philosophized, universalized), and thus comes to belong to the "philosophy of the people, by the people, and for the people."

Prigov frequently resorts to elevated scientistic terminology, insofar as it is *quasi*literate and vividly neutralizes the "intelligentsia vs. the people" opposition: "The Palicemen is invariant between the earth and the heavens." If the Paliceman has suddenly turned out to be a murderer, then a philosophically clear conclusion regarding him also ensues:

> He subverts not the laws of the state
> But the secret laws of the universe
> He deserves metaphysical punishment.

> Не государства он законы подрывает
> Но тайные законы мирозданья
> Метафизического он достоин наказанья.¹⁶

We might also note that the layout and punctuation of the Prigovian verse corresponds to this dual gesture of simplification/wisdomization. On the

---

15 Hegel, *Phenomenology of Spirit*, 133.
16 http://www.prigov.org/ru/texts/polnyy_spisok/apofeoz_milicanera___05.30.14.08.47.15.am.

one hand, Prigov either skips punctuation marks entirely, or uses them on a case-by-case basis, "higgledy-piggledy." For instance, he sets off similes and forms of address with only one comma instead of two, thus imitating a folksy carelessness, an incomplete education, the sense of "we never graduated any lycée." On the other hand, nearly all his lines begin with an uppercase letter, like in "big-time," classic poetry, "like in Pushkin." Once again, a dual gesture: that of debasement and elevation, illiteracy and pretentiousness.

> O, you alone, Paliceman
> As a pillar and symbol of the State
> And filled with passionate will
> Shall offer them, as in holy battle
> The support of thy strong arm

> О, только ты, Милицанер
> Как столп и символ Государства
> И волею исполнен страстной
> Возьмешь их, как в святом бою
> Под руку сильную свою[17]

In another well-known "didactic" poem by Prigov, a woman in a packed metro car kicks the lyric persona, and the latter, having answered her in kind, immediately begs her pardon:

> A woman in the metro kicked me
> It wasn't just a case of elbowing
> That one could take—but here she went too far
> And so the whole thing passed into the realms
> Of quite uncalled-for personal relations
> Naturally I kicked her back
> But at that moment begged her pardon—
> Being quite simply a superior person.[18]

---

17 http://lib.guru.ua/ANEKDOTY/prigow.txt.
18 Translated by Sally Laird; cited from Appignanesi, *Novostroika*, 26.

Женщина в метро меня лягнула
Ну, пихаться—там куда ни шло
Здесь же она явно перегнула
Палку, и все дело перешло
В ранг ненужно личных отношений
Я, естественно, в ответ лягнул
Но и тут же попросил прощенья—
Просто я как личность выше был[19]

This is one more example of the exultant, stripped consciousness, which responds to a minor incident with a proclamation of the sacred humane principle enjoining one to be a "superior person."

Prigov, of course, does not simply reproduce the style of a lover of platitudinous wisdom but exaggerates and defamiliarizes it, even as he remains within the framework of what he terms "shimmering aesthetics," which wavers as the distance between author and lyric persona is now elongated, now curtailed. This is a citational mode of unspecified borders, without an end-quote, oscillating between "another's" speech and "one's own." At the same time, Prigov is perfectly aware what sort of mentality he is subjecting to conceptualization. Here is the brief "Forewarning" to his collection *Atoms of Our Life* (*Atomy nashei zhizni*):

> Like all such previous opuses: Beasts of our life, People of our life, Events of our life, and this work tells, in fact, about the very same thing. About the very same substance that, always assuming different guises according to our ripped ability to perceive the entirety of this world as torn, appears to us as if different modes of one and the same essence.[20]

This act of everywhere discovering "one and the same essence" is just what turns our "ripped ability" into a stripped consciousness, insofar as it enforces a unity that is lacking. Thus through the ripped consciousness of the languishing and guilt-anguished member of the intelligentsia, we begin to hear the voice of the unconscious pushing its way powerfully through:

---

19   http://www.rulit.me/books/stihi-read-114429-1.html.
20   Prigov, *Kniga knig: Izbrannoe*, 593. This translation assumes the nonexistent word *razvorvanno* is supposed to read *razorvanno*, "rippedly, tornly."

"The most difficult thing" (Pierre went on thinking or hearing in his sleep) "consists in being able to unite the meaning of all things in [one's] soul. To unite all things?" Pierre said to himself. "No, not to unite. It's impossible to unite thoughts, but to *hitch together* all these thoughts—that's what's needed! Yes, *we must hitch together, hitch together!*" Pierre repeated to himself with inner rapture, feeling that precisely these and only these words expressed what he wanted to express and resolved the whole question that tormented him.[21]

Hitching, hitching things together—this is indeed what Prigov's overly thoughtful persona, following in the footsteps of Tolstoy's Pierre and Karataev, engages in. He experiences the intoxication of Sophia, he falls victim to wisdom-poisoning. Every trifle becomes overgrown with some sort of speculation, elicits a million questions of a metaphysical nature. "A figure on a meter"—what fields, what bird? Registering or formalizing a marriage is a form of living matter, whereas whatsoever lacks form, decays! This is a particular "Platonism" in which it is hard to distinguish between the ancient Greek and Tolstoy's Platon Karataev, and both these from the binge-thinking characters of Andrei Platonov. Right away and without any mediation, every particular is elevated to the general, or the other way around, practical particulars are deduced directly from some general speculation. What is lacking in this are the mediating links, a sober judgment as to the hierarchy of essences, their subordination, their gradual rather than instantaneous deducibility. Consciousness without such mediation is like a screw whose thread has been worn away; it gets no purchase, it is a stripped consciousness. While the ripped consciousness is able to accommodate two ideas without in any way associating them, the stripped consciousness, to the contrary, unites ideas of entirely different levels, instantly skipping from the general to the particular. There is a certain childishness in this; it is the sort of pensiveness that literally "seizes upon" everything in everything, and has no experience of making distinctions. It is as if a grown person were to begin to think for the first time, and was suddenly perplexed: why does the country "waste" a whole chicken just for me, am I really worthy of that? What did I do to earn it?

---

21 Tolstoy, *War and Peace*, 843–44.

c. The Banality of Abstraction: The Deeply Thoughtful Unconscious

In general, despite the superficial everydayness of its execution, Prigov's poetry is remarkably abstract; right away, in a single bound, it leaps to the level of generalization. "The cows were now beset by disease / Clearly they had committed an offense before God."[22]

In 1985 I went on a research trip sponsored by Moscow State University to study Old Believers, with whom I discussed their eschatological views. One of the discoveries I found most surprising was the extent to which the eternal and the temporary, the supernatural and the everyday, are compressed in folk consciousness. Signs of eschatological expectations may be conceived in the broad framework of centuries—and within a single current month, even a day. Omens of the end times may be seen in airplanes, tractors, electricity, radio, i.e., "novelties" at least a half-century old. At the same time, the commencement of the end times may be signaled by this summer's rains, or even specifically the rain that yesterday caused the cucumber seedlings to be overwatered. To quote some of my interlocutors' remarks: "The final millennium is at hand. Look, this summer the barley was ruined, the rains flooded it—that never used to happen" (V. Z.). "There was a particular rain, a magnetic one—this caused the cucumbers to go yellow and spoil" (F. Ser). Thus did my interlocutors complain about the vicissitudes of the weather, explaining how the end times had already come. "The father shall kill the son. That's just what's happening—a month ago near Zhitomir a father stabbed his son with a knife."[23]

Dmitrii Prigov's poetry is entirely capable of conveying this sort of "threadless" consciousness. The combination of the millennium and this summer, the coming end of the world and the yellowed cucumbers in the garden—this is an overlay of incommensurate proportions. The whole cycle "Banal Considerations on Banal Subjects" ("Banal'nye rassuzhdeniia

---

22 "Vot na korov nabrosilas' bolezn' / pred Bogom, vidno provinilis'..." These lines are from Prigov's 1999 collection "A ne stikhi li eto" ("Is this not verse"). It was probably never published, but was included in Prigov's poetry readings. I am grateful to Mark Lipovetsky for identifying this source from the script in his archive.

23 Transcripts of my conversations with Old Believers were published in my (unattributed) article "Staroobriadcheskii dnevnik," *Simvol* (Paris) 21 (July 1989): 99–156.

na banal'nye temy") is about the same thing. What are these subjects? The "reasonableness of ideals," the "firm foundations of life," the "all-conquering power of ideas," "freedom"—this is philosophical lyric, downright Tiutchevian or Zabolotskian. Or would be, except that Tiutchev's love of wisdom is that of the aristocrat, and Zabolotsky's that of the scientist or engineer, whereas Prigov's is precisely a folksy love of wisdom, and banal and philosophical in equal measure, for there is nothing more banal than philosophical commonplaces.

> You've hardly finished washing a dish, and
> Lo, there's a new one there
> Freedom's out of the question
> You wonder if you'll ever make it to old age

> Только вымоешь посуду
> Глядь—уж новая лежит
> Уж какая тут свобода
> Тут до старости б дожить[24]

There occur such states of pensiveness, especially in a child; you tap him on the shoulder, and he even flinches. "What's with you?" "Nothing, I was just thinking." This state of being numbed by lengthy pondering, aware of neither oneself nor anything around, is also characteristic of a philosophic people, a people capable, in a state of such speculative prostration, of demolishing half the world in one fell swoop without batting an eye. Prigov lyrically reproduces this state of powerful and unaccountable thought but at the same time gently taps the somnambulist on the shoulder: what's with you? what are you on about? His addressee flinches, and suddenly reveals an absolute void: not a single thought. Because it was his unconscious that was thinking and even philosophizing. This is not the philosophy of the unconscious but the unconscious of philosophy itself, which is carried out in concepts but which, at the same time, is just as elemental, as dreamy and vaguely primeval as mythology.

---

24 http://literatura.org/poetry/545-dmitriy-aleksandrovich-prigov-ono-vokrug-i-est.html.

In Prigov's interpretation, communism itself is a somnambulistic devotion to a certain beautiful half-unconscious idea, the reduction of all life in accordance with the exclamatory or interrogative "slogans of the soul": "Lord, what a city of / Paradise that would be!" or "What am I, better than everyone else?" Prigov's conceptualism reveals this *pensiveness* in the very substance of the Russian *unconscious*—which remains unconscious of *itself* precisely because it is steeped in thought, thinking without cease.

The Cyclical Development of Russian Literature[1]

The proclivity of Russian literature for paradoxes predetermines the cyclical model of its development. Contradictions are left unresolved: thesis and antithesis, sacred and profane, reality and dream, the ideal and the material, being and nothingness reciprocally change their places and are alternately affirmed or denied. But on a culture-wide scale, this does not lead to mediation or synthesis on a higher level. Russian literature revolves in a circle of the same problems and oppositions. For all the uniqueness of the current literary stage, it can nonetheless be said that "everything had been there in the olden days, everything will be repeated again, and sweet is only the moment of recognition" (Osip Mandel'shtam[2]). If we pause on this sweet moment of recognition, a kind of periodic table of the elements of Russian literature takes shape before us.

What did Russian literature begin with in the Modern Age, when it awoke from medievality? Before, there had been no literature to speak of; or rather, such literature as existed was merged with various types of instrumental writing (quotidian, didactic, scholarly, edifying, etc.). The new Russian literature begins with social and civil service, which in its first period, in the eighteenth century, is called classicism. Kantemir with his satires, Lomonosov with his odes, Fonvizin with his comedies, Radishchev with his revolutionary sermons: they are all in the service of the goals of the state, the good of the fatherland, the education of its worthy sons. Literature spreads out horizontally, addressing the consciousness of the reader-citizen, enlightening him with models of virtue and vice.

But then, as if reflecting some general law of creative development, Russian literature shifts from a social phase to a moral one. Individuality—its

---

1 This section was translated by Anesa Miller-Pogacar.
2 From Mandel'shtam's poem "I have mastered the science of parting" ("Ia izuchil nauku rasstavan'ia," 1918).

feelings and needs, its tears and tenderness—comes to the forefront. It was in this way that sentimentalism emerged, having undermined the dominance of social norms and criteria. Lomonosov gives way to Karamzin; the horizontal social plan narrows to a single point—the individual, who is entirely directed toward himself.

The next phase—the religious—is designated by a romantic tendency and associated with the name of Vasilii Zhukovsky. Once again, the point extends into a line but is no longer directed toward the social plane; rather it is a vertical, metaphysical line. The individual discovers his kinship with the super-individual, the otherworldly, the absolute. Poetry takes on a myth-making function, offers revelations from above; it becomes the expression of the inexpressible, the longing for the Ideal, the creation of the Temple.

Finally, with the appearance of its own norm and power, art closes in on itself. The vertical contracts, though now not to a point but to a circle: art exists not for the sake of the ascent to an external absolute. It is an absolute in itself—a language that speaks of the possibilities of language. In Russian literature, this is the phenomenon of Pushkin and the school of "harmonious precision" that he founded. At this point, art's other objectives—the service of society or morality—are done away with. In Pushkin's words, "Poetry is higher than morality, or at least it is something else altogether";[3] the artist is his own highest judge. According to Belinsky's accurate observation, the main thrust of Pushkin's work is its artistic quality: that which was once taken as a means—artistry—becomes an end in itself.

With Pushkin, the first cycle of the development of Russian literature is complete: having moved from the horizontal, through the single point and the vertical, it returns, in the circle, to itself, to literariness as such.

Then a new cycle begins—with the proclamation of those same ideas of social responsibility in heated polemics with the previous "schools," romantic as well as aesthetic. Belinsky ridiculed the epigones of romanticism, and Pisarev took aim even against Pushkin. The first phase of the new cycle—Gogol's "natural school," is to be seen as a "relentless exposure of the sores of

---

3 Pushkin, *Sobranie sochinenii v 10 tomakh*, 7:550.

The Cyclical Development of Russian Literature 393

social reality." Then there developed the physiological sketch, the denunciatory or social-critical novel, "realism" and "nihilism," revolutionary-democratic criticism, homage to the criterion of practical good, and the reestablishment of Radishchev and Fonvizin's socially enlightening tendency in literature.

But the social function of art does not satisfy the greatest writers, and already in the early work of Tolstoy and Dostoevsky, the moral-psychological imperative begins to predominate: not types, but individuals, the "dialectics of the soul" and "the freshness of moral feeling" (Chernyshevsky on Tolstoy). These impulses serve to reconstitute the sentimental phase in the second cycle of literary development, marked by the obvious influence of Schiller on Dostoevsky and of Rousseau on Tolstoy. In fact, to the very end, all of Tolstoy's work remains fundamentally moralistic; its goal is to exert a direct emotional effect on the reader, to "infect the reader with the writer's feelings" (as Tolstoy put it in his treatise *What is Art?*). And, in one way or another, the majority of Russian writers of the second half of the nineteenth century endeavored to come to terms with the same problem: the education of the soul, moral enlightenment, the awakening of conscience—from the revolutionary-populist moralism of Nekrasov and Nadson, to the humanist-individual moralism of Chekhov, Garshin, and Korolenko.

But already in Dostoevsky's work, Russian literature began to move into its next phase—the religious, which sees the world constructed along a vertical line, extending from heights to abysses. The religious function of literature was conclusively established by Vladimir Solov'ev and his followers in Russian symbolism, which was directly inspired by the legacy of romanticism (as Blok was inspired by Zhukovsky). Language became allusive, a kind of initiation into the secrets of higher worlds. Art became theurgy, that is, the transformation of existence in God's image, and all artistic-philosophical thinking of the early twentieth century moved in this current—from Merezhkovsky to Berdiaev and Florensky, from Andrei Bely to Viacheslav Ivanov.

Yet this cycle was also destined to close with an aesthetic phase. The increased critical attacks on symbolism accused the latter of disembodying and mystifying art, of turning it into myth and cryptography, whereas the task should be to return it to a magical plasticity, to language as such. This problem was addressed in a variety of ways in post-symbolist movements: acmeism, futurism, and imaginism all derived from the self-sufficient worth of the artistic vision. "Sublime clarity," "the self-spun word," "language art," "form as organism," "the image as an end in itself": all this brought literature along the new spiral, back to the work "as such." The formalist school of literary criticism also contributed to this trend, by conceiving of art as a device.

Thus, having passed through the same four phases—the social, the moral, the religious, and the aesthetic—Russian literature completed its second cycle of development.

The third cycle corresponds to the Soviet era and coincides with its boundaries. Yet it seems that even had there been no Bolshevism or October Revolution, literature would still have entered yet another cycle beginning with the horizontal, by posing social tasks and proclaiming a social mandate: proletarian culture, class loyalty, party loyalty, and the social face of the writer. After all, the cycles of the eighteenth and nineteenth centuries began in a similar way—why should the twentieth century be any exception? While there would not have been actual killings of disobedient writers, there would still have been ideological death sentences pronounced on works diverging from the horizontal or lapsing into previous phases of development, into a circle or a vertical. It is characteristic that the first phase of a new cycle is merciless with respect to the latter two phases of the previous cycle (the religious and the aesthetic)—summarily lumping them together as "decadence"—while adopting the first two (the social and the moral) and recovering them as part of its "classical heritage." Gogol and Tolstoy are revered, while Vladimir Solov'ev and Nikolai Gumilev are reviled or silenced. The social phase is lengthy: from the mid-twenties through the mid-fifties—and it is quite natural that, like the initial phase of the first cycle, one critic (Andrei Siniavsky) called it "socialist *classicism*." It is hardly necessary to list the greats of this period: beginning with Gorky and Maiakovsky, they were listed in all the textbooks—and quite deservedly so—as the "classics of Soviet literature."

But then, from the mid-1950s, from the period of the post-Stalin Thaw, the warming soul and the softening heart, the second phase began; and it would be difficult to find a better name for it than "socialist sentimentalism." Once again rigid classical canons come under critique, "sociologism" begins to seem "vulgar" and is rejected in favor of moral approaches based on the individual "soul" and "conscience." The unique human individual is the center of attention. "There are no uninteresting people in this world": this was the credo of Evgenii Evtushenko, one of the founders of this new sentimentalism. This credo could only be compared to Karamzin's immortal dictum that "peasant women know how to love too." Once again we find images of "little people"—tailors and stocking-makers—instead of generals and warriors. The principal demand made of literature is sincerity, arousal of feeling, confession. The principal direction—that of "moral seeking"—continued almost through the mid-eighties, already without hope of any findings. Voznesensky, Okudzhava, Aksenov, Andrei Bitov, Iurii Kazakov, Iurii Trifonov—all of them were formed by this principal direction, regardless of the paths they were to choose later. "Variety-hall poetry," "confessional prose," "urban prose," "the urban romance"—these were the signposts and milestones of the "sentimental education" of our literature in the fifties and sixties. And it was here that a second, mature period of the same movement came to replace youthful reverie—Solzhenitsyn's stern sermons on moral cleansing: "to live not by lies." In this category too would be Tvardovsky, *Novyi mir*, the poetics of bitter truth and the tortured conscience.

But literature moves on and, following some unknown law, once again makes the transition from a moral stage to a religious one, constructing a vertical metaphysical line over the single point of the moral individual. Chronologically, perhaps the end of the "Prague spring" and of *Novyi mir* marked this transition most clearly. Above all, this was telling in the case of Solzhenitsyn himself, in his personal transition from "moral socialism" to Christianity. Morality was exhausted as a sovereign force, a humanist impulse and "conscience without God."

Several periods may be distinguished in this metaphysical phase of our literature. The earliest was the phase of "quiet poetry" and "village prose," with their initial sense of resignation, the abdication of the "I," the embracing of age-old ways of life. But this religiosity is still of a naive, archaic, almost pagan model—with its cult of the earth, of nature, and of national roots. In its Orthodox version, it tends toward ritualization, and sacralization of the folk traditions of everyday life. Then came the turn to mythologism, no longer so morally bound and sermonizing, freely playing through the abysses and cliffs of the spirit, with the exoticism of Eastern religions and other esoterica—reincarnation, spells, demonic delusions, descent into the wells of times and spaces. Iurii Kuznetsov emerged in poetry, while in prose it was Anatolii Kim and Iurii Mamleev with their "fantastic realism." Chingiz Aitmatov traversed the same path from the moral tone of his early works to the metaphysical overload of his later ones.

Finally, the third and culturally most highly developed layer of this neoromantic movement consists of what we have already described as metarealism: the poetry and prose of Ol'ga Sedakova, Viktor Krivulin, Ivan Zhdanov, Elena Shvarts—and also, in a different way, of Tatyana Tolstaya and Mikhail Kuraev. In their work there is less of the color and drunkenness of myth, and more a sobering and intense peering into the transparent outlines of things, the ascent up the staircases of cultural parallels, entering into aborted embryos of cultures, their eternal archetypes. The conflict between reality and super-reality becomes ironically acute, as in Tolstaya, or washed in gnostic tones, as in Zhdanov—but in both cases, analogies with the two previous "vertical" epochs in Russian literature suggest themselves.

And further on, as experience would suggest, literature is "rounded off," as it enters the final phase—the aesthetic, where it becomes an encyclopedia of the possibilities of literature, a collection of signs and a crossroads of languages. The epoch of conceptualism arrives, when the mystic winds of the seventies begin to be perceived as the putrid fogs of the stagnation era, as the bequeathed "imperishables" of decayed and languishing souls. The word "vulgar" now clings to the preceding phases: if the metaphysicians deemed vulgar the *moralism* of the "sixties generation," who in their turn had condemned "vulgar sociologism," then the conceptualists see vulgarity in any kind of *mythologism* or metaphysical construction. Language is pure of the sin of content and must continue to purify itself, as it enters the zone of silence.

A striking feature of the new aestheticism is, in fact, its anti-aestheticism, which, in a sense, finds a parallel phase in the experiments of the futurists. The difference is that the futurists put great emphasis on the "transsensical," or nonrational, sound of words, their majestic ugliness, while conceptualism tends toward humble squalor. Whereas Kruchenykh youthfully thundered the nonsense words *"dyr bur shchil ubeshchur,"* Vsevolod Nekrasov's verse becomes senile muttering: "that is, this is it / this is what it is." Language is ashamed of its chattiness and seeks to hide deeper inside the oral cavity, even at the cost of stuttering and lisping.[4] Language has come up with so many monstrosities in the twentieth century, it has told so many deadly lies, that now it wants to forget itself and go to sleep, like speech as one dozes off.

The recent aesthetic phase cannot be reduced to conceptualism alone, which is but its "lower" stratum, while a "higher" one exists as well: not anti- but aesthetic proper. Alongside futurism there was acmeism. Likewise, the concluding phase of the current cycle includes prose and poetry that appear to be purely phenomenal, cleansed not only of social, moral, and religious tasks but also of conceptual minus-contents. Sensitivity is elevated to an attribute of the artist's supreme virtue: vision, hearing, touch—that is, all that would return aesthetics to itself, as a discipline of *sensitivity* (in the literal sense of the word "aesthetics"). In the work of Joseph Brodsky, one can sense a transition from the metarealism of his early collections to the phenomenalism of his later ones—not even so much a transition in and of itself as a retention and dynamic parity of the two different components. It is as if language does away with its metaphysical orientation through its own logic and finely honed syntax, though that orientation is restored precisely because of the transparency of the syntax, which cannot help but philosophize about the object in space—using noun cases and verb endings. In his best verses, Brodsky's world is ideally "superficial"—it is depth turned inside out, in such a way that not a single grain of matter, not a single step upward or outward separates metaphysics from physics and physiology.

This phenomenalism, a poetics of the pure *presence*[5] of the object on the iris of the eye and the tips of the fingers, is developed in the prose of Sasha Sokolov and Sergei Iourienen, in the poetry of Aleksei Parshchikov

---

4 The Russian word *iazyk* used here means both "language" and "tongue."
5 Hence another possible name for this literary current: "presentism," the poetics of the presence (vs. the "futurism" of the 1910s–20s).

and Il'ia Kutik. True, for the latter two, the logic of sensitivity, the "figure of intuition" and the "pentathlon of the senses" (the titles of Parshchikov's and Kutik's collections), are manifest not so much in the forms of metaphysics as in those of science, technology, or sport, as concretely applied thought, devices for mastering the object and mapping out space. This is characteristic of phenomenalism generally: the transformation of the scientific term into a metaphor, the appeal being its dry visual precision, fenced off from both the "overflow" of meanings in metarealism and their "ebb tide" in conceptualism. It is as if phenomenalism is deployed in a middle zone between myth and parody, between metaphysical seriousness and linguistic mischief, upon a surface that lies between the depth of the object and the comic inversion of this depth.

I think that in the literature of the emigre community this aesthetic middle is more fully represented than at home, where it is pushed aside by the extremes of metarealism and conceptualism, mystical enthusiasm and quasi-nihilist grotesque. In general, emigration itself—whether external or internal—is especially conducive to the presentation of objects as phenomena, whose ulterior, substantive nature is concealed and covered in haze, like the motherland that has been left behind. It was Nabokov—perceived in Russia in the perestroika years as the freshest literary news of the period since his death—who emerged as the precursor of this amazingly deep surface-writing. And on the whole, in being spatially removed, the emigration has been remarkably successful in lagging behind in the phases of time. It seems as if for seventy years, from Ivan Bunin to Sasha Sokolov, it has been preparing for the concluding, aesthetic phase—for merging with the principal course of the current, not just anywhere, but precisely at the mouth, right before it falls into the next and still unknown cycle.

It is possible, however, to surmise that the fourth cycle will also begin with a phase that will be strikingly social, whose anticipation took shape within the depths of perestroika and glasnost, although it could just as well have come into being without that influence, without any jolts from the outside. Having exhausted the circuitous and self-sufficient aesthetic model, literature again finds itself at the mercy of the horizontal—such is its destiny.

The Cyclical Development of Russian Literature 399

Thus, we observe the pattern of alternation of four phases of the development of Russian literature: the socio-ideological, the moral-humanist, the religious-metaphysical, and the aesthetic-conceptual. In order that all of this not be confused in the reader's mind, we might present a table of the cyclical development of Russian literature, with the reservation that it is approximate. The squares and columns are drawn in a highly provisional manner, and on more careful examination, they might turn into a painting, where each individual phenomenon would be a spot of color, a brushstroke across all straight lines.

The Periodic Table of Russian Literature (Cycles and Phases of Development)

	Social (the horizontal)	Moral (the single point)	Religious (the vertical)	Aesthetic (the circle)
Cycle 1 1730–1840	Classicism. The honor of nobility. Civic virtue. Service to the homeland. Obligation toward society.	Sentimentalism. The sensitive individual. The inner world. Sincerity, earnestness. Edification. Moral usefulness.	Romanticism. The superindividual, the beyond, the inexpressible. Myth and spirit. Pining for the heavens.	The pathos of the artistic. Harmonious exactness. "Poetry above morality." "We are born for inspiration."
Cycle 2 1840–1920	Critical realism. The natural school. The physiological sketch. "Types"; typical characters in typical circumstances. The denunciatory tendency. Social usefulness. Revolutionary democracy.	The new sentimentalism. Psychologism. Self-analysis. The "dialectics of the soul" and the "freshness of moral sensibility." Conscience. Guilt. Repentance. Denunciation of falsehood and vulgarity.	Symbolism. Art as theurgy. Myth-creation. The world-soul. The mysteries of otherworlds.	Acmeism. Futurism. Imaginism. The "self-spun" word. The creation of a new language. Art as device.

| Cycle 3 1920–90 | Proletcult. Socialist realism. The music of the Revolution. The pen as a bayonet. Loyalty to Party, class and the people. The hero as fighter and constructor. Educating the toiling masses in the spirit of socialism. | Socialist sentimentalism. Sincerity. Confessional prose. The poetry of the bared "I." The freshness of feelings. Self-expression. "We aren't screws." Moral searching. "To live not by lies." Conscience. Guilt. Repentance. | Neoromanticism. (1) "Village prose" and "quiet" poetry. Humbleness. The grassroots. The people. National roots. The faith of our forefathers. (2) Mythologism. Fantastic realism. The parable. Reincarnation. Doubles and werewolves. (3) Metarealism. Eidetics, pure forms, Platonic ideas. Contemplation. The religious content of culture. | (1) Phenomenalism. The logic of sensitivity. Things as they are. Surface = depth. Terms = metaphors. (2) Conceptualism. Play with empty language. Signifiers over and above the signified. Schemas and skeletons of culture. The concept as a work of art. (3) The rear guard. Zero-degree writing. The refuse of culture. Decentering. Entropy. Language as it is. |
| Cycle 4 1990–? | The new sociality. Metapolitics: play with the signs of various political systems. Political-literary-theatrical hybrids. | ? | ? | ? |

The Cyclical Development of Russian Literature 401

The most significant thing to note is the way in which the regular progression of the four phases in the historical movement of literature (horizontally) leads to a steady repetition and their correspondence through all three cycles (vertically). A "sweet moment" of recognition is afforded in the vertical columns, where Lomonosov is somehow revealed in Maiakovsky (the social, or classicist phase of the first and third cycles), Zhukovsky—in Blok (the religious, or romantic phase of the first and second cycles), and the poet Karamzin, perhaps, in Evtushenko (the moral, or sentimental phase of the first and third cycles).[6]

---

6 The cyclical development of Russian literature is discussed in more detail in my books *After the Future*, 71–97; and *Postmodern v russkoi literature*, 196–232.

Conclusion

a. Literature and Metaphysics

The "appetite for metaphysics ... distinguishes a work of art from mere *belles lettres*," writes Joseph Brodsky in his final collection of essays *On Grief and Reason*.[1] "Metaphysics" here means the attempt to comprehend the world as a whole, to pose the foundational questions of being and undertake an autonomous search for their solution.

As is well known, the word "metaphysics" was originally applied to those works of Aristotle that came "after physics" and investigated not sensorily perceptible phenomena but "being as being and the attributes which belong to this in virtue of its own nature."[2] Unlike the specialized sciences, metaphysics raises those eternal questions that scientific knowledge cannot answer. Why does the world exist? Is there a God? Where does evil come from, and why should we do good? Why are people born, what is the meaning of their lives, and why are they doomed to die? Is our will free, or is it the manifestation of some higher necessity unknown to us, of predestination?

Let us recall that when Lermontov's "fatalist" Pechorin asks Maksim Maksimovich's opinion of predestination, the latter declines to answer on the grounds that "he has no love for metaphysical debate."[3] Indeed, metaphysics has much that is unclear and unsettled but which is all the more vital to the soul for that. Intellectual history has seen numerous attempts to abolish metaphysics as a discipline ungrounded in science and foredoomed to ignorance or quasi-knowledge. But despite all the funerals held for metaphysics, the rumors of its death have always proved premature. Even if we have no definitive answers to metaphysical questions, the need itself to ask them, to go beyond the limits of sensory

---

1 Brodsky, *On Grief and Reason*, 101.
2 Aristotle, *Metaphysics*, 43.
3 Lermontov, *Geroi nashego vremeni*, 202.

being, to interrogate first principles and final meanings, remains abiding. Having laid the foundations of its radical critique, Immanuel Kant nevertheless acknowledged that metaphysics is inseparable from the primary aspirations of the human spirit: "That the human mind will ever give up metaphysical researches is as little to be expected as that we should prefer to give up breathing altogether, to avoid inhaling impure air. There will therefore always be metaphysics in the world; nay, everyone, especially every man of reflection, will have it."[4]

Literature, too, has its own metaphysics. A complexity and breadth of thinking addressed to the furthest reaches of human existence and beyond distinguishes literature from discourse meant to entertain, chronicle everyday life, or provide up-to-the-minute news. God and humanity, the spirit and the flesh, sanctity and sin, life and death, freedom and law, fate and chance—literature is pervaded with these metaphysical themes and concepts, often even regardless of the intent of authors themselves.

This does not mean that literature is a subsidiary of philosophy, simply conveying ideas in the form of images. Metaphysics is often seen as a subdivision of philosophy, one that investigates the laws and universals of creation, the nature and structure of reality. But metaphysics is not exclusively the privilege of philosophy. Religion and politics, language and music have their own metaphysics, their own vision of the first principles of being, its heights and depths. Thus is the field of "metaphysics" both *broader* and *narrower* than philosophy. On the one hand, metaphysics is only one subdivision of philosophy, along with epistemology, ontology, logic, ethics, aesthetics, etc. On the other, philosophy is only one of the fields of metaphysics, which may also be expressed in literature, theater, painting, etc. Consider, for instance, the metaphysical questioning in this stanza of Pushkin:

> Futile gift, random gift,
> Life, why are you given to me?
> Or why by a secret fate
> Are you condemned to execution?

---

4 Kant, *Prolegomena to Any Future Metaphysics*, 142.

Дар напрасный, дар случайный,
Жизнь, зачем ты мне дана?
Иль зачем судьбою тайной
Ты на казнь осуждена?[5]

This is one of the primary metaphysical themes: a person appears on earth not by his own will, but, having accepted this gift and attempting to discover the secret of its meaning, he is at the same time struck by the mystery of why this unasked-for gift is so quickly and again without asking taken away. Metaphysics is the realm of those questions we call not just eternal but also accursed, because they are irresolvable for the mind and torturous for the heart.

Of course, literary works do not contain too many directly metaphysical reflections; for Pushkin, for that matter, these are far less typical than for such philosophical lyricists as Fedor Tiutchev and Nikolai Zabolotsky. Usually the metaphysics of a literary work is expressed not in philosophical speculations but in the interplay of its imagery, the peculiarities of its style and choice of words and details, and in the call-and-response it engages in with works by other authors, sometimes at the remove of decades or centuries. Here you are dealing not with the author's directly expressed thought but the thought of a work itself, or even of a whole literature, a thought potentially alien or unknown to the author himself. It is up to the researcher to examine the great quantity of oblique evidence, of intra- and intertextual connections by which, through the writer, the language and the literature themselves think. But this is just what refines metaphysics as manifest in literature, ridding it of the subjectivity and preconception that often characterize it in the deliberate constructs of professional philosophers working with general concepts and categories.

Aleksandr Blok said that for a major writer, brief thoughts hastening from topic to topic are not enough—there should be a "long thought" (*dolgaia mysl'*) that permeates all their works. A major literature should also have its own long thought. The metaphysics of Russian literature is

---

5   Pushkin, *Sobranie sochinenii v 10 tomakh*, 2:208.

precisely its *long thought*, incarnate throughout the whole system of its imagery, inherited from writer to writer, from generation to generation.

The expression "the metaphysics of Russian literature" has a dual meaning: literature as the exponent of a certain metaphysical speculation—and as the object of metaphysical investigation. These two meanings coincide in this book. The metaphysicality of Russian literature itself is what renders this literature a worthy and necessary object of metaphysical analysis.

In 1906 the critic A. S. Volzhsky wrote: "Russian literature is the true Russian philosophy, an original, brilliant philosophy in the colors of the words, shining in a rainbow of thoughts.... At the heart of it, it has nearly always featured tireless work on the most important, undying, and significant problems of the human spirit; in it, the accursed questions have been a nearly constant presence."[6] This description is just as apt after a century that complicated Russian literature's philosophical questing when it attempted—politically, "revolutionarily"—to cut the knots of numerous metaphysical questions, managing only to draw them tighter still. The meaning of suffering, the right to rebel, freedom without equality and equality without freedom... Russian discourse of the twentieth century has borne the dual burden of these accursed questions, weighted by the consciousness of their hopelessness, and by the tragedy of a failed historical experiment whose instigator and first victim was Russia.

The metaphysics of nineteenth-century Russian writers—Pushkin and Lermontov, Gogol and Dostoevsky, Tiutchev and Lev Tolstoy—was studied first and foremost by Russian thinkers of the Silver Age: Rozanov and Merezhkovsky, Shestov and Berdiaev. The period for metaphysically interpreting and summing up twentieth-century Russian literature—a Silver Age of its own—should come now. Andrei Platonov and Mikhail Bulgakov, Boris Pasternak and Osip Mandel'shtam, Marina Tsvetaeva and Nikolai Zabolotsky, Mikhail Prishvin and Daniil Andreev, Vladimir Nabokov and Aleksandr Solzhenitsyn, Andrei Siniavsky and Joseph Brodsky, Andrei Bitov and Aleksandr Kushner, and in our own time Vladimir Sorokin and Viktor Pelevin, Ol'ga Sedakova and Dmitrii Prigov,

---

6 Volzhskii, *Iz mira literaturnykh iskanii*, 300–301.

Vladimir Sharov and Mikhail Shishkin—all of these writers, undoubtedly, have their own obvious or secret metaphysical theme, their own response to the mysteries of the Russian soul and the paradoxes of Russian history.

b. Metanarratives

The metaphysics of Russian literature may be imagined as a certain cohesive and consistent metanarrative (a "super-narration") that permeates the work of all writers and guides them to a certain supreme goal. The concept of the metanarrative was critically introduced by the French thinker Jean-François Lyotard in the book *The Postmodern Condition: A Report on Knowledge* (1979). Metanarrative is not an artistic narration but a holistic and all-encompassing worldview-system that explains all historical facts, all the phenomena of being, arranging them in a neat, linear sequence, like a plot that develops and leads to an appropriate finale—in this case, the embodiment of a super-goal or super-idea. Take this or that super-entity—the Absolute Idea or Reason, the Proletariat or Eurasia; the metanarrative knows just how it behaves, explaining its past and predicting its future. Among the West's reigning metanarratives, Lyotard names Christianity, Enlightenment (rationalism), and Marxism. According to Lyotard, the new age of postmodernity that came to the West in the 1970s undermines faith in any metanarratives and acknowledges the multiplicity of mutually untranslatable and even incompatible discourses and "paralogies." But in Russia, the metanarrative—singular, i.e., the Marxist one—ruled for so long that upon its ousting, the "holy place," as the Russian saying goes, "did not remain empty": several others have laid claim to its throne, competing among themselves. Even as it absorbs every variety of content, the totalistic structure of consciousness remains virtually unchanged.

Insofar as literature has been considered the basis of Russian culture and national identity for two centuries now, any metanarrative strives to rely thereon to demonstrate its explanatory and predictive power. Such a method of plotting Russian literature is quite familiar to us from Soviet-era textbooks that espoused the reigning Marxist metanarrative of historical progress, which naturally leads from social inequality through liberation and revolutionary movements to the supreme goal of building a communist society. Writers of the past took part in this plot as best they could: some hymned freedom, some showed compassion toward the lot of working people, some demanded that poetry show civic virtue, and some directly pointed the "way to the future" with characters who were revolutionaries, workers, and communists. This metaphysics of the "three stages of the liberation movement" has already receded into the past, but it has been easily replaced by other providential schemes that subordinate the whole movement of Russian literature to a certain super-idea.

One of these, as may easily be guessed, turns Russian literature into an applied Gospel reading, a learning-aid for Sunday school lessons. From Zhukovsky through Pushkin to Gogol, and beyond—bypassing the aesthetes, and in spite of the nihilists—to Dostoevsky and Tolstoy, to Chekhov's "The Student" ("Student") and "The Bishop" ("Arkhierei"), Russian literature is a quest for Christ, a quest for God in the human and the human in God. Lying in wait on its path were the devilish temptations and downfalls of revolution and its defrocked prophets: Blok, Gorky, and Maiakovsky. But Russian literature, having stumbled, is nevertheless, through the horror of crime and the pain of repentance, gradually returning to the path of faith: in Bulgakov's *The Master and Margarita*, in Pasternak's *Doctor Zhivago*, in the epic works of Solzhenitsyn devoted to the circles of a historical hell.

The visionary mystic-poet Daniil Andreev proposes another method of constructing a metaphysical discourse on Russian literature in his treatise *The Rose of the World* (*Roza mira*), on the universal theocracy of the future, which all human history has gone to pave the way for. Andreev's "metahistorical" narrative devotes much attention to Russian writers as "harbingers" of the various worlds of Illumination and prophets of the "heavenly Russia." In their fate and works—from Pushkin to Vladimir Solov'ev and Blok—he traces the spiritual peaks and valleys of Russian "metaculture," the struggle between the forces of darkness (the Prince of this world and the demons of the great state powers) and the forces of light, especially personified in female figures, incarnations of the planetary spirit Zventa-Sventana.

In the post-Soviet period, the most dogged claims to the role of super-interpretation have been made by "Eurasian" and "cosmist" discourses, each, of course, proposing its own consistent interpretation of

Conclusion 409

Russian literature. From the Eurasianist standpoint, modern Russian literature, despite having arisen in the eighteenth century under the influence of the West, has always sought independence from it. The central theme of this interpretation is the struggle between Slavophilism and Westernism, with both these parties turning out to differ mainly in the degree of their mistakenness. Slavophilism, that is, also pushed Russia toward Europe, albeit Eastern Europe, even as Russia, the heart of the whole Eurasian continent, encompasses both the Far East and Central Asia. In this discourse, the Eurasian consciousness is epitomized in the patriotic, great-power, imperial line of Russian literature: from Lomonosov, Derzhavin, and Pushkin, through the East-oriented interests and insights of Velimir Khlebnikov and Andrei Platonov, to the mystics, "state-builders" or "men of the state" (*gosudarstvenniki*), and "men of the soil" (*pochvenniki*) of the late twentieth century: Valentin Rasputin, Iurii Mamleev, Aleksandr Prokhanov, and the poet Iurii Kuznetsov. Sometimes associated with these figures are also the mythologically oriented writers of the Soviet East and Central Asia: Chingiz Aitmatov, Anatolii Kim, Timur Pulatov, Timur Zulfikarov, and others.

Finally, the cosmist discourse constructs its metaphysics of Russian literature on the basis of the philosopher Nikolai Fedorov's ideas regarding the "common cause" of resurrecting our ancestors, overcoming death, and rationally organizing and conquering outer space. Cosmism has also been inspired by Konstantin Tsiolkovsky, the mystic-utopian and father of spaceflight, and Vladimir Vernadsky, with his doctrine of the biosphere and noosphere. Like its Marxist counterpart, cosmist discourse is optimistic vis-à-vis historical progress, which it sees as stemming, however, not from the class struggle and the growth of productivity, but the struggle of human thought against inanimate matter. Cosmism seeks out ways to actively, teleologically evolve the universe as governed by technologically equipped reason. As projected onto Russian literature, this means a predominant interest in writers of a natural-philosophical and utopian cast, and an active-evolutionary and noospheric one, such as Fedor Tiutchev, Velimir Khlebnikov, Maksim Gorky, Sergei Esenin, Mikhail Prishvin, Nikolai Zabolotsky, Andrei Platonov, and the "village prose" school (*derevenshchiki*). Naturally, any writer creatively concerned with the thought of death and immortality, including Pushkin, Dostoevsky, and Lev Tolstoy, is also plugged into this resurrectionary plot.

And so, different approaches to Russian literature are possible as premised on whichever metaphysical idea is placed at the foundation of the metanarrative. Each metanarrative finds in Russian literature its heroes and antiheroes, its great writers and "seducers" or "reactionaries," its masterpieces and flops. Each of the approaches just mentioned—to put it provisionally, the Marxist, Christian, mystical-universalist (Andreevian), Eurasian, and evolutionary-cosmist (Fedorovian)—has its own truth, little or big. All these approaches may intersect and supplement one another; for instance, the Andreevian discourse of the "Rose of the World" may be plugged into the Fedorovian discourse of the "Common Cause," while Eurasianist discourse seeks to appropriate the statist aspirations of Soviet Marxism as their next phase. At times, some even seek to pass communism off as the international religion of our time and marry it with a mystical universalism, just as attempts have been made to unite Christianity and socialism.

We will not discuss here the relative merits and shortcomings of these approaches and all their possible combinations. We will rather pose the question: would it be possible to get by without any metanarrative at all, while at the same time keeping up with the metaphysical questionings to which Russian literature bids us?

c. Metaphysics Without a Metanarrative

Is metaphysics possible without a metanarrative? This is precisely the approach that has been proposed in this book. It consists of six sections, each of which encompasses its own knot of metaphysical problems, and correspondingly works out its own system of concepts by which to interpret them. It is of such knots that the metaphysical fabric of Russian literature is woven; but if you untie them all into a single thread, absorb them into a single metanarrative, the rich, multilayered pattern will disappear. In other words, instead of a *linear* approach, I propose a *nodular* one: not to straighten out the Russian metaphysical language according to the yardstick of some super-scheme, but to follow its curves, which are sometimes smooth, sometimes steep and tortuous.

Conclusion 411

Such a nonlinear approach gives rise to numerous unexpected questions; for instance, what do Akaky Akakievich and Prince Myshkin have in common? How is Goncharov's *Oblomov* evoked in Platonov's *Chevengur*? And more broadly, how does the echo of world literature get picked up and grow as Pushkin engages in a call-and-response with Goethe and Mickiewicz, Batiushkov with Hölderlin, Gorky with Freud, Platonov with Heidegger and Nabokov? We are interested not so much in direct influences and borrowings between works as their typological parallels and intersections, their dialogue in the grand spacetime of world culture.

Peculiar to the book is its attention to literature's cognitive "underside," the way—unlike philosophy—it poses eternal questions indirectly or "accidentally." I don't mean the questions asked directly by authors (*What Is to Be Done? Who Is to Blame?*), but those that stem from their styles, from the interaction of various works, from the resonance between distant images—convergences that, to the writers themselves, might seem unexpected, somehow even incongruous with their intent. We are more interested in the metaphysical "unconscious" of Russian literature than the philosophical and religious views (which are more or less known) of its creators.

Thus do I examine the patriotic theme in the famous lyrical digressions in *Dead Souls* as a development of Gogol's demonology ("Viy," "The Portrait"). Gogol raises aloft the grandiose and mysterious image of a proud, great-power Russia, but in this very image we uncover a motif familiar to us from the author's early works—that of witchery and devilry. We trace the continuity between the "little man" Akaky Akakievich and Russian literature's most sublime and beautiful character, the "Prince Christ" Myshkin of Dostoevsky's *The Idiot*. And at the same time, the continuity from Akaky Akakievich to one of this literature's most frightful characters, Chekhov's "man in a case," in whom we find the features of the "people-phobia" subsequently so characteristic of twentieth-century totalitarian figures—socialists and sociophobes rolled into one. We attempt to understand the poetry of Boris Pasternak and Osip Mandel'shtam in the context of Jewish religious traditions they inherited but could hardly have been fully conscious of. And one more example: Russian literature has a tradition of elevating the word to the level of "logos," the divine word, while the writer stands as prophet and teacher of life. However, eschewing its "human," informative function, and attempting to undertake an outright "divine" mission, the word turns into a magical or ideological spell, and ultimately into a figment. I trace this switch from logos to delusion and glossolalia in Gogol, Chekhov, Kharms, and Sorokin, who demonstrate the omnipotence and simultaneous nonentity of the word that has been turned into the inertia of mere speaking.

The purpose of examining all these paradoxes is not to "expose" writers as failing to understand their own texts but to demonstrate the interconnection between the *metaphysical images* and *artistic ideas* at work in the entire space of Russian literature. Instead of presenting this interconnection as a consistent ideological plot, a metanarrative, I focus on metaphysical meanings to the extent that they undermine any ideological interpretation of a work; thwart any attempt to take writers' direct statements on their own creation literally, or their imagery as the clear expression of some idea. Here we are interested in precisely what does not fit into the "intent" of a work—things that dilute or blur its logical and monologic unity, and lend its imagery a different, at times contradictory meaning. We are concerned with the realm of *artistic* metaphysics, as opposed to the doctrinal or speculative metaphysics expressed in systematically philosophical works.

Two words are key for this approach: the *metaphysics* of Russian *literature*. *Metaphysics*, and not the history, or theory, or aesthetics, or psychology of Russian literature. But also, the metaphysics of *literature*, and not of philosophy, or religion, or politics, or social ideology. The artistry of metaphysics depends precisely on the play of images and the richness of their allusive, ambiguous, allegorical, or unsayable meanings, which arise on the margins or the far side of direct statements. This is a sort of "apophatic," negative metaphysics of Russian literature, in the sense in which the concept of apophaticism is presented on the pages of this book—as a means of comprehending the unknowable or describing the inexpressible.[7] The metaphysics of literature is not what is stated outright

---

7 Apophaticism is the tendency in theology to conceive of God not positively, via the imagery of light, goodness, reason, etc., but through the negation of his very conceivability, his incommensurability with any substantive image or definition.

but what is kept silent about, preserved at the very bottom. As Thomas Carlyle put it: "In symbol there is concealment and yet revelation: here therefore, by Silence and by Speech acting together, comes a double significance."[8] Hence the metaphysicality of genuine literature—the sort that does not merely speak but is also silent, or more precisely, is silent through words and speaks through silence, that is, expresses itself with a double force, as a "silentilogue."

Writers in effect never say anything on their own behalf; it is their characters and narrators—stand-ins and masks—that speak. According to Bakhtin, "the creating figure (that is, the primary author) can never be part of any figure he or she has created. ... Nothing can be said on the writer's behalf. ... Thus does the primary author vest himself in silence."[9] A creator is not entirely part of the being he has created—this is why the artistic world (like the universe at large) includes mystery, something "out there" and "beyond." Artistic discourse is the realm of *signified silence*. Unlike the everyday word, to which definite things or actions correspond ("could you bring me a cup?"; "buy some bread"; "I'm going to the movies"), the artistic word lacks direct designata. This incidentally is what distinguishes someone who is simply writing from a *writer*, a master of the written. A writer creates a subtext or transtext, a realm of silence beyond the layer of text. As the writer Andrei Bitov attests: "I have always thought that literature works not with the word but with silence, with muteness. What is the telltale sign of the unexpressed, the inexpressible, if not the absence of words? The true writer never knows how to write."[10] If that is the case, then the commentator writes for, or rather, along with the writer. It is the task of the former to hear the silence in the depths of the word, and to convey its hidden meaning.

This book could thus have also been titled *What Is Russian Literature Silent About?* I don't mean the secrets it is keeping (for example, incidents and scandals in a writer's life) but the mysteries it shares with us such that we might respond to it. That being said, every national literature has its realm of mysteries and reticences. According to José Ortega y Gasset,

---

8 Cited from Brown, *Love's Body*, 190.
9 Bakhtin, *Estetika slovesnogo tvorchestva*, 353.
10 Bitov, "Raznye dni cheloveka," 6.

"every language has a different equation of manifestations and silences. Every people keeps silence on certain things in order to be able to say others. For *everything* would be unsayable. Hence the enormous difficulty of translation: in it one tries to say ... precisely what the language tends to silence."[11] It is difficult, moreover, to translate not just from one language to another but also texts within a single language: an artistic text, for example, into the language of philosophy or theory.

A common feature of all critical interpretations based on metanarratives is precisely the inability to hear the silence of literature. No mystery remains, nothing distinctively artistic or imaginative, capable of inducing wonder or resisting some preestablished scheme of thought. Whereas Aristotle, the father of metaphysics himself, believed that "it is owing to their wonder that men ... philosophize. ... [A] man who is puzzled and wonders thinks himself ignorant."[12] In this sense, the *metanarrative*, which explains everything and wonders at nothing, is opposed to *metaphysics*, which is born precisely of the greatest wonder, of puzzlement before what "everyone knows"; which finds itself snagged on that which habit, common sense, and know-it-all-ism pass by: where does the world come from? what is the purpose of life? what is a human being for?

If it is possible to designate some overall method to this investigation, then it has been an old, Aristotelian one. The metaphysics of Russian literature is *the totality of its wonderings at the world and our wonderings at it.* We are interested in every image or motif to the extent that it amazes us, incites us to form some new hypothesis, to reexamine generally accepted ideas and theories. Russian literature's "long thought" emerges as the contradiction or reticence in every particular work—the surprise, pitfall, tragic misunderstanding, grotesque twist, cutting irony, or slip of the tongue.

Hegel famously pronounced that art is thinking in images and therefore inferior to philosophy, which is thinking in concepts. But this is arguably a matter of difference rather than hierarchy. The relationship between thought and image is more controversial and ambivalent

---

11 Cited from Heisig, "Desacralizing Philosophical Translation in Japan," 51.
12 Aristotle, *Metaphysics*, 4.

than between thought and concept. Images not only convey or express thought but challenge it, defamiliarize it, present the very act of thinking as metaphorically "curved," strange and astonishing. Artistic metaphysics augments our mentality via the sabotage of any metanarrative; it is a pack of explosives planted in our readerly perception, in the (counter) logic of "amazing" imagery. Philosophical metaphysics is at its best when it provides the most convincing answers to perennial questions. Literary metaphysics is at its best when it offers the most challenging questions to perennial answers.

Works Cited

Abramovich, S. *Pushkin v 1833 g. Khronika*. Moscow: Slovo, 1994.

Aizlewood, Robin. "'Besy,' Disorientation, and the Person." In *Personality and Place in Russian Culture: Essays in Memory of Lindsey Hughes*, edited by Simon Dixon, 291–308. London: UCL School of Slavonic and East European Studies, 2010.

Aksakov, Sergei. *Years of Childhood*. Translated by J. D. Duff. New York: Longmans, Green, and Company, 1916.

Alekseev, M. P. "Zametki na poliakh: K 'Stsene iz Fausta' Pushkina." *Vremennik Pushkinskoi komissii* (1976): 91–97.

Andreev, Leonid. *Izbrannoe*. Moscow: Sovremennik, 1982.

Annenkov, P. V. *Materialy dlia biografii Pushkina*. St. Petersburg, 1855.

Annenskii, Innokentii. "Portret." In *Kniga otrazhenii* by Innokentii Annenskii, 13–20. Moscow: Nauka, 1979.

Appignanesi, Lisa, ed. *Novostroika / New Structures: Culture in the Soviet Union Today*. London: Institute of Contemporary Arts, 1989.

Aristotle. *Metaphysics*. Translated by David Ross. Roger Bishop Jones, 2012.

Arutiunova, N. D. "Fenomen molchaniia." In *Iazyk o iazyke*, edited by N. D. Arutiunova, 417–36. Moscow: Iazyki russkoi kul'tury, 2000.

Averintsev, S. S. *Poetika rannevizantiiskoi literatury*. Moscow: Nauka, 1977.

———. *Poety*. Moscow: Iazyki russkoi kul'tury, 1996.

Azadovskii, M. K. *Literatura i fol'klor*. Leningrad: Goslitizdat, 1938.

Bakhtin, Mikhail. *Estetika slovesnogo tvorchestva*. Moscow: Iskusstvo, 1979.

———. *Problems of Dostoevsky's Poetics*. Translated by Caryl Emerson. Minneapolis: University of Minnesota Press, 1984.

———. *Speech Genres and Other Late Essays*. Edited by Caryl Emerson and Michael Holquist. Translated by Vern W. McGee. Austin: University of Texas Press, 1986.

Barnes, Christopher. *Boris Pasternak: A Literary Biography*. Vol. 1, *1890–1928*, Cambridge: Cambridge University Press, 1989.

Barrow, John. *The Book of Nothing: Vacuums, Voids, and the Latest Ideas about the Origins of the Universe*. New York: Pantheon Books, 2000.

Barsukov, N. *Zhizn' i trudy M. P. Pogodina*. St. Petersburg, 1890.
Barthes, Roland. *The Pleasure of the Text*. Translated by Richard Miller. New York: Macmillan, 1975.
Belinskii, V. G. *Polnoe sobranie sochinenii v 13 t*. Moscow: Izd-vo Akademii nauk SSSR, 1953-59.
Berdiaev, N. "Religiia voskresheniia." In *Sobranie sochinenii* by N. Berdiaev, 3:242-301. Paris: YMCA Press, 1989.
_____. *Russkaia ideia: Osnovnye problemy russkoi mysli XIX veka i nachala XX*. Paris: YMCA Press, 1971.
Bethea, David M. *Joseph Brodsky and the Creation of Exile*. Princeton: Princeton University Press, 1994.
Bibikhin, V. V. *Iazyk filosofii*. Moscow: Progress, 1993.
Bitov, A. "Raznye dni cheloveka." *Literaturnaia gazeta*, 22 July 1987.
Blagoi, D. "Mitskevich i Pushkin." In *Ot Kantemira do nashikh dnei* by D. Blagoi, 1:289-318. Moscow: Khudozhestvennaia literatura, 1972.
Blok, A. *Dnevnik A. Bloka: 1911-1913*. Leningrad: Izdatel'stvo pisatelei v Leningrade, 1928.
_____. *Sobranie sochinenii v 6 t*. Leningrad: Khudozhestvennaia literatura, 1980.
Bondi, S. M. *Chernoviki Pushkina*. Moscow: Prosveshchenie, 1971.
Borges, Jorge Luis. *Labyrinths*. Edited by Donald A. Yates and James E. Irby. New York: New Directions, 1962.
Brat'ia Grimm. *Skazki*. Kiev: Molod', 1988.
Brodskii, Iosif. *Sochineniia*. St. Petersburg: Pushkinskii fond, 1995.
Brodsky, Joseph. *On Grief and Reason*. New York: Farrar, Straus, and Giroux, 1995.
Brovman, G. *Trud. Geroi. Literatura: Ocherki i razmyshleniia o russkoi sovetskoi khudozhestvennoi proze*. Moscow. Khudozhestvennaia literatura, 1974.
Brown, Norman O. *Love's Body*. New York: Vintage Books, 1966.
Buber, Martin. *Tales of the Hasidim: The Later Masters*. New York: Schocken Books, 1975.
Bulgakov, S. N. *Filosofiia imeni*. Paris, 1953.
_____. "Na piru bogov. Pro i contra. Sovremennye dialogi." In *Sochineniia* by S. N. Bulgakov, 2:564-626. Moscow: Nauka, 1993.
_____. *Unfading Light: Contemplations and Speculations*. Translated by Thomas Allan Smith. Grand Rapids, MI: W. B. Eerdmans Pub. Co., 2012.

Bunin, Ivan. *The Life of Arseniev*. Translated by Gleb Struve, Hamish Miles, Heidi Hillis, Susan McKean, and Sven A. Wolf. Edited by Andrew Baruch Wachtel. Evanston, IL: Northwestern University Press, 1994.

———. *Zhizn' Arsen'eva*. Moscow: Khudozhestvennaia literatura, 1966.

Burganov, A. "Derev'ia v skolz'iashchem potoke sveta." In *Arkhitektura moskovskogo metro*. Moscow, 1988. Available electronically: http://www.metro.ru/library/architecture/94/.

Cavanagh, Clare. *Osip Mandelstam and the Modernist Creation of Tradition*. Princeton, NJ: Princeton University Press, 1995.

Chaadaev, P. Ia. *Sochineniia*. Moscow: Pravda, 1989.

Chekhov, Anton. *Plays*. Translated by Elisaveta Fen. Hertfordshire: Wordsworth, 2007.

———. *Polnoe sobranie sochinenii i pisem v 30-i tomakh*. Moscow: Nauka, 1977.

———. *Selected Stories*. Translated by Richard Pevear and Larissa Volokhonsky. New York: Random House, 2009.

Chukovskii, Kornei. *Sobranie sochinenii v 6-i tomakh*. Moscow: Khudozhestvennaia literatura, 1969.

Dante. *The Divine Comedy: Hell, Purgatory, Heaven*. Translated by Peter Dale. London: Anvil Press Poetry, 1996.

Diurishin, D. *Teoriia sravnitel'nogo izucheniia literatury*. Moscow: Progress, 1979.

Dostoevskii, F. M. *Polnoe sobranie sochinenii v 30-i tomakh*. Leningrad: Nauka, 1972.

Dostoevsky, Fyodor. *The Adolescent*. Translated by Richard Pevear and Larissa Volokhonsky. New York: Knopf Doubleday Publishing Group, 2007.

———. *The Brothers Karamazov*. Translated by Richard Pevear and Larissa Volokhonsky. New York: Vintage Books, 1992.

———. *The Idiot*. Translated by Richard Pevear and Larissa Volokhonsky: New York: Vintage Classics, 2003.

———. *Poor Folk and Other Stories*. Translated by David McDuff. London: Penguin, 1988.

———. *White Nights and Other Stories*. Translated by Constance Garnett. New York: The MacMillan Company, 1918.

———. *A Writer's Diary*. Translated by Kenneth Lantz. Edited by Gary Saul Morson. Evanston: Northwestern University Press, 2009.

Dubnow, Simon M. *History of the Jews in Russia and Poland from the Earliest Times until the Present Day*. Translated by I. Friedlaender. Philadelphia: The Jewish Publication Society of America, 1916.

Eckermann, Johann Peter. *Conversations of Goethe with Eckermann and Soret*. Translated by John Oxenford. London: George Bell and Sons, 1874.

Eikhenbaum, Boris. "How Gogol's 'Overcoat' Is Made." In *Gogol's "Overcoat": An Anthology of Critical Essays*, edited by Elizabeth Welt Trahan, 21–37. Ann Arbor, MI: Ardis, 1982.

Engels, Friedrich. *Ludwig Feuerbach and the Outcome of German Classical Philosophy*. New York: International Publishers, 1941.

Epstein, Mikhail. *After the Future: The Paradoxes of Postmodernism and Contemporary Russian Culture*. Translated by Anesa Miller-Pogacar. Amherst: University of Massachusetts Press, 1995.

———. "Blud truda." In *Vse esse* by Mikhail Epstein, 1:122–42. Ekaterinburg: U-Faktoriia, 2005.

———. "Daniil Andreev and the Mysticism of Femininity." In *The Occult in Russian and Soviet Culture*, edited by Bernice Glatzer Rosenthal, 325–55. Ithaca, NY: Cornell University Press, 1997.

———. "Podzemnye khramy i ugol'nyi vek." In *Velikaia Sov': Sovetskaia mifologiia* by Mikhail Epstein, 55–63. Samara: Bakhrakh-M, 2006.

———. *Postmodern v russkoi literature*. Moscow: Vysshaia shkola, 2005.

———. *Religiia posle ateizma: Novye vozmozhnosti teologii*. Moscow: AST-Press, 2013.

———. *Russian Spirituality and the Secularization of Culture*. New York: Franc-Tireur USA, 2011.

Ermakov, I. D. *Ocherki po analizu tvorchesta N. V. Gogolia*. Moscow-St. Petersburg: Gosizdat, 1924.

Fedorov, N. F. *Sobranie sochinenii v 4 t*. Moscow: Traditsiia, 1997.

———. *Sochineniia*. Moscow: Mysl', 1982.

Fedotov, G. P. *Sud'ba i grekhi Rossii: Izbrannye stat'i po filosofii russkoi istorii i kul'tury*. St. Petersburg: Sofiia, 1991.

Fleishman, Lazar. *Boris Pasternak: The Poet and His Politics*. Cambridge, MA: Harvard University Press, 1990.

Florenskii, P. *Imena*. Khar'kov: Folio; Moscow: AST, 2000.

———. "Magichnost' slova." In *Sochineniia* by P. A. Florenskii, 2:252–73. Moscow: Pravda, 1990.

Florovskii, Prot. G. *Puti russkogo bogosloviia*. Paris: YMCA Press, 1988.

Foucault, Michel. *Madness and Civilization: A History of Insanity in the Age of Reason*. Translated by Richard Howard. New York: Pantheon, 1965.

Frank, S. K. *The Unknowable: An Ontological Introduction to the Philosophy of Religion*. Translated by Boris Jakim. Athens: Ohio University Press, 1983.

Freud, Sigmund. *Totem and Taboo*. Translated by Abraham A. Brill. New York: Cosimo Classics, 2009.

Gak, V. G. *Sopostavitel'naia leksikologiia*. Moscow: Mezhdunar. otnosheniia, 1977.

Galkovskii, D. *Beskonechnyi tupik*. Moscow: Samizdat, 1997.

Gastev, A. K. *Poeziia rabochego udara* [1918]. Moscow: Khudozhestvennaia literatura, 1971.

Geiman, B. "Peterburg v 'Fauste' Gete (k tvorcheskoi istorii 2-i chasti 'Fausta')." *Doklady i soobshcheniia Filologicheskogo instituta LGU*, no. 2 (1950): 64–96.

Goethe, Johann Wolfgang von. *Poetry and Truth: From My Own Life*. Translated by John Oxenford. Cambridge: Cambridge University Press, 2013.

———. *Faust, Part Two*. Translated with an introduction and notes by David Luke. Oxford: Oxford University Press, 2008.

———. *Faust: Der Tragödie erster und zweiter Teil*. Berlin: Herausgegeben von Karl-Maria Guth, 2015.

Gogol, Nikolai. *The Collected Tales*. Translated by Richard Pevear and Larissa Volokhonsky. New York: Penguin Random House, 2008.

———. *Dead Souls*. Translated by Richard Pevear and Larissa Volokhonsky. New York: Knopf, 1996.

———. *Selected Passages from Correspondence with Friends*. Translated by Jesse Zeldin. Vanderbilt, TN: Vanderbilt University Press, 1969.

Gogol', Nikolai. *Polnoe sobranie sochinenii v 14 tomakh*. Moscow: Izdatel'stvo Akademii nauk SSSR, 1951.

———. *Sobranie sochinenii v 7 t*. Moscow: Khudozhestvennaia literatura, 1984.

———. *Vybrannie mesta iz perepiski s druz'iami*. Moscow: Khudozh. lit., 1986.

Goncharov, Ivan. *Oblomov*. Translated by Marian Schwartz. New York: Seven Stories Press, 2010.

Gor'kii, M. "O M. M. Prishvine." *Krasnaia nov'*, no. 12 (1926): 230–33.

———. *Sobranie sochinenii v vos'mi tomakh*. Moscow: Sovetskaia Rossiia, 1990.

Works Cited   421

Gorky, Maxim. *Mother*. Translated by Isidor Shneider. New York: The Citadel Press, 1947.

Grabar'-Passek, M. E., and M. L. Gasparov, eds. *Pamiatniki srednevekovoi latinskoi literatury IV–IX vekov*. Moscow: Nauka, 1970.

Griboedov, A. S. *Gore ot uma*. Kharkov: Folio, 2006.

Grimm, Jacob, and Wilhelm Grimm. *The Complete Fairy Tales of the Brothers Grimm*. Translated by Jack Zipes. New York: Bantam Books, 2003.

Hegel, Georg Wilhelm Friedrich. *Phenomenology of Spirit*. Translated by A. V. Miller. Delhi: Motilal Banarsidass Publ., 1998.

Heidegger, Martin. *Being and Time*. Translated by Joan Stambaugh. Albany: State University of New York Press, 2010.

———. *Elucidations of Hölderlin's Poetry*. Translated with an introduction by Keith Hoeller. Amherst, NY: Humanity Books, 2000.

———. "The Origin of the Work of Art." In *Off the Beaten Track* by Martin Heidegger, 1–56. Translated by Julian Young and Kenneth Haynes. Cambridge: Cambridge University Press, 2002.

———. "What Is Metaphysics?" Translated by David Farrell Krell. In *Pathmarks* by Martin Heidegger, 82–96. Edited by William McNeill. Cambridge: Cambridge University Press, 1998.

Heisig, James W. "Desacralizing Philosophical Translation in Japan." *Nanzan Bulletin* 27 (2003): 46–62.

Hölderlin, Friedrich. *Sämtliche Werke*. Edited by Friedrich Sattler. Frankfurt am Main: Stroemfeld/Roter Stern, 1988.

Iakobson, R. *Raboty po poetike*. Moscow: Progress, 1987.

———. "Vzgliad na 'Vid' Gel'derlina." Translated by O. A. Sedakova. In *Raboty po poetike*, 364–86. Moscow: Progress, 1987.

Idel, Moshe. *Absorbing Perfections: Kabbalah and Interpretation*. New Haven, CT: Yale University Press, 2008.

Ilarion. *Na gorakh Kavkaza: Beseda dvukh startsev podvizhnikov o vnutrennem edinenii s Gospodom nashikh serdets cherez molitvu Iisus Khristovu*. Batallashinsk, 1907.

Jakobson, Roman. *Puškin and His Sculptural Myth*. Translated by John Burbank. The Hague: Mouton, 1975.

Joffe, J. A. trans., "Svyatogór," from the Elder Heroes. Revised by editor. In *Stories from the Classic Literature of Many Nations*, edited by Bertha Palmer, 185. London: Macmillan, 1898.

Kabakov, Il'ia. *Das Leben der Fliegen/The Life of Flies/Zhizn' mukh.* Cologne: Kölnischer Kunstverein, 1992.

———. *Dvorets proektov/The Palace of Projects.* London: Artangel, 1998.

———. *Sumasshedshii dom, ili Institut kreativnykh issledovanii.* Malmos: Rooseum, 1991.

Kant, Immanuel. *Prolegomena to Any Future Metaphysics.* Translated by Paul Carus. London: The Open Court Publishing Company, 1904.

Karlinsky, Simon. *The Sexual Labyrinth of Nikolai Gogol'.* Cambridge, MA: Harvard University Press, 1976.

Kazakov, Iurii. *Izbrannoe.* Moscow: Khudozhestvennia literatura, 1985.

———. *Vo sne ty gor'ko plakal: Rasskazy.* Moscow: Sovremennik, 2000.

Kharms, Daniil. *O iavleniiakh i sushchestvovaniiakh.* St. Petersburg: Azbuka-Klassika, 2000.

Kliuchevskii, V. O. *Sochineniia v 9 t.* Moscow: Mysl', 1987.

Kuzminskaia, T. A. *Moia zhizn' doma i v Iasnoi Poliane.* Tula, 1958.

Lenin, V. I. *Sochineniia.* Moscow: GIPL, 1952.

Lermontov, Mikhail. *Geroi nashego vremeni.* St. Petersburg: Azbuka-klassika, 2008.

———. *Stikhotvoreniia.* Moscow: Direkt-Media, 2014.

Levi, Peter. *Boris Pasternak.* London, Sydney: Hutchinson, 1990.

Lomonosov, Mikhail. "Predislovie o pol'ze knig tserkovnykh v rossiiskom iazyke." *Russkie pisateli o iazyke: Khrestomatiia,* edited by A. M. Sokusov. Leningrad, Gos. uch.-ped. izd., 1954.

Losev, A. F. *Filosofiia. Mifologiia. Kul'tura.* Moscow: Politizdat, 1991.

———. "Osnovnye osobennosti russkoi filosofii." In *Filosofiia. Mifologiia. Kul'tura* by A. F. Losev, 509–13. Moscow: Politizdat, 1991.

Losskii, N. O. *Istoriia russkoi filosofii.* Moscow: Vysshaia shkola, 1991.

Lotman, Iu. M. *Struktura khudozhestvennogo teksta.* Moscow: Iskusstvo, 1970.

Lotman, Iu. M., and B. A. Uspenskii. "Rol' dual'nykh modelei v dinamike russ-koi kul'tury (do kontsa XVIII veka)." In *Izbrannye trudy* by B. A. Uspenskii, 219–53. Moscow: Gnozis, 1994.

Maguire, Robert A. "Gogol and the Legacy of Pseudo-Dionysius." In *Russianness: Studies on a Nation's Identity (In Honor of Rufus Mathewson, 1918–1978),* edited by Robert L. Belknap, 44–55. Ann Arbor, MI: Ardis, 1990.

Maiakovskii, V. V. *Stikhotvoreniia: Kniga vtoraia.* Moscow: Direkt-media, 2012.

Maikov, L. N. *Batiushkov, ego zhizn' i sochineniia*. Moscow: Agraf, 2001.
Malmstad, John E. "Boris Pasternak: The Painter's Eye." *The Russian Review* 51, no. 3 (1992): 301–18.
Mandelshtam, Osip. *Selected Poems*. Translated by James Greene. London: Penguin Books, 1991.
Mandelstam, Osip. *The Complete Poetry of Osip Emilevich Mandelstam*. Translated by Burton Raffel and Alla Burago. Albany: State University of New York Press, 1973.
———. *The Moscow Notebooks*. Translated by Richard McKane and Elizabeth McKane. Newcastle upon Tyne, U.K.: Bloodaxe Books, 1991.
———. "On the Nature of the Word." In *The Complete Critical Prose and Letters*, 117–32. Edited by Jane Gary Harris, translated by Jane Gary Harris and Constance Link. Ann Arbor, MI: Ardis, 1979.
———. "Talking about Dante." Translated by Clarence Brown and Robert Hughes. *Delos* 6 (1971): 65–106.
———. *Poems from Mandelstam*. Translated by R. H. Morrison. London: Associated University Presses, 1990.
———. *The Poems of Osip Mandelstam*. Translated by Ilya Bernstein. New York: New Directions, 2014.
———. *The Prose of Osip Mandelstam: The Noise of Time. Theodosia. The Egyptian Stamp*. Translated, with a critical essay, by Clarence Brown. Princeton, NJ: Princeton University Press, 1965.
———. *The Selected Poems of Osip Mandelstam*. Translated by Clarence Brown and W. S. Merwin. New York: New York Review Books, 1973.
Mandel'shtam, Osip. *Kamen'*. Moscow: Olma-Press, 2003.
———. *Sobranie sochinenii v 2 t*. Moscow: Khudozhestvennaia literatura, 1990.
———. *Sobranie sochinenii v trekh tomakh*. Washington, DC: Inter-language Literary Associates, 1967.
———. *Sobranie sochinenii v 4 t*. Moscow: Art-Biznes-Tsentr, 1994.
Mann, Iu. V. *Poetika Gogolia*. Moscow: Khudozh. lit., 1988.
———. "Put' k otkrytiiu kharaktera." In *Dostoevskii—Khudozhnik i myslitel'*, edited by K. N. Lomunov, 284–311. Moscow: Khudozh. lit., 1972.
Markov, M. A. *O prirode materii*. Moscow: Nauka, 1976.
Marx, K., F. Engels, and V. I. Lenin. *O religii*. Moscow: Politizdat, 1983.
Mechnikov, I. I. *Etiudy optimizma*. Moscow: Nauka, 1987.

Merezhkovskii, Dmitrii. *Izbrannoe*. Kishinev: Literatura Artistike, 1989.

———. *V tikhom omute: Stat'i i issledovaniia raznykh let*. Moscow: Sov. pisatel', 1991.

Michurin, I. V. *Itogi shestidesiatiletnikh rabot po vyvedeniiu novykh sortov plodovykh rastenii*. Moscow: Sel'khozgiz, 1934.

Mickiewicz, Adam. *Poems by Adam Mickiewicz*. Translated by George Rapall Noyes. New York: Polish Institute of Arts and Sciences in America, 1944.

———. *Utwory dramatyczne*. Warsaw: Czytelnik, 1983.

Nabokov, Vladimir. *The Defense*. Translated by Michael Scammell in collaboration with the author. New York: Vintage Books, 1990.

———. *The Gift*. Translated by Michael Scammell. New York: Penguin Books, 1963.

———. *Invitation to a Beheading*. Translated by Dmitri Nabokov with Vladimir Nabokov. New York: Vintage Books, 1989.

———. *Pale Fire*. New York: G. Putnam's Sons, 1962.

———. *Sobranie sochinenii v chetyrekh tomakh*. Moscow: Pravda, 1990.

———. *The Stories of Vladimir Nabokov*. New York: Knopf Doubleday Publishing Group, 2011.

Nekrasov, N. A. *Polnoe sobranie stikhotvorenii*. Moscow-Leningrad: Gosudarstvennoe izdatel'stvo, 1929.

Nietzsche, Friedrich. *Daybreak: Thoughts on the Prejudices of Morality*. Translated by R. J. Hollingdale. Cambridge: Cambridge University Press, 1982.

Ostrovsky, Nikolai. *How the Steel Was Tempered*. Translated by R. Prokofieva. Moscow: Foreign Languages Publishing House, 1952.

Pascal, Blaise. *Pensées*. Translated by A. J. Krailsheimer. London: Penguin, 1995.

———. *Pensées: Notes on Religion and Other Subjects*. Translated by John Warrington. London: Dent and Sons, 1973.

Pasternak, Boris. *Doctor Zhivago*. Translated by Richard Pevear and Larissa Volokhonsky. New York: Pantheon Books, 2010.

———. *My Sister Life and the Zhivago Poems*. Translated by James E. Falen. Evanston, IL: Northwestern University Press, 2012.

———. *Sbornik stikhov*. Moscow: Ogiz, 1943.

———. *Sobranie sochinenii v 5 t*. Moscow: Khudozhestvennaia literatura, 1989.

———. *Stikhi 1936-1959: Stat'i i vystupleniia*. Ann Arbor. University of Michigan Press, 1961.

———. *Zapisi raznykh let*. Moscow: Sovetskii khudozhnik, 1975.

Pavlov, I. P. "Ob ume voobshche, o russkom ume v chastnosti." *Vestnik praktich-eskoi psikhologii obrazovaniia*, no. 3 (2009): 15–19.

Perry, Whitall N., ed. *A Treasury of Traditional Wisdom*. Cambridge: Quinta Essentia, 1971.

Plato. *The Laws*. Translated by R. G. Bury. Cambridge, MA: Harvard University Press, 1926.

———. *The Works of Plato*. Edited and translated by Floyer Sydenham and Thomas Taylor. 5 vols. London: Thomas Taylor, 1804.

Platonov, Andrei. *Chevengur*. Translated by Anthony Olcott. Ann Arbor, MI: Ardis, 1978.

———. *The Fierce and Beautiful World: Stories*. Translated by Joseph Barnes. New York: New York Review Books, 2000.

———. *The Foundation Pit*. Translated by Robert and Elisabeth Chandler and Olga Meerson. New York: New York Review Books, 2009.

———. *Izbrannye proizvedeniia: Rasskazy, 1934–1950*. Moscow: Khudozh. lit., 1978.

———. *The Portable Platonov*. Translated by Robert and Elisabeth Chandler et al. Birmingham: Glas, 1999.

———. *Sobranie sochinenii v 5-i tomakh*. Moscow: Informpechat', 1998.

———. *Soul and Other Stories*. Translated by Robert and Elisabeth Chandler with Katia Grigoruk, Angela Livingstone, Olga Meerson, and Eric Naiman. New York: New York Review Books, 2009.

Polsky, Howard W. and Yaella Wozner. *Everyday Miracles: The Healing Wisdom of Hasidic Stories*. London: Jason Aronson, Inc., 1989.

Prigov, Dmitrii. *Moskva: virshi na kazhdyi den'*. Moscow: Novoe literatur-noe obozrenie, 2017. Available electronically: https://books.google.com/books?id=ym52DgAAQBAJ&pg=PT268&lpg=PT268&dq.

———. *Napisannoe s 1975 po 1989*. Moscow: Novoe literaturnoe obozrenie, 1997. Available electronically: http://lib.ru/ANEKDOTY/PRIGOW/prigov.txt

Proust, Marcel. *In Search of Lost Time*. Vol. 1: *Swann's Way*. Translated by C. K. Scott Moncrieff and Terence Kilmartin. New York: Modern Library, 2003.

Pushkin, Alexander. *The Bronze Horseman: Selected Poems of Alexander Pushkin*. Translated and introduced by D. M. Thomas. New York: The Viking Press, 1982.

———. *Pushkin Threefold: Narrative, Lyric, Polemic, and Ribald Verse. The Originals with Linear and Metric Translations*. Translated and edited by Walter Arndt. New York: E. P. Dutton, 1972.

Pushkin, A. S. *Mednyi vsadnik*. In *Sobranie sochinenii v 10 tomakh* by A. S. Pushkin, 3:285–98. Moscow: Gos. izdatel'stvo khudozhestvennoi literatury, 1960. Available electronically: http://rvb.ru/pushkin/01text/02poems/01poems/0795.htm

———. *Skazka o rybake i rybke*. In *Sobranie sochinenii v 10 tomakh* by A. S. Pushkin, 3:338–43. Moscow: Gos. izdatel'stvo khudozhestvennoi literatury, 1960. Available electronically: http://rvb.ru/pushkin/01text/03fables/01fables/0799.htm

———. *Sobranie sochinenii v 10 tomakh*. Moscow: Gos. izdatel'stvo khudozhestvennoi literatury, 1960.

Radtsig, S. I. *Istoriia drevnegrecheskoi literatury*, 2-e izd. Moscow: MGU, 1959.

Rottenberg, Dorian. *Vladimir Mayakovsky: Innovator*. Moscow: Progress Publishers, 1976.

Rozanov, V. V. *Religiia. Filosofiia. Kul'tura*. Moscow: Respublika, 1992.

Sartre, Jean-Paul. *Words*. Translated from the French by Irene Clephane. London: Hamilton, 1964.

Selivanova, N. "Interv'iu s Viacheslavom P'etsukhom." *Izvestiia*, 15 November 1997.

Semenova, S. G. "N. F. Fedorov i ego filosofskoe nasledie: Predislovie." In *Sochineniia* by N. F. Fedorov, 5–52. Moscow: Mysl', 1982.

———. *Nikolai Fedorov: Tvorchestvo zhizni*. Moscow: Sov. pisatel', 1990.

———. *Preodolenie tragedii: "Vechnye voprosy" literatury*. Moscow: Sov. pisatel', 1989.

Shcherbatskoi, F. I. *Izbrannye trudy po buddizmu*. Moscow: Nauka, 1988.

———. *See also* Stcherbatsky, T.

Shestov, Lev. "Chto takoe russkii bol'shevizm?" *Strannik: Literatura, iskusstvo, politika*, no. 1 (1991): 47–59.

Shklovskii, Viktor. *Voskreshenie slova*. St. Petersburg, 1914.

Shklovsky, Victor. "Art as Technique." In *Russian Formalist Criticism*, edited and translated by Lee T. Lemon and Marion J. Reis, 3–24. Lincoln: University of Nebraska Press, 1965.

Sholem, Gershom. *Kabbalah*. New York: Schocken Books, 1974.

———. *Major Trends in Jewish Mysticism*. New York: Schocken Books, 1995.

Shrayer, Maxim D. *An Anthology of Jewish-Russian Literature: Two Centuries of Dual Identity in Prose and Poetry*. London: Routledge, 2007.

Snezhnevskii, A. V. *Spravochnik po psikhiatrii*. Moscow: Meditsina, 1985.

Soloshchenko, L. F. and Iu. S. Prokoshin, eds. *Golubinaia kniga: Russkie narodnye dukhovnye stikhi XI–XIX vv.* Moscow: Moskovskii rabochii, 1991.

Sorokin, Iu. S. *Razvitie slovarnogo sostava russkovo literaturnogo iazyka 50–90 godov 19-go veka.* Moscow: Nauka, 1965.

Sorokin, V. *Goluboe salo.* Moscow: Ad Marginem, 1999.

———. *Pervyi subbotnik.* Moscow: Ad Marginem, 2001.

Sontag, Susan. *A Susan Sontag Reader.* New York: Farrar, Straus, Giroux, 1982.

Sreznevskii, V. *Sborniki pisem I. T. Pososhkova k mitropolitu Stefanu Iavorskomu.* St. Petersburg, 1900.

Stalin, I. V. *Voprosy leninizma.* Moscow: Partiinoe izd-vo, 1934.

Stcherbatsky, T. *The Central Conception of Buddhism and the Meaning of the Word "Dharma."* Calcutta: S. Gupta, 1961.

Surkov, E. A. "Tip geroia i zhanrovoe svoeobrazie povesti N. V. Gogolia 'Shinel'.'" In *Tipologicheskii analiz literaturnogo proizvedeniia*, edited by N. D. Tamarchenko, 67–74. Kemerovo: Kemerovskii gos. universitet, 1982.

Swift, Jonathan. *The Basic Writings of Jonathan Swift.* Edited by Claude Rawson. New York: The Modern Library, 2002.

Terts, Abram. *Sobranie sochinenii v 2 t.* Moscow: Start, 1992.

Tolstoi, I. L. *Moi vospominaniia.* Moscow: Khudozhestvennaia literatura, 1969.

Tolstoi, L. N. *Polnoe sobranie sochinenii v 90 tomakh.* Moscow-Leningrad: Goslitizdat, 1925–58.

Tolstoy, Leo. *Anna Karenina.* Translated by Richard Pevear and Larissa Volokhonsky. New York: Penguin, 2004.

———. *Childhood, Boyhood, and Youth.* Translated by Michael Scammell. New York: Random House, 2002.

———. *The Death of Ivan Ilyich and Other Stories.* Translated by Richard Pevear and Larissa Volokhonsky. New York: Alfred A. Knopf, 2009.

———. *The Devil and Other Stories.* Translated by Louise and Aylmer Maude. Revised and edited by Richard F. Gustafson. Oxford: Oxford University Press, 2009.

———. *Last Steps: The Late Writings of Leo Tolstoy.* Translated by R. F. Christian et al. London: Penguin UK, 2009.

———. *Resurrection.* Translated by Louise Maude. Oxford: Oxford University Press, 1999.

———. *War and Peace*. Translated by Richard Pevear and Larissa Volokhonsky. New York: Vintage Classics, 2008.
Toporov, V. N. *Issledovaniia po etimologii i semantike*. Moscow: Iaziky slavianskoi kul'tury, 2004.
Triolet, Elsa. *Mayakovsky, Russian Poet*. Translated by Susan de Muth. New York: Hearing Eye, 2002.
Tryon, E. P. "Is the Universe a Vacuum Fluctuation?" In *Modern Cosmology and Philosophy*, edited by John Leslie, 222–25. Amherst, NY: Prometheus Books, 1998.
Tsvetaeva, Marina. "Istoriia odnogo posviashcheniia." In *Sobranie sochinenii v trekh tomakh* by Osip Mandel'shtam, 3:306–344, Washington, DC: Inter-Language Literary Associates.
———. *Proza*. New York: Chekhov, 1953.
Turgenev, I. S. *Polnoe sobranie sochinenii i pisem v 30 t*. Moscow: Nauka, 1982.
Twain, Mark. *The Adventures of Huckleberry Finn*. Berkeley: University of California Press, 1985.
———. *The Adventures of Tom Sawyer: The Original Text Edition*. Edited by Allen Gribben. Montgomery, AL: NewSouth Books, 2012.
Tynianov, Iu. N. *Arkhaisty i novatory*. Berlin: Priboi, 1929.
———. *Poetika. Istoriia literatury. Kino*. Moscow: Nauka, 1971.
———. *Problema stikhotvornogo iazyka* [1934]. Moscow, Sovetskii pisatel', 1965.
Uspenskii, B. A. "Mifologicheskii aspekt russkoi ekspressivnoi frazeologii." In *Izbrannye trudy* by B. A. Uspenskii, 2:53–128. Moscow: Gnozis, 1994.
Volzhskii, A. S. *Iz mira literaturnykh iskanii*. St. Petersburg: Izdanie D. E. Zhukovskago, 1906.
Vygodskii, M. Ia. *Spravochnik po elementarnoi matematike*. Moscow: Nauka, 1966.
Weiner, Adam. *By Authors Possessed: The Demonic Novel in Russia*. Evanston, IL: Northwestern University Press, 1998.
Weintraub, Wiktor. *The Poetry of Adam Mickiewicz*. The Hague: Mouton, 1954.
Weiskopf, Mikhail. "The Bird Troika and the Chariot of the Soul: Plato and Gogol." In *Essays on Gogol: Logos and the Russian Word*, edited by Susanne Fusso and Priscilla Meyer, 126–42. Evanston, IL: Northwestern University Press, 1992.
Wellek, René. *Concepts of Criticism*. New Haven, CT: Yale University Press, 1963.

Wilde, Oscar. *The Picture of Dorian Gray*. London: Bibliolis, 2010.
Wittgenstein, Ludwig. *Tractatus Logico-Philosophicus*. Translated by C. K. Ogden. New York: Harcourt, Brace, and Co., 1922.
Yevtushenko, Yevgeny. *The City of Yes and the City of No, and Other Poems*. Translated by Tina Tupikina-Glaessner, Igor Mezhakoff-Korjakin, and Geoffrey Dutton. Melbourne: Sun Books, 1966.
Zhirmunskii, V. M. *Sravnitel'noe literaturovedenie: Vostok i Zapad*. Leningrad: Nauka, 1979.

Index of Subjects

A
aestheticism, 140, 246, 396
afterlife, 111, 225-27
air, 5, 62-63, 67-69, 73-74, 132, 159, 187-88, 190, 237, 248, 275, 362, 367, 404
Antichrist, xiv-xv, 18, 20, 22, 24, 137
atheism, xvi, 181-86
autocrat 44-46

B
banality, 83, 291, 364, 388-390
being; beingness; beingfulness, xiii, 3, 13-14, 18, 22, 26-27, 49-50, 83, 145, 149, 159, 215-27, 231-33, 276-80, 287, 294, 389
bipolarity (manic-depressive disorder), 251, 261-67
blacksmith, 68, 190
bogatyrstvo (Il'ia Muromets, Sviatogor), 262
boredom, 12-13, 205, 241, 244, 248

C
Caucasus (Armenia, Georgia), 369
childhood, 125-57, 160, 162, 256, 332
chiming, 61-62, 64-66
Christianity, xv-xvi, 112, 172, 181, 348-349, 357, 359, 395, 407, 410
chronotope, 63, 66-67, 69, 72-73
citation; citational mode, 364, 386
comic, the, and the tragic, 43, 46-49, 97, 100, 174, 398
comparativistics, 3-4
conceptualism, 103n4, 293, 375, 390, 396-398
consciousness, 9, 11, 48, 50-51, 53-54, 70, 74, 87, 92, 106, 128, 130-31, 135, 138, 140, 144, 150, 156-57, 170, 180, 187, 205, 209, 224, 229, 232, 249, 263, 273, 277, 284, 310, 313, 315, 363, 375-76, 379-88, 391, 406-407, 409
cosmism, 101, 330n30, 409
cycles, the cyclical, 127, 391-401

D
death; deathening, xiv-xv, 16, 22-24, 26, 57, 78, 83n38, 101, 107-9, 111, 118, 144, 152, 159-69, 172-73, 177, 210, 213, 225-26, 233-238, 243-46, 250, 254, 256, 259-60, 285, 293, 310, 316, 394, 398, 403-404, 409-10
dehumanization, 136
demon, the demonic, xvii, 14-18, 20-22, 56, 58-59, 61-64, 66-67, 69, 71-72, 74, 77-78, 81-83, 102, 109-10, 118, 135, 151, 191, 396
demonic irony, 15-18
demonology, 56-70, 411
devil, xv-xvi, 13, 17, 21, 25, 62-63, 65-69, 77, 81, 95-96, 110, 110n15, 112, 118, 137, 190, 192, 408, 411
dialectic, xiii, 97, 129-30, 146, 191, 195, 336, 393
disease, 91, 143, 156, 166, 266, 388
dream, dreamer, 5, 26, 39, 42, 42n11, 44, 48, 51, 66-67, 79, 110, 131-34, 143, 150, 157, 246, 248-51, 253, 255-61, 263-264, 303, 315, 319, 321, 330, 334-335, 357, 369, 389, 391
dualism, 245, 251

E
ecstasy, 54, 88, 187, 266, 323, 355
elements, 4-15, 17-18, 27, 34-43, 45, 48, 50n21, 51, 62, 69, 72-73, 83, 150, 181, 195, 223-24, 229, 275, 333, 338, 341, 347, 365, 367, 374, 391
emptiness, xv, 83, 160, 165, 211, 243, 248, 294, 321n14
erotics, eroticism, 70-74, 81, 112, 186-91, 196, 198, 257
eunuch, 232-33, 243, 246-47
Eurasianism, 407-10
existential, the, 89, 91, 223, 228, 239, 242, 246-48, 250, 348

F
fairy tale, 29-30, 33, 42-43, 46, 49, 126, 151, 259-60
family, xiv, 15, 44, 46-47, 73, 94, 115, 143, 145, 148, 150, 152-154, 173-74, 176, 183, 220, 373

father, fatherhood, xiv, 58, 101-2, 108-9, 111, 127, 130, 142, 144-48, 153-54, 162, 167, 169-70, 178-79, 181-84, 188, 192-94, 196-98, 207, 234, 245, 259, 272, 361, 374, 388
partricide, 178-79
Faustian, the, 10, 12, 20, 25-27
folklore, 126, 368, 376

G
gaze, 56-62, 72, 78, 82, 140, 154, 156, 162, 177, 224
ghost, 62-64, 66, 96, 109-10, 118, 368
glossolalia, 286, 286n14, 287, 412
Gnosticism, 247-248, 250, 396
grotesque, 49, 103n4, 398, 414

H
hagiography, 95-96, 109-10, 116, 168-69
handwriting, 88, 90, 93-94, 98, 105, 213
happiness; and unhappiness, xiv, 12, 59n14, 64, 99, 120, 155, 173-76, 254, 258, 318
Hasidism, tzaddik, 347-60, 367, 372n49, 373n51
Hebrew, 341, 343, 347, 362n32, 374
heroics, 93, 96, 151-52, 187, 249, 257-58, 265
holy fool, 171, 342, 348-49
homeland, 10, 140, 249, 317, 319-20, 360, 369, 373-74

I
ideal, xiv-xv, xvii, 10, 54, 82, 87, 95-96, 98, 101, 103, 111, 133, 135, 144-45, 150, 160, 178, 180, 182, 241-42, 246, 254-55, 281, 389, 391-92
ideocracy, 325, 329, 333
ideology, 147, 196, 199-200, 280-81, 284, 329, 335, 363, 383, 412
idol, 20-21, 24-25, 63, 211-12
idyll, 14-16, 44, 47, 70, 99, 137, 145, 149, 252
incest, 183-184, 187, 190, 192, 195-96, 198
interpretation, 73, 81, 94, 103, 135, 183, 192, 224n15, 248, 274n9, 340, 357, 363-64, 370, 390, 408-409, 412, 414
irony, xiv-xv, 15-18, 51, 53-56, 78, 81-84, 175, 190, 362, 414
irrational and hyperrational, 13, 324, 331, 372n49

K
Kabbalah, 33, 338-347, 353

L
labor, toil, 4-11, 13-14, 16, 26, 91, 110, 119, 152, 169, 183, 186-87, 187n13, 188-90, 198, 234, 236, 238, 244, 246-47, 249, 252-54, 256, 258, 267, 286
landscape, 39, 45, 66, 70, 72-74, 77, 138, 152, 218, 271, 356, 367
language, 55, 84, 114, 120, 131-33, 136, 180, 184, 193, 195, 199-200, 212, 215, 219, 228, 239, 242, 272, 275-78, 280-82, 282n3, 283, 289, 301, 307-10, 313-14, 337-47, 361, 363-64, 371, 374, 392-93, 394, 396-97, 404-5, 414
letter, character, 88-95, 98, 101, 103-5, 107, 113-14, 117, 119, 122, 177, 206, 207n5, 264, 319, 338, 341, 346, 348, 373, 385
light, 16, 43, 55, 58, 61-4, 78, 91, 156, 167, 183, 188, 204-216, 209, 212, 221, 240, 243, 250, 266, 275, 310, 315, 319, 331, 349, 353-54, 357-358, 361, 367, 372, 379, 408
"little man", 44-46, 96-97, 98n9, 99, 118, 411
logos, 221, 273, 275, 293, 346, 411-412

M
madness; poetic and philosophical; insanity, ideomania; noostasis, 22, 25, 45-46, 98-99, 125, 133, 177, 313-37, 382
poetic and philosophical, 322-27
insanity, 320, 337
othermindedness, 314n2, 336-37
ideomania, 329, 335
irrational and hyperrational, 13, 324, 331, 372n49
as method, 327-33
noostasis, 325, 327
see also reason
magic, 5, 55, 59-63, 65-66, 69, 74, 111-12, 116, 139, 194, 204-207, 249, 262, 278, 281, 283-84, 287, 309, 393, 412
"man in a case," 113-14, 119-22, 411
maniac, 121, 261, 264, 328-29, 382-83
Marxism, 179, 183, 196, 329-30, 407, 410
mat (profanity), 180-82, 191-96, *see also* profanity
materialism, xiii, 179-84, 187, 191-95, 198, 246, 281, 382
Mediterranean (Greece, Italy), 319-320
Mephistopheles, 5-6, 12-18, 25-26, 46
metanarrative, 407-10
metaphysics, 4, 204-205, 231, 313, 397-398, 403-407, 410-15

432 Index

metarealism, 396–98
miners, 187–89
morality, 126, 135, 148, 229, 325, 392, 395
mother, the maternal, 95, 108–9, 113, 119, 134, 146, 168–69, 179–85, 188–99, 217, 239, 242, 326, 373–74
motherland, 71, 78, 80, 244, 277, 398
mystery, 48, 59, 140, 213, 215, 233, 235–38, 278, 301, 303, 306, 405, 413–414
myth, mythology, 50–51, 101, 130, 137, 151, 192, 263, 267, 392–93, 396, 398

N

Nabokovian, the, 203–205, 207–208, 210–14
name; name-glorifying (onomatodoxy), 24–25, 56, 70, 78, 81, 95, 102–3, 108, 121, 142, 161, 163, 169–70, 188, 192, 204–207, 224, 239, 245, 251, 259, 275, 277
nature, 5–6, 21–22, 30, 48–49, 63, 67, 71, 83, 135–36, 138–40, 146–47, 151–52, 157, 170, 213, 215, 222, 224–27, 234–35, 243–44, 246, 249, 261, 266, 292–93, 300, 304–305, 310, 313, 315, 329, 331, 342, 348, 362, 364–65, 368, 375, 383, 387, 395, 398, 403–404
   art and, 49
   childhood and relation with, 130, 136, 138, 147, 151, 355
   as humanity's judgment, 368
   Lenin's view, 199
   Maiakovsky's view, 234
   Mandel'shtam's view, 370–71
   Mother Nature, 179–81, 183–84, 188–89, 192, 194, 196, 198–200
   Pasternak's view, 357–360
   power of, 9, 200
   power over, 11, 14, 101, 111
   revolt against, 22
   and technology 234
negative aesthetics, 54–55, 83
night, 16, 18, 62–63, 66–69, 71, 80–81, 95, 116, 134, 153, 165, 188, 221, 224, 232, 250, 272, 359, 365
nirvana, 221–25
nonbeing, nonexistence, 69, 211, 213, 216–17, 220–23, 225, 227, 231–33, 247
nonnon (*netka*, in Nabokov), 215–19
nothing, nothingness, 14, 28, 47, 50, 66, 68, 74, 88, 93, 104, 113–16, 118, 142, 149, 152, 160, 162, 164–165, 169, 171, 174, 180, 182, 185, 191, 213, 215, 218–23, 225, 227–29, 231–233, 235, 243–44, 246–50, 252, 254–55, 259, 264, 271–72, 274, 278, 280, 287, 289–91, 301–302, 314, 324, 348–50, 366, 375, 381, 389, 391, 413–14

O

Oblomagin (literary type), 251, 261–67
Oblomovka, 251–56
Oedipus complex, 150, 181–86
orphanhood, 148, 234, 244
othermindedness, *see* reason
otherworld, 58, 205, 248, 292, 321n14, 392

P

paliceman (in Prigov), 384
paradox, xiii–xiv, xvi–xvii, 28, 116, 140, 146, 164, 183, 222, 251, 271, 333, 380, 391, 407, 412
parody, 46, 48, 97, 100–1, 107, 290, 398
patriotism, 54–55, 70–74, 190
phantom, 29, 51, 63, 66, 70, 73, 110–11, 144, 218, 225, 247–48 250, 293, 302
phenomenalism, 397–98
philosophy, 108, 183, 193, 195, 199, 215, 228–31, 233, 284, 314, 325–26, 329, 330, 375–81, 384, 389, 404, 406, 411–12, 414
   German, 228–31
   philosophism, 375–81
Platonic, the, 56, 95, 113, 143, 181, 257, 323
Political, the, and the mystical, 302–307
profanity, 191–195
project, 7, 11, 13, 16, 103n4, 111–12, 228, 235, 327, 330–33, 335, 357
prototype, 29, 50n21, 77, 97, 101–2, 105, 107
psychiatry, 330, 332
psychoanalysis, 184

Q

quietude, 271–75, 296, 299, 304, 307
quotation, 331–332, 362

R

reason; othermindedness, xiii–xiv, 11–12, 23, 46, 100, 107, 111, 125–26, 130, 132, 135, 160, 204, 215, 246, 248, 258, 281, 308, 313–16, 321n14, 323–24, 327, 331, 333–37, 345–46, 355, 370, 379, 409, *see also* madness

Index 433

repetition, 46–47, 102–103, 103n4, 109, 111, 121, 161, 168, 226, 284, 335, 401
resurrection, 22, 102–103, 107–109, 111–12, 177, 228, 233–35, 238, 246, 330, 335n38, 410
riding, 62, 67–72, 74, 153, 190
ringing, 61–62, 64, 71, 318
romanticism, 126, 130, 133, 154, 315, 392–93
Russian literature, xiv, xvi–xvii, 13, 21, 29, 48, 50, 58, 74, 83, 87, 90, 92, 100–1, 108, 122, 128–30, 132, 137, 139, 141, 149, 212, 228–31, 246, 251, 259, 262–63, 291, 297, 301, 347, 364, 391–94, 396, 399, 405–414

S
saint, 95–96, 105, 107–109, 111, 135, 168–69, 348–49
Satan, the satanic, 18, 20, 24, 26, 59, 66, 96, 135, 137
scribe, 90–92, 94, 101, 105, 107, 114, 362, 362n32
sculpture, statue, 20–21, 45, 49, 110, 335
sea, 4–12, 16–17, 22–23, 26, 34–35, 38, 41–43, 46, 51, 63–64, 127, 146, 277, 294
seashore, 5, 8, 11–12, 30
secondariness, 14, 363–364, 364n35
sentimentalism, 392, 394–395
silence, 83, 107, 114, 142, 252, 255, 271–75, 278, 285, 287, 289, 291–97, 299–300, 302–308, 310, 313–14, 321n14, 396, 413–14
social phobia, 115–116, 116n2, 121–22
soil, 5, 9–10, 14, 19, 21, 128, 140, 142–43, 146–49, 151, 191, 193, 200, 213, 409
Sophia, sophiology, 55, 181, 387
spark (in Hasidism), 347–360
speech, 122, 151, 176, 193, 239, 266, 271–72, 275–76, 278, 284n8, 286n14, 287–93, 295, 300, 303–9, 313, 319–20, 339–40, 346–47, 356, 374, 376, 386, 397, 413

State, the, xvi, 15, 46–47, 49, 73, 136, 162, 230, 288, 306, 354, 382, 391, 409
statue, 20–21, 45, 49
St. Petersburg, 11, 19, 22–24, 27, 33, 68, 88, 106, 249
subject and object, 239–43

T
Talmudism, the Talmudic, 348, 354, 360–74
Technology, 234, 247, 250
thing; allthing and allbody, 381–87
totalitarianism, 262, 325
Tower of Babel, 33–34, 34n9
toys, 142–143, 164
tragic, the, and the comic, 43, 46–49, 97, 100, 174, 398
trembling, 45, 54, 132, 137, 250, 354

U
unconscious, the, xv, 81, 121, 128, 130–31, 142, 146, 156, 170, 189, 195, 249, 253, 260, 263, 357, 362, 374–76, 378, 380, 386, 388–90
underground, 184–85, 191, 261

V
vacuum 16, 24, 103, 156, 217, 221–25, 243–245, 247–248, 278, 282, 294–95, 389
void, 16–17, 24, 68, 103, 156, 217, 221–22, 224, 243–45, 247–48, 278, 282, 294, 395, 389
verbiage, 278, 308

W
warrior–dreamer, 251, 256–61
weeping, 23, 64–66, 155, 171
winter, 106, 138, 170, 183, 267, 288, 290, 366–68,
wisdom, 11, 55, 93, 176, 181, 275, 306–307, 356, 359, 369, 375, 378, 383–84, 386–87, 389
witch, 21, 56–60, 62–65, 67, 69–72, 74–75, 78–82, 190
word, 274–79, 287–95, 307–10

Index of Names

A
Aitmatov, Chingiz, 154, 396, 409
  The White Steamship (Belyi parokhod), 154
Akhmatova, Anna, xv
Aksakov, Sergei, 128, 138–42, 150, 152, 156
  The Childhood Years of Bagrov the Grandson, 138
Aksenov, Vasilii, 153, 395
Andreev, Daniil, xv, 406, 408,
Andreev, Leonid, 272, 328
Arutiunova, Nina, 272
Askol'dov, Sergei, xvi
Averintsev, Sergei, 91, 305, 362, 363, xvi
  "The Fate and Tidings of Osip Mandel'shtam," 372

B
Ba'al Shem Tov (Besht), 372
Bakhtin, Mikhail, 81, 176, 272, 310, 338, 413
Baratynsky, Evgenii, 14, 363, 369–70
Barrow, John
  The Book of Nothing: Vacuums, Voids, and the Latest Ideas about the Origins of the Universe, 221
Barthes, Roland
  The Pleasure of the Text, 303–304
Batiushkov, Konstantin, 314–22, 334, 363
Belinsky, Vissarion, xiv, 54, 74, 307, 392
Bely, Andrei, 132, xiii
Berdiaev, Nikolai, xvi, 111, 307, 375, 376
  The Russian Idea, 307
Bibikhin, Vladimir, 297, 299, 300, 306
Bitov, Andrei, 395, 406, 413
Blagoi, Dmitrii, 4, 19
Blatty, William Peter
  The Exorcist, 137
Blok, Aleksandr, 74, 77–80, 171, 258, 305, 393, 401, 405
  The Fairground Booth (Balaganchik), xv
  The Stranger (Neznakomka), xv

"The New America" ("Novaia Amerika"), 78
Bloy, Léon, 28
Bradbury, Ray
  "Zero Hour," 136–37
Brezhnev, Leonid, 184
Brodsky, Joseph, 282, 310, 397, 403, 406
Büchner, Ludwig, 191
Bulgakov, Mikhail, 406
  The Master and Margarita, 408
Bulgakov, Sergei, 194, 215, 223, 278, 308
Bunin, Ivan, 128, 140–44, 152, 156, 398

C
Carlyle, Thomas, 413
Chaadaev, Petr, xiv, 213, 264, 277, 307
  Philosophical Letters, xiv
Chekhov, Anton, 113–15, 118–19, 122, 149, 206, 290, 294, 301, 393, 411–12
  Cherry Orchard (Vishnevyi sad), 291–93
  "The Man in a Case," 113–114
  Uncle Vania (Diadia Vania), 290
Chukovsky, Kornei, 327–29
de Coster, Charles
  Legend of Thyl Ulenspiegel and Lamme Goedzak, 135

D
Dal', Vladimir, 302
Dante, 315–16, 345, 362–63
Dickens, Charles, 145, 149
  Oliver Twist, 134, 141
Ďurišin, Dionýz, 3
Donner, Richard
  The Omen, 137
Dostoevsky, Fedor, xiv, xvii, 29, 42, 48–52, 78, 87–90, 93, 95–100, 101, 105–8, 128, 133–35, 137, 142, 143, 145, 236, 266, 278, 291, 293, 294, 300, 310, 375, 376, 393, 406, 408, 411
  The Brothers Karamazov, xiv, xvii, 133n9, 236, 291.

Index   435

Diary of a Writer, 142
The Idiot, 88n1, 89, 96, 411
Poor Folk and Other Stories, 97n8
Poor People (Bednye liudi), 97
The Village of Stepanchikovo and Its Inhabitants, 97
White Nights and Other Stories, 98n10
Dubnow, Simon, 373

E
Esenin, Sergei, 206, 345, 364, 409
Evtushenko, Evgenii, 298–99, 395, 401

F
Faulkner, William, 147
  The Sound and the Fury, 133
Fedorov, Nikolai Fedorovich, 101–112, 228, 231, 233–38, 245–46, 250, 330, 335, 410
  Philosophy of the Common Cause (Filosofiia obshchego dela), 102
Fedotov, Georgii, 273
Florensky, Pavel, 171, 181, 277, 284
Florovsky, Georgii, 111–12
  Pathways of Russian Theology, 273, 307
Freud, Sigmund 150–51, 178–79, 183, 200
  Mass Psychology and Analysis of the "I," 178
  Totem and Taboo, 178

G
Gak, Vladimir
  Comparative Lexicology, 282
Galich, Aleksandr, 303, 305
Galkovsky, Dmitrii, 289, 302, 308
Gastev, Aleksei, 186–88
  Poetry of the Worker's Blow (Poeziia rabochego udara), 186
Goethe, Johann Wolfgang von 4, 7–15, 18, 25, 229, 315
  Faust, Part Two, 5, 8, 25–27
  Truth and Poetry, 125
Gogol, Nikolai, xiv, 74, 78, 81–84, 87, 95–96, 101, 104, 106, 108–10, 120, 190, 203, 206, 278, 280, 394, 406, 408, 412
  Dead Souls (Mertvye dushi), xiv, 54–73, 81, 84, 211, 280, 411
  The Inspector-General (Revizor), 53, 291
  "May Night, or The Drowned Maiden," 21
  "Nevsky Prospect" ("Nevskii Prospekt"), 53

Selected Passages from Correspondence with Friends, 83–84, 97, 100
  "The Overcoat," 113–14, 116–18
  "The Portrait" ("Portret"), 21
  "Viy," 21
Golding, William
  Lord of the Flies, 136
Golubkov, Dmitrii, 155
Goncharov, Ivan, 256
  Oblomov, 251, 411
Gorbatov, Boris
  Donbass, 187, 196
  Before the War (Pered voinoi), 187
Gorky, Maksim, 149, 178, 182, 188–89, 196–98, 206, 327, 394, 411
  Petty Bourgeoisie, 196
  The Petty Bourgeoisie (Meshchane), 188, 196
Greenwood, James
  The Little Ragamuffin, 134
Grimm, Jacob, and Wilhelm Grimm, 34–35, 41, 49–51
Gumilev, Nikolai, 394

H
Han Yu, 28
Hegel G. W. F., 414
  The Phenomenology of Spirit, 384
Heidegger, Martin, 228–29, 231–39, 242–43, 245, 250, 305, 323, 411
  Being and Time, 228
Hemingway, Ernest, 147, 151, 153
Hesse, Hermann, 229
Hitchcock, Alfred
  The Birds, 136
Hoffmann, E. T. A., 21–22
Hölderlin, Friedrich, 314–20, 323, 336
Homer, 318, 363
Hugo, Victor
  Les Miserables, 134
Husserl, Edmund, 313

I
Iourienen, Sergei, 397
Ïurišin, Dionýz, 3
Ivanov, Viacheslav, 347, 393

J
Jakobson, Roman 20–21, 320
  "The Statue in Pushkin's Poetic Mythology," 20

K

Kabakov, Il'ia, 103, 293–94, 302, 330–33, 335
  Institute for Creative Research, 330–31
  The Palace of Projects, 330, 332–33
Kafka, Franz, 28, 338
Kaganovich, Lazar, 185, 200
Kant, Immanuel, 226, 229–31, 327, 404
Karlinsky, Simon
  The Sexual Labyrinth of Nikolai Gogol, 70
Kataev, Valentin 138, 140
  A Solitary White Sail, 150
Kazakov, Iurii, 153–55, 395
  "The Little Candle," 154
  "You Wept Bitterly in Your Sleep," 154
Kharms, Daniil, 288–91, 412
  "Grigor'ev and Semenov," 288
Khlebnikov, Velimir, 132, 347, 409
Kierkegaard, Søren 28, 137
Kim, Anatolii, 396, 409
Kliuchevskii, Vasilii, 266
Krivulin, Viktor, 396
Kuraev, Mikhail, 396
Kushner, Aleksandr, 406
Kutik, Il'ia, 398
Kuzminskaia, Tatyana, 165
Kuznetsov, Iurii, 396, 409

L

Lawrence, D. H., 187
Lenin (Ul'anov), Vladimir, 120, 179–83, 191, 198–99, 256, 265, 281, 283, 284, 286
Lermontov, Mikhail, 126–28, 131, 261, 347, 403, 406
Leskov, Nikolai, 142, 262
Lossky, Nikolai, 108
Lotman, Iurii, xvi, 102, 109
Lucretius
  On the Nature of Things, 180
Luria, Isaac, 346, 353
Lyotard, Jean-François
  The Postmodern Condition: A Report on Knowledge, 407

M

Maiakovsky, Vladimir, xv, 206, 234–35, 238, 240, 281, 304, 394, 401
  About That (Pro eto), 234
Makarenko, Anton, 148–49
  Pedagogical Poem (Pedagogicheskaia poema), 148
Mamleev, Iurii, 396, 409
Mandel'shtam, Emil, 347
Mandel'shtam, Osip, xv, 121, 189, 203, 235, 236, 276–78, 280, 288, 294, 305, 338–340, 342–43, 345, 360–74, 406, 411,
  The Noise of Time, 374
Mann, Thomas, 229
Markov, Moisei, 218
Mechnikov, Ivan, 165
Melville, Herman
  Moby Dick, 152
Merezhkovsky, Dmitrii, xvi, 300–301, 327–28
Mérimée, Prosper, 21
Mickiewicz, Adam, 18–23, 26, 33–35, 49
  Forefathers' Eve, 18, 33, 49–51, 411
Miller, Henry, 187
Mindlin, Emil, 360
Moleschott, Jacob, 191

N

Nabokov, Vladimir, 156, 203–205, 207–209, 211–27, 246–50, 338, 406
  Camera Obscura, 208
  The Gift (Dar), 207
  Laughter in the Dark, 208
  Pale Fire, 210
  "Ultima Thule", 215–21, 224–27
Nekrasov, Nikolai, 142, 206, 296–99, 339, 393
Nekrasov, Vsevolod, 397
Nietzsche, Friedrich, 314
Novikov, Nikolai, 126

O

Okudzhava, Bulat, 395
Olesha, Iurii, 132
Ossian, 363
Ostrovsky, Nikolai, 240, 251
Ovid, 363

P

Parshchikov, Aleksei, 397–398
Pascal, Blaise, 324
Pasternak, Boris, 131–132, 260, 338–40, 343–52, 35461, 364–369, 371–74, 406, 411
  Doctor Zhivago, 183, 408
  "Fairy Tale" ("Skazka"), 259

Liuvers's Childhood (Detstvo Liuvers), 132
"Spring" ("Vesna"), 344
Paustovsky, Konstantin, 138, 151
Pavlov, Ivan, 309
Pelevin, Viktor, 406
Pisarev, Dmitrii, 158-159, 193, 392
Plato, 180, 181, 215, 257, 322-323, 325, 327, 333-37, 400
  Laws, 333-35
  The Phaedrus, 323
  The Republic, 335
Platonov, Andrei, xv, 132, 228-229, 231-64, 282, 376, 378, 387, 406, 409, 411
  Chevengur, 119-21, 228, 251-57, 262, 299, 411
  The Foundation Pit (Kotlovan), 232, 241-42, 262, 282
Poe, Edgar Allen, 21, 363
Polanski, Roman
  Rosemary's Baby, 137
Pososhkov, Ivan, 193
Prigov, Dmitrii Aleksandrovich, 299, 375-90, 406
  Deep Book or *Dove Book (Golubinaia kniga)*, 380
  The Makhrot' of All Rus (Makhrot' vseia Rusi), 381
Prishvin, Mikhail, 151, 178, 198, 406, 409
  The Ruler's Road (Osudareva doroga), 151
  Shiptimber Grove, 151
Prokhanov, Aleksandr, 409
Pulatov, Timur, 409
Pushkin, Alexander, 6-27, 29-36, 41-44, 48-52, 64-65, 77, 80, 87, 126-27, 158, 175, 203-207, 213, 229-30, 257, 297, 300, 315, 321, 323, 335-337, 339, 341, 347, 354, 363, 385, 392, 404-406, 408, 411
  The Bronze Horseman (Mednyi vsadnik), 4, 8, 10-16, 18-19, 22, 28-31, 33, 35, 39, 42, 46-48, 50-51, 206, 230
  The Captain's Daughter (Kapitanskaia dochka), 230
  History of Peter the First (Istoriia Petra I), 18
  A Scene from Faust, 8, 12-13, 17
  The Stone Guest, 21
  The Tale of the Fisherman and the Fish (Skazka o rybake i rybke), 29-51

R
Rasputin, Valentin, 409
Rozanov, Vasilii, xv, 51-52, 229, 301-302, 406
  The Endless Dead End (Beskonechnyi tupik), 302
Rozov, Vladimir, 4

S
Salinger, Jerome David
  The Catcher in the Rye, 147
Sartre, Jean-Paul, 143-45, 147
  Words, 143
Sedakova, Ol'ga, 203, 396, 406
Semenova, Svetlana, 103, 106, 234
Sharov, Vladimir, 407
Shcherbatskoi, Fedor, 223
Shepilov, Dmitrii, 283
Shestov, Lev, 229, 281
Shishkin, Mikhail, 407
Shklovsky, Viktor, 163-64, 177, 344-47
Sholokhov, Mikhail 147-48
  Quiet Flows the Don (Tikhii Don), 147
  Tales from the Don (Donskie rasskazy), 148
Shvarts, Elena, 396
Siniavsky, Andrei, 59, 394, 406
  Strolls with Pushkin, 158
Sokolov, Sasha, 397-98
Sologub, Fedor, 328, 382
  The Petty Demon (Melkii bes), 382
Solov'ev, Vladimir, xiv, 111-112, 181, 408
  "A Brief Tale of the Antichrist," xiv
Solzhenitsyn, Aleksandr, 306, 395, 408
Sontag, Susan
  Against Interpretation, 303
Sorokin, Vladimir, 190-91, 284-87, 308, 382, 406, 412
  Blue Lard, 190
  The Norm (Norma), 382
Strakhov, Nikolai, 177
Surkov, Evgenii, 95
Swift, Jonathan 325-326
  A Tale of a Tub, 325

T
Taymanova, Marianna, ix
Tiutchev, Fedor, 300, 303-306, 310, 363, 369-371, 389, 405-406, 409
Tolstaya, Tatyana, 396

Tolstoy, Aleksei, 138
Tolstoy, Lev, 108, 127–132, 137, 142, 146, 149, 156, 158–169, 171–177, 203, 374, 387, 393–394, 406, 408, xiv
  "Alesha-the-Pot," 167–173
  Anna Karenina, 161, 173–176
  Childhood (Detstvo), 128–130, 138
  The Death of Ivan Ilyich, 160–167
  "On Shakespeare and Drama," 158
  War and Peace, 130, 161
Toporov, Vladimir, 180–81
Trifonov, Iurii, 395
Tsiolkovsky, Konstantin, 409
Tsvetaeva, Marina, 360, 366–367, 406
Turgenev, Ivan 152, 197, 277
  Notes of a Hunter (Zapiski okhotnika), 152
Twain, Mark, 145–47, 149
Tynianov, Iurii, 96–97, 100, 131–132, 344–45, 364
  Dostoevsky and Gogol: Toward a Theory of Parody, 96

U
Ul'ianov, Vladimir, 283, *see* Lenin
Uspensky, Boris, xvi, 192, 194

Uspensky, Gleb, 299

V
Vernadsky, Vladimir, 409
Vogt, Karl, 191
Voltaire, 230
Volzhsky (Glinka, Aleksandr), 406
Voznesensky, Andrei, 395
Vygotsky, Lev, 151

W
Wilde, Oscar, 140
Wittgenstein, Ludwig
  Tractatus Logico-Philosophicus, 271, 273
Wolfe, Thomas
  Look Homeward, Angel, 147

Z
Zabolotsky, Nikolai, 369, 389, 405–406, 409
Zeno, 28
Zhdanov, Ivan, 396
Zhirmunsky, Viktor, 4
Zhukovsky, Vasilii, 319, 392–93, 401, 408
Zinov'ev, Aleksandr
  The Madhouse (Zheltyi dom), 329–30
Zulfikarov, Timur, 409

www.ingramcontent.com/pod-product-compliance
Lightning Source LLC
Chambersburg PA
CBHW071355300426
44114CB00016B/2069